Active Duty

Public Administration as Democratic Statesmanship

Edited by
Peter Augustine Lawler
Robert Martin Schaefer
David Lewis Schaefer

ROWMAN & LITTLEFIELD PUBLISHERS, INC.
Lanham • Boulder • New York • Oxford

ROWMAN & LITTLEFIELD PUBLISHERS, INC.

Published in the United States of America
by Rowman & Littlefield Publishers, Inc.
4720 Boston Way, Lanham, Maryland 20706

12 Hid's Copse Road
Cumnor Hill, Oxford OX2 9JJ, England

British Library Cataloguing in Publication Information Available

Library of Congress Cataloging-in-Publication Data

Active duty : public administration as democratic statesmanship / [edited by]
    Peter Augustine Lawler, Robert Martin Schaefer, David Lewis Schaefer.
        p. cm.
    Includes bibliographical references and index.
    ISBN 0-8476-8646-9 (cloth : alk. paper). — ISBN 0-8476-8647-7
(pbk. : alk. paper)
        1. Public administration—United States. 2. Public administration.
    3. United States—Politics and government. I. Lawler, Peter Augustine.
    II. Schaefer, Robert Martin. III. Schaefer, David Lewis, 1943-   .
    JF1338.A3U53 1998   98-9907
    351—dc21   CIP

Printed in the United States of America

∞ ™The paper used in this publication meets the minimum requirements of American
National Standard for Information Sciences—Permanence of Paper for Printed
Library Materials, ANSI Z39.48–1984.

Contents

Acknowledgments

Peter Lawler wishes to thank Kathy Gann, Lynsey Morris, and Matt Barrett for various editorial chores at Berry College.

Robert Schaefer appreciates the assistance of Kristel Hoy, Allison Knight, John Buaas, and Judy Criswell at the University of Mobile. He also is grateful to the Earhart Foundation for its kind support.

David Schaefer expresses his gratitude to the National Endowment for the Humanities for a fellowship that supported his research while he was working on this and other projects.

The editors especially thank Stephen M. Wrinn, acquisitions editor, and Lynn Gemmell, production editor, at Rowman & Littlefield Publishers, for their support and patience.

Chapter 1 by Herbert J. Storing was previously published in *Bureaucrats, Policy Analysts, Statesmen: Who Leads?* (Washington, D.C.: American Enterprise Institute, 1981). Reprinted by permission with minor revisions.

Chapter 5 by David Lewis Schaefer is a revised version of material previously published in *Administration & Society* 19, 4 (February 1988), pp. 371–98, copyright © 1988 by Sage Publications, Inc. Reprinted by permission.

Chapter 6 by Jeremy Rabkin was previously published in *Saving the Revolution: The Federalist Papers and the American Founding* by Charles R. Kesler (New York: Free Press, 1987). Reprinted by permission with minor revisions.

Chapter 8 by Robert Eden was previously published in *Polity* 28, 3 (Spring 1996), pp. 357–94. Reprinted by permission with minor revisions.

Chapter 11 by Donald J. Maletz was previously published in *Ad-

ministration & Society 23, 3, pp. 374–94, copyright © 1991 by Sage Publications, Inc. Reprinted by permission.

Chapter 12 by William D. Richardson and Lloyd G. Nigro was previously published as "Administrative Ethics and Founding Thought: Constitutional Correctives, Honor, and Education" in *Public Administration Review* 47, 5 (September/October 1987), pp. 367–76. Reprinted with permission from *Public Administration Review* © by the American Society for Public Adminstration (ASPA), 1120 G Street NW, Suite 700, Washington, D.C. 20005. All rights reserved. Reprinted with minor revisions.

Chapter 13 by John A. Rohr was previously published in *International Political Science Review* 9, 3 (1988), pp. 167–78. Reprinted by permission of Sage Publications Ltd, with minor revisions.

Preface

This collection of essays is designed to contribute to the education of present and prospective American civil servants. For students of public administration and others, it is an introduction to understanding the political role of the American civil service. The common concern that unites the diverse approaches of the authors is the conception of public administration as a particular kind of political activity. The authors relate administrative issues to the broader questions of political life, which involve political judgment and responsibility, the Constitution and constitutionalism, and the promotion of human liberty and the common good. They aim to encourage and assist the public administrator to become a democratic statesman.

The contemporary prejudice against the view that public administrators need this sort of education comes chiefly from two sources: the civil service reform movement of the late nineteenth century and the thought of Woodrow Wilson, the founder of the American discipline of public administration. Battling against the corruption of the spoils system, the civil service reformers sought to establish a professionally competent governmental bureaucracy. The work and tenure in office of the professional administrators was to be made immune from the pressures of partisan politics. The great achievements of the reformers were the Pendleton Act of 1883, which laid the groundwork for today's politically neutral, merit-based civil service system, and the Hatch Act of 1940, which aimed to remove federal civil servants from the influence of partisan pressures.

Wilson sought to separate administration from politics in a more fundamental sense. Aiming to promote both professional competence and democratic accountability, he portrayed the public administrator's task as essentially nonpolitical. Along with the Progressive writers who followed his lead, he described the job of the civil servant as simply the duty to implement efficiently the people's will as conveyed to him from his elected political superiors. While the administrator ought not to substitute his political judgment for that of his superiors, Wilson held, the people in turn should refrain from interfering with his efficient performance of the task of implementation.

By attempting neatly or systematically to separate administration from politics, Wilson and the other reformers believed they were solving a fundamental problem of democracy. Good government, as *Federalist* 70 asserts, depends on efficient administration. "Popular" administration—the democratic, Jacksonian spoils system—produced bad government, incompetence, and corruption. Democracy, the American experience seemed to show, requires an elite, technically trained administrative class. But if democracy is to prevail, administrative expertise must not be allowed to become political power.

At a practical level, much can be said for the legacy of civil service reform. Americans now benefit from a highly professional and comparatively honest system of government service. The city manager system of municipal government championed by the Progressives has also often produced good government in smaller American cities.

A fundamental problem with the separation of politics from administration, however, is the misleading view it gives to civil servants about the nature of their work. Not long after the triumph of the reform movement, scholars discovered that the politics–administration dichotomy was unrealistic. It did not accurately portray what administrators were doing. At least for higher-level administrators, the discretion that is indispensable for responding effectively to diverse circumstances and changing situations unavoidably involves influencing and making public policy. As government gets bigger and more complex, entering more extensively into the details of daily life, the political power of public administrators seems inevitably to grow.

Scholarly attempts to recognize and legitimate this administrative exercise of political power democratically or constitutionally have run into other difficulties. Some political scientists argue that the American civil service actually "represents" the people more accurately than the class of elected politicians, because its demographic profile is more like that of the American people as a whole. But demographic representation is clearly not political representation. An African American, for example, can hardly be trusted to rule on behalf of all African Americans simply because he shares their racial characteristics. The individual's political views are not simply or reliably determined by his or her race (or gender, religion, ethnic group, socioeconomic status, etc.). In any case, there is no conceivable mechanism that could assure that bureaucrats are fully adequate mirrors of the American people in their diversity.

Another justification of administrators' exercising political will came out of the 1960s: the New Public Administration movement. This movement began with the view that administrators who serve merely as instruments for the will of others act "inauthentically." (Consider, said the new public administrators, the craven defense of Nazi bureaucrats that they were "just following orders.") Administrators should be encouraged to do their duty as human beings, to do what they believe to be right, even without the niceties of formal legislation or edicts from their elected superiors. Civil servants, in this view, have opportunities to act not only politically, but even "heroically."

Those who promoted the New Public Administration doctrine assumed that all authentic choices would favor greater equality, environmental purity, and a larger and more active government. They soon saw the need, however, to secure a deeper grounding for the individual administrator's "values." Hence, the more enduring tendency of the New Public Administration was the search for "philosophical" justifications for advancing the administrator's public policy preferences—goals favored by an educated, enlightened minority—against recalcitrant majorities. Administrative scholars had recourse to new theoretical principles, such as those set forth in John Rawls's influential philosophical treatise *A Theory of Justice* (1971), as a ground for challenging majoritarian politics. They praised Rawls's redistributive "difference principle" as well as the courts' innovative forms of constitutional principle, which generated such doctrines as that of "welfare rights." The New Public Administration came to depend on a "new constitutionalism."

We doubt that the movement of administrative theory from uncritical majoritarianism to principled self-actualization represents genuine progress. The hierarchical, formal nature of modern bureaucracy, along with the technical training of many administrators, tends to make civil servants into "systematizers." Both their attachment to formal rules and the technical principle of efficiency incline or compel them to reduce the diversity of human experience to a more manageable order or uniformity. Public administrators tend to be repelled by the disorderliness of democratic politics as it is actually practiced, and especially by messy and unenlightened political interference with the performance of their duties. Both administrative standardization and the principled, political impulse of our intellectual elites may have an inherent bias to promote a bigger, more centralized, more meddlesome government that weakens the opportunity and capacity of ordinary citizens for personal and political choice. The mixture of administrative and egalitarian principle thus threatens to culminate in what Alexis de Tocqueville called "soft" or apathetic despotism.

The antidote we propose to moderate this potentially antiliberal mix is a form of liberal education, designed to develop the character and judgment of a statesman. Such an education begins not with abstract "philosophical" principle, but with consideration of the political choices actually made by the American Founders on behalf of liberty. It calls attention to the differences between the Founders' thoughtful choices and those recommended by their seemingly more principled, sometimes radical critics, beginning perhaps with Wilson. Liberal education for administrators also includes the development of one's own ability to articulate reasonable public policy and to contribute to informed political discussion.

This book has three sections. The first provides an orientation to some of the issues and problems facing American public administrators today. The contributions to the second section relate the practice of public administration to the political institutions created by the Constitution. The third section is devoted to the relationship between public administration and personal responsibility.

Part One

Some Fundamental Concerns

Introduction

This first section provides an orientation to the issues and problems facing public administrators in America's liberal democracy. The unifying theme of this volume is well illustrated by Herbert Storing's essay (chapter 1). Storing relates the task of the public administrator to that of the statesman, highlighting both the reasons why administrative statesmanship is a central task of modern, liberal government and the reasons for the decline in Americans' understanding of statesmanship. Administrative statesmanship, he argues, should be grounded in an understanding of constitutionalism rather than in purportedly "scientific" methodologies that attempt to supplant the civil servant's prudential judgment.

Peter Lawler turns our attention in chapter 2 to Tocqueville's recognition of democracy's hostility to liberty on behalf of equality. Tocqueville fears that the combination of the love of equality with the science of administration may destroy what is genuinely distinctive and admirable about human liberty. The administrator should resist the inclination of administration toward impersonal control on behalf of human liberty.

Marc Landy and Charles Rubin address in chapter 3 the problem of how bureaucrats should handle the dissemination or popularization of scientific knowledge. Administrators, they contend, should think of themselves as civic educators, stimulating informed and rational deliberation about public policy issues. Landy and Rubin present a case study of failure in civic education by administrators in the Environmental Protection Agency. The absence of scientific consensus on global warming allowed certain administrators to engage in apocalypse-mongering in pursuit of a questionable partisan agenda.

In chapter 4, Richard Green considers the problem of adhering to the norm of impartiality in light of the public administrator's "mixed role" as part clerk and part statesman. He proposes a dialectical analysis of authoritative sources, or a reasonable balancing of the competing intellectual and political claims for the administrator's loyalty.

David Schaefer critically considers in chapter 5 Theodore Lowi's highly influential solution to the supposed American problem of excessive delegation of power to unaccountable interest groups: "juridical democracy." Schaefer gives evidence to doubt the solution and even to question the genuine existence of the problem. Juridical democracy is really a neo-Wilsonian project to reform American political life radically through systematization and centralization. Lowi's thought is distorted by a principled animus against the combination of statesmanly prudence and citizen self-interest that characterizes constitutional liberty.

1

American Statesmanship: Old and New

Herbert J. Storing

"Statesmanship" is almost un-American. The word has an elitist and obsolete ring. I will use it, nevertheless, both because it is service-able enough to refer to the practice (and the theory of the practice) of government rather broadly understood, and because I want to try to rehabilitate, to some extent, an older view. I shall be concerned not so much with the practice of statesmanship as with the way Ameri-cans in significant public office, from the president down through at least the upper levels of the bureaucracy, understand their public roles (to use a much more fashionable term).

My beginning point is the observation that there is a strong ten-dency to resolve the role of the public official into two simple ele-ments: populism, or radical democracy, and scientific management. Since I will be trying to follow some very accessible, though often vaguely understood and expressed, ideas to their roots, I shall not begin with any attempt at precise or elaborate definition— premature definition obscures the interesting questions. I refer to the broad sets of ideas these terms immediately call to mind. They are admittedly vague and they will need refinement and explana-tion, but they will turn out, as our common language so often does, to identify rather well the kernel of the principles involved. These elements not only tend to characterize American "statesmanship" (and it is precisely because they characterize it that the word "statesman-ship" no longer seems to fit), they also are responsible for its char-acteristic narrowness.

I do not claim that American statesmen always *act* in terms of these principles. Indeed, one of the facts of their lives is that they find that

5

they cannot do so. They act in many ways as statesmen have traditionally acted, as leaders trying to deal with problems justly and prudently on their merits. But they have, to a very large extent, lost the understanding of the legitimacy of nonpopulist, non-scientific-management decision making. They "do" statesmanship in the broader and more traditional sense, but they do not understand it. Therefore, they often do not do it very well. While there is truth in the frequent criticism that our representatives and (especially) our officials are unfeeling and arrogant in their indifference to opinions and concerns other than their own, the more profound phenomenon, I think, is their lack of confidence in their own judgments.

They are rather good at articulating consensus. They are usually reasonably good at implementing clear-cut goals. Much of the time, however, there is no consensus to articulate, or it is foolish or unjust. Most of the time, the goals are not very clear or are in conflict, and their implementation has to be pursued under conditions that do not stand still for the principles of scientific management to be applied. Nonpopulist, nonscientific concerns seem even in American democracy to be at the heart of statesmanship; yet the American statesman is likely to believe that they are not really his proper business, even when he spends most of his time with them. The result is that these nonpopulist, nonscientific sides of American statesmanship tend to be done poorly and, even when done well, tend to be done under cover.

While I shall not here be much concerned specifically with presidential statesmanship, President Jimmy Carter does provide an instructive case in point. It has become almost a truism that Carter, who [initially] seemed such an exotic in presidential politics, [was] emphatically in the mainstream. His first presidential campaign was built around the two themes that I have suggested are the dominant themes of contemporary American statesmanship: populism and scientific management. The American government was to be brought up to the level of the American people by opening up that government and making it more responsive to the healthy good sense and compassion of the people. ("Make the government as good as the people.") Carter's second theme—the answer to the question of what the candidate would actually *do* when he had opened up the government to the popular impulse—was the promise to reorganize thoroughly the whole government, to reduce the great number of agencies, to cut away at excessive bureaucracy, and to improve and eliminate vast inefficiencies. In short, the promise was to make the government an efficient instrument for doing what the people, now again in control of their own government, want done. Once we became accustomed to the style and the accent, we saw that what was distinctive about the Carter campaign rhetoric was precisely the clarity with which it expressed the distinctive themes of American statesmanship.

There are two qualifications to these observations. First, I have not referred to another strand of the Carter rhetoric, namely, a version of Protestant fundamentalism. In this he is, again, representative of American statesmanship as a whole. In leaving the religious strain of American statesmanship out of account, I admit the incompleteness of my sketch, while also indicating my opinion that this strain would not turn out to be bedrock. A second qualification is closer to my present concern. For better or worse (and opinion on that varies sharply), once in office President Carter did not behave the way his campaign rhetoric indicated that he would behave. True, the populist style was ably, even brilliantly, maintained, and the president pressed hard the theme of technical efficiency, in his reorganization plans, his energy proposals, his decision to drop the development of the B-1 bomber, and so forth. Yet, in substance, President Carter acted very much as other middle-of-the-road presidents have usually acted, attempting to respond to specific policy questions prudently and on their merits, within limits enclosed by popular opinion, but with a willingness to stand against popular opinion and to lead it when that seems wise and possible.

It is arguable that President Carter understood quite well the limits of populism and scientific management and built a rhetoric from them, in quite a clear-headed way, in order, first, to secure office, and then, once in office, to provide the shell for a much broader, more traditional statesmanship. The thrust of this chapter is to doubt the feasibility, at least on any significant scale or over any considerable period of time, of a statesmanship in which there is such a sharp difference between style and substance.

At the level of scholarship or "theory," almost all political scientists understand American statesmanship in terms of some combination or variant of the two principles I have identified. Compared with this basic agreement, their disagreements, which seem so compelling in the discipline, are secondary. Scholars in public administration debate the principles of efficient management, the connection between efficiency and "responsibility" (which is understood as responsiveness ultimately to popular will), and the extent to which the science of administration can be divorced in theory and practice from the requirements of democratic responsiveness. Students of American politics debate how adequately the American system collects and orders and gives effect to public opinion. A human-relations expert criticizes the formal-organization tradition for inadequately perceiving the human requisites of true efficiency.[1] Richard Neustadt criticizes the President's Committee on Administrative Management for its preoccupation with administrative arrangements and its failure to see the importance of the president's task of persuasion and consensus building.[2] The pluralists criticize the antielite theorists for their simplification of democracy and their failure to see the varied and subtle texture of American society. The differences among academic students of American politics are great and the debate is vigorous and often illuminating. Nonetheless, with very rare exceptions (including some parts of the fast-disappearing discipline of constitutional law), the bedrock of principle from which all else derives in American politics is seen to be popular opinion and scientific management. The articulation of these principles and their relation to one another is the whole substance of American politics.

These themes of populism and scientific management are pervasive and deep. They are not, I repeat, always the terms in which American statesmen act; they are not always explicit in specific policy discussions; they are often ignored or overridden in specific decisions. But they are the general terms in which American statesmanship presents and understands itself and is understood both by the people at large and by those whose business it is to study and understand it.

The Decay of Democratic Statesmanship

That there has been a broad change since the beginnings of the American republic in both the theory and practice of what may loosely be called democratic statesmanship is widely agreed, and the rough outlines of that change are not in much dispute. American political society, and with it American statesmanship, has become much less elitist or, in the older term, aristocratic, and much more democratic or popular. The general view is that this is an improvement, a maturation, a sloughing-off of elements alien to American democracy properly understood. I will try to establish that from the point of view of the Founders this change represents a decay, and that this point of view makes sense. I will also try to give some account of the main elements of that decay before reflecting on its broad significance.

The indispensable beginning point is to take seriously the Framers' commitment to popular government. This commitment stands out boldly in almost all they said and did; and yet it is seldom seen today for what it was. Part of the reason for this is our tendency to assume that people (and especially "elites") always act for reasons other than those they profess. Even if we overcome that paralyzing and self-defeating premise, we stumble on the Framers' persistent and often sharp criticisms of democracy. They seem to be either hypocritical or half-hearted in their commitment to popular government.

The explanation at this level is simple and, it seems to me, altogether compelling. Martin Diamond spent much of his scholarly life trying to show that the Framers' devotion to popular government was the devotion of a true friend who sees the defects of a friend, studies them, and combats them so that they should not destroy the thing he loves.[3] Popular government is good, but it is problematic. It is not, in this, different from any other kind of government, as James Madison explained so well to Jefferson (who understood the point, though he understood it differently from Madison). Each government has an evil tendency that is connected to its own vital principle. In a monarchy it is the king who must be watched; in an oligarchy, the rich; in a popular government, the people. Democracy is a problem in the United States precisely because of the extent to which the people are made the ruler. The beginning point, then, is that popular government is good but problematic in its own way, the specific danger being majority foolishness or tyranny. Democratic statesmanship must be understood, above all, in the light of that great danger, which implies its great task.

At the time of the American founding, the traditional solution to this problem was to build into the government representation of social elements that could check one another, and particularly the *demos,* with the aim of securing the benefits of all and resisting the dangers of each. The American Constitution of 1787 rested on a rejection of this traditional solution. Part of the reason was the unavailability in the United States of the elements of the traditional mixed regime, and especially of a hereditary aristocracy. We do not, the American Founders often said, have the materials for such a mixture. A deeper reason, and the reason most of the Americans thought their solution to the problem was superior even to the admirable and time-tested British regime, was that in the modern mixed regime there was inherent a degree of deception, of resting the working government on appearances rather than on fundamental truths. The traditional mixed regime, as the Americans knew it from Blackstone and Montesquieu, softened the truth of original human equality with the willingness of people to take their places in a natural-seeming hierarchy. It relied heavily on a traditional class of leaders disposed to public service and popularly accepted as entitled to it. The problem was how to secure the benefits of the traditional mixed government without the materials and without the myths and deceptions that such governments involve. The Constitution of 1787 was the Founders' answer.

From the point of view of traditional mixed government, this Constitution looks "democratic"; from the point of view of simple democracy it looks "mixed." Both of these terms were sometimes used by the Founders, but the more common and accurate designations were "popular" and "complex." James Wilson caught the essence, I think, in this characterization:

> In its principles, Sir, it is purely democratical; varying indeed, in its form, in order to admit all the advantages, and to exclude all the disadvantages which are incidental to the known and established constitutions of government. But when we take an extensive and accurate view of the streams of power that appear through this great and comprehensive plan, when we contemplate the variety of their directions, the force and dignity of their currents, when we behold them intersecting, embracing, and surrounding the vast possessions and interests of the continent, and when we see them distributing on all hands beauty, energy and riches, still, however numerous and wide their courses, however diversified and remote the blessings they diffuse, we shall be able to trace them all to one great and noble source, THE PEOPLE.[4]

This government is popular but not simply popular. It does not, however, rely on mystery or myth to check the fundamental popular impulse. "Nondemocratic" elements are at work (though not nondemocratic social entities, in Wilson's description), but they are out in the open. This government is like a glass-enclosed clock. Its "works" are visible to all and must be understood and accepted by all in order to function properly. Not many of the Framers were quite as confident as Wilson of the reasonableness of the people, but the government they constructed was nevertheless understood by them all to be unusual in the relatively small demands it placed on a political aristocracy and in the relatively great demands it placed on the people. The Senate was to make its distinctive contribution, for example, not because it consists of people presumed to have some superior title to rule or people with huge social influence derived from family tradition or wealth, but mainly because the interest of the men in the Senate is constitutionally tied to certain "senatorial" duties and because the people would *see,* over a relatively short time, the benefits of such a non-popular institution.

There were men of the founding generation who found this solution facile and feeble. Alexander Hamilton's reservations are the most pertinent for our present purpose. Hamilton feared that there would be nothing in the new government (and the new society) strong enough to check or channel the reigning popular impulse. Hamilton doubted the effectiveness of the Virginia Plan (put forward in the Constitutional Convention by Madison, Edmund Randolph, and others) to check the excesses of democracy that had been experienced in many of the states. "A democratic assembly is to be checked by a democratic senate, and both these by a democratic chief magistrate," Hamilton wrote.[5] This looked to him like "pork still, with a little change of the sauce."[6]

While Hamilton labored brilliantly to explain and to defend and to operate this Constitution, his earlier reservations revived, as is well known, as he saw what he thought to be the weakness of the elements in the Constitution designed to check democratic foolishness and injustice. Alexis de Tocqueville confirms this view, but at the same time presents a wider or at least a different horizon. Even more directly pertinent are the more modest administrative histories of Leonard D. White. It is striking that when White looked at the actual conduct of the government in the early years, including both the Federalist and Jeffersonian periods, it was characterized by what he called "administration by gentlemen."[7] The federal government in its early years was operated by a relatively small group of men who were socially prominent and who took their bearings from English notions of the right and, more especially, the obligation of members of the class of gentlemen to serve their country by conducting its affairs, and to do that with wisdom, honesty, and public spirit. To the extent that White is correct, it appears the actual conduct of government then depended crucially on the existence of the political influence of a class of gentlemen, with an ability and a commitment to prudent statesmanship for which the framers of the Constitution had made no provision. Once the residual, English-based gentry was used up, there was little to preserve or maintain it, and the underlying populism—Hamilton's "pork"—took full command.

I exaggerate, of course. The constitutional scheme of checks and balances continued to function (indeed, in a certain sense, came into its own) under the Jacksonians. If the gentry was swept aside, if demagoguery thrived, the results were still mixed. Andrew Jackson's claims for the democratic presidency (accompanied by a certain notion of administration) were challenged, deflected, blunted by men in the Senate and the courts acting much as Madison expected they would act. But I am here following one strand of American history and American political thinking. It is not the only strand; it may or may not turn out to be the strongest and most persistent one; but it does seem to be the one most clearly tied to the self-understanding of American statesmen. It became increasingly difficult as the nineteenth and twentieth centuries wore on for American statesmen to see themselves politically as anything more than mouthpieces of popular opinion.

The story we are recounting is completed, in the decisive sense, with civil service reform, which is the end of democratic statesmanship and the beginning of the contemporary decay of practical statesmanship. The Jacksonian doctrine of rotation in office (and the Jacksonian program in general) was meant to take the government out of the hands of the few and give it to the many. As rotation declined into spoils, however, it seemed that the result had been to turn over the government from an honest and competent aristocracy to a dishonest and incompetent one. Indeed, the concern of the civil service reform movement that began to build after the Civil War was fundamentally with government dishonesty rather than with government incompetence. Like the Jacksonians, the civil service reformers' concern was political and moral; and like the Jacksonians, the civil service reformers sought to remove an illegitimate and corrupting obstruction that had grown up in the way of the free, healthy, spontaneous expression of the political will of the American people. The reform movement is today often described as having been "elitist" and antidemocratic. It involved a "good-government" elite attempting to destroy the vulgar, corrupt, unsystematic, but democratic functioning of patronage-based political parties. This is not inconsistent with the civil service reformers' view of themselves as returning to the principles of the Founders. But what both this self-understanding and this sociological view of the civil service reform movement missed is that the reformers had rejected, or forgotten, the central element in the Founders' statesmanship, namely, a sense of the problematic character of democracy. In this fundamental sense, they stood with the Jacksonians against the Founders.

Even that, however, is not precise enough. Democracy was in a way still seen as problematic by the reformers, but the focus of the problem had shifted for them from politics to administration. They believed that democracy itself is not unproblematic (the problem here is clearing away the rubble of various kinds that obstructs it), but its implementation *is* unproblematic.

This prepared the way for the next and, as it were, final step in the development of American statesmanship, the science of administration or scientific management. Before turning to that, however, it may be useful to summarize and to reflect on the significance of this development. Leonard D. White described this whole development as a healthy working through of the basic principle of the American republic (again, Tocqueville's similar but more critical account is pertinent). As White saw it, bringing into focus a very widespread view, the development ran as follows: first came the Federalist period, characterized by elitist politics plus sound administration; then the Jacksonian period, characterized by democratic politics and unsound administration; and now, a "new Hamiltonianism," characterized by the return, as a result of civil-service reform, to the sound administration of the Founders but now in the service of democratic politics.[8] This view misses three major considerations: (1) The old Hamiltonianism was not antidemocratic, but it was concerned with the problematic character of democracy. (2) Democracy is still problematic; and losing the sense of that problem (however much the Framers may have missed solving it), the new Hamiltonianism is shallow in the decisive respect. (3) The administrative theory and practice of the old Hamiltonianism, although it was indeed related to scientific management, had a commonsense quality that may have given it more severe limits in some respects than modern administrative science but also a breadth and soundness that today's understanding of administration lacks. To that second aspect of the decay of American statesmanship I now turn.

The Decay of Rational Statesmanship

When Woodrow Wilson called in 1887 for a new science of administration, he saw himself as building upon and to some extent restoring the work of the Founders. With the decisive victory of liberal democratic theory, the making of the U.S. Constitution, and the repair of the major defect of that Constitution in the Civil War, the great task of regime building and constitution making was finished. There would still be a need to extend liberal democracy to other parts of the world and a continuing need to modify and repair its constitutional structure. Nonetheless, the locus of the decisive problems of government had shifted from questions of constitution making and high politics to questions of administration. Wilson sought, then, to turn attention from largely obsolete and fruitless political controversy to the pressing and still unsolved problems of running the Constitution. Political theory had had its day; the task for today and tomorrow was the development and application of administrative theory. Wilson proposed that the democracies look to the systematic development of administration that had taken place under more autocratic governments, with a view to developing and learning to use the science of administration, the fundamental premise of which is that there is "but one rule of good administration for all governments alike."[9]

In many important ways, Wilson's proposal and the project of administrative science and practice that followed from it were indeed extensions of the Founders' own project. In the most crucial sense, it can be said that, for the Founders, the problem of government is a matter of administration. Government was no longer seen as a grappling with various and conflicting claims to rule, claims to determine the ends and character of social life. Instead, they believed the legitimate end of government is fixed: the securing of individual rights. In question, in terms of both forms of government and their operation, are the arrangements and policies that under given circumstances would be the best means to that fixed end. This is the reason that discussions, by the founding generation, of forms of government have the curiously shallow quality that has frustrated so many analysts. Monarchy no longer "rode tilt against democracy," as Woodrow Wilson put it.[10] There were still differences, and forms of government were still important (see *Federalist* 70), but they no longer carried anything like their traditional freight. Government was no longer seen as directing and shaping human existence, but as having the much narrower (though indispensable) function of facilitating the peaceful enjoyment of the private life. In this view, government and the whole public sphere are decisively instrumental; government is reduced to administration. Questions of forms of government, too, become instrumental. Much less is at stake in a dispute between "democracy" and "monarchy," for example. The question is merely what kind of governmental arrangements will, under given conditions, be most likely to secure the aggregate of individual liberty, which it is the business of any government to secure. (This is why constitutional and administrative questions, in contrast to political questions, are closely related for Wilson.)

"Statesmanship" in such a government is diminished in proportion. It can reasonably be called administration, though it may be administration of a rather high and demanding kind. The moral demands on statesmen in such a government are reduced to a commitment to serve the "permanent and aggregate interests of the community," as Madison called them.[11] The intellectual demands are reduced to the formulation and implementation of appropriate means to fairly limited ends. To the American Founders, however, even these demands seemed too great. The moral demands on the statesman were further reduced by putting him in a constitutional position, so far as possible, where his private interests would coincide with his public duty. The whole complex system of checks and balances and related constitutional devices have this aim. The intellectual demands (our special concern here) would be reduced through the development of the sciences dealing with the main areas of the statesman's (now rather limited) concerns. Thus, to the Founders, the science of economics—or rather political economy—is queen; derivative from this are the subordinate sciences of, for example, military administration, governmental budgeting and accounting, and the arrangement of public offices. The American statesman of the future would be not a George Washington but a Robert Morris, a man whose private interests were closely tied to his country's fortunes and whose statesmanship consisted of the knowledge that a merchant and financier has of the way society works.

In sum, then, the American Founders' view of statesmanship could be described as follows. There is never needed that kind of statesmanship that had formerly been regarded as its essence: great, way-of-life-setting, character-forming political leadership. That kind of leadership was based upon a misapprehension of political life, a failure to understand its decisively instrumental function. There may be needed, however, rarely but occasionally, what might be called high American statesmanship, or high liberal statesmanship, comparable to that of the Founders themselves. The requirements here are an extraordinary (and perhaps ultimately inexplicable) devotion to public duty and an understanding of the principles of governmental structure and operation of the broadest and deepest kind. Note that this statesmanship is still, in a fundamental sense, "administrative"; it ministers to the private sphere essentially by securing private rights. Most of the time, however, an even narrower statesmanship will be sufficient: the activities of reasonably decent and well-informed people, guided by the constitutional system and by moral and prudential maxims derived from widely understood principles of political economy, military science, public finance, and so forth.

Just as the popular principle became radicalized, so did the "science" of government or administration become radicalized. The Founders' maxims of administrative statesmanship became Wilson's "one rule of good administration for all governments alike," which in turn became Frederick Taylor's "one best method," and that in turn became the "maximizing" model (and all of its various elaborations and qualifications) of contemporary decision-making science.

Taylor is perhaps the crucial turning point. He insisted that his techniques—such as time-and-motion studies—must never be separated from the broader "philosophy of scientific management." That philosophy was a simplification of modern liberalism. Taylor saw scientific management as the working principle of a whole social system in which there is ultimately social harmony among apparently competing groups and individuals. He believed that once the true principles of organized activity are discovered and applied through scientific management, political and social conflict, which is based upon ignorance and misunderstanding, will be dispelled. Compared with the Founders' view of American statesmen, Taylor's administrative statesman is relatively narrow.

The context of the older statesmanship was still a political or constitutional order that was, indeed, expected to limit the statesman's horizon; but that horizon was, nevertheless, a political one, and that was reflected in the statesman's everyday judgments. For Taylor, on the other hand, the context is a presumed natural harmony. There is ultimately no need for politics—either as providing a broad political order within which economic activity is pursued or (therefore) adjusting competing and (in terms of mere self-interest) irreconcilable demands. Taylor did not entirely escape the need for the more traditional moral and political judgment. The increase in pay for Schmidt, the carrier of iron hogs, was not to be in proportion to his greater efficiency (which resulted merely from his willingness to accept the commands of the scientifically informed supervisor); it was to be enough to stimulate him to raise the level of his private life, but not so much as to demoralize him.[12] It is not clear where the standard for such judgments comes from in Taylor's scheme (though it should be noted that it is not clear either where the standard for equivalent decisions by traditional liberal statesmen comes from). Nor is it clear why the scientific manager does not attempt to pay Schmidt as little as possible in order to keep an unfair share of the benefits of increased efficiency for himself. The whole problem of the fidelity of the statesman, with which the Framers were so deeply and, on the whole, effectively concerned, was largely ignored by Taylor. Not surprisingly, Taylorism came to be, or at least was widely thought be, an instrument of management. It became part of a broader political context, for which Taylorism itself could not account and to which it could not direct itself.

This "philosophy" of scientific management, which seemed to Taylor so fundamental, quickly dropped away, distorting Taylorism in ways that seemed to have been invited by Taylor (as Taylorism distorted the administrative thought of the Founders). What was left was the pool of techniques of scientific management, the best known of which are time-and-motion studies, and the notion of what he called the "one best method."

Now, among the various methods and implements used in each element of each trade there is always one method and one implement which is quicker and better than any of the rest. And this one best method and best implement can only be discovered or developed through a scientific study and analysis of all of the methods and implements in use, together with accurate, minute, motion and time study. This involves the gradual substitution of science for rule of thumb throughout the mechanic arts.[13]

This notion, which is basic to scientific management and all its heirs, would have seemed strange to the Founders with their more commonsense notions of administrative science. Yet, it could be argued that Taylor was merely making clear and explicit what the earlier science implied: that the theoretical challenge is to develop that science of "management" in the broadest sense that will ultimately or in principle utterly displace the ad hoc, muddled, and inefficient lore of the traditional craftsman, as well as the ad hoc, muddled, and inefficient judgment of the traditional statesman.

What I have called scientific management in the broadest sense has taken a further large step beyond Taylorism, but in the same direction. Taylor can be understood as radicalizing the Founders' attempt to free the statesman from major concern with the broadest ends of his activities. The statesman provided for by the Founders "works" the system without having to try to follow his decisions to their broadest ends; the Taylor manager similarly develops his science secure in the knowledge that better means will naturally lead to good ends. In these ways, both the Founders' statesman and Taylor's statesman are substantially relieved of responsibility for considering the highest or broadest ends. In the concrete situation, however, both are emphatically end-oriented. Taylorism is a science of means to given ends. The science was instrumental in the way administration had always been understood to be instrumental, as subordinate to given ends. The rationale of practical statesmanship became severely narrowed, but it was not transformed.

This traditional way of thinking about administration has the great advantage that the given ends guide and limit the search for means. That advantage, however, is purchased at a price that is scientifically unacceptable. The standard scientific formula becomes: Given a comprehensive measurable statement of ends, there is but one best means. It became increasingly clear that such a requirement is not only impossible in practice (that is not regarded as fatal), but also inadequate in principle. "Ends" are misleading reflections of prescientific judgmental statesmanship. What common sense calls "ends" are ultimately mere wants, and one cannot be expected to know what one wants until one knows what one might have and at what cost. The very language of means-ends is not merely imprecise or approximate, it is essentially misleading. The decisive break comes with its replacement by something like a "behavior-alternative" model (what are my possible courses of action and which do I want?) or a utility-maximization model freed from the teleological implications of the means-ends formula, but now at the price of crushing informational and calculational demands and utter subjection to essentially arbitrary preference.

This independence from ends, and its accompanying benefits and problems, is what characterized the most recent version of scientific management. It is surely true, as earlier laborers in the vineyard of scientific management complained, that such fashionable schemes as "systems analysis" and planning, programming, and budgeting systems (PPBS) are in many ways less new and original than they claim. However, there is today a rather widespread understanding of the fact that what scientific management has been moving toward is not statesmanship, and not even administration or management, but rather economizing in the true sense.

The contribution of "systems analysis" is to clarify and elaborate the proposition that all practical rationality, the rationality of administration, the rationality of choice, is economic rationality. "It should go without saying that all decision-making persons or groups attempt to economize, in the true sense of the word. That is, they try to make the 'most,' as they conceive of the 'most,' of whatever resources they have."[14]

With this understanding clearly in mind, the new science of choice can overcome the two great defects of traditional statesmanship, which even the earlier forms of scientific management had not altogether corrected: its preoccupation with ends and its inability or unwillingness to replace mere maxims of action with objective measurement. In his preoccupation with given ends—those that seem important at the moment or those he is administratively responsible for—the traditional statesman or even the fairly sophisticated "manager" has failed to see the essentially economic character of all decision making. Thus, one of the men who helped to apply the new understanding to the Department of Defense, where it has had its greatest (though still disputed) success, explained that in 1961 military planning was in "disarray" because of the separation of military planning and fiscal planning. Military plans were made more or less incrementally and in terms of certain presumed military needs and objectives, with the price tag tacked on afterward. With the help of PPBS, the economic character of the decisions was recognized. Thus costs and national security objectives were linked at the outset, while systems analysis provided quantitative information on various possibilities.

Although it is not always easy to understand just how far the claims of systems analysis extend, in general it can be said that greater sophistication about the economic underpinnings and techniques of quantification has been accompanied by greater sophistication in claims about practical applicability. The proponents of systems analysis are, generally, considerably less expansive than Taylor, for example, in the extent of their claims to replace traditional commonsense judgment. They emphasize that quantitative analysis can clarify and make more intelligent, but cannot displace, the nonscientific decision of the responsible administrator. Both implicitly (for example, in the "end" implications of "program" budgeting) and explicitly (for example, in various models of what Herbert Simon called "satisficing"),[15] the proponents of systems analysis concede and even grapple with the limits of their science. If the practical claim is muted, the theoretical claim is even sharper and more comprehensive. Systems analysis admits, indeed emphasizes, that it can never absorb completely the "practical" side of practical reason. At the same time, it clearly affirms that it does in principle comprehend the "rational" side of practical reason. Systems analysis (or the science of the economics of decision making) is not all that there is to practical reason in decision making, but it is all there is to the *reason* of practical reason.

Some Commonsense Corrections

Does this more or less historical analysis help us to understand contemporary issues of American statesmanship? It seems to me that it does. It encourages us to revive for consideration some rather obvious, useful commonsense observations about American statesmanship—what it is and what it ought to be. It also leads into some less obvious, more fundamental theoretical issues, the practical thrust of which is much more obscure, but which are probably determinative in the long run.

Populism

It is not difficult to grasp and to be persuaded by the need a democracy has of regulation and guidance in the face of some of its own tendencies toward foolishness and injustice. If we can add to our rather sharp consciousness of the dangers of "elites" a recollection of the dangers of majorities, our statesmanship will be better grounded. Indeed this lesson has never been forgotten in practice. What has been neglected is its understanding and justification in principle. Government still acts in opposition to simple democracy (when it secures the rights of minorities and individuals, for example), but mostly we talk as if the solution to the problems of democracy is more democracy. That is why there is a persistent *tendency* to resolve more or less complex notions of American democracy into some kind of simple populism.

This simplistic talk at the level of principle tends to undermine more prudent views at the level of practice. Even the modern Supreme Court, the strongest bastion of nonpopulist principle, has an increasingly difficult time giving an account of itself. Nevertheless, in the courts there is still a self-conscious and principled capacity to resist mere majoritarianism, weakened as this may have become. In the other parts of the government, such a capacity is much less evident. One of the results is, I think, an undermining of the statesman's confidence in his own judgment, in the legitimacy of relying on his own judgment even in the face of popular disagreement. The further and even more harmful result is that the people at large are constantly taught by their statesmen's rhetoric that their opinion is the touchstone of politics. Because this is not the case in practice, and cannot be the case in any respectable regime, the contradiction strains the system, driving true leadership underground and depriving the system of popular confidence. The whole doctrine of elitism, in both its popular and scholarly forms, owes much to the absence in our public rhetoric (and behind that in our scholarly understanding) of a justification of the role of an "elite," a not simply responsive statesmanship, in American democracy.

The danger of populism to popular government has to be met, I think, at two levels. At the level of institutions, the problem is basically recovering (perhaps in different forms) the lessons of the Framers. I have mentioned the Supreme Court, and it is surely vital to our whole constitutional system that the broad understanding and acceptance of the legitimacy of such a contrademocratic institution, as Alexander Bickel called it, not be lost; or if it has in principle been lost, that it be recovered.

Another institution that has seemed promising to me in this regard is the bureaucracy, which, for all its limitations, does introduce into the political system elements of stability, intelligence, and equity that are not altogether dissimilar to the qualities intended to be provided by the original Senate. The advantage of the bureaucracy from this point of view is its very invincibility (a democracy has a much harder time dispensing with the bureaucracy than with the Senate, as Max Weber—with somewhat different intentions—has shown). The disadvantage is the bureaucracy's narrowness and its strong tendency toward the merely technical, a tendency strengthened under modern doctrines of scientific management. A properly schooled bureaucracy might, however, be a solidly based source of the intelligence, stability, equity, and public-spiritedness that a democracy needs.

But institutional arrangements are probably not sufficient, and the degree to which the Founders relied on them may partly explain the power of the populist principle. The institutions require what I have argued has been seriously lacking, namely public justification and, therefore, continued legitimacy in the eyes of the people, who are the ultimate rulers. What some of the Founders neglected is that in a popular government, however much it is modified with various "sauces" (and the bureaucracy is a fairly penetrating one), the people have to be reasoned with by their statesmen. This means reasoning not only at the level of specific policies but also at the level of constitutional principle. Precisely because the American government is so transparent, relatively speaking, so little reliant on lords, kings, and priests, American statesmen must keep alive its basic rationale. At the least this means not playing the easy game of populist rhetoric, which cannot but undermine, in the long run, the capacity of the system to act well. At the most it means finding ways of reinforcing and deepening the people's commonsense understanding that government, even popular government, is more than a matter of registering and implementing dominant opinion.

This task of leadership is crucial, and it provides a kind of test of contemporary statesmen. Any American statesman whose public face is populistic is not performing his highest duty, no matter how prudent and successful his specific policies may be. This points us, however, to the deeper consideration to which I have made reference. The founding generation, people and leaders alike, could grasp the principle of checks on popular opinion and could make informed judgments about specific institutions and policies because they were persuaded of the truth of the foundation and end of that government. That there can be majority tyranny is a notion that makes sense to people who see government as designed to secure inalienable rights. If this truth is denied or lost sight of—as is surely the case today—it becomes exceedingly difficult to hold any ground against the populist impulse.

The loose relativism that today penetrates popular political ethical understanding tends to support the kind of loose populism I have been examining and criticizing. Such relativism is the ultimate obstacle to any thoroughgoing mitigation (by which I do not mean some kind of aristocratic displacement) of simplistic democracy. The great popular—and final—challenge today is, "Who's to say?" The question implies not only that it is extremely difficult and dangerous to give anyone (or any governmental institution) the power to "say" what is right or what is to be done, but that there is in principle no way to "say" what is right or what should be done. Liberal government exists in a tension between popular control and individual rights. With the washing away of the ground of individual rights, consent in one form or another seems to be only place for a statesman to stand.

If this describes the popular view, the scholarly view is fundamentally identical. Almost the whole range of dispute among scholars about how American democracy does and should work takes place within the "consent" arena. What is popular consent? How is it articulated, and how is it to be most accurately recorded and responded to by government? These are the agreed issues. There are occasional forays outside the field of populism, but their feebleness tends to support my broad point. The "new public administration," for example, has been dissatisfied, mainly on political grounds, with the subordination of the old public administration to dominant public opinion. The *ground* on which the new public administration might resist popular opinion is a treacherous bog consisting of supposed silent or suppressed majorities (a path out of the bog and onto the safe ground of populism again), or an almost undefended commitment to socially disadvantaged people (as the definition of social equity and social consciousness), or a more or less simple existentialism, which the new public administration is not the first to see is the main alternative to democratism. If sheer preference or commitment is all there is, why not mine?

Scientific Management

Just as a serious examination of the insufficiency of populism yields a number of commonsense corrections, so does the serious examination of the insufficiencies of scientific management. But as contemporary populism points to the underlying issue of natural rights, so contemporary scientific management points to the underlying issue of the nature of human reason. In this case it may be more helpful to touch (with some apprehension) on this underlying issue before turning to some commonsense thoughts about statesmanship or practical reason. We are not going to be much helped here by the thought of the American Founders. They were far less articulate and self-conscious in their thinking about practical reason, or decisionmaking, or the science of government, than they were about the political side of government. Their thrust was in the direction of systematic science, but this science did not seem to be inconsistent with, or likely to replace, traditional prudence. We who live with the sometimes unintended results of their work and thought need to try to recover and reflect upon some of their more or less hidden assumptions.

Our problem is to understand practical reason or, in the contemporary term, "rational" decision making. The issue is well framed in Simon's forceful and influential attack on the maxims of so-called practical judgment. Simon's argument is that these maxims, which are supposed to guide practical reason and which are the glory of the "practical man," are in fact empty because they are self-contradictory.

For every maxim there is a countermaxim: look before you leap; he who hesitates is lost. The sum of practical rationality here is zero. If the practical man decides well (for example, if he maximizes his values), either he is lucky or he is proceeding according to a rationality more systematic and scientific than he knows, which it is the business of the science of decision making to elaborate and extend. (This is a theoretical elaboration of Taylor's scientific management.)

The issue here is, what *is* rational decision making? I think many of the critics of scientific management have given up the game too easily, granting a Simonian understanding of what rational decision making is but contending that the sphere of rationality in decision making is much more limited than Simon and others suggest. Practical judgment turns out to be either an accommodation to practical political necessities or an unavoidable arbitrariness. (It is the willingness of systems analysis proponents to admit these limitations on practical rationality that has typically muddled the issue in the current literature.) I think the attack must be carried further.

I will not claim victory here, but I do want at least to open the question of whether scientific management misunderstands the essence, if not the scope, of practical rationality. I will frame the issue as a proposition: the two critical principles of the current understanding of practical reason, or rational decision making—the notion of the "one best method" and the assumption that all practical reasoning is essentially economic reasoning—do not make good sense.

As already suggested, the crux of scientific management is the notion of "one best method." Does it not make more sense to say that practically there often *is* no one best method? The road to the one best method is not the road to rationality but to insanity. There are many cases where it just does not matter much which one of alternative choices is made (whether, for example, to ride elevator A or elevator B). It is not rational to worry or calculate much about something that does not matter much, even if one could conceive of and even perhaps discover some marginal benefit one way or the other (elevator A is closer to the entrance and thus more used and thus more worn—or is it therefore better maintained?). In other cases, the difference between alternative possible choices may matter very much, but there may be practically no way to know which one is better. It is likely that the outcomes cannot be known in crucial respects. There is, of course, a good deal of thinking and research on decision making under conditions of uncertainty, but again the premise of this thinking is that these conditions *limit* rationality. My suggestion is the commonsensical and, I think, practically indispensable notion that one of the most important elements of practical reason—or "rational" decision making—is precisely how well or poorly such limits are grappled with. The person who insists on calculating, and constantly postpones decisions in order to get more information and make more predictions and calculations, is acting *irrationally* in any sensible view, though he is merely persisting in a rational pursuit according to the strict economizing model. Simon speaks of "bounded rationality," yet he more or less admits that it is only because of these irrational boundaries that any given exercise of rationality makes any sense at all. Simon's main response to the insanity of the maximizing model is what he calls "satisficing," which is a much more commonsense (and, incidentally, traditional means-end) approach in which the decision maker is satisfied with the decision that is "good enough" instead of insisting on maximizing. That seems altogether, may we say, reasonable. But for Simon it is a necessary falling short of reason. We "satisfice" because we have not the wits to maximize. If we can maximize, we would be silly to "satisfice." On the contrary, I think we "satisfice" because we have the wits to know that we *cannot* maximize and that we would be insane to try to do so. The notion of the "one best method," that human rationality is the maximization of utility, is, as I have tried to show in an extended analysis of Simon, a fragile bridge suspended between two great fires, the arbitrariness of preference and the insanity of infinite calculation, by which it is consumed.[16]

The second side of the contemporary view of practical reason is the contention that all practical reasoning, all rational decision making, is essentially economic. That does not mean that there is any claim that all people do act as economizers—or even that anyone actually does it (it turns out to be quite impossible); but so far as they are rational they are economizers. The genius of "economic" rationality is that it is unqualifiedly comprehensive and it is also a purely instrumental science. All "ends," "values," are reduced to "utility," which provides the ultimate test of the science of rational choice without threatening its purely instrumental character. Clearly, there is some truth in this whole understanding. To take the previously given example of military planning, it is surely correct that for military planners utterly to ignore questions of cost does involve their avoiding the "hard management choices" that must be made. In government, at least, every decision (well, almost every decision) can be and at some point must be reduced to a decision about budget, about economizing. Clearly, economizing is involved in practical reasoning, is necessary to it; the question is whether that is all there is to it or whether that is truly its essence.

Consider the experience and the character of the Office of Management and Budget (formerly the Bureau of the Budget). The centrality and independence of the OMB are undeniable. It is hard to imagine a government without such an institution performing such a function (though it is perhaps not quite as hard to imagine as we might today think, and the effort might be instructive). It is easy, moreover, to agree that the director of the OMB, whoever that person may be, is the superior, despite the lack of cabinet position and the lower salary, of most heads of departments. But is it imaginable that the OMB should govern—would that be reasonable? My point is simple, but I think very pertinent to the present issue. It is surely important that generals be compelled to face the issue of cost/benefit, and the people who do that compelling are as vital in practice as that element of practical rationality is vital in principle. But must not generals remain generals? Could the OMB defend the country? Could it conduct foreign relations? Could it protect individual rights?

What we need to consider here is the effect of economic thinking and whether its claim to be practical rationality makes sense. Is not the beginning of military rationality some kind of understanding of an adequate defense, rather than some abstract notion of maximizing utility or even the rather less abstract notion of "more bang for the buck"? Are not similar understandings the essential basis for practical rationality in other spheres? The legitimate rights of minorities ought to be secured. Old people ought to be able to live decently. All of these raise or point to economic questions, but they are not "economizing" in themselves. The question is whether such end-oriented views are not independent, indispensable bases of practical rationality.

The crux in practice is what kind of decision results from one view or the other. Grant that a general will make bad decisions if he utterly ignores questions of cost (which the fact of limited resources makes it extremely difficult to do). But then consider what kind of decision the economist is likely to make. Is he not likely to be easily shifted from a "utility" that is costly to one that is less so? Is he not likely to prefer utilities and costs that are measurable over those are not? I do not claim that the economists necessarily make such errors in practical reasoning—any more than it can be claimed that the general is necessarily irresponsible or indifferent to cost/benefit—but that is the tendency.

One of the common criticisms of scientific management in various forms, including systems analysis, is its indifference to structure and institutions and, at the same time, its thoughtless tendency to foster centralized institutions. The basis of this criticism is the traditional fear that the centralization fostered by the pursuit of administrative efficiency will threaten democracy. It should be noted that the claim that scientific management has a centralizing tendency is controversial. Some defenders of systems analysis have contended that it is neutral with regard to structure and indeed can foster decentralization. Taking advantage of an ambiguity that is unresolved in Weber's account of bureaucracy, they contend that the development of objectively rational bases of decision reduces the dependence on (personal) authority and therefore on hierarchy. In Weberian terms, the stronger and more comprehensive the definition of jurisdiction, the weaker can be the lines of hierarchical authority (subject, of course, to the necessity of enforcing jurisdictional definition that is relatively unexplored by scientific management). But in practice, surely, and, as I have tried at least to suggest, in principle also, scientific management is centralizing. It is centralizing in the sense that Taylor understood perfectly well, that the crucial and governing activity is the development of the science itself, which can only occur (except derivatively) at the top. It is centralizing, further, to the extent that gaps in the science make it necessary to resort to central *authority* to support the science itself. And it is centralizing to the extent that (presuming a comprehensive science) there remains a continuing need to *enforce* the rational design of the science.

Scientific management radicalizes the claim for "unity" in administration. When Andrew Jackson defended his removal of subordinates even contrary to congressional legislation, he presented a view of administration as well as a view of democracy. Administration was seen as residing crucially in the president, with the administration serving as his eyes and hands. The Whig view, on the other hand, rested not only on a different (more "pluralistic") view of American politics but also on a different view of administration. The Whigs saw public administration not as a closed hierarchy leading to the top but as pools of official discretion, loosely connected but largely independent. Jackson and the Whigs were primarily concerned with what today we would call the issue of responsibility—Jackson, to the president; the Whigs, to the law. But the implicit views of public administration are especially interesting here, and the Whig view in particular since it is the one that seems always to lose. This view emphasizes the importance of the exercise of experienced, informed, responsible discretion as the heart of administration. Sound discretion, not obedience to higher command, is the essence of good administration, though both, of course, are always involved. Administrative structures should be built to provide the right conditions for this informed good judgment—independent regulatory commissions are a case in point. The Whig view of administration is modeled, one might say, on the judge. (One could describe modern administrative science as the decisive displacement of the judge as the model administrator by the administrative assistant—even, increasingly, in the courts themselves.) A major aspect of the Whig model was the notion of the judge's responsibility, but I want to point to another side, the kind of practical reason the judge exercises. His judgment here is confined and guided by more or less severe limits of the law, but within these limits the judge is expected to secure a personal grasp on the whole and to exercise his best judgment. The judge is thus, characteristically, assisted by law clerks, whose very immaturity, transience, and small numbers reinforce the judge's personal responsibility and judgment.

It seems reasonably clear that any government, to be well administered, needs a judicious combination of these two principles—each may appropriately predominate in its own time and place. But what we need to recover is an understanding of the claim of what can be called the judicial model of rationality. Partly because of our failure to grasp the reason of that model, it always tends to lose out in a contest with centralized, hierarchical rationality.

Perhaps the most striking omission in scientific management is any concern with the moral side of decision making, especially of political decision making. There is some current renewed interest in the ethics of administration or decision making, but it tends to result either in (fringe) codes-of-ethics thinking, the assumption of which is that ethics surrounds practical decision making but does not really enter into it; or in (sterile) case studies of the confrontation of (arbitrary) public policies and (arbitrary) personal preferences.

What we can roughly but usefully call the moral side of public decision making was for the American Founders the major concern; today the intellectual side has occupied almost the whole ground. Yet in any kind of practical situation, the question of the fidelity of the decision maker is crucial. The question that Taylor could not answer (or could answer only by assuming a simplistic harmony)—why will the scientific manager not try to exploit his workers?—was for the Founders the vital issue of statesmanship.

Robert Hutchins once observed of university administration that the intellectual problems, adapting means to ends, are small compared with the moral problems.[17] A fairly simple example: It is on the whole easier to know that someone does not deserve academic tenure than it is to decide not to give it to him. As I cast my mind back on the many administrative situations I have been involved in, I am struck by the importance of the moral character of the people in charge. I think of a small army unit that constantly threatened to come unhinged under the leadership of an intelligent and able but weak commander and that was held together only by the stern, able, but mule-skinner army morality of an old, extremely inefficient master sergeant. I think of political science departments whose fortunes (so far as they are not determined from the outside) seem to wax and wane far more in rhythm with the integrity and moral stature of department heads than with their administrative ability in the usual sense. I do not mean to assert the simple-minded proposition that good people make good administrators, or even that good administrators need to be good people— although that is not a bad place to start. I think that one could defend the proposition that moral stature is vital to administration or statesmanship of any consequence. And that is precisely what is lacking in our statesmen trained in and oriented to scientific management. They are no more really bad men than really good ones; rather, they tend to be morally uninteresting children. That dimension—moral stature—is missing or severely truncated.

The reference to Hutchins suggests another commonsense correction of the scientific-management view of statesmanship, namely that the good statesman has a good understanding of and commitment to the ends of his organization, whatever they are. University presidents these days tend to be bookkeepers and brokers among their various "constituencies." That may, often, be good enough, but such administrators work in the shadow of people who knew what universities are for and how any particular university fits into that broad function. Greatness in a president of the United States, in a president of a university, in a general of the army, or in a chief of a governmental bureau is determined among other things by the grasp he has of the *ends* of the organization. A fairly loose grasp may be sufficient most of the time, but even mundane statesmanship is rooted in some such understanding. If an ordinary public servant does not need the grasp of the American regime of a Lincoln, he does need, as John Rohr suggests, at least the grasp of a reasonably competent student of some parts of American constitutional law.[18]

A final commonsense observation, harder to explain and defend, and for that reason more directly pertinent to the underlying question of practical reason, is that the essence of statesmanship is to be found in the old distinction between line and staff. The curious thing about decision-making theory is that it is not about decisions but about getting ready to make decisions. The rationality of scientific management is the rationality of the staff, but it does not reach, does not treat whatever it is that is finally decisive. Decisiveness is, after all, universally acknowledged to be central to good administration of any consequence, yet it has no place in decision-making theory.

(Editorial note: The following is an outline that Herbert Storing prepared of the conclusion to this essay, which he died before completing.)

Conclusion

Authentic American statesmanship has decayed, but it decayed (as it were) from within.

1. Premise: statesmanship is in the service of the private sphere. This means that the activity of statesmanship is not seen as "fulfilling" and tends to be held in low esteem.

2. This is magnified by the American Founders' effort to rely on this instrumental statesmanship as little as possible.

3. Radicalization of the popular principle.

4. Radicalization of the science as government principle.

Thus, statesmanship is not much respected; it doesn't much respect itself ("civil servants" want to be "professionals" or even "government employees" rather than "civil servants").

Statesmanship tends to narrow itself to the role of the respectable technician, leaving the big decisions to "politicians" who in turn have to find their justification in being spokesmen of the popular will.

There is an alternative tradition, growing out of what the Framers did rather than what they said.

They were pulled between the private and public lives; usually they chose the public, and not merely out of duty (and anyway, what's the basis of that?).

There is also a strain of popular recognition of the need for non-technical leadership and of leaders who see that need and try to meet it; but there is always a presumption against that which has been radicalized.

Notes

This essay by Herbert Storing was originally published in 1981. We are grateful for permission from the American Enterprise Institute to reprint it here with minor revisions.

1. See Chris Argyris, "The Individual and Organization: Some Problems of Mutual Adjustment," *Administrative Science Quarterly* 2 (June 1957): 1–24. (Here and in some other notes, the editors have supplied references for sources to which we believe Professor Storing was alluding in this essay.)

2. See Richard E. Neustadt, "Approaches to Staffing the Presidency: Notes on FDR and JFK," *American Political Science* Review 57, no. 4 (December 1963): 855–63; also, *Presidential Power: The Politics of Leadership from FDR to Carter* (New York: Wiley, 1980), 112–14.

3. See William A. Schambra, ed., *As Far as Republican Principles Will Permit: Essays by Martin Diamond* (Washington, D.C.: AEI Press, 1992); also Diamond, *The Founding of the Democratic Republic* (Itasca, Ill.: F.E. Peacock, 1981).

4. John Bach McMaster and Frederick D. Stone, eds., *Pennsylvania and the Federal Constitution, 1787–1788* (Lancaster: Historical Society of Pennsylvania, 1888), 11.

5. Max Farrand, ed., *The Records of the Federal Convention of 1787*, rev. ed. (New Haven: Yale University Press, 1966), I, 310.

6. Ibid., 301.

7. See Leonard D. White, *The Federalists: A Study in Administrative History, 1789–1801* (rpt. ed., New York: Free Press, 1965), esp. chaps. 21, 25; *The Jeffersonians: A Study in Administrative History, 1801–1829* (New York: Macmillan, 1951), esp. chaps. 24, 35.

8. See White's introduction to Lynton K. Caldwell's *The Administrative Theories of Hamilton and Jefferson,* as quoted in Louis C. Gawthrop, *The Administrative Process and Democratic Theory* (Boston: Houghton Mifflin, 1970), 5.

9. Woodrow Wilson, "The Study of Administration," *Political Science Quarterly*, 56 (December 1941; rpt. of 1887): 502.

10. Ibid., 482.

11. See Hamilton, Madison, and Jay, *The Federalist* 10 (Middletown, Conn.: Wesleyan University Press, 1961), 57.

12. See Frederick Winslow Taylor, *The Principles of Scientific Management* (New York: Harper and Brothers, 1911), 43–47, 74.

13. Ibid., 25.

14. Richard N. McKean, "The Role of Analytical Aids," in Gawthrop, *Administrative Process and Democratic Theory*, 253.

15. Herbert Simon, *Administrative Behavior: A Study of Decision Making Processes in Administrative Organization*, 2d ed. (New York: Macmillan, 1957).

16. "The Science of Administration: Herbert A. Simon," in Herbert Storing, ed., *Essays on the Scientific Study of Politics* (New York: Holt, Rinehart, and Winston, 1962), 63–150.

17. See Robert Maynard Hutchins, "The Administrator," in *Works of the Mind*, ed. Robert B. Heywood (Chicago: University of Chicago Press, 1947), 135–56, at 140.

18. See John Rohr, *Ethics for Bureaucrats* (New York: Marcel Dekker, 1978).

2

Tocqueville on Administration and for Administrators

Peter Augustine Lawler

Alexis de Tocqueville's *Democracy in America*, written in the 1830s, remains the best book on the American way of life. Tocqueville describes that way of life as democratic or egalitarian, but not completely so. He shows that the Americans love not only equality, but liberty, and he writes to defend that love of liberty against egalitarian or democratic excesses. His view is that the development of what we call public administration might well be one of those excesses. The spirit that guides the science of administration, devoted as it is to the efficiency or control that comes with the imposition of impersonal or egalitarian rules to regulate all of human life, is naturally opposed by the spirited love of liberty.

I have two purposes in this chapter. The first is to consider what Tocqueville says about administration. *Democracy* has two volumes, and his approach to administration changes somewhat from volume 1 to volume 2, because he changes his view somewhat about the chief threat to liberty from democracy. I go on to consider what is most important about what Tocqueville says for American public administrators, his explanation of why Americans continue to find liberty lovable. That knowledge is indispensable for using one's political discretion well, for doing what one can to perpetuate human liberty in our time.

Administrative Decentralization versus Tyranny of the Majority

In volume 1, the main threat to liberty is called "tyranny of the majority." An activist majority might suppress minority dissent and individual resistance. Tocqueville's concern here is primarily that of the American Framers as expressed in *The Federalist*. With the danger of majority faction in mind, he describes and praises the Americans' "administrative decentralization." What he really praises is their administrative ineptitude, their lack of a science of administration. He says that "in the United States the majority, though it often has a despot's tastes and instincts, still lacks the most improved instruments of tyranny" (262).[1]

Tocqueville holds that tyranny of the majority is the American theory of government. There is and ought to be "no power capable of resisting" the majority's will as expressed in the legislature. Not "even the authority of reason" can resist, because the majority "claims to be the unique organ of reason" (89). The distinction between rational and majority rule is undemocratic. So the majority is limited only by the limits it imposes on its own will, by action it decides not to, cannot, or cannot imagine itself taking.

The Americans so far have neither the inclination nor the ability to regulate all of life according to the majority's sovereign will. The majority is "ignorant of how art might increase its scope" of power, of how an efficient, centralized administration might allow it more fully to exercise control (263). The majority suffers, from a purely democratic perspective, from a failure of thought and imagination.

In America, the "sovereign commands" of the majoritarian "central government" are "carried out by agents who often do not depend upon it and cannot be given direction every minute." They are the relatively independent and incompetent officials of local administration. They function as "so many hidden reefs retarding or dividing the flood of the popular will" (262–63). As long as Americans leave administration decentralized with independent local officials, they will not be able to regulate effectively the details of individual lives. Endeavors requiring "continual care and rigorous exactitude for success" are usually beyond the competence and focus of American administrators (92). So America suffers from tyranny of the majority much more in principle than in practice.

Tocqueville finds wisdom, even if unconscious, in the American majority's lack of concern with details. In fact, no "central power . . . can . . . alone see to all the details of the life of a great nation" (91). That "task exceeds human strength." But Tocqueville also says it is possible to impose "an external uniformity" on people's behavior. Such success leads one to love uniformity "for itself without reference to its objectives" (91). Administrative efficiency becomes valued for its own sake, and all disorder is feared indiscriminately. Here we cannot help but think of the dissidents'—Vaclav Havel's and Aleksandr Solzhenitsyn's— description of communist tyranny, which aimed simply to eradicate diversity or plurality from the world. The particularly democratic temptation, an extreme version of which we saw in communist ideology, is to combine the administrator's scientific propensity to increase the scope of his comprehension and control by submitting everything to impersonal rules with the egalitarian view that justice means treating everyone in the same way. The dissidents report that communism achieved external conformity, but hardly ever genuine belief in the lie of ideology.[2]

Administrative centralization really can impose order on the details of daily life. It can "maintain the status quo." It can, in effect, put people to sleep, a condition "which administrators are in the habit of calling good order and public tranquility." But such administrative imposition "excels at preventing, not at doing." When personal responsibility and resolute action are required, government is "reduced to impotence" (91). Administrative stability is actually unstable, because it undermines the capacity of a particular people and particular individuals to respond effectively to the changes that will inevitably challenge them. People will not act responsibly unless they are regarded as free. They are animated by self-direction far more than by obedience to rules not of their own making (92). A nation that has abandoned disorderly freedom for administratively imposed uniformity is "ready for conquest." It lacks the "public virtues" that inspire personal resistance, because its inhabitants are already "subjects," not "citizens" (94).

So Tocqueville has both negative and positive teaching on administrative decentralization, which he prefers for its *"political* advantages," not its administrative ones (93). Negatively, he praises its inefficiency for limiting the will of the majority, for preventing tyranny. Positively, he sees that that same inefficient inattention to detail arouses "civic spirit," giving citizens enough freedom to take pride in and responsibility for their own affairs. He observes the paradox that in America, "the force behind the state is much less well regulated, less enlightened, and less wise, but it is a hundred times more powerful than in Europe." The source of that power is personal effort: "Without doubt there is no other country on earth where people make such great efforts to achieve social prosperity." Individuals associate voluntarily to take responsibility for what administrators do not: "I know of no other people who have founded so many schools or such efficient ones, or churches more in touch with the religious needs of the inhabitants, or municipal roads better maintained" (92). Institutions suit people's needs because they are popularly originated and maintained.

Because in America the government's "means of action" or administration "are limited," individuals know they can and must rely largely on themselves. The "efforts of private individuals combine with those of the authorities" to "accomplish things which the most concentrated and vigorous administration would be unable to achieve" (95). Administrative decentralization blurs the line between and so combines public and private action. Tocqueville gives the example of the posse, or "inhabitants of a county . . . spontaneously forming committees with the object of catching the criminal and handing him over to the courts." Because local authorities have so few means for securing criminal justice, people know they cannot be "mere spectators" if justice is to be done (96).

In Europe, Tocqueville says, government's aim is to administer justice impersonally through the use of centralized authority. Local citizens need do and can do nothing. So they take no interest in or responsibility for the punishment of criminals, and a "public official stands for force," not "for right" (95). In America, by contrast, the police, prosecutors, and so forth are few in number, limited in power, and inefficient in method. "Nonetheless," Tocqueville observes, "I doubt whether in any country crime so seldom escapes punishment." Because local citizens share in the administration of justice, the criminal "becomes an enemy of the human race and every human being is against him" (96). The law stands for right, not mere force. The paradox is that when justice is connected with personal responsibility, it then seems less personal, or less merely the arbitrary will of those with power.

The source of this particularly American efficiency is not "uniformity or permanence of outlook, minute care of details, or perfection of administrative procedures." It lies in the "robust," because "somewhat wild" or disorderly, "striving and animation" of free citizens (92–93). Tocqueville contrasts the French "commune" with the American "township." In the former, thanks to Napoleonic centralization, the "accounting system is excellent," but people are "overtaken by such invincible apathy that society there seems to vegetate rather than live." They have no reason to give any thought to and so are mired in "profound ignorance of their true interests." The American townships have "untidy budgets lacking all uniformity," but also "an enlightened, active, and enterprising population." Tocqueville is astonished by the connection between the Americans' disorderly finances and their prosperity, and between the "immaculate budget" of the French and their "wretchedness" (92–93n.51).

Tocqueville remembers that the purpose of "good government is to ensure the welfare of a people and not to establish a certain order in the midst of their misery." So he "gladly" accepts the disorder and neglect of administrative decentralization, "compensated" as it is "by so many benefits" (93n.51). This robust resistance to order can be understood really to be resistance to tyranny of the majority. Individuals are confident enough in their own judgments to be patriotic without submitting blindly, to unite around "common interest," including tyranny's resistance, and to be willfully aroused against uniformity or homogenizing egalitarianism as an end in itself (96). But this spirit of resistance strengthens, not weakens, the individual's attachment to government. The combination of his own, responsible efforts, with those of administrators means that he can take pride in, or not feel detached from, what is achieved in the name of the public good (93).

But Tocqueville means to leave us fearful about the future of human liberty in America. Liberty seems to depend on a combination of administrative ineptitude and some deficiency in egalitarian imagination. There is every reason to anticipate what actually happened in American history. The science of administration would improve, increasingly more of the details of life would be subject to centralized administration in the name of efficiency and egalitarian justice, and the imagination would conceive of more possibilities for government regulation. Tocqueville says that the combination of administrative centralization and America's democratic political institutions could well produce a "despotism . . . more intolerable than in any of the absolute monarchies of Europe. One would have to go over into Asia to find anything with which to compare it" (263). The efficient, detailed implementation of majority will, so praised by the Progressives of our century and found at the core of our distinction between political will and administrative science, Tocqueville compares to Oriental despotism.

As Tocqueville explains, "no nations are more liable to fall under the yoke of administrative centralization than those with a democratic social condition" (96). There is an obvious, overwhelming connection between democracy and centralization. Democratization reduces the complexity of aristocratic social order to "nothing . . . but equal

individuals mingled in a common mass" (97). After the abolition of
social distinctions or diversity in the name of equality, there seems to
be no foundation for resistance to the centralization of all power in
the government that represents all equally. The spirit of democracy
opposes the spirit of decentralization, because the latter depends upon
and perpetuates a spirited resistance to uniformity, upon what Tocqueville regards as the aristocratic love of human particularity, the
love of some particular human beings to the exclusion of them all.

The Americans and the English, Tocqueville observes, have a prejudice in favor of "local freedom" because they did not have the lev-
eling, centralizing revolution of the French. The French Revolution
was consistently motivated by hatred of everything aristocratic, and
the Americans do not see that their local institutions are really, in
part, aristocratic inheritances. They inconsistently incorporate them
into their democratic chauvinism (97–98). Tocqueville makes it extremely hard to see why administrative decentralization will not decay over time in favor of a more consistently egalitarian or uniform
conception of justice.

Tocqueville's Ambivalence

We also leave Tocqueville's laudatory account of administrative
decentralization in volume 1 somewhat confused. The danger it coun-
tered is said to be an overbearing majority, which is limited only by
administrative ineptitude. But Tocqueville also worries about the danger
of an enervated, apathetic citizenry, about its inability to resist the
tyranny of a meddlesome central government acting in the majority's
name. Is the primary danger popular activism against minorities and
individuals? Or is it popular apathy or spiritlessness? Is the tyranny
to be feared an aroused majoritarianism? Or is it a seemingly impersonal central authority imposing uniform rules on a docile, will-less,
increasingly massified population?

The question of which form of tyranny or despotism is the greater
danger must be answered in order to evaluate administrative decentralization. If it is tyranny of the majority, the result, finally, is ambivalence, and one might question the extent of Tocqueville's praise
of local activism. *The Federalist*, for example, seems to be more on
the side of administrative centralization than not, despite its inclination to leave many details to state and local government. Tyranny of

the majority, for its authors, is more likely on the state and local level, where homogeneous majorities readily find themselves and where there are no barriers to their oppression. Against that tyranny, its racism, sexism, meddlesome religious moralism, and so forth, much administrative control has moved to Washington over the years, arguably to some extent in accord with the intent of the Framers.

The greater professional training or expertise of national administrators also arguably produces more of a devotion to justice and rights than the wild "redneck" chauvinism that sometimes animates local administrators. Although local populations in America may be relatively enlightened, are they really as enlightened as professional administrators? Tocqueville praises the posse, but we also know about lynchings. He does mention the "gross instances of social indifference and neglect" sometimes encountered in America, and even rare "major blemishes" that "appear completely at variance with the surrounding civilization" (92).

But such inconveniences, although hardly minor and certainly unjust, are worth bearing if the main threat to freedom is apathy. Local activism, even with its incompetence and limited but genuine majoritarian tyranny, must be maintained against the democratic grain of centralization. Tocqueville's suggestion, in this light, is that *The Federalist* was simply wrong about what is most required to perpetuate human liberty in America.

Apathetic, Despotic Degradation

Volume 2 of *Democracy* resolves the tension between the twin dangers of activism and apathy. There Tocqueville is not at all concerned with aroused majoritarianism, and he no longer refers to the tyranny of the majority. He is now concerned only with the unprecedented despotism that may come when individuals surrender control of the details of their lives, and, thus, responsibility for and even thought about their futures, to gentle, apparently benevolent schoolmaster-administrators (691–93). That "*general apathy*" is "the fruit of individualism" (735–36), the malady of the heart, characteristic of democracy, that causes one to be incapable of love or hate (506–8). Tocqueville says "our efforts" should be directed not primarily against despotism but against the apathy that engenders it (735–36).

Individualism, Tocqueville says, is fundamentally the result of a "misguided judgment": The social, heart-enlarging experiences of human beings make them more miserably discontented than anything else (506–7). Human beings would be better off without those experiences. So individualism is a judgment in favor of the brutish contentment that comes with total unconcern for the future in Rousseau's state of nature. Tocqueville sees that democratic thought culminates logically in Rousseau's theoretical negation of all human distinctiveness, and his suggestion is that democratic practice moves in the direction of that thought, unless resisted by the artful efforts of lovers of human liberty.

Tocqueville's change in outlook from volume 1 to volume 2 seems to mirror American history, or the progress of democracy. The Framers thought the main danger to rights or liberty would be an overbearing majority. But we today are not particularly concerned about the specter of class warfare, demagogues rousing people into a frenzy, or even fundamentalist tyranny. The few card-carrying members of the ACLU who are still mainly animated by such concerns seem quaintly out of touch. Most analysts today "fear an apathetic or disabled majority that does not claim its rights or cannot exercise them."[3] Those on the right worry about dependency, drugs, welfare, and the middle class, and so about individuals who cannot or will not take responsibility for their own lives. Those on the left complain about individuals so withdrawn and insensitive that they are incapable of acting on behalf of the unfortunate.

Almost everyone seems distressed about the low turnout of voters, the lack of citizen involvement, and the stupefying power of television and popular music to absorb people in "private fantasies" or what Rousseau called reveries. Those on both the left and right, although obviously not everyone, also criticize the growing influence of the New Age therapeutic culture, which aims to keep individuals from being touched by their experiences of their individuality by showing them, Buddhist-fashion, that such anxious and contingent experiences of particularity are an illusion. Individualism, we see, is much more of a problem in our time than in Tocqueville's, and we marvel at his prescience about democracy's development.

Human action, Tocqueville observes, is becoming more regular, uniform, and methodical. "Variety is disappearing from the human race" (615). Not only are human beings behaving more similarly and predictably, even the difference between human and nonhuman reality may be in the process of disappearing. Democratic theorists prefer deterministic or systematic explanations of human behavior, ones that deny or abstract from human liberty and responsibility. The main reason for their preference is that such explanations are homogeneous or completely egalitarian. Not only do they not privilege the thought and action of particular, extraordinary individuals, they claim to show that what animates human beings is no different from what animates all the animals or all that exists (493–96). Such explanations, Tocqueville says, perniciously and untruly deny or miss genuine manifestations of human liberty (451–52, 495, 544). But he also acknowledges that systematic or deterministic science is becoming more true as democracy develops (494). Human beings are progressively less likely to demand to be recognized or to be recognizable as individuals (626, 631–32).

In aristocracies, human beings were distinguished in many ways, and the aristocrat's sense of his individuality or liberty was strong and amply supported, although it was not unlimited. So the aristocrat, Tocqueville says, conceived of the idea of rights, a proud assertion of independence against others and the social whole (663). That idea is what "is rapidly disappearing from men's minds." Replacing it in Tocqueville's time is "the idea of the omnipotence and sole authority of society at large" (669). The personal idea, one that defends one's particular liberty and responsibility, is being replaced by the impersonal one, the one compatible with and served well by administrative science or bureaucracy. The idea of rights, originating in the aristocrat's proud experience of ruling himself and others, is replaced by one that suggests that no one in particular is responsible or rules.

Aristocrats, Tocqueville says, do justice or more than justice to natural human distinctions. But they are so enamored with human particularity or inegalitarian individuality that they find it almost impossible to conceive of general ideas, ways of thinking that reveal what all human beings have in common with each other and with all that exists (439). So the "notion of a uniform rule imposed equally on all members of the body social seems to have been strange to men's thoughts in ages of aristocracy" (668). It did not occur to them that it might be more just and efficient to impose uniform rules on everyone, and so their science of administration or bureaucracy could not progress.

With the decay of aristocratic social distinctions in the face of egalitarian skepticism, the dissolution of "the ancient fabric of European society," human beings have become both less different and less aware of differences. They have come to think readily, too readily, with general ideas (437). So European governments "nowadays . . . wear themselves out imposing uniform customs and laws on popula-

tions with nothing yet in common" (689). Their thought is oriented
by an imagined uniformity not yet in existence. Their general or impersonal ideas do not yet adequately describe human reality. Their
ideas are in part impositions that aim to eradicate the diversity which
they cannot comprehend.

Aristocrats intensely love and hate particular human beings. They
are strongly attached to some to the unjust or arbitrary exclusion of
others. They often cannot even recognize the humanity of nonaristo-
crats, those outside their circle of concern (563–64). The particularly
democratic love is not of particular human beings, but of the general
idea or abstract principle "equality." Only God can love all human
beings equally and intensely; only He can see us all as we really are.
For human beings, limited as we are in thought, feeling, and imagination, love becomes less particular or intense as its scope increases
(437). Corresponding to the democratic love of equality is "hatred of
privilege" (672). Democrats hate love that prefers or privileges one
or some over others. They hate human love as it actually exists,
which is why they judge in favor of individualism, an apathetic, pas-
sionless existence. That democratic hatred, Tocqueville observes, actually
grows with progress toward equality, because "amid the general uniformity, the slightest dissimilarity seems shocking" (673). The democratic love is for the perfection of uniformity. So its hatred is for
anything that cannot be comprehended and controlled by impersonal,
administrative rules. The hatred of privilege favors the concentration
or centralization of power in government. Whatever is conceded to
"the state" is taken from unequal individuals. Because the state or
the sovereign impersonally represents us all equally, its power does
not arouse hatred or envy (673). The more it controls, the more uniform our lives will become.

The great danger to liberty in democratic times is that the devotion
of democrats and that of the "central government" are the same. The
government "worships uniformity" because it is infinitely easier to
subject "all men indiscriminately to the same rule" than to make rules
that actually "suit men" in their diversity. Both the government and
democratic citizens hate unequal, disorderly manifestations of human liberty. So they have "a secret and permanent bond of sympa-
thy," forming a "community of feeling" against "individual independence" (673). They both feel that the experience of liberty is not a
human good. The increase of centralized, homogenized, governmental
control over all the details of human life is the "natural" progress of
democracy (674). The "instinct for centralization" has been "the one

permanent feature" of democratic development. So "one can say that the older a democratic society, the more centralized will its government be" (672n1).

Tocqueville adds that "the art of despotism" in democratic times has been "simplified," even "reduced to a single principle" (679). Government's justification for the centralization of power is the love of equality. Rulers either must actually have that love or convince citizens that they do. The pursuit of equality is the fraud used by despots in democratic times to maximize their own power. It allows them to control their subjects more completely than subjects had ever been controlled before. The government's professed devotion to egalitarian uniformity leads "those same men who from time to time have upset a throne and trampled kings beneath their feet to bend without resistance to the slightest wishes of some clerk" (688).

The Science of Administration

The method used to pursue the egalitarian and despotic goal of complete uniformity is "the science of administration." Tocqueville notes the "immense improvements" in that science by the European governments of his time. He asserts that "there is no country in Europe in which public administration has become not only more centralized but also more impulsive and minute." It "meddles" in affairs formerly regarded as private; it extends indefinitely the sphere of its control. With the science of administration "the state itself . . . increasingly takes control of the humblest citizen and directs his behavior even in trivial matters" (680). Charity, education, and religion have been brought under administrative control; "functionaries" have taken responsibility "for forming the feelings and shaping the ideas of each generation" (681). Through them "princes" now do more than govern: "They seem to hold themselves responsible for the behavior and fate of subjects as individuals." Through guidance and instruction, princes "will, if necessary, make them happy against their will" (681). The aim of the prince and his administrative functionaries is to produce perfectly orderly, predictable subjects, to eradicate the willfulness that comes with discontent. The discipline imposed here is that of the "schoolmaster," the expert who tells his students what to think and feel for their own good (681, 691).

The despotic use of the science of administration "degrades rather than torments" subjects by depriving them of their free or willful exercise of personal responsibility. By "cover[ing] the whole of social life with a network of petty, complicated rules that are both minute and uniform," it "daily makes the exercise of free choice less useful and rarer . . . rob[bing] each citizen of the proper use of his own facilities" (692). Such a people "slowly falls below the level of humanity," because human beings are defined by their exercise of their liberty, by their spirited, responsible and sometimes immoderate choices (694). Tocqueville says that the goal of this brand of "orderly, gentle, peaceful slavery" is to "entirely relieve" people "from the trouble of thinking and all the cares of living" (692).

That people might gradually surrender their thought about and responsibility for their futures to schoolmaster-administrators for their own good suggests that the psychological explanation of love of equality given so far has been too abstract. Not only do democratic citizens hate the manifestations of the unequal individuality of others, they come to experience their own individuality as hateful. The democratic destruction of aristocratic hierarchy and other social ties leaves the individual "both independent and weak." That new independence fills the individual temporarily with "confidence and pride," but soon he feels his weakness and vulnerability, his need for help from others to secure his existence. But with the dissolution of social ties and duties, and so the deterioration of love, his "fellows" seem equally "impotent and cold" (672).

The impotent individual turns to that "huge entity," centralized government, that "alone stands out above the universal level of abasement" (672). He expects government to do what his friends, fellow citizens, and family used to do. But finally he is looking for more than day care, social security, and welfare. The individual in democratic ages becomes obsessed with time, because he has been skeptically deprived of various aristocratic illusions about immortality. Everything seems mutable; despite his constant calculation the future is beyond his control, and he cannot divert himself effectively from the inevitability of death (537). He is "frightened by" his apparently "limitless independence." His unsupported individuality wears him out and eventually becomes hateful (444).

Because thoughts about the future seem to do nothing but make them miserable, democratic individuals "easily fall back into a complete and brutish indifference about the future" (548). They readily conclude that they are better off surrendering all calculation about the future to administrators. Finally, they would rather not be touched by awareness of their mortality, their individuality; they would rather lose themselves in the moment. As Rousseau says, the most egalitarian conclusion is that human beings are better off when they are brutishly unaware of time.

The best Tocquevillian analyst of American democracy in our time has been the philosopher-physician-novelist Walker Percy. According to Percy, Tocqueville's core observation was that the Americans are Cartesians without ever having read a word of Descartes. Their view of the world is pop Cartesian.[4] They understand the world and themselves in terms of a popularized, deterministic science articulated by experts. These experts, counselors, therapists, administrators, Phil Donahue, Carl Sagan, and so forth say that human beings are no different from the other animals. They should be happy in good or prosperous environments, and miserable in bad or impoverished ones. Any experience that causes them to be miserable in the midst of prosperity should be dismissed as a misery-producing illusion. Therapy means changing the environment that produces such unproductive moods.[5]

Tocqueville himself suggests how democracy produces the rule of scientific experts. He says that democracy makes the individual too intellectually weak, too uncertain and disoriented, to resist public opinion. The rule of public opinion seems not to be undemocratic, because it appears to be the rule of no one in particular (434–36). But democratic public opinion itself is shaped by its tendency to be expressed in the language of impersonal or deterministic science (477–82). That language is articulated by experts, who claim not to rule on the basis of their own judgments but only to express the objective authority of science. The expert shaping of public opinion also appears to be the rule of no one in particular.

Percy makes clear what individuals attempt to surrender when they give up their personal sovereignty or responsibility to impersonal expertise. He says what terrifies people most is not sex or crime or poverty. They have trouble "knowing who they are or what to do with themselves." Their perplexity increases when they are not doing what "*they*, the experts" say they should be doing. The experts cannot explain why wealthy, intelligent, and attractive people should be miserable and unproductive for "no apparent reason."[6] The pop Cartesian experts are the *they* described by the philosopher Martin Heidegger: "*The 'they' do not permit us anxiety in the face of death.*"[7] Their expertise means to keep one from being touched by one's awareness of mortality. Their judgment is that that experience is not good for human beings.

According to Percy, the Cartesian experts mean to deprive the individual of what constitutes his freedom, his sovereignty, his capacity to live in the light of the truth. Percy's own judgment is Tocqueville's: Such personal experiences lie at the core of human liberty, and human beings really can live well with some help while facing death. Percy notices that the experts have not been able to deprive Americans of the anxious restlessness of self-conscious mortality, and Tocqueville himself describes the Americans as anxious and restless, even melancholic and disgusted with life, in the midst of prosperity (535–38). Tocqueville and Percy describe the failure, so far, of the expert science of administration completely to shape human experience and take control of the details of particular lives. What Phil Donahue, Carl Sagan, the politically correct administrator, and so forth say does not yet conform to what Americans actually experience.

Percy denies that experts can eradicate human misery. They end up making some Americans, at least, feel more miserably dislocated than ever before by depriving them of language through which they can articulate their personal experiences of self or soul. Tocqueville similarly writes of the tendency of democracy to eradicate the theological and metaphysical dimensions of language (477), and of the Americans' deepening inability to divert themselves from the needs of the soul (535–38). His fear, in fact, is that the Americans may well surrender the details of their lives, their responsibility for the future, to administrators precisely because their lives have become so anxious and restless (548). Because the Americans find the experiences of individuality, of self-conscious mortality, to be so hard, they may willingly give them up in favor of a life that is too easy truly to be human. Because they sometimes find liberty hateful, they may come to prefer complete equality, which is necessarily subhuman.

Tocqueville imagines the perfection of unprecedented, democratic despotism, the despot's control of all the details of peaceful, orderly, subhuman lives. Allied with and at the service of the despot is the administrative scientist or expert, who holds that such control is for the individual's benefit. The individual, the expert asserts, would be better off living with a childish, irresponsible indifference for the future. He would be better off freed from the miserable burden of anxious calculation, and from being touched by his knowledge of his mortality. He should live only in the enjoyment of the moment, and he should be freed from those restless experiences that deprive him of that enjoyment (692).

Opposed to the despot and the expert is the lover of liberty for its own sake, despite that misery. In that category Tocqueville places only a few, "the true friends of liberty and of human dignity," who artfully resist the movement toward democracy (699, 674). He does not favor an unjust and futile attempt to reinvigorate aristocracy, but only the perpetuation of the liberty that is possible in democratic ages (695). He says, "The individual should be allowed to keep the little freedom, strength, and originality left to him. His position in the face of society should be raised and supported. Such, I think, should be the chief aim of any legislator in the age opening before us" (701). The task of the legislator or statesman is to provide individuality with assistance or support, because if left unsupported it becomes unendurable.

The Love of Liberty

The public administrator, on the basis of his scientific or technical education and his professional pride, tends to become a pop Cartesian expert.[8] But if the administrator reads Tocqueville, he might become a true friend of liberty or a statesman. Insofar as he is able to exercise independent judgment or discretion, he will act either to use his expertise to relieve citizens of their freedom and responsibility, or he will do what is possible to support and encourage experiences of individuality or personal responsibility. What can be done to keep liberty lovable for Americans? That is the question the American engaged in political life, including the administrator, ought always to ask. Knowledge of what makes liberty lovable for human beings, along with the actual love of liberty, are necessary supplements to the science of administration in the education of public administrators in a nation dedicated to liberty.

Tocqueville observes that Americans do love liberty, because they are able to exercise it in the context of the fortunate perpetuation of institutions inherited from aristocratic ages. The first Americans were English, and they brought with them England's "free institutions and virile mores," which originated in aristocratic pride. These institutions, fortunately, were not leveled by any "great democratic revolution" or "war between the various classes" (675). The Americans are in the crucial respect considerably less democratic than the French. "The American destiny," Tocqueville asserts, "is unusual; they have taken from the English aristocracy the idea of individual rights and a taste for local freedom, and they have been able to keep both these things because they have had no aristocracy to fight" (676). What

Tocqueville says about the extreme consequences of democracy's development does not yet apply to the Americans. Meddlesome, puerile administration has perfected itself in Europe, not America.

Tocqueville discusses the Americans' inheritance of the "free institutions" of local government as part of their "combat" against individualism. He does so in part 2 of volume 2 of *Democracy*, where his subject is the effect of the movement toward democracy on love or the heart, and so also the maladies specific to democracy that threaten the heart's functioning. It is because love of equality opposes human love as it actually exists that democratic progress, unresisted, culminates in individualism. The Americans engage in such resistance or combat because they are not simply democrats. They love not only equality but liberty, each other, and God.[9]

The Americans actually employ two weapons in their combat against individualism. The first is "free institutions," the second is "interest rightly understood." Free, local institutions are the practical, political combat employed by "the lawgivers of America," largely the English (509–13). Interest rightly understood, the doctrine of American moralists, is theoretical (525–28). The latter presupposes the success of the former. Moralistic theory supports American political practice, aiming to help secure the legislators' work.

Both forms of combat aim to enlarge the American heart. How free institutions do this is not hard to see. But the doctrine of interest is explicitly and pridefully heartless. We have to consider how a pridefully heartless doctrine aids the enlargement of the heart. The moralist's doctrine, it turns out, is less concerned with interest itself than with the relationships among interest, pride, and love in a comprehensive strategy to resist democracy's antiliberal excesses. We have to consider the first form of combat to find the place of the second.

Tocqueville begins his chapter on free institutions by showing the connection between individualism and despotism. Here he anticipates *Democracy*'s conclusion. The "vices" of despotism, which the despot calls virtues, contract the heart or keep human beings from loving one another. All the despot needs to maintain his power unimpeded is apathy or "indifference" (509).

Democratic people "have a particular need" for the experience of political freedom to resist despotism's progress. They must be compelled, against their inclination, "to take part in public affairs," to be citizens. When "common affairs are treated in common," the individual learns the limits of his self-sufficiency. He "notices he is not as independent of his fellows as he used to suppose." He needs them, and to get their help he must help them. Political indifference is not in one's interest or even possible (510).

What begins as calculation of interest ends in love. The individual calculates that he gains the cooperation of others most effectively with "their goodwill and affection." He sees that it is in his interest to be loved by others. But that love will not come unless he acts to "disguise" his pride, contempt, and egoism, the pretentious passions that constitute his perception of self-sufficiency. By fooling others, he cannot help but fool himself to some extent. "Those frigid passions," Tocqueville says, "that keep hearts asunder must then retreat and hide at the back of consciousness." The individual compelled to act as if he were a citizen actually becomes one (510).

The free institutions of local government, of which decentralized administration might be considered a part, artfully create ties that exist much more readily or seemingly naturally in an aristocracy. One's imagination and so one's heart are extended to and filled by others. This awakening of the social passions, love and pride, affects human beings unequally. More pride is aroused in some than in others, and the extraordinary pride of a few arouses love in many. This aristocratic orientation becomes obvious when Tocqueville notices that "Under free government most public officials are elected" (510).

The possibility of winning elections attracts "men whose great gifts and aspirations are too closely circumscribed in private life," those with the ability and prideful passion to distinguish themselves. This ambition also "makes a man care for his fellows"; he needs their votes. Again calculation turns readily into affection and love. Tocqueville even says that the candidate "often finds his self-interest in forgetting about himself." Self-interest and selflessness are intertwined, because the best way to appear to care is actually to care (510).

The stimulation by election of political ambition is a social and so heart-enlarging passion. "Eagerness to be elected" is what most powerfully "forges permanent links among a great number of citizens who otherwise might have remained forever strangers to one another." The natural aristocrats, those with a prideful love of human liberty, create the ties that combat individualism. Those who are less inclined to be content with the individualist's apolitical life attract the political interest and affection of those who are more content. Aristocratic or political interest and pride arouse democratic love (510).

The Americans have incorporated their aristocratic inheritance of the institutions of local government into their view of democracy. It is what gives them a relatively liberal view of democracy. But like

their chauvinistic attachment to administrative decentralization, it
remains vulnerable to egalitarian criticism. America over time has
centralized in the name of justice. Largely gone are the particularistic
and passionate local institutions Tocqueville described. Local democracy is activist democracy. It readily arouses pride and love and so
difference, inequality, hatred, and injustice. National democracy—because
it is more consistently impersonal and egalitarian or just—tends to
be apathetic democracy.

Local democracy depends more on personal responsibility, the exercise of which is somewhat unpredictable. National democracy depends more on the predictable uniformity of bureaucracy. Politically
inspired love and pride have almost disappeared, because Americans
can no longer connect their interests to effective political action. They
too rarely have the political experiences that readily turn calculation
into affection.

Arguably, administrators today should use their discretion to promote plans to "devolve" some of the responsibility of government to
the states and localities. The implementation of such plans may well
produce some injustice. As Tocquevillians, perhaps we can say that
they are the price one pays to arouse some political passion, and to
restore political liberty. But Tocqueville was especially worried about
American racism, which he viewed as a monstrous form of injustice,
and he saw the connection between it and the states' decentralizing
assertion of self-government. He would have welcomed almost any
effective remedy to it (355–63).

Perhaps Tocqueville might have recommended the statesmanship
of House Speaker Newt Gingrich. Gingrich, in his first speech as speaker,
praised the centralization or nationalization of the 1960s that aimed
at racial justice. He made it clear that today's decentralization presupposes the success of that centralization. Returning power to the
states and localities today will be much less likely to produce particularly racist policy.

But Tocqueville might also have been very skeptical of any attempt
to return vitality to local institutions once it has been lost. His effort
was largely to preserve the aristocratic inheritances in America that
had survived the transition to democracy. He did not recommend the
creation of new, free institutions. Because of their habitual skepticism in the service of equality, democrats lack the imaginary resources for such creativity (445, 485). So far only a few observers have
noticed that Gingrich's American revolution or realignment, if it succeeds, would be the first directed against equality's excesses.

How the doctrine of interest well understood contributes to the Americans' proud love of liberty is more difficult to see. This doctrine, which Tocqueville describes as the teaching of American moralists, is that everything human beings do should be the product of enlightened calculation in pursuit of material enjoyment. The Americans enjoy explaining that it accounts for all their activity: "It gives them pleasure to point out how an enlightened self-love continually leads them to help one another and disposes them freely to give part of their time and wealth for the good of the state" (526). They complacently think they show how citizenship need not depend on love or thoughtless self-sacrifice.

What the Americans enjoy explaining is that they are consistent thinkers and free actors. Their rational will is the basis of their independence. They have freed themselves from natural and imaginary propensities to be attached to others. They know the truth that every human being is separated from others by bodily need, and that life is nothing but doing what one can to satisfy one's own needs.

So Tocqueville makes it clear that the American doctrine is a form of boasting about one's liberty. Before their enlightenment, in aristocratic ages, human beings were unfree. Their imaginations formed illusory bonds of dependence. They were blinded by the illusions of love and duty, which aristocrats manipulated to control others. The result was injustice rooted in ignorance. The Americans use their minds, the democratic method of consistent, skeptical thinking, to dispel the illusions and liberate their wills to overcome injustice, each individual in his own case.

But Tocqueville contends that the Americans do not accurately explain why they do what they do. He says, with some irony, that they "often do themselves less than justice." He notices them sometimes abandoning themselves, "carried away" by natural impulses and really serving others. They are, like people "elsewhere," partly selfish and partly not (526). Interest may explain some, but never all, of what human beings do. From an aristocratic perspective, the Americans are inclined to be better or more selfless citizens than they say. The American's response to Tocqueville would be that Tocqueville does him less than justice. The American always resists the call of the heart. Despite the appearance of self-sacrifice, all social and political relationships are his own construction and so within his own control.

We remember that Tocqueville had already explained how the heart-enlarging effects of the free institutions of local government transform the pursuit of interest. Given the effect of such experience, which makes their heartless moral doctrine inaccurate, why do American moralists support the doctrine at all? Why do they encourage the American people, in effect, not to tell the whole truth about their experiences?

The American doctrine, as a form of boasting, is also a cover or disguise. Americans deny that they really love, but sometimes, as a result of their political involvement, they really do. The fact of their love offends their sense of liberty or pride. They do not want to acknowledge their dependence, which limits their liberty. So Tocqueville affirms the doctrine of interest because it allows the American to explain away the true effects of his heart-enlarging experiences. It verbally disguises his impulsive affection for others, aroused by his political life. By doing so, it makes it easier for him to have such experiences. His love need not seem to be incompatible with his pride. A heartless moral doctrine disguises and so protects what enlarges the heart.

Here again, public administrators might look to the example of Gingrich, to the prideful inadequacy of his public argument. He attempts to justify as many of his policy choices as possible according to the doctrine of interest, as good for the pursuit of prosperity and personal economic independence. But for him the doctrine is clearly a boast and a cover. His responsible, antibureaucratic choices exhibit a love of political liberty that no doctrine of enlightened self-interest could ever adequately articulate. Tocqueville shows why the speaker should be praised, not blamed, for not acknowledging his own and our dependence. Political theorists today sometimes see the connection between acknowledgments of dependence and apathy, but almost never do they see the one between prideful assertions of self-interest and active, and sometimes even selfless, citizenship.

But we cannot forget the interdependence of the two forms of combat against individualism. The doctrine of interest is praised by Tocqueville as a way of protecting local political life. In the absence of that life, the goodness of the prideful doctrine of interest becomes far more questionable. Tocqueville cannot help but notice the troubling inconsistency of the Americans' moralistic defense of their liberty. For them, liberty is the consistent pursuit of material enjoyment, but it is not enjoyment itself. Once one enjoys, one is no longer free, because one gives way to instinct or impulse, or gives up self-control. So the Americans seem to say proudly that they pursue enjoyment, but never enjoy. They seem to explain a nonmaterialistic motivation in materialistic terms. They say all there is, is bodily need, but their restless, insatiable pursuit of its satisfaction is evidence of their liberty from that need. But a life without enjoyment could hardly be lovable, and the attempt actually to live it makes the preference for apathetic individualism over liberty seem perfectly reasonable.

Religion and the Family

The doctrine of interest protects, in a largely democratic context, the heart-enlarging effects of America's lucky aristocratic inheritance of free, local political institutions. A wider glance at *Democracy*'s volume 2 shows that the doctrine performs the same function for two other American inheritances, religion and the family. These institutions also fortunately enlarge the American heart and make liberty lovable. So they also combat individualism. They are also vulnerable to self-centered, democratic criticism of inegalitarian dependency generated by the imagination.

Tocqueville begins his description of the American application of the doctrine of interest rightly understood by saying that "However hard one may try to prove that virtue is useful, it will always be difficult to make a man live well if he will not face death" (528). He opposes the experts who would recommend the pursuit of enjoyment as a diversion from one's self-conscious mortality. He adds that the Americans actually agree with him.

Tocqueville observes, with irony, that Americans actually take pride in extending the doctrine of interest to their religious duties and their relationship with God. He notices that their view of religious practice is "so quiet, so methodical, and so calculated that it would seem that the head rather than the heart leads them to the altar." They calculate how best to achieve "eternal felicity," as if they could even bring that under their control. Their aim is to give the minimum amount of attention to religious duty and still gain eternal life. They do not want to sacrifice more than is necessary for the pursuit of happiness or enjoyment in this world (529–30).

The Americans' doctrine is, in effect, a proud denial that they either love God or are anxious about their contingency or mortality. Even God and death need not limit one's independence. They "affect no vulgar indifference to a future state," because they hold it is possible to plan for all of one's future (529). Obviously enough, if they really lived according to their doctrine they would not really be facing death.

Egalitarian skepticism dissolves even love of God. Christianity, as

Tocqueville says, is a most egalitarian religion. All human beings are equal under God. But Christianity also teaches human love of and dependence upon God, and human duties to each other flow from that love. That attachment and dependence limit one's liberty, and they depend on evidence apparently generated by the imagination. They originate, in Tocqueville's own view, in the imaginative arousal of love made possible by aristocratic social conditions (439, 443–46, 483–84). So he strikingly calls the Americans' religion their "most precious inheritance from aristocratic times" (544). The best hope for the future of the love of God, which seems necessary if human beings are going to love one another and liberty itself, is to perpetuate whatever religion a particular democracy may have fortunately inherited.

Tocqueville affirms the Americans' application of the doctrine of interest to religion because it is not a true or complete description of their religious longing or action. The application is only largely true in the sense that interest may really be what usually leads human beings to religion. But interest never explains all of religious practice (529). The Americans' claim that they are free from anxiety about death and longing for God's love is a boast. That anxiety and longing are the main causes of their restlessness in the midst of prosperity. Their pursuit of enjoyment really is an increasingly less successful diversion from their increasingly anxious longing (535–38).

Tocqueville also observes Americans acting as if they really do love God. On the seventh day they are able to rest, taking time to contemplate God and their souls. They are then temporarily but truly free from both calculation of interest and personal anxiety. They have some confidence, sometimes, that they are somehow immortal. That experience is a source of pride indispensable for the love of liberty or individuality (529, 542–45). The Americans' boast that they have reduced religion to the domain of interest actually protects their religious experiences from skeptically democratic criticism.

So public administrators today ought to see the truth in what has become the conservative argument that religious belief supports liberty and the pursuit of prosperity. The American claim to have reconciled the spirit of Christianity with that of capitalism is not altogether true. It is a boast and a cover, one to be protected. Administrators ought also to resist the welfare-state tendency to expand the reach of government in ways that constrain religious practice. Most of all, they ought not to let their love of egalitarian justice or impersonal efficiency undermine organized expressions of people's love of God.

Tocqueville also makes it clear enough that the family, even in its

American, democratic form, is another aristocratic inheritance. His presentation of that fact is quite indirect. His initial emphasis is on how democracy has transformed relations among family members. In the short term, the movement toward democracy has increased familial love by liberating it from the proud reserve of aristocratic formalities (586–89).

But the development of democracy, as we see so clearly today, eventually threatens the family's very existence. It cannot be held together by love alone, and the love of one's particular family members is undermined by love of equality. The family is necessarily exclusive, and its existence will always be a barrier to the achievement of perfectly egalitarian justice.

Today the emphasis is often on the unjust subordination the family has imposed on women. Tocqueville's conclusion is that the superiority of American women is the cause of the endurance of the American family (603). They submit, in his description, to a transformed but genuine form of patriarchy, justified by the doctrine of interest rightly understood. That doctrine causes the American view of marriage to be strangely unerotic. The Americans' distrust and disparagement of romantic love is another instance of their "continual sacrifice of pleasure for the sake of business," or their pursuit of prosperity for the sake of pleasure (592). The Americans explain that that pursuit is most efficient when labor is divided between men and women. "They have applied to the sexes the great principle of political economy which now dominates industry" (601).

Tocqueville observes that American women's work is in the home, the men's business and politics. But the husband still rules the family under the law, and the wife is socially subordinate and almost literally locked up in the home. The Americans do allow the women the choice of whom to marry, and even whether or not to marry. But they are educated to use their freedom well, and they know that marry they must if they are to secure what happiness and dignity is possible for them in this world. One reason American women are superior to American men is that they acknowledge freely that human beings must submit, or acknowledge their dependence, if they are to live well with their liberty (590–97).

American women, Tocqueville shows, humor the pride of men. But they know that male pride is really chauvinism, and they secretly view it with some contempt. Women are the source of morality and defenders of religion. They shape the souls of children and even their husbands. They assume the responsibility of socializing or humanizing

men, making love and contentment possible in a vulgarly selfish age.
So they are responsible for the perpetuation of human happiness and
dignity by making life something more than liberty conceived as anxious restlessness ending only in death. By constraining liberty with
love, they make liberty lovable (291, 592–93, 598, 600–603).

American men pay their women lip service, but in fact they are
largely unaware of the extent of their dependence. They certainly do
not acknowledge how anxious and miserable they would be without
women's self-denying efforts. Their doctrine of interest rightly understood, with which they explain their family ties, is again a prideful
cover, allowing them not to acknowledge the conjugal and familial
love and sense of duty they really experience (594–603).

The family Tocqueville describes may be largely gone today, a victim
of democracy's development, especially women's liberation. But it is
not completely gone. Women still sacrifice more than men for the
children's sake, and perhaps that is because they are more inclined by
nature to do so. They still humor male pride to some extent, and certainly
men are still more reluctant to acknowledge their dependence. Even
today's more egalitarian family is under attack, primarily in the name
of the perfection of women's liberation. Government policy, driven
mainly by equality and efficiency, is not the family's particular friend.
Yet the natural superiority of women requires social and political support
to be effective.

The sociologist David Popenoe has made the Tocquevillian observation that life has gotten both better and worse for Americans over
the last generation. There has been genuine and rapid progress in the
direction of justice defined as "inclusivity." One aspect of that progress
has been the "legal, social, and financial emancipation of women."
But there is also social and moral deterioration, more crime and greed,
less trust, and a general confusion about moral standards. Families
are failing, and more people are lonely. The average middle-class
American is "more fearful, anxious, and unsettled," more full of "individual anguish," and so on balance less happy.[10]

There is now, as Tocqueville predicted, too unconstrained a perception of freedom or choice, too much of life is dissociated from the
domain of social duty. Too much human experience, in effect, has
been turned over to the doctrine of interest. This emotional detachment or movement toward individualism Popenoe traces primarily to
the decline in the number of stable, affectionate nuclear families. If
women are no longer defined primarily by the task of habituating or
socializing children, it is unclear who in particular is charged with

raising them. Most of all, today's parents cannot find adequate time to raise children.[11]

Public administrators should join the growing consensus that the strong, two-parent, heterosexual family is the best suited for preparing and sustaining individuals for the responsible exercise of liberty. The experiences of love and dependence are required for the proper development of the American mixture of personal independence and familial, political, and religious responsibility. "Recent sociological studies," William Galston summarizes, "confirm a strong correlation between family solidarity and the sense of obligation to a wider community or society." So the decline of the two-parent family produces "a growing subset of the population that cannot discharge the basic responsibilities of citizenship in a liberal democracy."[12]

Studies also show that, even for most adult Americans, family life remains the greatest source of happiness and personal satisfaction. A stable marriage, Popenoe notices, "is good for one's physical and mental health."[13] It limits one's restless anxiety with love. Men still need their wives to experience such order more than women need their husbands. Because familial love is still what makes life worth living for most Americans, administrators should do what they can to support it, even at the expense of equality and efficiency. They should do what they can to assist American women in employing their natural superiority in resisting democracy's inhuman or individualistic excesses.

Conclusion: Administration as Democratic Statesmanship

The Tocquevillian paradox is that excessive independence generates excessive dependence. So the modern, democratic process of liberation from all forms of authority in the name of equality seems to be culminating in bigger, more powerful, and more meddlesome government than ever before. What big government does, above all, is constrain individual choice, and it most readily grows when individuals feel especially in need of such constraint. Big government is welcomed by those who feel isolated, disoriented, and personally powerless, those who lack the resources to choose well.[14]

Administrators cannot help but be inclined to administer, to control impersonally the lives of others in the name of justice and technical competence. But Tocqueville shows them why they should act against their administrative inclination on behalf of their love of human

liberty. They should devote themselves to perpetuating personal responsibility in a quite impersonal and irresponsible time.

Notes

1. Page numbers in parentheses refer to the Lawrence translation of *Democracy in America* (Alexis de Tocqueville, *Democracy in America*, ed. J. P.
Mayer, trans. G. Lawrence [Garden City, N.Y.: Doubleday, 1969]).
2. For an introduction to Solzhenitsyn's and Havel's dissident thought,
see my "The Dissident Criticism of America," *The American Experiment:
Essays on the Theory and Practice of Liberty*, ed. P. Lawler and R. Schaefer
(Lanham, Md.: Rowman & Littlefield, 1994).
3. Harvey C. Mansfield Jr., *America's Constitutional Soul* (Baltimore:
Johns Hopkins University Press, 1993), 177. This paragraph and the next are
indebted to Mansfield's astute chapter 13.
4. Lewis Lawson and Victor A. Kramer, eds., *More Conversations with
Walker Percy* (Jackson: University Press of Mississippi, 1991), 232–33.
5. Most of Percy's analysis found here is taken from *Lost in the Cosmos: The Last Self-Help Book* (New York: Farrar, Straus, and Giroux, 1983).
For elaboration, see my *"Lost in the Cosmos*: Walker Percy's Analysis of
American Restlessness," *Poets, Princes, and Private Citizens*, ed. J. Knip-
penberg and P. Lawler (Lanham, Md.: Rowman & Littlefield, 1996).
6. Walker Percy, *The Thanatos Syndrome* (New York: Farrar, Strauss,
and Giroux, 1987), 88.
7. Martin Heidegger, *Being and Time*, trans. J. Macquarrie and E. Rob-
inson (New York: Harper and Row, 1962), 297–98.
8. See Michael W. Spicer, *The Founders, the Constitution, and Public
Administration: A Conflict in World Views* (Washington, D.C.: Georgetown
University Press, 1995) with the refinements in Spicer's argument suggested
by Donald J. Maletz in his review (*American Political Science Review* 90
[March 1996]: 205–6).
9. From this point onward, I draw upon my "Tocqueville on Pride, Interest, and Love," *Polity* 28 (Winter 1995): 217–36.
10. David Popenoe, "The Family Condition of America: Cultural Change
and Public Policy," *Values and Public Policy*, ed. H. Aaron et al. (Washington, D.C.: Brookings Institution, 1994), 90.
11. Ibid, 104.
12. William A. Galston, "Liberal Virtues and the Formation of Civic Character," *Seedbeds of Virtue*, ed. M. Glendon and D. Blankenhorn (Lanham,
Md.: Madison Books, 1995), 56.
13. Popenoe, 98. See also James Q. Wilson, *The Moral Sense* (New York:
Free Press, 1993).
14. See Harvey C. Mansfield and Delba Winthrop, "Liberalism and Big
Government: Tocqueville's Analysis," unpublished paper.

3

Public Administration and Policy Deliberation: The Case of Global Warming

Marc K. Landy and Charles T. Rubin

For better or worse, public administration cannot be understood simply in terms of the reflexive execution of the laws. Flawed though they may be, public agencies have a valid claim to being repositories of impartial information and expertise. This fact takes on increasing importance as the public at large becomes increasingly mistrustful of all large institutions and increasingly prepared to believe that any and all factual claims placed before it are misleading and partisan. Corporations, labor unions, and Congress are regularly given first place on the public's list of least-trusted institutions. And there is growing recognition that even so-called public-interest groups and other nonprofit organizations have private interests capable of distorting the information they place before the public.[1] If public agencies cannot play the honest broker, there are diminished hopes that reason can be deployed in the service of sound policy. Under these circumstances, the question becomes not whether bureaucrats should exercise leadership in policy formulation, but how to reconcile bureaucratic initiative and constitutional democracy.

The most dangerous path would be for bureaucrats, no matter how noble their motivation, to think of themselves as independent agents promoting their own policy agendas. The nonelected official may not legitimately substitute his or her judgment for that of constitutionally sanctioned judicial or legislative bodies.

Instead, we suggest, bureaucrats should think of themselves as civic educators. Their most essential republican task is to provoke and stimulate deliberation among a wider public concerning the central policy issues at stake. Since they are not properly placed to provide

the ultimate answers, they can serve to pose the right questions. Those
questions can provide an intelligible framework for policy determinations by constitutionally responsible bodies.[2]

Asking the right questions is not simply a technical matter. In fact,
the most difficult question to ask involves determining which of the
technical attributes of a problem are most relevant for framing policy
consideration. This task requires deliberation among those with relevant expertise, such as scientists, engineers, lawyers, and economists,
etc. The right question is the fruit of the mutual instruction that takes
place as participants work back and forth between the norms and theories
they subscribe to and the specific facts at hand. They explore the
alternative formulations they find most compelling as their grasp of
the situation improves. Asking the right question is not a contest between
interests, but an inquiry that profits from the contributions of several
minds reflecting different professional perspectives.

Obviously, this portrait is of an ideal type rarely if ever perfectly
embodied in any real policy deliberation. Nonetheless, it is an ideal
to be aimed for. The closer the approximation, the better the outcome. What follows is an examination of a specific policy deliberation involving the Environmental Protection Agency (EPA) and various
scientists whom it commissioned to consider the issue of global warming.
By closely examining key features of this deliberation, we will assess
how closely it approximated the ideal type and what the intellectual
and institutional barriers were to a closer approximation.

The Rise of Global Warming

In a very short space of time, global warming went from being a
very obscure issue to occupying a high position on the public agenda.
In the late 1980s, it became the stuff of newspaper headlines, television scrutiny, congressional hearings, and myriad national and international conferences. The EPA has placed it high on its list of most
serious environmental problems. Although the Bush administration
greatly expanded research funding to investigate the issue, the president was pilloried not only by environmental groups, but also by
Congress and the editorial pages of leading national dailies for not
doing a great deal more. The Clinton administration has been only
somewhat more aggressive in its policy recommendations. But under
the leadership of Vice President Al Gore and the State Department's

Timothy Wirth, it has raised the rhetorical level of concern over warming to new heights within the federal government.

Policy scholars have been trained to expect that a problem will rise on the public agenda only if it meets the triple criteria of *serious, certain,* and *soon.* The global warming question fails two and possibly all three of these tests. Climate change is not likely to occur soon. Even those most concerned about it agree that its palpable effects will not be felt for decades. In fact, great uncertainty exists about whether it will happen at all. While it is true that dire consequences could follow from a drastic increase in global mean temperature, the inability to assess the likelihood of such an event makes it very difficult to determine how seriously to take the problem.

Perhaps the quick rise of global warming as an issue reflects the results of a successful policy decision that recognized that *certain* and *soon*—in neither case sufficient criteria for sound public action— were inappropriate criteria. Abandoning the certainty principle might reflect a recognition that nothing is really certain. Risk and uncertainty lie at the very heart of modern environmental problems. Nor is it always wise to wait to act until the full brunt of a problem is being experienced. Far better to nip some problems in the bud than to wait until they reach a crisis stage.

But it is equally plausible that this heightened attention to global warming reveals less admirable attributes of the policy deliberation that produced it. Perhaps the government has been pressed into taking premature action by unwarranted hysteria. Such "apocalypse abuse" could have been fomented either by those with something personal to gain, or by those who have an animus against the sort of industrial society that is fueled by the hydrocarbons that are the main roots of the purported problem. Or perhaps the intellectual assumptions that underlie the scrutiny and interpretation of the evidence are deeply flawed. Perhaps all three of these factors are at work. Only by examining the public record of how the global warming problem has been defined can one understand why the call to action has been so positively received and determine whether it is justified.

To resolve these questions, we focus on early major studies of global warming and how policy advocates and public agencies interpreted them at the time for the purpose of defining the "global warming problem" and making concrete policy recommendations. We scrutinize two large studies of global warming done by the Environmental Protection Agency's Office of Policy, Planning, and Evaluation: *The*

Potential Effects of Global Climate Change on the United States (1989) and *Policy Options for Stabilizing Global Climate* (1990). As is usually the case with scientific research, the EPA's work builds on the work of others. In this instance, studies by the National Academy of Sciences (NAS) have had an important role in legitimizing the prominent position of global warming on the federal policy agenda.

The quality of global warming policy deliberation depends largely upon the soundness of the two fundamental intellectual constructs upon which it rests—scientific consensus and scenario building. Following the lead of the NAS, the EPA reports employed a specific decision rule, scientific consensus, to justify giving attention to this issue. This decision rule was applied by the NAS and the EPA to assess evidence obtained on the basis of two specific methodologies: climate modeling and scenario building. Therefore, to evaluate the quality of the policy development process, it is necessary to understand how the EPA and NAS employ climate modeling and scenario-building, and the meaning of a "scientific consensus" based on these methods.

The Meaning of Scientific Consensus

All honest accounts of the greenhouse effect acknowledge substantial uncertainties in any attempt to predict the climate of the future. Since in this area one cannot speak of unambiguous scientific truth, those who want to make the case for action must refer to some other standard in order to bolster that part of their case that depends on what science can tell us about the climate many years hence. The EPA chose to assert that a "scientific consensus" exists about various aspects of global warming. What does that mean?

In *Potential Effects* we read, "Although there is consensus that increased greenhouse gas concentrations will change global climate, the rate and magnitude of change are not certain (see box entitled Climate Change)."[3] The cited box is a summary of a summary statement from the National Research Council's 1987 report *Current Issues in Atmospheric Change.* Similarly, in *Policy Options* we find, "There is scientific consensus that increases in greenhouse gas emissions will result in climate change (Bolin et al., 1986; NAS, 1979, 1983, 1987; WMO, 1985)."[4] Here we have five reports that are used to define consensus. Bolin et al. and WMO (World Meteorological Organization) are attempts to synthesize and assess the scientific "state of the art" at the time of their publication. NAS 1987 is the report mentioned above; NAS 1979 is a report called *Carbon Dioxide and Climate: A Scientific Assessment*; and NAS 1983 is titled *Changing Climate*.

These two passages suggest that for the EPA, "scientific consensus" means that certain scientific associations have produced reports that, if they are interpreted accurately, substantiate the point in question. (As we will see, accurate interpretation cannot be taken for granted.) Therefore, to judge the weight that should be given to such claims, it would be necessary to know the substance of the reports, the nature of the organizations that have produced them, and the way in which they were produced. For example, do the reports put out by the NAS actually define a scientific consensus?

The NAS is not only one of the most prestigious scientific honor societies in the United States, but also a crucial adviser to the U.S. government. The special relationship it has to the government adds to its prestige. Established by Congress in 1863 as an independent organization on the model of European academies such as the Royal Society, the Academy's charter states that it "shall, whenever called upon by any department of the Government, investigate, examine, experiment, and report upon any subject of science or art. . . ."[5]

The service so offered is, in recent years at least, only very rarely the performance of original experimentation or investigation. Rather, the NAS's "typical mode of operation" is as follows:

[A] federal agency which needs help with a problem will ask the Academy for advice, the Academy will reach out into the scientific community to find experts capable of analyzing the problem, these experts will convene periodically as a committee, and ultimately the committee will produce an advisory report which is submitted to the agency for its consideration in making a decision.[6]

Flexibility seems to be the hallmark of the choice of those who serve on NAS and NRC committees, as is evident even from the following "in-house" description of the process:

Prospective committee members are identified in a variety of ways, most of which involve suggestions from individuals considered knowledgeable in the fields in which nominees are sought. Most suggestions for committee members come from individuals, not from institutions, organizations, or agencies of government. Committee members are nominated by commissions, offices, and boards, and are approved by the chairman of the National Research Council.[7]

The chairman of the NRC, who must approve appointments, is also the president of the NAS.

Clearly, committees thus formed can vary widely in quality, depending on the clarity of the question they are being asked to address, and the capacities of the people who at a given time are asked, willing, and able to serve. In relatively recent years, the NRC has strengthened its procedures for review of committee reports prior to their release. But once the reports are issued, the immense prestige of the academy stands equally behind all of them.

This prestige itself is important as a means by which scientific consensus comes to be defined. So when the EPA cites various NAS reports as definitive of a scientific consensus, it is hardly doing anything extraordinary. But what actually stands behind the citation? Let us look in a little more detail at the background for these simple and authoritative-sounding references. Do the reports themselves claim to be doing what the EPA employs them to do? This question has two parts. Does the form these reports take justify using them to define scientific consensus? And what is the substance of the consensus that they are said to support? We will take up each question in turn.

Current Issues in Atmospheric Change (1987) came about because in June 1986, eight senators, whose request in September of that year prompted the two EPA reports considered here, wrote to Dr. Frank Press, president of the NAS. Professing alarm over "some of the most extraordinary statements ever made by respected and reputable scientists and scientific organizations" about the potential harm that could be done by global warming, they solicited the aid of the NAS

in collecting and analyzing this data [about global warming], as well as communicating it to the Congress and the public in an understandable way. One option would be to conduct a one or two-day workshop for Members of Congress, their staffs, and the press, which would identify research priorities and evaluate current evidence.[8]

This workshop was held 30–31 October 1986. It appears from the list of attendees that no member of Congress came. Instead, staff members and representatives from various agencies (but no members of the press) heard presentations from nine scientists. The published report

was developed on the basis of the workshop presentations, and it represents the consensus of the workshop participants. The summary should thus be viewed as a symposium proceedings rather than as a standard NRC report, which reflects the deliberation and scientific consensus of a carefully selected committee over an extended period of study.[9]

In this instance, then, the document does *not* purport to define a broad scientific consensus. But in passing, it suggests some standards that, if met, might allow a more appropriate use of that term: the committee must be carefully selected and it must study and deliberate over an extended period. Do the other two NAS works cited by the EPA meet these criteria?

Carbon Dioxide and Climate (1979) (usually called the Charney report) was produced pursuant to a request to the NAS by the Director of the executive branch's Office of Science and Technology Policy (OSTP) to assess "the scientific basis" for studies predicting a warmer earth, and "the degree of certainty that could be attached to their results."[10] The NAS convened the Ad Hoc Study Group on Carbon Dioxide and Climate, consisting of nine scientists, who met 23–27 July 1979. Their very brief report—only seventeen pages of text—fulfills its charge primarily through a relatively technical peer review of the strengths and weaknesses of five general-circulation models of global climate—at best, a narrow interpretation of their charge. As such, the report might serve as part of an ongoing process by which a consensus is developed. But it shares the limitations of *Current Issues*. That the committee was labeled ad hoc suggests an informality about selection even beyond what is customary at the NAS, and in any case, it gathered for only a brief period and considered a limited issue. So here, too, it is not clear that the report deserves to be considered as definitive of a scientific consensus.

Changing Climate (1983) is by far the most ambitious, and in many respects the most thoughtful, of the three reports cited here. It was produced in response to a directive in the Energy Security Act of 1980 that the OSTP request the NAS to produce

a comprehensive study of the projected impact, on the level of carbon dioxide in the atmosphere, of fossil fuel combustion, coal-conversion and related synthetic fuels activities authorized by the Act, and other sources. Such study should also include an assessment of the economic, physical, climatic and social effects of such impacts.[11]

The nine-member Carbon Dioxide Assessment Committee (CDAC) met four times over a space of two years. The final 490-page report included articles written with the assistance of a number of scholars not formally on the CDAC, along with selections from a study (*Carbon Dioxide and Climate: A Second Assessment*) that was produced by a different panel. The preface speaks of the volunteer efforts of thirty outside reviewers.

Here it might seem most reasonable to speak of a report that represents a scientific consensus; the committee produced a detailed and in-depth study over an extended period of time. But *Changing Climate* places an interesting construction on this point. The report consists of two parts: a relatively brief synthesis portion, and the bulk of the report, made up of papers by individual authors. As explained in the preface, only the synthesis section—about one-sixth of the whole—represents a committee consensus without "major dissents."[12] The papers by individual authors are just that.

The various caveats and limitations that their authors place on these NAS reports suggest at the very least that, formally speaking, the EPA may be claiming rather more for them than the NAS authors themselves would claim. But if the form of the reports does not always seem to justify giving them such significance, what about their content?

Is it indeed the case—whatever modesty and caution scientists may insist on applying to their work—that the substance of the consensus the EPA asserts is supported by the NAS reports it cites? Let us note that the proposition they are being asked to substantiate ("that increases in greenhouse gas emissions will result in climate change") is quite general. Indeed, it is nearly tautological. "Greenhouse" gases do not come with tags on them saying "I am a greenhouse gas." What is a greenhouse gas, except one whose radiation-absorbing properties give it the potential for producing climate change, such that more of it will make climate change more likely?

At this level of generality, the NAS reports certainly support the proposition that the EPA wants them to support. But it is the very generality of this consensus position that limits its significance. Will the climate change a great deal, or a little? Will the change be on balance for the better, or the worse? Will it happen sooner or later? Should we take one kind of action, another, or none at all? These are the kinds of questions that policymakers must address. The consensus position, left at face value, hides important problems and disagreements more than it serves even as a beginning for a discussion of appropriate policies.

We begin an examination of this point by looking at *Changing Climate* as the most comprehensive and thoughtful of the reports under

consideration here. Its relatively small synthesis portion could represent a hard core of the knowledge that is central to any greenhouse
policy. Or it could be a summary of what is indisputably known about
global warming and its effects. Are either of these adequate descriptions of the "large core of views, findings, conclusions, and recommendations" that "all members could wholeheartedly and responsibly
endorse"?[13]

The discussion in the synthesis portion can be divided into three
parts: a look at how, why, and to what extent climate might change in
response to increasing levels of carbon dioxide (CO_2), a discussion of
the potential effects of climate change, and a set of policy recommendations. A close look at each section suggests that the "large core" of
views that could be agreed upon has much more to do with questions
and uncertainties than with knowledge and prediction.

Thus, when it comes to asking how much CO_2 is likely to be emitted over the next decades, there seems to be no question that the amount
will be increasing. But how much and how fast? "There are no strong
signs of convergence toward a single, widely accepted projection or
set of assumptions. . . ."[14] As a result, for "purposes of understanding
future outcomes and weighing policy choices, the past efforts reviewed
leave open important questions" that "do not allow a judgment as to
the accuracy with which a forecast is made."[15] It is for that reason
that authors attempted estimations whose purpose was "not to resolve
uncertainties but to represent current uncertainties as realistically as
possible."[16]

Given an estimate of how much CO_2 will be emitted, what will
that do to atmospheric concentrations of the gas? (Not all emitted
CO_2 remains in the atmosphere; some is taken up by terrestrial life
and by the oceans.) It is likely that CO_2 concentrations will increase.
But how much and how fast? There is "uncertainty and conflicting
evidence about the preindustrial concentration [of CO_2], fossil fuel
emissions, the biotic contribution, and ocean uptake. . . ."[17] As a result, the authors suggest that it is most useful to try to represent the
uncertainties, that is, to examine how different assumptions about how
CO_2 is taken up or emitted result in different resulting atmospheric
concentrations.

If CO_2 in the atmosphere increases, what will be the impact on
climate? It is agreed that some surface warming is to be expected, but
how much and how fast? On this crucial point the synthesis portion
does not commit itself, resting content with the summary presentation
of a range of possibilities produced by various models and reports. It

does note that the specific regional effects of any general warming cannot "at present" be predicted.[18]

If increased CO_2 concentrations mean warming, can we detect any evidence of warming given increasing levels of CO_2 that have been observed over the past one hundred years or so? "[W]e do not believe that the overall pattern of variations in hemispheric-mean or global-mean temperature or associated changes in other climate variables either confirms or contradicts model projections. . . ."[19]

With all these uncertainties in hand, it is hardly surprising that in the twenty pages of the synthesis section's seventy-six pages that are devoted to the possible effects of global warming on agriculture, water supplies, and sea level, the authors admit that any assessment of impacts is based on "enormous" uncertainties.[20] It is also not surprising that the examination of each area of impact is based on slightly different assumptions about the speed and degree of warming.

Finally, twenty-seven of the synthesis portion's pages are taken up with policy recommendations. Like many scientists, the authors of this report believe that the uncertainties they agree upon are no reason not to start doing something about global warming. But what to do? Some fourteen pages—over half—are given over to outlining the research that needs to be done to fill in the many blanks in our knowledge. And, as we shall see later, the remaining recommendations suggest a cautious approach to defining the "global warming problem" and to making policy in the face of this ignorance.

Is *Changing Climate* perhaps unusual in its caution? Do the other reports taken separately or together tell us more of what we need to know to make policies to ameliorate or reverse potential global warming? Let us look more broadly at how they collectively attempt to define the issue. Take, for example, the measure by which the extent of global warming to be expected is most often summarized—the mean global surface temperature increase in the event of a doubling of atmospheric CO_2, or the equivalent in greenhouse gases of all kinds. All the cited reports agree that in this event we should expect an increase of from 1.5 to 4.5 degrees Celsius. Consensus reigns. But what does that tell us? At the bottom of this range, the likely impact produced by the warming would be minimal; at the top, it would be potentially catastrophic for some parts of the world. A consensus over such a wide range is not a solid basis for deciding what, if anything, needs to be done.

Furthermore, what level of confidence are we to put in this prediction? The Charney report calls the stated range "most probable."[21]

Current Issues calls the range "very probable."[22] The executive summary of *Changing Climate* says simply that CO_2 doubling "would cause" such a temperature increase, with "values in the lower half of this range . . . more probable" than values in the upper half.[23] But it is not clear that the Executive Summary is part of the synthesis report. The synthesis portion identifies this range as the result of various models, but does not clearly endorse or assign a probability to that range.[24]

A further complicating factor is that conclusions from both the Charney report and *Carbon Dioxide and Climate: A Second Assessment* (1982) are incorporated into *Changing Climate* as chapter 4, whose topic is "Effects on Climate." These two reports are in agreement on the range in question, with the proviso that *Second Assessment* interprets the Charney report "to imply a 50 percent probability that the true value would lie within the stated range."[25] In other words, the result was as likely to be outside the range as inside it. Further, the placement of these reports in the structure of *Changing Climate* suggests that they, like the other nonsynthesis portions of the report, represent positions for which there was not necessarily "unanimity of conclusions."

Do all of these statements somehow represent the same estimation of likelihood? Did all panel members have the same thing in mind when they agreed to these "consensus" formulations? Or do not the reports clearly indicate that the consensus range is really an estimate of what was *not* known about global warming over the seven-year period covered by them?

Furthermore, what is the *significance* of an increase in average surface temperature of the sort that this range suggests? Here the reports seem to be in agreement again. As stated in *Changing Climate*:

> consider, for example, the most frequently quoted index—change in global average surface temperature. This crude measure of climate tells us about what temperature change to expect for specific regions and nothing about the type of climate that would be experienced.[26]

The Charney report agrees that "we do not consider existing models to be at all reliable in their predictions of regional climatic changes,"[27] while *Current Issues* notes, "We have little confidence in predictions about the many details of the forecasts: local changes by city or state, exact shifts of desert regions or of extent of monsoons, changes in river flows, or overall economic impacts."[28] Here we see explicitly that there is a consensus about what is *not* known. Furthermore, *Current Issues* proves to be at odds about what could be known both with *Changing Climate*, because it did attempt to examine overall economic impacts, and the EPA's *Potential Effects*, which is given over to estimating regional effects of climate change.

If the estimated change in global average surface temperature is so unilluminating, why is it the stock-in-trade both of consensus formulations and of popular concern over greenhouse warming? *Changing Climate* notes that the figure is used so much because "for many models it is the only result with much scientific validity."[29] As we have seen, however, this validity is at best probabilistic. The report acknowledges that the measure "may well suggest the nature of our unease,"[30] making its significance more affective than analytical. In any case, if we know little about the impact of such an increase "on the ground" in any given area, we have little basis for formulating policies that could respond to such a change before it happened.

What, then, do the reports suggest about how to think about responding to such a change, given the uncertainties? Is there any consensus on this point? The Charney report is almost silent on this topic, presumably because

it appears that the warming will eventually occur, and the associated regional climatic changes so important to the assessment of socioeconomic consequences may well be significant, but unfortunately the latter cannot yet be adequately projected.[31]

Yet the foreword to the Charney report, by a scientist who did not serve on the study group, asserts without saying what should be done that "A wait-and-see policy may mean waiting until it is too late."[32] Signals appear to be mixed.

The synthesis portion of *Changing Climate* presents a highly nuanced discussion of what should be done, so much so as to be difficult to summarize fairly. This difficulty reflects the fact that whereas the other reports assume a certain level of CO_2 and attempt to describe the consequences of that concentration for climate, this report takes on the much more difficult task of predicting future CO_2 levels, as well as trying much more than the other two reports to address the consequences of climate change, and policy options regarding it.

Still, the authors agree that "Overall, we find in the CO_2 issue reason for concern, but not panic."[33] The report notes how problematic it is to try to define an issue with so many ramifications simply as "the CO_2 problem," and stresses "its ties to other social, economic, and environmental problems."[34] "Viewed in terms of energy, global pollution and worldwide environmental damage, the 'CO_2 problem' appears intractable. Viewed as a problem of changes in local environmental factors—rainfall, river flow, sea level—the myriad of individual incremental problems take their place among the other stresses to which nations and individuals adapt."[35] Indeed,

It is probably wiser not to act aggressively to "solve the CO_2 problem" right now when we really do not know the future consequences or context of CO_2 increase. In trying to consider the world of 50 or 100 years from now, we cannot be sure that we can tell the difference between solutions and problems.[36]

Despite the fact that the report wants to link CO_2 with precisely the kind of changes it acknowledges we know least about, it nevertheless recommends a variety of steps to address the prospect of warming, beyond further research.

Last, *Current Issues* does "not presume to answer such a value-laden question" as *when* we should act.[37] Instead, it asserts that future knowledge is unlikely to force a major revision of current findings about global warming, even though its major recommendations involve strengthened research and further thorough study. Still, "many of the workshop participants believe that steps should be taken now to slow emissions or mitigate the potential impacts of the rising atmospheric trace gases discussed in the workshop"—thus answering the question that "we" would not presume to answer.[38]

In addition, *Current Issues* takes an argument about the complexity of the specific results of climate change such as was made in *Changing Climate* and uses it to promote a greater sense of crisis. Warming, it notes, might have conflicting effects on agriculture: good in some ways, harmful in others, good in some areas, bad in others. "These competing influences may mask shifting effects on individual farmers, regions, or even small nations. A farmer of Illinois or Kansas, bankrupted by a carbon dioxide–induced drought, would take little comfort in the higher yields harvested by Canadian wheat farmers."[39] Still, since the report acknowledges that regional effects are least well understood, it is hard to see how we can now make policy that has a reasonable chance of protecting even individual farmers.

What Consensus?

In short, the substance of the "consensus" position properly understood makes it less a solid foundation on which to build science or
policy than an attempt to describe what is still missing in that foundation. It is very useful to identify what one needs to learn, and if
this were the limit of the explicit claims made on behalf of the consensus, it would be hard to object to it. The problem is that a consensus like this one is open to a dual use in the debate over greenhouse
policy. Some will say that action would be premature given the lack
of knowledge, while others will assert that waiting for more knowledge before acting will leave us with a less tractable problem. At
such a stage, then, the attempt to approach greenhouse policy though
the medium of a "scientific consensus" is unlikely to be productive.

This situation should not be surprising. In an area of science with
many unknowns, just what is a matter of "consensus" is what scientists themselves debate, in painful awareness that even consensus
positions are not necessarily the final truth. There will be powerful
forces that resist the conformity that is implicit in "consensus," and
hence in the democratic policymaker's hope that policy can be predicated on some "consensus." Indeed, it seems in this particular case
that such consensus as exists in these reports could be summarized in
the proposition that effective greenhouse policy—which implies the
sort of knowledge of particular effects under specific circumstances
that is currently lacking about the consequences of global warming—
is going to be very difficult to make.

In its more meaningful respects, then, "scientific consensus" is at
odds with the rhetorical purpose for which it is employed—creating
a sense of broad agreement and urgency behind acting to "deal with"
the greenhouse effect. The EPA's *Potential Effects* report is thus a
little more honest about the significance of consensus than *Policy
Options,* since it admits that "the rate and magnitude of change are
not certain."[40] But whereas many popular presentations rest content
with such problematic arguments from authority, the authors of both
these reports must deal with the fact that their more sophisticated
readers will be well aware of the limits of scientific consensus. In
order to construct policy recommendations, they must somehow build
on the highly generalized consensus to make appear certain what is
uncertain in those reports. At this more sophisticated level, the consensus is just a jumping-off point for the development of scenarios in
the EPA reports.

Scenarios and Predictions

Like a number of environmental groups, the World Resources Institute has published a book about the greenhouse effect intended for popular consumption, *The Greenhouse Trap*. It summarizes one finding of the EPA reports under study here by saying that the "most immediate impacts" of global warming on the United States would likely be in agriculture and forestry. "Greatly decreased forest yields, crop losses, and 'moving' grain belts are among the predictions" made by the EPA, according to WRI.[41]

The summary is accurate in all but one crucial respect: the report that was cited, *Potential Effects,* made no predictions. Indeed, it specifically says it is analyzing "plausible scenarios of future climate change" and presenting "indications of the impacts that could occur as a result of global warming" rather than making predictions.[42] As a result, even where WRI uses conditional language to present EPA conclusions, it is still misleading. In the context of attempts to predict, conditionality implies a judgment of probability. But in presenting scenarios, the EPA explicitly refuses to assign probabilities to the events it discusses.[43]

Treating scenarios as predictions has become a common feature of global warming discussions. What is a scenario, and how does it differ from a prediction? Why did the EPA choose to develop scenarios rather than attempt to predict the future? Answers to these questions are important to understanding how proposed greenhouse effect policies are studied and justified.

In one sense, creating scenarios has been a tool of policymaking ever since people asked themselves the question "What if?" in reference to some contemplated course of action. For at their simplest, scenarios are nothing more than attempts to work out in a thoughtful way the possible consequences of a given set of assumptions.

But as a "method" employed by the social sciences, scenarios owe much to the work of Herman Kahn and his Hudson Institute think tank during the 1960s. Indeed, the *Oxford English Dictionary* supplement attributes the first use of the term in this specialized sense to Kahn. He employed scenarios in the study of international relations and in futurology, but most notoriously in his work on nuclear war.

Kahn always described scenarios as "an aid to the imagination."[44] They enable analysts to get a sense of a "large range of possibilities" and prepare the way for systematic investigation of those possibili-

ties.[45] They suggest key issues, questions, and choices with a detail
that would be impossible if the analysis remained at a more abstract
level. And they allow consideration of the complex interactions among
different aspects of a problem or situation. Finally, scenarios can be
used as artificial "'case histories' . . . to make up to some degree the
paucity of actual examples."[46]

But Kahn consistently stressed that the scenario was "not used as
a predictive device."[47] Scenarios must strike a balance between stimulating and disciplining the imagination. On the one hand, they must
be grounded in a plausible representation of the present, and of the
forces that will produce the future. On the other hand, since history
is replete with surprises, they must not be limited to the merely plausible or conventional.

Of course, Kahn's understanding of the nature and limits of scenarios need not govern the research of the EPA. But in fact, it seems
that in many ways the EPA follows Kahn's lead. There is repeated
acknowledgment that scenarios are not predictive devices, and the EPA
reports are intended to serve purposes that Kahn attributed to scenarios. They investigate a range of assumptions about the impact of CO_2
on climate in such a way as to direct future research and analysis.
Finally, in their specification of unknowns and the assumptions that
fill in for those unknowns, they employ just the kind of "if-then" thinking
that scenarios are designed to promote.

Nevertheless, there are also important differences. The extensive
employment of computer modeling and quantitative analysis means
that the EPA scenarios are intended as far more than the literary and
pedagogical devices Kahn developed; every attempt has been made to
turn them into tools of rigorous quantitative analysis. And the apparent precision of the results is used to do far more than guide future
research and analysis. The ability to examine questions of technical
feasibility in great detail has prompted the EPA to draw policy conclusions from the scenarios despite its own formal disavowal of the
intention of doing so.

This tension results not simply from misusing the scenario methodology set forth by Kahn, but from a problem that was implicit in
that methodology, the problem of the conflicting requirements of
imagination and analysis. As analytical tools seem to become more
rigorous with the advent of computer modeling, their tendency to rely
on, and to hide their reliance on, imagination becomes increasingly
problematic.

Let us examine, for example, one of the policy "findings" from

Policy Options, tracing back some of the various assumptions from which it is derived.

The most direct means of allowing markets to incorporate the risk of climatic change is to assure that the prices of fossil fuels and other sources of greenhouse gases reflect their full social costs. It may be desirable to impose emission fees on these sources according to their relative contribution to global warming in order to accomplish this goal. Imposing fees would also raise revenues that could finance other programs.[48]

The executive summary of *Policy Options* is rather more detailed on this "other programs" point than the body of the report, noting that a carbon fee could be used to "reduce other taxes, reduce the national debt, and/or support other national goals."[49]

Full social-cost pricing of energy has been on the environmental agenda for many years now. Our question is, how do scenarios support its utility for addressing greenhouse emissions? What steps are involved in generating the information upon which this recommendation is presumably based? First, *Policy Options* estimates future emissions of CO_2—to the year 2100—in the absence of policies to address greenhouse warming. This is the purpose of the two "base case" scenarios, involving a "slowly changing world" (entailing slow GNP growth, slow technological change, and a carbon-intensive fuel mix) and a "rapidly changing world" (rapid GNP growth, rapid technological change, very carbon-intensive fuel mix).[50] While the existence of two such scenarios indicates the gross uncertainties about future economic growth, population growth, and technological change, there are many uncertainties subsidiary to these larger ones. Among those pointed out in the report itself is the absence of certainty that activity levels assumed in the models of the various economic sectors (e.g., industrial or agricultural) harmonize with the economic assumptions of the scenario as a whole. Further, capital markets (i.e., the availability of capital for investment in various areas) are not explicitly considered, a matter of some importance to developing nations' ability to reduce greenhouse emissions. And it is assumed that "aggressive" research and development (R&D) will lower the costs of alternative energy sources, an assumption that goes to the heart of the economic impact of substituting less carbon-intensive energy sources for more.[51]

These are all, as it were, "macro-uncertainties." But we can go still further. The amount and kind of energy used will play a major role in greenhouse emissions. The scenarios attempt to model all kinds of energy use, such as its use for air transportation. This analysis requires looking at future demand for passenger travel, which the model takes to be "a function of demand in 1985, growth in real income, and the income elasticity of demand."[52] The demand is translated into kilometers traveled, which in turn is translated into energy required for that amount of travel. This method seems reasonable enough. But the projection goes out some one hundred years. Imagine what an attempt to model global transportation needs for the year 2000 would have looked like in 1890. Would it likely have been right about how, where, and when people travel? If the EPA has reasons to doubt that the next hundred years will bring changes of the same magnitude, they are not given in the report.

But let us return to the big picture. In the attempt to study future emissions of CO_2, the stabilizing scenarios change the picture of the rapidly and slowly changing worlds by adding (among many other measures) substantial carbon fees on fossil fuel production in proportion to their carbon content so as to encourage conservation and the switch to alternate, less carbon-intensive energy sources (as well as to help balance the federal budget). It is at this crucial step that we find some of the most interesting unknowns and assumptions. First and foremost, as the executive summary notes, "the appropriate levels for setting greenhouse gas fees are unknown."[53]

Why, then, were the modeled tax levels chosen? The modeling effort could be said to be a preliminary estimate of what greenhouse fees should be. On the other hand, *Policy Options* here, as in the case of many other proposals it considered, did not attempt to estimate the "full social costs and benefits" of full social-cost pricing.[54] This far-from-trivial omission means that really we are no closer than before to knowing the appropriate greenhouse "fees," because, whatever their impact on emissions, we do not know that the levels chosen are economically sustainable. This lacuna is all the more remarkable given the fact that the scenarios assume both that energy efficiency improvements are likely to occur even without substantial energy price increases, and (as already noted) that R&D alone will bring down the price of alternative energy sources.[55] If true, to what extent do these assumptions call into question the need (in other than a symbolic or revenue-producing sense) for carbon taxes? If false, then the EPA has probably done its case a disservice by understating the likely impact of such taxes on emissions reductions.

But let us press on. What is the likely result of these proposed taxes? Estimates of the effects of a carbon tax vary wildly. For any given level of taxation, the models employed produce a range of estimates of reduction where the highest is nearly seven times the lowest. The closest estimates among the three models employed differ by a factor of two.[56] Yet *Policy Options* gives no direct indication as to which figure was used to estimate the reductions in carbon emission. Nevertheless, the amount of forgone carbon has to be converted into its effect on warming. The first step is an estimate of the atmospheric concentrations of CO_2 a given level of emissions would produce, since not all the emitted CO_2 ends up in the atmosphere. At this level, there are controversies, for example, about the effect of increased CO_2 levels on plant growth, and hence on the ability of plants to absorb it, as well as about the extent to which the ocean acts as a "sink" to absorb CO_2. To date, atmospheric models are notoriously bad at modeling processes involving the ocean. Still, estimates for CO_2 concentrations are produced.

Finally, these atmospheric concentrations of CO_2 help shape the calculation of the extent of greenhouse warming. At this last level, we introduce into the scenarios all of the well-known uncertainties about climate modeling. In the end, however, the EPA estimates that, relative to the rapidly changing world, the carbon taxes would reduce warming by about 5 percent. The rapid-reduction tax rates would produce an additional 2 percent to 3 percent reduction in warming.[57]

It may be some indication of the degree of confidence that the many authors of *Policy Options* had in results that build assumption on assumption in this way that the discussion of "internalizing the cost of climate change risk"[58] is not, as one might expect, an analysis of the scenarios per se. Instead, there is a general discussion of the extent to which energy demand is responsive to increases in energy prices, and of the extent to which financial mechanisms are useful for creating markets for energy efficiency and conservation.[59] As it turns out, they may or may not be. The striking fact is that no part of this thematic discussion of the issue depends in any way on the results of the scenarios.

Yet somehow, social-cost pricing is vindicated. The problem here is not only that the "finding" depends on a lengthy chain of debatable assumptions. In many instances, if one looks hard enough, these assumptions are admitted to be questionable. And in the world of policymaking, it is often difficult to avoid such long chains of inference. The way the finding is generated and presented is misleading, using computer and mathematical analyses that produce readily quantified results. The appearance of precision may mislead the layman—and that is important—but the layman is unlikely to see the results in that form, anyway. Against the impression he will get from news reports that the EPA reports were an exercise in prediction, this false precision pales in importance. In any case, the more one is the kind of person who would read the whole report, the less likely it is to mislead.

These two difficulties are quite significant, however, when combined with a third, which is the undisciplined use that *Policy Options* makes of imagination. Any thinking about the future requires some imagination, but if it is to be more than daydreaming, that imagination must be directed into consistent paths. The authors of *Policy Options* are aware of both the need and the difficulty of making scenarios depend on mutually consistent assumptions. They attempt to do so for those factors that can be readily quantified. But not all assumptions can be so quantified. Our look at social-cost pricing, for example, raised questions about the wellsprings of technological change. Does technological change have an impetus of its own, or is it called forth by economic conditions, or by political fiat? Does technology develop in response to problems, does the perceived severity of a problem influence what technological solutions are deemed acceptable, or do nascent technological abilities help to define new problems? At what point do technological changes combine to produce new ways of life or life choices, such that one cannot any longer project on the basis of current trends or assumptions?

Policy Options answers these questions in a variety of ways, even in our own limited example. Sometimes it imagines that energy R&D has a life of its own, sometimes that it must be encouraged by economic conditions or government action. Its view of air travel takes a "conservative" stance on likely technological change; might not high-speed communications drastically reduce business travel? But alternative energy sources like solar power and biomass are seen as capable of rapid development that would produce significant differences in the way we produce energy. Failure of imagination in one case, and excessive imagination in the other?

Perhaps it can be said that such catholicity of perspective on the motive forces of technological change is true to life. But if our experience is that these questions can be answered in mutually contradictory ways, that suggests one reason for the indeterminacy of the future.

The assumptions of scenarios would then always be so arbitrary that the enterprise would have little meaning.

This problem of the use and misuse of imagination for scenario building arises also in *Potential Effects*. Given that report's more explicit concern for general methodological questions, it is no surprise that the issue comes up in a somewhat more self-conscious, but curiously inverted, way.

When the executive summary of *Potential Effects* explains why the scenarios presented cannot be considered predictions, there is a careful explanation of some of the limitations of climate study results, and the limits of our knowledge about the changes that warming might bring for natural ecosystems. But the concluding two paragraphs are of particular interest:

> With some exceptions, we did not generally examine human responses and adaptations to effects of climate change. The report was intended to examine sensitivities and potential vulnerabilities of current systems to climate change. Many other changes will also take place in the world at the same time that global climate is changing. We cannot anticipate how changing technology, scientific advances, urban growth, and changing demographics will affect the world of the next century. These changes and many others may singularly, or in combination, exacerbate or ameliorate the impacts of global climate change on society.
>
> The results are also inherently limited by our imaginations. Until a severe event occurs, such as the drought of 1988, we fail to recognize the close links between our society, the environment, and climate. For example, in this report we did not analyze the reductions in barge shipments on the Mississippi River due to lower river levels, the increases in forest fires due to dry conditions, or the impacts of disappearing prairie potholes on ducks; all these impacts were made vivid during 1988.[60]

What is interesting about these two paragraphs is the unrealized tension between them. Let us leave aside the irony that the very things that *Potential Effects* says cannot be anticipated are just the sort of thing *Policy Options* attempts to anticipate. In any case, *Potential Effects* is revealed as having made what might charitably be called an extraordinarily imaginative assumption—that in the face of any climate change that might happen, human beings will not constantly make incremental adjustments. When the study concludes that the "findings collectively suggest a world different from the world that exists today,"[61] we can well believe it, because the assumption that little will be done to prevent change is built in. In the fifty or so years that the report covers, the world would look very different even *without* climate change if we were not constantly making "responses and adaptations" to natural forces.

At the same time, *Potential Effects* in effect chastises itself for its own lack of imagination, and in a sense justly. It is indeed true that scenarios are as limited as our imaginative abilities, but what does that tell us about scenarios as an analytical tool? We can always imagine one more consequence, if we put out minds to it; we can always imagine some connection between events. Left as stories or as jumping-off points, as they were by Kahn, scenarios retain in an obvious way the mark of their origins. But the more sophisticated they are in a quantitative sense, the easier it is to forget we are looking at the results of our imaginations, played out in however much detail scientific tools can provide. For these tools do not guide and direct those imaginings; they simply flesh them out.

What guides the imagination? For most of us, most of the time, it is our hopes and fears. It is apparent that *Potential Effects* is directed more by fears than hopes. The failure throughout the report to consider ongoing responses and adaptations is an attempt to present the worst case. Likewise, the report is much more concerned about imagining the factors that would make the impact of warming more rather than less of a problem. The nine "systems" that it examines, ranging from forests to agriculture to electricity demand to urban infrastructure, were chosen *because* they were judged to be "particularly affected by climate change."[62]

As a result, *Potential Effects* treats a massive number of particular changes, and repeated recommendations are made, particularly to federal agencies, to consider just the kind of planning for responses and adaptations that the report assumes will not happen. In other words, the assumption behind the report is that to cause such matters to be taken seriously, it is necessary first to imagine the worst of what would happen without them. However, if the scenarios are intended as general guides to policy investigations, are they not being treated as predictions—for why would one want to look into something that is not likely to happen? Furthermore, the more particular and specific the projection of the effects of global warming, the less likely the projection is to be well grounded in current models of such effects. Here again, the ultimate burden seems to fall on imagination.

The way these two reports complement each other is a tribute to the confusion about what they can legitimately be regarded as having shown. *Potential Effects* suggests all sorts of impacts; some we might want to prevent, some not; some are disastrous, some benign; some reversible or meliorable, some irrevocable. But *Policy Options* does not treat these impacts individually, instead presenting global schemes for emission reductions. The implied link is that we simply don't want most of the things mentioned in *Potential Effects* to happen. What have we done, then, but imagine a future that we don't want? That's a very human thing to do; it is the stuff of alien invaders setting out to destroy the earth. But policies do not get made to prevent "The Day the Earth Stood Still." The more we are prompted to act on these greenhouse imaginings, the more we do act on them, the more we implicitly treat them as predictions.

So even those writing the scenarios become somewhat confused about what they have accomplished. When the results fall into the hands of EPA spokesmen, the limits of the scenario method fall even farther behind. When *Policy Options* began circulating in draft form, EPA spokeswoman Linda Fisher is said to have commented, "We look at the report as good news, because it says there are things we can do" about global warming.[63] Is she not suggesting a high level of confidence that the measures outlined in the report will work as the scenarios suggest? And does this assurance not implicitly turn the scenarios into predictions of what will happen if we implement certain policies? A few months later, EPA administrator William Reilly put a different spin, but also a predictive one, on conclusions in *Policy Options*. Speaking before the Los Angeles World Affairs Council, he said that "under our most optimistic control scenario, we could reduce global warming in the year 2025 by only one-fourth" of the expected increase.[64] The statement treats a scenario in the report as if it were a plan for action, including predictions of the effects of putting that plan into place.

Is it any wonder, then, that news media pick up the story of these reports as a story about prediction? And, despite methodological protestations to the contrary, perhaps that is precisely the effect these reports were designed to have. The scenario method as implemented by the EPA gives their reports the "deniability" they need to be credible with the limited audience that will be concerned about the technical merits of the case being made. But it produces results that are guaranteed to call into play the passions of those for whom global warming is the latest, best hope of the environmental crusade.

Conclusions

Was this example of global warming policy deliberation a success or a failure? We suggest it was a failure because it rested upon two inappropriate analytic premises. A scientific consensus did not exist in any form that was truly applicable to policymaking. The consensus that did exist concerned what was *not* known rather than what was known. Furthermore, the use of scenarios was inappropriate because it treated an exercise in imagination as if it were a valid means for making predictions.

Since further research is so crucial for addressing this issue, our finding concerning the manner in which current scenario-based research is conducted, and, in particular, the manner in which it is translated into policy-relevant statements and reports, is particularly disturbing. Most disturbing of all is the depiction of a scientific consensus regarding both the likelihood and the magnitude of the problem. Much of what passes for consensus represents language that is sufficiently ambiguous to enable scientists who actually harbor significant differences of opinion to sign a particular committee report or joint statement without violating their professional scruples. Policy entrepreneurs are then left free to cast these documents to a wider public with whatever partisan gloss they see fit.

Such a procedure ill serves the causes both of policy and of science. From a policy standpoint, it promotes hasty and excessive action by overstating the degree of expert support for a dire view of future warming. But it also slows the progress of scientific investigation by blurring the lines of expert disagreement, and therefore makes it more difficult to determine what the most promising lines of further inquiry might be. As a result, funding may be misdirected.

At one level, this problem is insoluble. It is the nature of committees to dampen dissent and seek a common ground. Furthermore, it is the nature of members of such committees to seek to please their sponsors, especially (as in this case) if those sponsors have significant control over present and future funding opportunities, or if the opportunity to participate on such committees is itself viewed as a sign of professional standing. We do not believe that, as a result of such pressures, scientists routinely sign reports they consider false. But there are strong incentives for papering over disputes, for overlooking aspects of reports readily subject to misinterpretation, and for being less than aggressive in criticizing the purposes to which sponsoring agencies or organizations subsequently put the work.

One alternative to this excessive pressure for an unproductive conformity among experts would be to replace the committee model with that of a court. Much attention has in fact been given to the idea of "science courts," but we do not share that enthusiasm. All institutional forms have their own biases. Courts are based on advocacy. Just as committees create pressure for uniformity, so courts create a pressure for partiality among those who submit evidence before them. In a society that is already excessively litigated and replete with adversarial decision-making forums, the adoption of yet another one hardly sounds like a step in the right direction. Furthermore, while the best courts provide procedural fairness, ferreting out the truth is not really their long suit.

Rather than looking for such an institutional "fix," it would be better to accept the unpleasant truth that in a modern, commercial, democratic society, science, politics, and partisan interests will tend to be intertwined. Scientists will seek—and have every right—to advance their agendas as citizens, as members of public and/or private bureaucracies, and as representatives of their particular scientific specialties. In this last guise, they are often competing with members of other research disciplines not only in terms of how best to explain the world, but for the resources to develop such explanations. One does not have to give up on the goal of scientific objectivity to recognize that it was easier to maintain when science was less a part of everyday, commercially oriented life, and when scientists were for the most part members of a leisured class who could afford to pursue knowledge for its own sake. Scientists will have a much harder time being disinterested in a society that sees its prosperity and success as, in large measure, based on their activities.

We do not mean to suggest that scientific findings are reducible to the interests of the people who produce them. But as matters stand now, the pretense of scientific objectivity is a readily available shield behind which self-seekers can hide while they strive to advance their own agendas. A wider appreciation of the factors that compromise scientific objectivity might serve to deter the abuses that can result from them. As the public is whipsawed between the results of one study this week and a contradictory one the next month, a growing cynicism about science develops that might more appropriately be targeted against scientists who present incomplete or speculative findings to the public before their peers. More skeptical citizens and legislators would be less willing to plan for the remaking of civilization every time a new risk appears on the horizon.

Paradoxically, by expecting less we might even get more. The quest for scientific disinterestedness is not simply a myth; hence a greater awareness both within and beyond the scientific community of the forces that compromise it could lead to greater efforts of self-policing. If scientists don't enjoy being politicians (more or less in disguise), then the dissonance created by a more overt awareness of the dangers of their present situation might push them defensively in the right direction. Under stronger professional pressure, the shield of disinterestedness might shrink so as to protect only those who deserve it.

But the current political and economic pressures on scientists are too great to be alleviated solely, or even primarily, by improved self-scrutiny. We have heard the private lament of scientists about the caution they must exercise not to offend or challenge the orthodoxies of the funding networks too many times to believe that it is merely sour grapes. The answer to such dangerous pressure, which strikes at the heart of scientific integrity, is hardly going to be a unified, centralized "science policy." Better to encourage a greater proliferation of scientific voices at the same time that one improves the capacity of government to provoke rather than smother scientific deliberation.

Perhaps the single most useful reform pointing in this direction would be to expand the availability of private sources of scientific research funding. Greater diversity of funding sources means that more dissident researchers will have access to needed resources. More dissident research means greater debate. However, although widening the investigative net holds the promise of yielding better understanding, that will happen only if a more stringent enforcement of procedural and formal discipline of scientific research is imposed. Here again, greater debate may prove useful. Procedural and formal requirements help to make debate productive, but they are also enforced by debate, as failures in these regards become ground for criticism. The need to expose and defend scenario premises would be a fine way to situate the imagination within its proper limits. In sum, such discipline means that even as we risk the closer tie between science and private interest that increased private funding may produce, we create conditions to minimize the dangers of that tie.

Government, too, has a role in fostering and disciplining the complex process of scientific debate. It is a role that is not served when lawmakers seek to score points off those who testify in hearings, or force them to oversimplify complicated issues. Likewise, it is not performed when bureaucrats seek to smooth over disagreements for

the sake of a unified, final "product." To fill this role effectively requires that officials recognize that their primary responsibility is not
to try to wring premature consensus out of divergent views, but to
facilitate an ongoing process of scientific deliberation. Rather than
dampen dissent, they should be asking questions that serve to focus
and clarify the issues that remain unresolved. Then they can serve as
effective and responsible educators of both the public and their politically responsible superiors, providing a careful overview of what is
known and what is not, and how best to conceptualize the probabilities and magnitudes of the risks to be faced.

To be able to perform such a mission requires, first of all, that
it be viewed as the proper one for public officials to perform.
This necessitates a change in the prevailing climate of opinion within
federal agencies, which both abets and rewards policy "entrepreneurship." It is this climate that will make it seem to some that we are
foolish to believe in the possibility of governmental disinterestedness,
particularly in light of our skepticism about scientific disinterestedness. But whatever may be true of global climate, there is certainly
such a thing as political "climate change." As long as middle- and
senior-level administrators believe that they are expected to "create
policy," that is what they will do. They will continue to use their
imaginations to find the most effective worst-case possibilities, and
seek out science and scientists whose findings justify the policy initiatives they favor.

If, on the other hand, public administrators were to understand that
their job is mainly to provide what Hugh Heclo has called "politically neutral and professional competent performance" for their politically responsible superiors, they would be far more likely to act that
way.[65] The point is not to pretend that all politics and ideology can
be wrung out of government in favor of comprehensive "management"
or "administration." Rather, disinterested behavior on the part of public
servants depends on how they understand their role, and this understanding will be strongly affected by the training they undergo and
the incentives they receive.

It is a small but decisive step from "discovering" that bureaucrats
often function as policy entrepreneurs, to celebrating that development. Such a subtle but important shift has in fact taken place in the
posture that the study and teaching of political science and public
administration have adopted toward public executives. Such people
are now frequently described as "public managers" rather than "civil
servants," as if to say that government agencies should pursue lines

of "business" that are to be "managed" in order to produce a product for the public, just as private businesses do. The contrast with the earlier locution, which suggests a role subordinated to the polity and its needs, could hardly be more marked.

If we have public managers, then we must expect them to act in the entrepreneurial fashion that is a vital part of business management. Thus, recent graduates of programs in public administration or policy are likely to enter government service under the impression that part of their job is to know their "line" of policy and make sure that they can "sell" it. Why not teach them instead that, whatever the place of policy entrepreneurship in public life, their primary role is to be skeptical civil servants, provokers of deliberation, and providers of thoughtful analysis to their political superiors?

The reward structure that civil servants face would have to reinforce this self-conception. Salary increments should not go to those beating the drums for a pet idea, but to those who most effectively serve the public by asking inconvenient questions of experts, and developing sensible criteria by which to judge competing explanations and policy strategies.

The irony is that if such a sea change could be accomplished, many constituencies of the bureaucracy would find it quite easy to live with. It would provide the president with an "out" from pressures to take precipitous action. It would give members of Congress a place to get the disinterested information they need, and the responsible media a whole raft of "issue debate" stories of the sort they claim to be looking for. Also, it would relieve a certain tension within the bureaucracy itself. The old conception of bureaucrats as civil servants dies hard. Not everyone can be happy with the expectation that they become policy entrepreneurs, and many might look with favor upon trading the job of salesman for one that is more intellectually demanding.

We acknowledge that this proposal represents the public administration equivalent of balancing the budget. It is something that, in principle, most people, even congressmen, would like to see happen— but only if it did not impede the realization of some cherished policy objective. Yet what is the alternative? In an era of budgetary constraints, the continuation of what has become business as usual is costly both to the budget and to our political culture. In order to get their piece of the pie, policy entrepreneurs must continually exercise their imaginations to fan the flames of public hysteria. As the perceived problems grow in seriousness, so must the proposed solutions be inflated. How then, if we know what these terrible problems are and know what to do about them, could our failures to do so be explained by anything but the idiocy or knavery of the powers that be? Confidence in government understandably weakens when government is seen to lurch in and out of engagement with issues that in fact were not yet well enough defined or understood to allow anything more than symbolic action in the first place. Apocalypse-mongering simultaneously creates great expectations and continual disappointments; it thus leads to a public that is cynical about what it is told without being genuinely skeptical, alienated by the messengers rather than maintaining a prudent caution about the message. In such an atmosphere, the chances of adopting policies that are favorable to the long-term economic and political viability of the nation are slim indeed.

Notes

The authors gratefully acknowledge a grant to Charles Rubin from the Carthage Foundation, which has made possible some of the research in this chapter.

1. Cf. Michael S. Greve and Fred L. Smith, *Environmental Politics: Public Costs, Private Rewards* (New York: Praeger, 1992).

2. This point is developed in Marc K. Landy, Marc J. Roberts, and Stephen R. Thomas, *The Environmental Protection Agency: Asking the Wrong Questions from Nixon to Clinton* (New York: Oxford University Press, 1994).

3. Joel B. Smith and Dennis Tirpak, eds., *The Potential Effects of Global Climate Change on the United States* (Washington, D.C.: U.S. Environmental Protection Agency, Office of Policy, Planning, and Evaluation [PM-221], 1989): xxv (EPA-230-05-89-050).

4. Daniel A. Lashof and Dennis A. Tirpak, eds., *Policy Options for Stabilizing Global Climate* (Washington, D.C.: U.S. Environmental Protection Agency, Office of Policy, Planning and Evaluation, 1990), 1.

5. *Questions and Answers about the National Academy of Sciences, National Academy of Engineering, Institute of Medicine and the National Research Council* (Washington, D.C.: National Academy of Sciences, April 1990), 1.

6. Phillip M. Boffey, *The Brain Bank of America: An Inquiry into the Politics of Science* (New York: McGraw-Hill, 1975), 3.

7. *Questions and Answers*, 14.

8. Participants in the Workshop on Atmospheric Change, *Current Issues in Atmospheric Change* (Washington, D.C.: National Research Council, 1987), 33.

9. *Current Issues*, vii–viii.

10. Ad Hoc Study Group on Carbon Dioxide and Climate, *Carbon Diox-*

ide and Climate: A Scientific Assessment (Washington, D.C.: National Academy of Sciences, 1979), vii.

11. Carbon Dioxide Assessment Committee, *Changing Climate* (Washington, D.C.: National Academy Press, 1983), 492.

12. Ibid., xv.

13. Ibid., xv.

14. Ibid., 9.

15. Ibid., 10.

16. Ibid., 12.

17. Ibid., 19.

18. Ibid., 30.

19. Ibid., 33.

20. Ibid., 40.

21. *Carbon Dioxide and Climate*, 2.

22. *Current Issues*, 9.

23. *Changing Climate*, 2.

24. Ibid., 28.

25. CO_2 Climate Review Panel, *Carbon Dioxide and Climate: A Second Assessment* (Washington, D.C.: National Academy Press, 1982), 51.

26. *Changing Climate*, 50–51.

27. *Carbon Dioxide and Climate*, 17.

28. *Current Issues*, 25.

29. *Changing Climate*, 51.

30. Ibid., 51.

31. *Carbon Dioxide and Climate*, 3.

32. Ibid., viii.

33. *Changing Climate*, 61.

34. Ibid., 62.

35. Ibid., 3.

36. Ibid., 62.

37. *Current Issues*, 25.

38. Ibid., 26.

39. Ibid., 17–18.

40. *Potential Effects*, xxv.

41. Francesca Lyman et al., *The Greenhouse Trap* (Boston: Beacon Press, 1990), 5.

42. *Potential Effects*, xxvii.

43. Ibid., 57.

44. Herman Kahn, *Thinking about the Unthinkable* (New York: Avon Books, 1962), 150.

45. Ibid., 151.

46. Herman Kahn and Anthony J. Wiener, *The Year 2000: A Framework for Speculation on the Next Thirty-Three Years* (New York: Macmillan, 1967), 263.

47. Ibid., 264.

48. *Policy Options*, chap. 7:1.

49. Ibid., executive summary, 31.
50. Ibid., chap. 6:8.
51. Ibid., chap. 6:20.
52. Ibid., technical appendix A, 23.
53. Ibid., executive summary, 31.
54. Ibid., executive summary, 31.
55. Ibid., chap. 6:20.
56. Ibid., chap. 7:53.
57. Ibid., chap. 6:56, 58.
58. Ibid., chap. 7:13.
59. Ibid., chap. 7:13–22.
60. *Potential Effects*, xxix–xxx.
61. Ibid., xxx.
62. Ibid., 3.
63. "EPA Plan Targets Global Warming," Pittsburgh *Press*, 14 March 1989, A10.
64. "Greenhouse Worries EPA Chief," Pittsburgh *Press*, 28 June 1989.
65. Hugh Heclo, *A Government of Strangers: Executive Politics in Washington* (Washington, D.C.: Brookings Institution, 1977), 246.

4

Impartiality and Administrative Statesmanship

Richard T. Green

It is common in the United States to think of civil servants as impersonal and impartial functionaries—official clerks who are supposed to dispassionately serve us and carry out the will of our policymakers. We also like to criticize these people as inefficient, legalistic, and unresponsive to the public and their political representatives. We recognize that uncaring and rigid attitudes may accompany impersonality and impartiality, and this bothers us.

At the same time, we applaud when civil servants resist superiors who tout ill-conceived plans or manifest corrupt intentions. We also want them to be innovative and expert at handling some of our most intractable problems. We expect them to find or create jobs for the unemployed, ameliorate the effects of poverty and ill health, protect our environment, reduce crime, improve education, and much more. We demand that they protect and regulate as well as serve, and that they promote fidelity and accountability to our governing system in the process. In short, we also expect public servants to act like statesmen.

These role expectations conflict, of course. It is very difficult to be both clerk and statesman. As a result, some frustrated officials complain of a fickle public demanding the impossible. Some students of government describe the public as schizophrenic, unforgiving, illogical, irrational, and unreasonable. And many citizens will agree with these assessments when confronted by them. Yet almost everyone, even the most jaded public servant, is resigned to accepting these and other conflicting expectations as a permanent feature of our political culture.

91

This acceptance is a good thing, because in many ways these expectations reflect sound political instincts. It is sensible to expect faithful obedience from subordinate public officials, but not blind obedience. It is reasonable to give them discretionary powers for the sake of developing varieties of policy and administrative expertise. It is also prudent to exercise nervous oversight for the sake of limiting their powers. We Americans have believed, at least since our country's founding, that we must build contrary tendencies into our governments—to check and balance power—to give it with one hand, and limit it with the other.

These sensibilities, however, give little comfort to civil servants and citizens when they find themselves torn by resulting cross pressures. Nor do they lend much insight on their own for understanding how to balance or integrate conflicting roles properly—how to be both clerk and statesman. Perhaps we should not concern ourselves too much with comfort, for that can lead to complacency and the avoidance of tension, when tension is the very thing we wish to engender. Understanding how to integrate these roles, though, is vital for both citizens and public servants, and this chapter contributes toward that end.

Connotations of Impartiality

An important key to understanding how to balance the roles of clerk and statesman lies in the concept of impartiality. It is a vital attribute of wise and legitimate decision making. Deciding impartially, however, can mean different things. Various meanings are employed in public life, and some are less helpful than others for our purposes.

Neutrality

People often think of impartiality as neutrality. Public officials, it is held, should avoid imposing their own opinions in favor of those expressed by elected representatives and their political appointees. This populist version is often accompanied by a technocratic formulation that states that public servants should apply value-neutral techniques derived from science and the professions to achieve the ends prescribed by law. In either case, public servants become mere instruments of policymakers.[1] Public administrators have been heavily influenced by these instrumental approaches during the twentieth century.

One still hears administrative officials claim that they "only carry out policy, not make it."

This view of impartiality consigns the public servant exclusively to the role of technical clerk, entirely ignoring public expectations of statesmanship. It also overlooks a vast empirical literature that demonstrates that public administrators do shape public policy in countless ways. The literature indicates that even street-level officials such as police officers and social workers exercise substantial policy-determining discretion.[2]

The neutrality approach presents a convenient but deceptive dodge for public servants. They can divert challenges to their discretionary powers toward higher political officials by claiming only a technical role in the policy implementation process. In effect, they may claim that they are merely clerks following orders. In ethics, this is commonly known as the Eichmann excuse—after Adolf Eichmann, the German bureaucrat who claimed he merely followed Nazi orders as a technocrat in designing and implementing the extermination camp system. The only source of responsibility in this view lies outside of oneself and up the hierarchy. This extreme view became common throughout the Western world in the early twentieth century, and spawned a rather heated debate over whether administrative responsibility should be focused upon external authority or one's conscience.[3] Claims to neutrality will not work if we seek to balance clerkship with statesmanship. Blindly obedient public servants are incapable of limiting their obedience to appropriate matters, because that requires conscience and judgment independent of their superiors.

Impersonality

We also often think of impartiality as involving impersonality. If officials maintain an impersonal attitude toward those they serve, then they will treat them more equally and without prejudice. This meaning is heavily reinforced by modern bureaucratic theory. Max Weber, the great German sociologist writing at the turn of the century, provided a comprehensive theory in which impersonality played a key role. In his model, impersonality was enhanced through a variety of organizational principles. First, all ranks are held "in position" rather than "in person." That is, individuals are identified by their position in the organization, such as "clerk stenographer" or "engineering technician." If moved to a new position, they become identified with that new position, and shed the old one. Individuals are fit to jobs as if they are cogs in a machine. If they don't work well, they can be replaced by new cogs. Like parts on an assembly line, they are interchangeable. Thus, personality and personalism fade away in favor of a machinelike image of operating structures and processes.

Second, in Weber's account, the proliferation of rules in the organization reinforces impersonality. Rules define what employees do and how they do it. Strict adherence to the rules means that everyone occupying a job class performs the same duties in exactly the same way. Thus, obeying the rules means downplaying any unique qualities of personality in the performance of one's work. People who display personal idiosyncrasy in their work are usually punished in some way to guarantee general conformity of behavior.

Finally, hierarchy and clear chains of command reinforce the idea that organizational responsibility lies outside of oneself. Employees are responsible only for their own work, and therefore should not meddle in affairs that transcend it, despite any qualms or pangs of conscience. This conjures up the image of a single person at the top being in control of the whole organization, and of focusing all accountability ultimately upon that person. The organization is his or her instrument.

Today we often project this image onto presidents, agency heads, and chief executive officers of corporations. Anything that happens, whether good or bad, is attributed in the end to the person at the top. The officials below, who actually do the vast bulk of the planning and work, seem to disappear in an impersonal sea of anonymity and deference.

Impersonality, like neutrality, emphasizes clerkship and excludes statesmanship among subordinate officials. It encourages blind obedience by destroying personal ownership in the results of organized or cooperative effort. The worst extremes of this attitude were again manifested in Nazi Germany, where many thousands of officials contributed to organized efforts at mass murder, and then denied their culpability because their roles were allegedly minor and distant from the actual results. We experience many less extreme examples today that nevertheless have profound effects.

Our current disdain for government bureaucracy is fed in part by the cold impersonality and procedure-bound habits of some officials. They seem indifferent to the actual effects of their policies and procedures. We want them to treat us equally, but we also want the treatment to be effective and sensitive. We want to be treated respectfully and decently, and an impersonal manner often seems offensive as a result. We want officials to act coolly and firmly under pressure, but also with a demeanor that shows that they care about our needs and respect us. This is no easy task, and the bureaucratic principle of impersonality seems incompatible with such prudence and care.

Impersonality is not highly regarded by most government employees, either. They don't like being treated like replaceable cogs in a machine. As a result, they have taken steps to mitigate at least some aspects of impersonality. For example, the professionalization of many government occupations over the past fifty years has shifted much employment to rank-in-person status.[4] Professionals identify themselves by permanent titles of "rank," such as doctor, nurse, attorney, forester, engineer, professor, and military officer. They carry these titles into every position, and share privileges of membership in professional associations, which regulate the characteristics of professional practice from outside the employing agencies. This gives them some autonomy from rule-bound hierarchies.

Agencies dominated by professionals also often display collegial organizational structures that differ markedly from traditional bureaucratic hierarchy.[5] In short, many of our modern governmental organizations are not bureaucratic at all in the Weberian sense.

This does not mean that professionals necessarily make their service to the public more personable, but they do attend more carefully to the results of cooperative efforts in the agency. They are less apt to think of their work as a minor contribution, and are therefore more disposed to accept rather than evade greater responsibility. Occupational groups seeking professional status (such as nurses, police officers, and social workers) openly display these attitudes when they seek to acquire more complex work responsibilities and shed simpler ones. In the process, they anticipate receiving more respect and personable treatment from clients, colleagues, and superiors.

This desire for recognition of the person in the job is a factor that some of the American Founders tried to provide for in the design of our governing system. James Madison wrote in *The Federalist Papers* of his hope that the constitutional design would tie "the interests of the man . . . to the constitutional rights of the place."[6] He wished to engage the personal motives of the individual official by giving him sufficient power and incentive to check those who would encroach upon his own duties. In addition, both Madison and Alexander Hamilton emphasized the importance of getting officials to stake their reputations on their offices, which meant that they would have to attend to the integrity of related offices as well. For many of the

Founders, loss of reputation seemed a fate worse than death. Concern for reputation entailed consideration for how future generations would look upon their work. They thought of fame as high esteem and recognition by those who would see the effects of their work well beyond their time.[7] Officials attracted to the pursuit of fame would therefore try to anticipate the long-term effects of their work upon the country. The involvement of personality in this sense promotes responsibility and accountability, and is indispensable for cultivating statesmanship. Impersonality, by contrast, dissipates ambition and separates the official from collective responsibility. It will not serve to balance clerkship with statesmanship.

Mediation

Another common approach to impartiality entails mediation as the primary means of administrative decision making. This approach comes from America's pluralist political ideology, which emphasizes the interplay of contending interests in our political system. Conventional pluralist wisdom holds that administrative officials should mediate among the contending interest groups who compete for an agency's protection, resources, or other valuable services. Playing the impartial broker involves a largely passive role, in that the contending interests bring their differences to the table while the bureaucrat simply facilitates compromises. Agency officials, in the pluralist view, may sometimes have to impose a compromise of their own making on the interest groups, but the terms usually still fit the situation as defined by the groups. This keeps the range of compromises within limits acceptable to the groups. If not, they will appeal to higher authorities, such as courts, legislators, and higher executive officers, to rein in the agency.

Mediation as an administrative style now pervades American public administration at all levels of government. It helps administrative officials avoid conflict, and encourages them to view their role as largely facilitative. Its passivity often complements claims to neutrality in administrative decision making. Mediators merely help others reach a decision, and ostensibly refrain from making policies of their own. In this way they can also claim to be more democratic and responsive in decision-making. Public-choice theorists have given this approach renewed vigor in recent years by adding economic arguments for refraining from the use of discretionary power in favor of market-style choice for constituents. Administrators simply explore and provide a range of program policy alternatives through survey feedback.

The Total Quality Management and Reinventing Government movements are based heavily upon this approach. Managers are expected to empower "customers" or the public rather than themselves. Unfortunately, problems arise as the popularity of the mediational approach grows. From the standpoint of statesmanship, it is too passive. There are times when aggressive, uncompromising strategies are needed. Though mediation is certainly an important dimension of administrative decision making, it hardly exhausts the gamut of professional responsibilities. Mediating at the wrong times or in the wrong situations can result in dereliction of duty to the public. Neville Chamberlain, Britain's prime minister from 1937 to 1940, exemplified this problem when he applied his mediational style in dealings with Adolf Hitler, who would indulge Chamberlain's pursuit of negotiations to buy time and keep the British unprepared for conflict. Then he would act with force to induce British appeasement. While Chamberlain took negotiations seriously, Hitler merely used them to further his uncompromising agenda. Chamberlain was forced to make serious concessions to Hitler in hopes that he would eventually negotiate in good faith. He never did.

This problem abounds in less drastic but still serious public matters today. Administrators often try to negotiate with groups that have amassed substantial political and economic power. They are strongly encouraged to do so by elected officials currying favor with those groups. As a result, concessions are made that may work against broader public interests. Theodore Lowi describes this phenomenon as "interest-group liberalism." A small number of interest groups can come to dominate an agency's agenda, effectively making policy without the guidance of law.[8] Adopting a mediational style does make administrators more responsive and pliable to these narrow interests, but is this the kind of responsiveness we want?

Another problem arises when mediation replaces strategic vision. This results in what is known as policy gridlock. Public officials spend all their time mediating disputes and fail to keep any guiding mission or standards in mind. They try to satisfy every group, and end up pleasing no one. Some even turn this consequence into a virtue. "If everyone is mad, I must be doing something right!" To meet expectations, these administrators may adopt a mission statement with vacuous language, and then proceed under its cover to uphold a status quo of mediational drift. Such a strategy usually flows from an exaggerated fear of conflict that would ensue from the assertion of meaningful standards.

Mediation serves, at least in appearance, to diminish the role of the administrator in making decisions. That is certainly appropriate at times, but cultivating it into a habitual style of management leads to the neglect of statesmanship, and sometimes to outright dereliction of duty.

Detachment

We also think of impartiality as a form of detachment. This means standing apart or aloof from objects or circumstances. We typically associate this kind of impartiality with judges. We want them to be detached from the cases and controversies they must decide in order to ensure some objectivity or independent perspective.

Administrators must act as judges in a variety of circumstances, and in that role must seek a degree of detachment as well. For example, administrative law judges are often employees of the agency that is party to a dispute, but are usually shielded from any involvement in the dispute until they are called upon to adjudicate it. Similarly, agency heads or commissioners may stay aloof from a case until it rises to their level of appeal.

Conflict-of-interest laws also make detachment necessary for some administrators. In this case they must separate aspects of their private affairs (such as certain business activities) from their public duties in order to avoid the temptation or appearance of swaying public decisions for their own private gain.

More generally, public administrators often wish to remain detached from the heat of agency and interest-group politics in order to maintain a more balanced perspective toward the public needs the agency meets and how it meets them. This is especially true of higher-level administrators. Typically, these officials spend much of their time dealing with outsiders to the agency, trying in part to assess how the agency is viewed. They spend so much time doing this that lower-level agency officials may often think of them as outsiders as well.

Behavioral studies and systems analyses have shown that all complex organizations display segmented and stratified layers that provide varying degrees of detachment for the sake of accommodating differing organizational functions and perspectives.[9] For example, middle managers perform functions and adopt perspectives that differ dramatically from those of top-level and street-level officials, and they are generally found in offices physically separated from these other layers of operation.

Professionals also gain significant levels of detachment through their control over standards and methods of professional practice. Employing agencies must defer to these, or risk public censure by the professional association. They do not want to be castigated for interfering with professional judgment.

Detachment differs from the previous connotations of impartiality because it does not necessarily entail passivity. An official can aggressively pursue an agenda and yet remain somewhat detached. Judges, for example, adopt legal philosophies and political opinions that are reflected in their court decisions. We may disagree with their particular philosophy or viewpoint, but this does not deter us from thinking of them as remaining impartial in the sense that they are detached or independent from the parties to the case. Rules of procedure (criminal and civil) are designed to ensure that such detachment exists throughout the life of the case in the courts.

Administrators similarly have viewpoints and agendas of their own, whether they are appointed politically or through the civil service. We expect political appointees to adopt the general views of their elected superiors, but we are not surprised to see them differ with them as well. Most elected officials understand at the outset that they will be appointing strong-willed officials having agendas of their own. In many cases that is the primary reason for their appointment. Elected officials do not want mere clerks running agencies. Indeed, it is not unusual for an elected official to appoint former political rivals. (One example is President Bill Clinton's appointment of former Republican Senator William S. Cohen to serve as his secretary of defense.) Hence it is not surprising that appointees commonly seek substantial degrees of detachment, even from their elected superiors, very soon after their appointment. Over the past fifty years, political appointments have also increasingly been based on professional credentials rather than strict personal or partisan loyalty, and this increases the appointee's desire for detachment.[10]

Moreover, not all political appointees serve at the pleasure of elected officials. Some (for instance, members of the Federal Reserve Board) have fixed terms that may be shortened only by legislation or for cause, such as malfeasance. Others, such as federal judges, have terms that continue "during good behavior," which means until retirement or death in most cases. Appointments such as these guarantee substantial degrees of detachment.

Civil service administrators enjoy detachment by virtue of their legal protection from partisan manipulation. For example, they cannot be removed at will or for overtly partisan reasons. Nor are they allowed to participate directly in political campaigns. Their detachment is intended to maintain partisan neutrality, though this does not mean that civil servants are or should be neutral about all policy matters, or even about some partisan matters. For example, they may openly oppose some aspects of a political party's agenda for an agency on the grounds that it is poorly designed, or that it ignores administrative capabilities. Civil servants would fail to act responsibly if they ignored the important connections between political agendas and the means for their implementation.[11]

Furthermore, these officials have to choose which superiors they will follow when conflicts among them ensue. Our constitutional system of separate powers and checks and balances guarantees that such conflicts will arise. For example, should an administrator uphold the partisan agenda of his executive branch superiors, or a conflicting agenda of legislative superiors? If the courts are brought into the fray, their rulings must generally be followed instead. Civil servants often find themselves in the middle and they must ultimately decide to follow one side or another. Decisions of this sort demand judgments informed by statesmanship rather than clerkship, and depend heavily for their success upon significant degrees of detachment.[12]

Professionals, too, have distinctive views and active policy agendas shaped largely by needs, dispositions, and values inherent in their work. Their positions are typically highly responsible, and their professional detachment, often protected by law, enables them to exert significant influence over agency law and policy. They also assert their influence directly on political parties through their professional associations. Parties today are very sensitive to the influence of numerous professional organizations.

Detachment, then, is one aspect of impartiality that accommodates both clerkship and statesmanship, and is common to our structure and traditions of governance. It is a necessary condition for improving judgments of complex issues. However, detachment alone neither improves nor justifies judgment. It gives little indication of what aspects of statesmanship are legitimate in our system and how it is to be balanced with clerkship.

Justice

The final and most important connotation of impartiality involves justice. The concept is subject to a wide variety of meanings, and includes various subordinate elements such as fairness, equity, and due process. A well-known distinction, commonly applied in our governing system, is between just results and just process. We clamor for getting what we think we deserve from public decisions, as well as for being treated fairly in the process of their formulation. Administrators have to make careful judgments about both matters, especially when their decisions affect constitutional rights.

Other relevant characteristics of justice also pertain to this analysis, including completeness, integrity, proportionality, and having adequate or reasonable grounds for decision.[13] Each of these attributes connotes an aspect of thoroughness, which we expect from those making public decisions. We demand completeness in the sense of exploring all matters relevant to a decision. We require integrity in the sense that decisions should balance or harmonize conflicting but legitimate criteria. For example, we want the Environmental Protection Agency to clean up the environment without unduly hampering economic development. We want proportionality in the sense that solutions should "fit" problems appropriately. For example, in courts we hope that punishments will fit crimes. In regulatory agencies, we want to avoid both underregulation and overregulation. In military and diplomatic agencies, we want strategies and tactics carefully scaled to the scope of the disputes faced in order to avoid the undue escalation of international conflict. Finally, we expect sound judgments about the appropriate grounds for making public decisions. In sum, we want public officials to make right or just decisions by "giving everything its due."

Justice is the only aspect of impartiality that directs our attention to the substance, as well as conditions, of effective and legitimate public decisions. It demands the positive exercise of discretion and complex judgment associated with statesmanship, and yet may also entail the restraint expected of clerks. A number of theorists have developed insights in recent years to help explain this.

Leif Carter, in his textbook *Reason in Law*, provides an excellent starting point. He offers a theory of impartiality based upon the idea that one "decides the claims of others before an audience," and that this "means in the end [officials] must, to appear impartial, conform to audience expectations of the process of decision."[14] Carter relates his theory to lawyers and judges, and their audience—the community. The theory applies equally to civil servants, though their decisions

often involve more than deciding competing claims. All public officials hold their positions under the authority of law, and share with
lawyers and judges the responsibility for ruling according to the law.

For Carter, ruling impartially means that decision makers must satisfy
the public that they have "reconciled and harmonized" four basic elements of public decisions: the relevant facts of a situation, the rules
applicable to the situation, the social conditions of the period, and
appropriate moral values.[15] Decision makers need not please every
party to a decision if they can demonstrate that they have attempted
to reconcile these factors. People who lose from a government decision often that agree they were treated fairly or justly if they believe
such conditions were met.

Carter's point is that decisions made in this fashion display a kind
of *completeness* and *integrity* or *balance* that the public recognizes
and expects. They provide *adequate and reasonable grounds* for making
decisions over us and on our behalf.

Inherent in decisions of this sort is the idea that the official must
look beyond his own will for appropriate criteria of judgment. Such
restraint does not mean that the decision maker must be neutral, impersonal, or strictly mediative. Rather, it may mean actively pursuing
certain values or agendas, but these must transcend the individual's
own preferences and ultimately reside in a broader, collective sense
of justice.

The process by which an official transcends his own will entails
submission of ideas and agendas to a broader arena of discourse and
decision. This public arena is constituted of those who deserve access, either personally or through representation, and of a variety of
authoritative sources of accepted truth, wisdom, or entitlement. These
include, but are not limited to, the Founders' intent, legislative intent, precedent or past practice, current public opinion, authoritative
texts, and enduring values. The participants interact with each other
and with these authoritative sources in trying to achieve just or impartial decisions.

Authoritative sources are, of course, subject to interpretation and
argument. Officials must weave their interpretations into persuasive
accounts or "stories" that others will find acceptable, if not compelling, grounds of decision. They may choose to base their decisions on
just one or a few sources, but it is vital, to achieve impartiality, that
they address others as well, especially those that offer conflicting criteria.
Brief consideration of some of these sources will help to illustrate
how clerkship and statesmanship may be balanced.

We often hear public officials claim the congruence of their policies and decisions with the Framers' intent or legislative intent. They
invoke names and ideas in our country's past, especially the founding
era, because we the people treat these as an enduring, authoritative
source of insight about how to live and govern wisely. These claims
may be disputed in terms of accuracy, and by rival claims deemed to
rest on higher or more compelling grounds. Both sides, however, must
join in a conversation with our past by at least confronting what one
side or another invokes as authoritative, historical intent. An argument about what the intent of a law, administrative rule, or constitutional provision was, and why it remains or does not remain salient
to a particular decision, brings past and present together in public
deliberation.

Public administrators are obliged to give past figures and ideas
their due in proposed decisions. This obligation stems in part from
their oaths to uphold the Constitution and laws of the country. Our
constitutional system is built upon values and ideas framed in over
two hundred years of political discourse.[16] It therefore presents decision makers with a rich and varied source of insight as well as authority. Officials are not required to base their decisions exclusively
on this source, for other authoritative factors may also pertain, but
they should argue this point, and do so before the appropriate audi-
ences. If they do, the public will more readily judge their decisions to
be impartial.

The text or "plain meaning" of relevant law constitutes another
authoritative source. We want to believe that every law provides a
coherent and determinate source of meaning. Many traffic laws (regulating speed, right of way, etc.), for example, offer fairly plain meanings.
Such laws make consistent enforcement possible, and thereby enable
citizens to anticipate the likely effects of their actions. When such
plain meaning exists, administrators must give it its due, arguments
about original intent notwithstanding.

Not all laws have plain meaning, however, and even some that have
it come up against overriding values, changing contexts, or resurrect-
ed intentions that lead us eventually to alter them, or to at least make
exceptions. Many laws contain intentionally ambiguous meanings.
Legislators make laws to achieve a general and future effect, and this
commonly requires broad terms that must be adapted to changing
circumstances by administrators. Furthermore, many of the problems
addressed in law have an abstract nature. What does it mean to regulate "impure drugs" or to "ensure a fair and orderly market"? The

abstract nature of these things hardly makes them less real. If anything, they are more grave than many so-called concrete issues because they entail so much more meaning for our lives. The more meaningful something is, the more difficult it is to grasp its "plain" meaning.

Such laws, however, still may convey intelligible meanings that stand on their own merits, independent of their authors' intentions. For example, laws regulating transportation safety may be applied to new modes of transport not originally anticipated by lawmakers. Laws on privacy and confidentiality may have to be reinterpreted in light of the emerging computer information highway system. These laws may contain sufficiently broad and coherent purposes to justify application to new sets of problems. The important point is that the justifications must be argued in light of original intent and other potentially relevant sources of authority in order to achieve impartiality.

Current values comprise yet another authoritative source. The prevalence of opinion surveys and claims of electoral mandates for change reveal our devotion to this source. It is safe to say that current values dominate most public officials' minds, because of their proximity. Other authoritative sources often require more elaborate investigation and thought to become compelling. For example, original intentions, precedents, and authoritative texts require substantial investigation, and their salience is often not as readily apparent as current opinion. Furthermore, if current opinion is strong, it will be difficult to make concerns stemming from other sources convincing. Impartiality demands, however, that other sources at least be considered, in part because they help us develop a richer perspective on our current values. It is difficult to make wise decisions in the heat of political controversy. The other sources provide avenues for intellectual detachment that enable officials to see current matters from a broader, more balanced perspective.

Taken alone, each authoritative source is subject to cogent criticism. For example, Framers' intent is very difficult to assess because the Constitution had so many Framers, and they had diverse opinions on most issues. Many constitutional provisions resulted from political compromises rather than intellectual consensus. Which Framers should we then follow? Which should be given their due? When were they arguing a case they didn't really believe in, but were supporting because of some compromise or a desire simply to play devil's advocate? Furthermore, some of our most influential Founders (Thomas

Jefferson and James Madison, for example) stated explicitly that they did not want future generations to be bound by their specific deliberations. We also often discover that intentions clearly differ from "intelligible purposes" and "plain meanings" that subsequent interpreters find in the same laws.

These problems pertain equally to legislative histories, and lead some officials to disregard original intent altogether. They go too far, however, because we may still gain important insight from the speeches and writings of lawmakers. Some of their ideas and designs retain lasting importance. We can also make rough but usable historical judgments about the relative influence of various framers and legislators on the content of our laws. We are justifiably critical of officials and scholars who abandon an authoritative source completely. It is not uncommon to find officials who express single-minded devotion to one or another authoritative source. Some judges, for example, advocate strict devotion to original intent, while others wish to abandon it in favor of a jurisprudence devoted to changing values. From the standpoint of impartiality, however, we should expect them to adopt a more receptive attitude about other sources because they may hold legitimacy and insight.

The philosopher Hans-Georg Gadamer made this same point with his theory of the hermeneutical circle. "All that is asked is that we remain open to the meaning of the other person or of the text."[17] This attitude reflects an ability to learn and a disposition to change one's mind in light of new insight. It suggests a certain humility and deference to multiple sources. Gadamer observes that the openness we desire "always includes placing the other meaning in a relation with the whole of our own meanings or ourselves in a relation to it." His hermeneutical circle describes this dialectical process of continuously reconsidering one's "pre-understandings" by considering the understanding of many relevant others.[18]

William Eskridge Jr. and Philip Frickey, borrowing from Gadamer's hermeneutic philosophy, have crafted a model of statutory interpretation that is useful here:

> Our model holds that an interpreter will look at a broad range of evidence—text, historical evidence, and the text's evolution—and thus form a preliminary view by testing various possible interpretations against the multiple criteria of fidelity to the text, historical accuracy, and conformity to contemporary circumstances and values. Each criterion is relevant, yet none necessarily trumps the others.[19]

In this dialectical process of judging which interpretation to follow, the decision maker can consider a wider variety of supporting arguments from multiple authoritative sources. He may not find agreement among all the sources, but openly confronting that fact in each case is itself a sign of genuine impartiality.

Eskridge and Frickey also observe that decision makers may, over time, form a hierarchy of authoritative sources based upon the level of abstraction and range of arguments each one provides. In their assessment, a good argument derived from true textual analysis of a statute will often hold more sway because it is more focused and concrete. The trade-off is that textual analysis has a more limited range of meaningful arguments than more abstract sources such as legislative history, precedent, or intelligible purpose. Such hierarchies, however, are not fixed, and become suspect if too rigidly applied. The important point, as the authors stress, is that interpretation is a fluid or dynamic intellectual process rather than a mechanical one.[20]

Public administrators, I suggest, must engage in the same sort of dialectical analysis of authoritative sources in order to achieve impartiality. However, they will probably order their hierarchies of criteria from these sources differently from the way lawyers and judges do. Scientific and technical expertise, for example, will often hold more sway as authoritative sources than those mentioned above. But their authority is subject to limitation and criticism too. Recent rhetorical studies of scientific endeavors show that the scientific community develops its knowledge through an unfolding process of argument about the efficacy of its members' claims. Scientists employ a rhetoric of inquiry as well as a logic of inquiry.[21] Thus, science cannot stand alone as an authoritative source any more than the others can. It must be integrated with the others into administrative decision making.

Thus, giving these various sources their due requires that officials must transcend their own will. They must cultivate an openness to changing their minds in light of what the sources tell them. They must search, listen, and argue carefully. It may be helpful to think of these various authoritative sources as aspects or dimensions of justice. No single voice expresses it alone, and we often disagree among ourselves about it. The American community reflects many voices—from past, present, and future. It is a task of administrative statesmanship to exercise and uphold this dialectical process through the myriad and subordinate institutions we create to sustain our way of life.

Administrative Statesmanship

It remains, in conclusion, to explain that *administrative* statesmanship is a drastically limited version of the original concept. Our desire to saddle administrative officials with conflicting expectations of clerkship and statesmanship makes this necessary. Given the liberal regime we have created over two hundred years, it may also be very convenient.

The term "statesman," as originally conceived, referred to a great ruler who exhibited the rare combination of virtue and wisdom. To have virtue meant that an individual had achieved an integration of excellences of intellect and character that entitled him to make decisions for all, with or without benefit of law.[22] He embodied such virtues as courage, justice, temperance, and prudence, which enabled him to secure the common good with his subjects' willing consent. Wisdom entailed the ability to reason about practical affairs in ways that elicited broad consensus and established justice for all.

It was understood early on that true statesmen are rare. Early treatments of the subject described an ideal regime (which has never existed) created and sustained by these ideal leaders. Plato, fearing lawless rule by nonstatesmen, recommended that regimes based on rule of law become the acceptable (second-best) alternative.[23] One hoped for statesmen to emerge in the founding of a regime to give it wise law and order (a constitution) for subsequent generations to follow.

It remained for judges and other subordinate officials to maintain respect for this constitution over time through education, sanctions, and other institutional supports. As Gary Jacobsohn argues, this responsibility entails gaining knowledge of the statesmanlike wisdom in the Constitution, making the authority of law paramount, and preserving it for the future. Officials who succeed at this may be said to act in statesmanlike fashion, though in a very limited sense. They should not disregard the law in their pursuit of a greater good, as an ideal statesman could in theory, and their role is more educative than innovative. They may be aggressive in pursuing this responsibility, but will also restrain themselves and others when they see the wisdom (or authoritative sources) of the laws threatened. Jacobsohn aptly describes this attitude as "activist restraint."[24]

Jacobsohn applies this reasoning to judges, but subordinate administrative officials play such critical and extensive roles in modern regimes that it would be foolish to exempt them from sharing this responsibility. We may apply an additional limitation, though, which becomes increasingly appropriate as we move lower in the ranks of officialdom.

Mark Moore distinguishes between being a statesman and performing acts of statesmanship. We needn't require officials to *be* statesmen. The qualities of statemen are too rare, and their powers too awesome. However, we do want officials to perform occasional acts of statesmanship that remind us of the wisdom of our governing system. Moreover,

> if our political processes hurl near-statesmen together and extract from them a choice that would have been beyond the capability of any one of them, then statesmanship can occur without individual statesmen. So, it is some mix of the qualities of people serving in the government and the processes that bring those people together that will determine the frequency of acts of statesmanship.[25]

It is in this context that impartiality, which emphasizes detachment and justice as its primary characteristics, becomes most vital. First, the American Constitution, through its system of checks and balances, provides for multiple sources of quasi-autonomous or detached competence and judgment. John Rohr illuminates this fact by identifying twenty-two different types of appointment to office provided in the Constitution.[26] The Founders designed the federal government not only to limit power, but also to gather the best-qualified citizens to serve in it, and encourage them to use their capacities cooperatively to our benefit.

Direct election gives this system its most apparent republican character, but it is tempered with twenty-one other modes of appointment that remove most officials from direct control by the current populace. This enables them to consider other authoritative sources that contribute to our sense of justice. Hence, the American people rule, but not just the current populace.

Additionally, our vast administrative infrastructure, which emerged in the United States during the twentieth century, reflects the Constitution's emphasis on diffused powers through its pluralistic structure.[27] Our bureaucracy is divided among levels of government and a host of agencies competing for power and turf. As typified by the relation among the three superior branches, these agencies share powers both in order to check each other and to cooperate in complex public endeavors. For example, multiple law enforcement agencies (such as the FBI, ATF, and local police departments) simultaneously compete for resources and powers while working cooperatively on specific enforcement programs. Redundancy often becomes a virtue, rather than merely an expensive vice. It enables us to limit the power of any single agency while combining multiple perspectives to address complex issues. It is through these profuse combinations of capacities that we may also hope to encourage more frequent and cooperative acts of statesmanship. This goal requires making the various authoritative sources for administrative decisions more widely known and used in these circles. The idea of impartiality, properly understood, is especially attractive in this regard because it is something to which officials commonly aspire, and it can be squared with both clerkship and statesmanship.

Notes

1. These insights are developed more thoroughly by Herbert Storing in "American Statesmanship: Old and New," in *Bureaucrats, Policy Analysts, Statesmen: Who Leads?* ed. Robert A. Goldwin (Washington, D.C.: American Enterprise Institute, 1981), chap. 6. (See chap. 1, this volume.)

2. See especially, Michael Lipsky, *Street-Level Bureaucracy: Dilemmas of the Individual in Public Services* (New York: Russell Sage, 1980).

3. This debate became known as the Friedrich-Finer debate, after Carl Friedrich, a well-known political thinker who argued for conscience, professional standards, and other internalized sources of moral guidance, and Herman Finer, who argued for the external accountability approach. See Carl J. Friedrich, "Public Policy and the Nature of Administrative Responsibility," in *Public Policy,* ed. Carl J. Friedrich and E. S. Mason (Cambridge, Mass.: Harvard University Press, 1940), 165–75; and Herman Finer, "Administrative Responsibility in Democratic Government," *Public Administration Review,* 1, 4 (Summer 1941): 335–50.

4. For a more elaborate treatment of professionalization in government, see Frederick C. Mosher, *Democracy and the Public Service,* 2d ed. (New York: Oxford University Press, 1982).

5. For an interesting analysis of the variety of organizational structures existing in government agencies today, see Karen M. Hult and Charles Walcott, *Governing Public Organizations: Politics, Structures, and Institutional Design* (Pacific Grove, Calif.: Brooks/Cole, 1990).

6. *Federalist* 51.

7. For an in-depth analysis of the meaning of reputation to the Founders, see Douglass Adair, *Fame and the Founding Fathers* (New York: Norton, 1974).

8. See Theodore Lowi, *The End of Liberalism: The Second Republic of the United States,* 2d ed. (New York: Norton, 1979).

9. For excellent examples of this literature, see Hult and Walcott, *Govern-*

ing Public Organizations, and James D. Thompson, *Organizations in Action* (New York: McGraw-Hill, 1967).

10. For an in-depth treatment of the relations between political executives and appointees, see Mosher, *Democracy and the Public Service*, and Hugh Heclo, *A Government of Strangers: Executive Politics in Washington* (Washington, D.C.: Brookings Institution, 1977).

11. See John P. Burke, *Bureaucratic Responsibility* (Baltimore: Johns Hopkins University Press, 1986) for an in-depth discussion of this point. He argues cogently that subordinate public administrators share responsibility for (1) restoring failing officials to their proper roles and functions, (2) maintaining the integrity and quality of the policy-formulation process, and (3) maintaining the integrity and quality of the policy-implementation process.

12. See John A. Rohr, *To Run a Constitution: The Legitimacy of the Administrative State* (Lawrence: University Press of Kansas, 1986) for an elaborate historical and constitutional development of these points.

13. See the *Oxford English Dictionary* and compare "impartial" with "just" and "justice."

14. Leif H. Carter, *Reason in Law*, 4th ed. (New York: HarperCollins, 1994), 230.

15. Ibid., 230–31.

16. John Rohr has developed an elegant constitutional theory of professional administrative responsibility around this idea. See John A. Rohr, *Ethics for Bureaucrats: An Essay on Law and Values,* 2d ed. (New York: Marcel Dekker, 1989), and *To Run a Constitution*.

17. See Hans-Georg Gadamer, *Truth and Method*, trans. G. Barden and J. Cumming, 2d ed. (New York: Crossroad, 1975), 238.

18. Ibid.

19. William N. Eskridge Jr. and Philip P. Frickey, "Statutory Interpretation as Practical Reasoning," *Stanford Law Review*, January 1990, 321–84, quote at 352.

20. Ibid.

21. For example, see J. A. Schuster and R. R. Yeo, eds., *The Politics and Rhetoric of Scientific Method* (Boston: Reidel, 1986); Donald N. McCloskey, *The Rhetoric of Economics* (Madison, Wis.: University of Wisconsin Press, 1985); Lawrence J. Prelli, *A Rhetoric of Science: Inventing Scientific Discourse* (Columbia: University of South Carolina Press, 1989), and Richard T. Green and Robert C. Zinke, "The Rhetorical Way of Knowing and Public Administration," *Administration & Society*, 25, 3 (November 1993): 317–34.

22. For a thorough explanation of the classical understanding of virtue, see David L. Norton, *Democracy and Moral Development* (Berkeley: University of California Press, 1991).

23. See Plato, *The Statesman*, for one of the most thorough and insightful treatments. For additional insight, see A. E. Taylor, *Plato: The Sophist and the Statesman* (London: Nelson, 1961), and Leo Strauss, "Plato," *History of*

Political Philosophy, ed. Leo Strauss and Joseph Cropsey (Chicago: Rand-McNally, 1963), 7–63.

24. Gary J. Jacobsohn, *Pragmatism, Statesmanship, and the Supreme Court* (Ithaca, N.Y.: Cornell University Press, 1977), 148–51, 162–72. Also see Rohr's *To Run a Constitution*, 101–10 for a fascinating analysis of Thomas Cooley's statesmanship as first head of the Interstate Commerce Commission. Cooley exemplified impartiality and activist restraint. As a former Michigan state judge, Cooley understood the nuances of constitutional powers and wisdom, and applied them in simultaneously vigorous and restrained fashion. He fought for broad regulatory powers over railroad practices, and yet refused to exercise certain statutorily conferred powers because he believed, and argued cogently, that they violated the Constitution.

25. Mark H. Moore, "Statesmanship in a World of Particular Substantive Choices," *Bureaucrats, Policy Analysts, Statesmen: Who Leads?*, ed. Robert A. Goldwin, (Washington, D.C.: American Enterprise Institute, 1980), 20–36, 21.

26. Rohr, *To Run a Constitution*, 185, 260–61.

27. This point is also developed in Rohr, *To Run a Constitution,* 171–94.

5

Theodore Lowi and the Administrative State

David Lewis Schaefer

In his 1986 memoir, *The Triumph of Politics*, David Stockman, Ronald Reagan's first budget director, attested to the insight he had gained in understanding the problems of contemporary American government from Theodore Lowi's *The End of Liberalism*, which he aptly termed "one of the more seminal works of modern American political science."[1] This judgment by the libertarian-leaning Stockman exemplifies the way in which the appeal of Lowi's book, despite its author's overt preference for "the values of traditional liberalism" over those of "conservatism" (291),[2] has transcended the conventional liberal-conservative dichotomy. Lowi argues that the categories of liberal and conservative have become irrelevant for understanding contemporary political issues, and acknowledges the influence on his thought of the "classical" liberal political economist Friedrich Hayek, whose work he believes has wrongly been dismissed by contemporary liberal theorists (xiv, 43–49, 300n). Yet, far from sharing Hayek's aim (and the goal Stockman himself once aspired to achieve) of reducing the scope of the government's domestic responsibilities, Lowi assures his readers that his critique of liberalism entails no support for the "contraction of modern government toward some nineteenth-century ideal" (300). Indeed, Lowi regards the New Deal as having "establish[ed] the principle *for all time* in the United States that in a democracy there can be *no* effective limit to the scope of governmental power." He hopes that "the mere question of more government or less government . . . will be completely discarded" (since "[w]e already have more, and twentieth-century democracies will tolerate nothing less"), in favor of

113

the "older and almost forgotten ones" of the proper character, ends, and forms that government should have (xv–xvi, emphasis added).

In a more recent book updating his thesis entitled *The End of the Republican Era*, Lowi acknowledges that his position would require some reduction in the size of the federal government, but he continues to stress both his own liberalism and his indebtedness to Hayek.[3] Although the newer work elaborates the consequences of what Lowi identifies as the faults of twentieth-century liberalism, including the danger (in Lowi's view) that the "Republican era" that followed the decline of the Democratic coalition may undermine the American republic itself, *The End of Liberalism* contains Lowi's fullest account of the problems of liberal governance and of the administrative state it has engendered. Hence the present chapter will focus chiefly on that book.

The common ground seemingly uniting Lowi's proposed reformation of liberalism, which he terms "juridical democracy," with the classical liberalism of Hayek and his followers is their shared emphasis on the rule of law. Law is understood by both Lowi and Hayek in contradistinction to the exercise of arbitrary discretion by government officials. But whereas for Hayek, strict adherence to the rule of law standard would require the elimination of all governmental activities that aim to promote the good of particular classes of the citizenry at the expense of others,[4] for Lowi the function of that principle is to prevent the improper devolution of legislative authority from elected officials to bureaucrats who lack direct accountability to the people (304, 311–12).[5] Such devolution, he contends, has engendered the transformation of the American regime into a "Second Republic," the operations of which are grounded in a "public philosophy" that he labels "interest-group liberalism." This system enables particular societal groups to bend government policy to favor their interests, in a manner that is concealed from public view by its informality. Only through a renewed concern with the importance of legislative "forms," which dictates that bureaucratic discretion be limited by statutes drafted with appropriate specificity, as well as by a codified system of administrative rules, Lowi argues, can the legitimacy of liberal government be restored (50–63, 281, 297–304, 311–12).

Serious questions have been raised by scholars such as James Q. Wilson both about the claim that regulatory agencies have typically fallen victim to the "clienteles" with which they deal (112, 281) and about the feasibility of the reforms by which Lowi proposes to overcome that problem.[6] But the issue of feasibility is ultimately less crucial

than that of justice or principle. In *The Politics of Disorder*, a work
that elaborates the thesis of *The End of Liberalism*, Lowi accuses
critics who dismiss his proposed reforms as impractical of having
been so "enveloped" by the existing system that they fail to appreciate the virtues of a true, "formal democracy."[7] The very "belief system" that attaches political leaders to the existing regime, he contends,
"is the source of the pathology" that needs to be attacked. Hence any
divergence of American political practice from its proper forms does
not undermine the legitimacy of those forms, but demonstrates the
need to alter governmental practice to fit them (297–98).

My purpose here is to address Lowi's claim that the broad delegation of administrative authority deprives government policies of legitimacy, and that the "forms" of American constitutional democracy
require a radical limitation of such authority. It is widely acknowledged that the scope of the federal government's activities, and consequently the size and power of the bureaucracy that administers them,
are far broader than the Founders anticipated. But if (with the older-
but-wiser David Stockman) we moderate the hope, regardless of the
desirability, of radically contracting those activities to their pre-New
Deal level, what remains to be considered is how far the less formal
or legalistic mode of administering them typically practiced by federal agencies is truly liable to Lowi's charges, and whether "juridicial
democracy" is indeed more faithful than the system Lowi criticizes to
the principles of American constitutionalism.[8]

Interest-Group Liberalism
and the "Second Republic"

Lowi traces the origin of interest-group liberalism to the expansion of federal activity during the New Deal period, which rendered
what he describes as the original American "public philosophy" of
capitalism irrelevant to our national circumstances. Whereas capitalist ideology presupposed a "self-regulating society" with minimal
domestic governmental activity, the development of American society
during the nineteenth century destroyed the conditions in which such
a system could maintain itself. Hence the contemporary "dialogue"
between liberals and conservatives, Lowi holds, is an empty one, since
both sides agree on the need for governmental intervention, differing
only about which interests government should favor (3–4, 42–52).

Interest-group liberalism, according to Lowi, is an amalgam of capitalism, which it absorbed, with "statism" (that is, the acceptance of an activist government) and pluralism (22). Even though the amalgam is a product of twentieth-century political developments, Lowi traces the foundations of its pluralist core to the insights of Alexis de Tocqueville and James Madison (in *Federalist* 10) about the operation of modern industrial society. Tocqueville and Madison articulated the fact that "industrialization produces social diversity along with extremes of wealth and poverty." Hence in one respect, the pluralist model served to defend the capitalist system, inasmuch as it refuted the Marxian claim that capitalism engenders the simple domination of a homogeneous class of workers by a homogeneous class of capitalists. But at the same time, "the pluralist model cuts equally against capitalist theory," inasmuch as "It renders absurd the capitalist notion that government is the only source of power and control." By highlighting the dispersion of power among a variety of social groups, pluralist theory demonstrates that "power and control" are "ubiquitous." Hence "It rightly rejects any and all notions of a natural distinction between the functions of government and the functions of nongovernmental institutions" (31–33).[9]

Lowi applauds pluralism for having "helped bring American public values into the twentieth century by making the state an acceptable source of power in a capitalist society." Yet even while pluralism liberated its adherents from the myth of a self-regulating society in the sense of one requiring little governmental intervention, he contends, it gave renewed vitality to that myth in another sense: that of an "automatic political society" in which the interests of the people as a whole are secured as a result of group competition *within* the political process. Pluralism, in sum, is hostile to "the idea of separate government," that is, of a government that takes seriously its responsibility to arrive at an independent conception of the public good, and to employ the public power to promote that end (36–37, 40).

Lowi distinguishes the pluralism espoused by Madison from that popularized by twentieth-century political scientists such as David Truman and Arthur Bentley on the ground that the latter conception lacks Madison's awareness that group interests may conflict with the public interest. Whereas Madison viewed group competition as a means to "neutralize many of the most potent power centers" in society so as to protect the government "from control by any 'majority,'" contemporary pluralism regards groups as inherently good, and aims to accommodate rather than regulate them. Hence pluralism now shuns the formalism of law, which requires that all groups be subjected to uniform and publicly known standards, in favor of informal procedures that facilitate group bargaining (36–37, 55).[10]

It is thus *by means of* statutes drawn so loosely that they allocate excessive discretionary authority to administrative agencies that particular social groups are enabled in Lowi's account to circumvent the rule of law and advance their interests at the expense of the public good. This practice illegitimately extends the practice of representation from the legislative process to the administrative one, in such a way as to frustrate the popular expectation that "laws [will] quickly make a difference to the problems around which the representation process had been activated." The extension of representation into the administrative process, to which various groups have unequal access, negates popular representation and hence democratic legitimacy (63).

Lowi is one of numerous scholars to have criticized pluralism during the post–New Deal era on the ground that the ostensibly "countervailing" competition of groups conceals a systemic bias that enables the influential few to dominate the many.[11] The distinctive feature of Lowi's argument is his proposed remedy. By *restricting* representation to the legislative as distinguished from the administrative process, Lowi aims to make democratic representation more effective, and specifically to defend "the powerless . . . against the powerful" (298). Since such alternatives to legislative formalism as personal political leadership, interest-group politics, and administrative decentralization all favor the status quo because of the advantages they give to the powerful, Lowi concludes that juridical democracy "is the only weapon available . . . to bring about radical transformation of society in order to eliminate injustices."[12]

Lowi represents the conversion of the American government into a "second republic" as illegitimate not only on account of its substantive consequences, but also because the transformation occurred informally, rather than through a new constitutional convention (271). Curiously, however, he offers almost no examination of the original constitutional order created by the American Founders. In fact, despite berating the pluralists for failing to appreciate the reality and (potential) autonomy of the state (36–37), Lowi himself represents the American regime as the byproduct of nonpolitical factors: specifically the Industrial Revolution and capitalism, with its attendant ideology of "the invisible hand" (3).[13] The "capitalist ideology," which according to Lowi was the strongest determinant of American "constitutional practices and governmental life" until well into the twen-

tieth century, was so extreme, in his account, that it denied the very
need for "administration" (defined as "rationality applied to social
control") (5, 21). The "most important" characteristic of the original
constitutional structure, in Lowi's view, was not the separation of
powers or the rule of law, but the principle of federalism, which ensured that "the states did almost all the governing" (272). Since such
a characterization implies that the Founders failed to provide for a
national government adequate to the range of responsibilities that
twentieth-century regimes must undertake, it follows that the Constitution can furnish little guidance for enabling the federal government
to execute its necessary role today.

Lowi's interpretation of the original American "public philosophy"
as one of pure laissez-faire seems to be belied, however, by his own
treatment of two of the most influential authors of the Constitution
and shapers of the American political tradition. As already noted,
Lowi specifically exempts Madison from his criticism of pluralist
doctrine, since Madison appreciated the need for government to *regulate* the activities of groups, rather than simply reflect an autonomous process of group bargaining. He similarly observes that Alexander
Hamilton devoted a substantial portion of his *Report on Manufac-
tures* to "attempting to refute [Adam] Smith as regards the application of laissez-faire principles" to the United States (4). Although
Lowi claims that Hamilton "won his battles but lost his war" to enlarge the economic functions of the national government (4), the ultimate expansion of those functions in the twentieth century might
suggest the continuing relevance of Hamilton's thought to our situation.[14] Similarly, even if Madison saw faction as (potentially) more of
a problem than some twentieth-century pluralist theorists do, it is less
obvious that the *practice* of pluralist politics in the contemporary
United States represents a fundamental deviation from the intentions
of the Founders.

The real reason for Lowi's near-disregard of the Founders' thought
and intentions, I believe, is that there is a significant gap between
those intentions and his doctrine of juridical democracy. Lowi's conception of such traditional liberal principles as the rule of law and
the separation of powers considerably alters their original sense. Nor
do Madison's strictures concerning the dangers of faction support Lowi's
critique of interest-group politics. The true ancestry of Lowi's argument against "pluralistic" administration is to be found not in the
founding documents of American constitutionalism, I suggest, but rather
in the conception of the relation between politics and administration

originally advanced by Woodrow Wilson in the late nineteenth century. That conception, I shall argue, not only deviates considerably from the Founders' intentions, but also threatens to weaken the security that the Constitution provides for individual liberty and civic harmony.

"Juridical Democracy" versus the Constitution

On the surface, Lowi's argument for curbing the allocation of broad discretion to administrative agencies aims at a restoration of the separation of powers embodied in the Constitution. He applauds the Supreme Court's 1935 *Schechter* decision ruling unconstitutional Congress's excessive delegation of authority to the National Recovery Administration, and regrets that the Court has failed to apply the principles of that decision subsequently (93). But Lowi's account of the separation of powers differs from the one set forth by Madison in *The Federalist*. In *Federalist* 47, Madison upholds that principle as a necessary bulwark against despotism, holding that "the accumulation of all powers, legislative, executive, and judiciary, in the same hands" would constitute "the very definition of tyranny." He goes on to argue, however, that the separation of powers by no means requires an absolute separation of *function* among the three branches of the federal government. Indeed, a *partial* sharing of functions is essential to provide the "checks and balances" that enable each branch to protect its independence.[15]

While the separation of powers as a formal principle constitutes a check against the tyrannical concentration of power in any one branch of government, Madison subsequently explains (in *Federalist* 48) that in a "representative republic" such as the United States, "where the executive magistracy is carefully limited, both in the extent and the duration of its power; and where the legislative power is exercised by an assembly, which is inspired by a supposed influence over the people with an intrepid confidence in its own strength" and which is likely to share the people's own passions, the greatest danger of tyranny arises from the legislature itself. As Madison's recapitulation of the argument of *Federalist* 10 immediately following his account of checks and balances suggests, the danger of legislative tyranny is itself a reflection of the threat of *majority* tyranny that was addressed in the earlier essay. The goal of justice, understood as protecting the rights of all individuals, requires that the greatest security in a popular government be taken against the abuse of power by a popular majority.[16] Hence the partial division of functions among the three branches of government is primarily aimed, according to Madison, at preventing the excessive concentration of power in the part of government most directly tied to popular passions. Thus understood, Madison's argument harmonizes with Hamilton's justification of the president's relatively long term of office in *Federalist* 71 as necessary to buttress the president's resistance to temporary popular passions and humors. Presidential independence is needed to ensure that "the deliberate sense of the community," but not transient popular impulses that run contrary to the common good or to the rights of individuals, will determine the conduct of the government. The Senate, similarly, is intended to embody "the cool and deliberate sense of the community," thus operating "as a defense to the people against their own temporary errors and delusions."[17] And federal judges are given "permanent tenure" so as to buttress an "independent spirit" in them that is essential "to guard the Constitution and the rights of individuals from the effects of . . . ill humors" that may arise among "the people themselves" when they lack adequate opportunity for "deliberate reflection."[18]

The most obvious contrast between Lowi's and *The Federalist*'s treatments of the separation of powers is the lack of any overt concern on Lowi's part about the dangers of simple majoritarianism, or the need to buttress executive independence.[19] Rather than aiming to limit the power of popular majorities to violate the rights of minorities, Lowi seeks "to centralize the political process" so that the government is clearly put "on one side as opposed to other sides" and enacts laws that "deliberately set some goals and values above others" (92–93). Far from echoing Madison's fears about an excessive concentration of political power, he criticizes contemporary liberalism for having "promoted . . . deconcentration of democratic power" (297). Whereas the Founders aimed to safeguard individual rights against legislative tyranny through such devices as enabling judges to interpret "unjust and partial laws" narrowly so as to mitigate their severity and confine their operation,[20] Lowi sometimes writes as if the principle of rule of law entailed outright legislative supremacy. For the Founders, by contrast, the legislature is itself subordinate to a more "fundamental law," the Constitution.[21] Hence the rule of law, properly understood, requires checks on the power of the lawmaking body.

Despite Lowi's concern that government policies should promote justice, the meaningfulness of this concern as a security for individual rights is vitiated by his avoidance of giving any "particular definition of justice" (311). Without attempting such a definition, Lowi believes it is still possible to demonstrate that interest-group liberalism cannot generate justice, simply because it "lack[s] the *sine qua non* of justice," namely, a disposition to derive a particular action "from a preexisting general rule or moral principle governing such a class of actions" (296). Arguing that his proposed juridical democracy is superior to interest-group liberalism simply because it "leads to a justice-oriented politics" (311)—that is, a politics that is expressly concerned with the choice among first principles—Lowi is strangely oblivious to the dangers of such politics, which the Founders consciously set out to avoid. Whereas Madison cites the "zeal" for differing opinions about such matters as politics and religion as a source of faction, and hence a cause of injustice if its effects are unmoderated by the political system,[22] Lowi is inexplicably confident that heightened controversy over principles will produce "increments of justice" (311).

Lowi holds juridical democracy to surpass interest-group liberalism not only by pushing issues of principle to the forefront of politics, but also by its capacity to give effect to decisions on such issues once they have been reached. Here again, however, Lowi's position cannot but trouble the friend of individual liberty. While criticizing the pluralists for falling victim to the illusion that "government need not be coercive," he is less than clear in *The End of Liberalism* about what checks should in fact limit what he terms "the awesome coerciveness of government" (55). Despite his disinclination to identify juridical democracy with any particular understanding of justice, he does claim that that principle "has very clear and profound substantive implications" on a variety of issues, such as the intolerability of racial segregation "in any form." This confidence enables him to elaborate how federal policies could achieve the "complete destruction of the fiction of local citizenship and the sanctity of local corporate boundaries" by enacting "the strongest and most authoritative of laws" (267–68), and how "a properly moral and legal attitude toward power could render the federal government capable of overcoming rural conservatism and suburban reactionism and fear in the state legislatures" (263). Morality, according to Lowi, dictates that the objections of both whites and blacks to mandatory school busing be ignored (266), and that members of both races be compelled "to adjust, rather than to escape" from the application of such policies (258, 267). Whatever his own views of busing, the partisan of liberty may well wonder whether the issue is adequately resolved by Lowi's blanket assurance that all such policies "would simplify immensely the expansion of the rights of the individual in the United States" (263). That assertion apparently rests on the identification of justice or morality with equality rather than liberty, such that the government enjoys a comprehensive power to attack any "privilege" that is not universally enjoyed.[23]

Lowi's illustration of how restricting opportunities for interest-group bargaining would facilitate the enforcement of coercive policies aimed at social transformation provides further evidence that the goal of his ostensible restoration of the constitutional separation of powers is not, as it was for Madison, the protection of individual liberty. His frankest statements to this effect may be found in *The Politics of Disorder*, where he defines juridical democracy as "formal democracy, a majority rule democracy limited *only* by the absolute requirement that government be run as closely as possible according to the way it says it is run."[24] Lowi denies the need, or the efficacy, of any checks on a democratic government's actions, except for the stipulation that those actions follow forms that facilitate the greatest public awareness of the policies it adopts:

> In any democracy—plebiscitary, republican, or bureaucratic—majorities must ultimately overcome minorities. The only effective check against majority tyranny (or any other kind of tyranny) is the requirement that it or its agencies act only through governments duly constituted with laws that citizens can know about clearly before they or the agency enter into the action.[25]

In this passage, Lowi minimizes the significance of just the distinction on which *The Federalist*'s case for American republicanism rests: the differentiation between plebiscitary democracy (termed by Madison "pure" democracy) and representative or republican democracy.[26] Although it is tautologous to say that in a democracy, "majorities must ultimately overcome minorities," it makes all the difference, in the Founders' view, whether the majority that triumphs is a deliberative one that is compelled to take account of the long-term effects of its actions on the good of the country and the rights of minorities, or whether any majority, however ill-informed or stirred by passion, can have its way.[27] According to *The Federalist*, it is only by means of the plurality of interest groups in a large, commercial republic, along with such devices as representation and checks and balances, that the danger of majority tyranny can be overcome. Such a concern is absent from Lowi's argument. Only in appearance is the legal formalism that he favors a restraint on the majority will, since the very function of such formalism is to make the actions of government more clearly visible to the majority—and hence enable it more surely to employ government's coercive powers to achieve its goals.[28]

Lowi's implicit deprecation of checks on a popular majority's will other than the majority's own judgment links his position with that of Woodrow Wilson. In an 1879 essay urging the adoption of the parliamentary form of government in this country, Wilson identified the political system affording "the largest measure of real liberty" with that "which is most susceptible to the control of [the people's] sovereign will."[29] Lowi's wish to bring issues of principle to the forefront of political debate, with a view to the enactment of legislation that clearly sets "some goals and values above others" (93, 267, 311), similarly echoes the intention Wilson expressed in the same essay to promote a "responsible" party system that would embody "an open war of principle against principle" ending in "the triumph of one opinion over all opposing opinions."[30] Lowi's dismissal of those who fear "to centralize the political process" (93) was prefigured by Wilson's deprecation of critics who would sound "the alarm-bell of *centralization*" against his proposed transformation of the constitutional separation of powers.[31] And the critique of administrative discretion in *The End of Liberalism* mirrors the views Wilson expressed in a 1908 address, "Conservatism, True and False":

> [T]rue conservatism demands . . . [that] [t]he control of the government should be exercised by process of law and not by administrative discretion. . . . This is the true meaning for us of the old Jeffersonian principle, "as little government as possible." For us that maxim means as little government by executive choice and preference, as little government of the kind that varies the footing upon which interests are dealt with, which chooses its measures differently, instance by instance. . . . It means as little government by discretionary authority as possible. It is not hostile to regulated and equalized freedom or to any process of law which is a calculable process of rule and proceeds by defined standards.[32]

The Wilsonian foundations of "juridical democracy" can be seen most clearly in Wilson's influential essay on "The Study of Administration." The central intention of that essay was to promote an improvement in the practice of public administration in America by

encouraging the application in this country of advances in administrative science that had been developed in the despotic regimes of
continental Europe. Crucial to Wilson's argument is the distinction
he drew between the spheres of politics and administration. While
emphasizing the need to avoid importing, with European administrative techniques, the authoritarian political principles that those techniques had thus far been employed to serve, Wilson argued that there
was no essential connection between the two, precisely because politics and administration are separable functions. Since "the field of
administration is a field of business," distinct both "from the hurry
and strife of politics" and, in general, from "the debatable ground of
constitutional study," it ought to be possible to apply the "business
methods" developed in the French and German administrative systems without borrowing any of their *political* principles.[33] The chief
obstacle to administrative improvement in America in Wilson's view
is the American people's failure to appreciate the distinction between
the proper spheres of politics and administration. While embracing
"popular sovereignty" as a political principle, Wilson laments the
disposition of the people to be "meddlesome" in the *execution* of decisions arrived at by their elected leaders. Although the influence of
public criticism in "superintending the greater forces of formative policy"
is "altogether safe and beneficent, altogether indispensable," when it
is allowed to interfere "in the choice of the daily means of government" it amounts to a "clumsy nuisance" that prevents administrators
from being properly held accountable for their actions.[34]

While Wilson's distinction between politics and administration
contains far more ambiguity than can be discussed here,[35] it soon became
popularized, through the work of Frank Goodnow and others, into
what Herbert Storing has aptly pictured as a two-pyramid theory of
democratic government. According to that model:

> The will of the people flows up through the pyramid of politics where
> it is collected by political parties and formed into programs of legis-
> lation. The programs of the majority party then flow down through
> the administrative pyramid where they are implemented in the most
> efficient manner. . . . The civil servant is not supposed to make pol-
> icy. He decides, according to scientifically established technical cri-
> teria, the best, that is, most efficient, way to accomplish any given
> ends. Those ends are set by his political superiors who are responsi-
> ble through the party to the people.[36]

Over the past sixty years, the politics–administration dichotomy has been subjected to thoroughgoing and widespread criticism, largely for its empirical inaccuracy. Civil servants, it is widely recognized, inevitably exercise "political" discretion. But Lowi's argument is evidence that that dichotomy, and the attendant two-pyramid model, continue to exercise a powerful *prescriptive* influence on American political science.[37] Lowi's critique of the delegation of broad authority to administrative agencies rests on the complaint that "broad delegations are a menace to formal organization and to the ideal of the neutral civil servant," since they make "a politician out of a bureaucrat" (304). The true principles of democracy require, by contrast, that broad political power be exercised only by leaders who are "directly responsible to the largest electorates," since they—unlike appointed civil servants—can easily be "peacefully cashiered" by the people themselves (163). The two-pyramid model recurs in Lowi's distinction between the stages of policy formulation and implementation: by "misapplying" the notion of "popular decision-making" to the latter stage, he charges, interest-group liberalism actually "undermines popular decisions." Giving people "access" to the administration of laws that have already been enacted by a democratic legislature amounts to "a basic disrespect for democracy," he maintains, since it prevents "liberal leaders" from "wield[ing] the authority of democratic governments with the resoluteness born of confidence in the legitimacy of their positions" (295).

As the foregoing quotations suggest, Lowi's conception of juridical democracy sometimes bears a discomfiting resemblance to the Leninist doctrine of democratic centralism: the principle that decisions of policy, once democratically arrived at, must be executed in strictly hierarchical fashion. Like Wilson, Lowi represents the tendency of the American people to intermix politics with administration as the product of a delusion about the means of giving effect to their will. Thinking that they are making the bureaucracy more "responsive," they actually prevent the elected officials to whom they have delegated political power from using that power effectively on their behalf. But is it true that severing "politics" from administration, as both Lowi and Wilson recommend, would enhance the power of the people? And would a major restriction of the political role of federal civil servants promote the goal of constitutional legitimacy?

I believe that Lowi's argument rests on a misconstruction of the sense in which the American government rests on the consent of the people. That argument threatens to substitute a part of the people for the whole—so that policies are judged to be legitimate purely by their conformity to the presumed wishes of a popular majority (as expressed in elections) rather than by their regard for the rights of all members of the citizen body. Here again, a quotation from *The Federalist* is apropos:

> Justice is the end of government. It is the end of civil society. It ever has been and ever will be pursued until it be obtained, or until liberty be lost in the pursuit. In a society under the form of which the stronger faction can readily unite and oppress the weaker, anarchy may as truly be said to reign as in a state of nature, where the weaker individual is not secured against the violence of the stronger; and as, in the latter state, even the stronger individuals are prompted, by the uncertainty of their condition, to submit to a government which may protect the weak as well as themselves; so, in the former state, will the more powerful factions or parties be gradually induced . . . to wish for a government which will protect all parties. . . .[38]

The central point of this passage is that a government that operated only to satisfy the wishes of "the stronger faction"—in a democracy, the majority—would not even truly serve the interest of that faction. Since individuals whose rights are consistently abridged will continue to seek justice, even at the expense of liberty, it is in the interest of a popular majority itself to insure that the legitimate claims of the minority are given their due so as to maintain their loyalty to the regime.[39] Hence Madison, in *Federalist* 10, applauds the beneficial effects of pluralistic competition among a multiplicity of factions, not (as Lowi recognizes) because he assumed that an "invisible hand" guaranteed that such competition would by itself generate just results, but because it is essential to the goal of breaking up potential majority factions. Only by this means can the people's elected representatives (collectively responsible to diverse constituencies) be enabled to achieve a reasonable accommodation between popular demands and the requirements of justice and the common good.[40]

As Lowi's critique attests, the practice of group competition that Madison hoped to encourage is alive and well in the United States today. But while such features of the Founders' system as the separation of powers and the independent, unitary chief executive continue to exert an important influence on our politics, certain changes both constitutional (the Seventeenth Amendment) and extra-constitutional (the failure of the Electoral College to work as intended) have eliminated or radically modified some of the devices they established to promote a properly deliberative democratic statesmanship. For that very reason, the friend of American constitutionalism ought to look favorably on any alternative institution that may promote such statesmanship. A prime candidate for this role, as Herbert Storing has argued, may be the federal bureaucracy itself. As Storing notes, several features of the present-day federal civil service—its members' comparatively long tenure in office, their accumulated knowledge, and their relative independence from direct popular control—might enable it, at its best, to serve a political function analogous to that which the Founders intended the Senate to perform: "to add stability and moderation to the national councils"; "to think in terms of the long-range interest and reputation of the country"; and to embody "the cool and deliberate sense of the community," as distinguished from "momentary [popular] humors" that may run contrary to justice or the sound policy.[41]

For Lowi, the exercise of discretionary political power by the civil service is morally suspect because it lacks the publicity and uniformity of statutory law or codified administrative regulations. To the extent that his concern is simply to emphasize the need for procedural fairness in the development of administrative policy (xvi), the point is unexceptionable. However, this need is already widely recognized, and considerable efforts to satisfy it have been maintained for several decades.[42] Indeed, the pendulum may already have swung too far in the direction of judicial supervision of administrative procedures, as Jeremy Rabkin contends, thus elevating judicially defined claims of individual right (or partisan views of the "public" interest masquerading as claims of right) over the determination of the public good that is arrived at through the political process and the efforts of administrators to arrive at a coherent policy.[43] And Lowi's broader claim that it is inherently illegitimate for members of the civil service to use the broad discretion granted them by law to moderate the substantive thrust of government policy is highly questionable.[44]

Lowi's position rests, as we have seen, on the supposed "irresponsibility" of civil servants, by contrast with their elected superiors, to the public. But to what extent, in a large, commercial, representative republic such as ours, are most acts of legislation given much consideration by the public? And are administrative actions that seriously impinge on major public interests really *less* subject to popular scrutiny (aided by Congress and the media) than legislative ones?[45] When

Lowi complains that "regulators are powerless without the consent of the regulated" (77), is he not in fact objecting to the representative principle itself?

Interest-Group Politics and American Democracy

Having questioned whether "juridical democracy" gives adequate consideration or security to the interests of political minorities, I am thus driven to ask whether Lowi's proposed reforms are truly more *democratic* than the system they are intended to replace. Lowi himself acknowledges at one point that those reforms are in a sense "elitist," in that they concentrate "great powers" in the hands of officeholders who are "directly responsible to the largest electorates"—though he claims that this reflects the "elitist tendencies" of democracy itself (163). And he later indicates that his true concern is less with whether laws are formulated by elected assemblies rather than by "the aristocratic Supreme Court through judicial review or technocratic agencies that engage in early rule-making," than simply with replacing discretionary government *by* that of "rules" (310).[46] The real function of juridical democracy is not so much (if at all) the democratization of governmental authority, as the *systematization and centralization* of policymaking and execution.[47] Such centralization, combined with Lowi's rejection of principled limits on the scope of government, is ultimately intended to remove all obstacles to the "radical transformation of society" at which he aims.[48]

Herein, I think, lies the secret of the seemingly paradoxical appeal of Lowi's thesis to libertarian ideologues like the young David Stockman. Despite the gulf that may separate their substantive goals, intellectuals who aim at political reform on the grand scale share a distaste for interest-group politics, precisely because of the relatively petty stakes over which it is fought, the manifestly self-interested motivation of most participants, and the absence of the "open war of principle against principle" for which Woodrow Wilson wished. Just as Lowi laments that interest-group liberalism generates a rationalization of the status quo that amounts to "administrative boredom" (312–13), Stockman was appalled to discover that American public policy "was not a high-minded nor even an ideological endeavor, but simply a potpourri of parochial claims proffered by private interests parading in governmental dress," utterly lacking in "higher principles" or "broad idealism."[49] The spirit that underlies these complaints is an aristocratic rather than a democratic one. Both its appeal and its dangers were articulated by Tocqueville in his account of the distinction between "great" and "small" political parties:

> What I call great political parties are those whose adherents are more attached to principles than to consequences, to generalities rather than to particular cases, to ideas rather than to personalities. Such parties generally have nobler features, more generous passions, more real convictions, and a bolder and more open look than others. Private interest, which always plays the greatest part in political passions, is there more skillfully concealed beneath the veil of public interest; sometimes it even passes unobserved by those whom it prompts and stirs to action.
>
> On the other hand, [since] small parties . . . are not elevated and sustained by lofty purposes, the selfishness of their character is openly displayed in all their action. . . . That is why, when a time of calm succeeds a great revolution, great men seem to disappear suddenly and minds withdraw into themselves.[50]

Tocqueville acknowledges that great parties, such as the United States had until Thomas Jefferson's victory, are superior in "morality" to "small," interest-based ones. But because they "convulse society" by the extent of their disagreements, great parties are less conducive to the people's happiness and well-being than small ones. Ambitious American politicians are compelled to create issues out of mere "questions of detail," he observes, because of the salutary absence of religious or class hatreds to be exploited in this country.[51] Echoing Tocqueville's observation of the disappearance of strongly principled parties from the American scene, Lowi contended at the time he published *The End of Liberalism* that the erstwhile "great debate" of principle between liberals and conservatives over the scope of government had become irrelevant to present-day political realities. His claim (as of 1979) was that America had arrived at a consensus, in fact if not in name, that there can be no fixed limits to that scope.[52] Yet his goal was to resuscitate a politics of principle, one that would make it possible to confront such issues as "the problem of scarcity and of inefficient distribution of wealth under capitalism" by promoting an alliance "between the poor and the powerful" (232, 234). Under juridical democracy, "elites" whose authority derives from their being "directly responsible to the largest electorates" would marshal great powers that the people would be unable to check, except by replacing them with other elites at the next election. The stakes in each election would thus rise considerably.[53]

While American political parties have sometimes served to articulate great issues of principle (notably during the pre–Civil War and New Deal periods), we may join in Tocqueville's doubt whether the national well-being would be promoted by encouraging such potentially violent and bitter political divisions on a regular basis. The very perpetuation of the rule of law seems to presuppose the existence of a broad consensus on the ends of law, such that the political process does not ordinarily pit one class or group against another in a "zero-sum game."[54]

Above and beyond this issue, however, one may question whether promoting a "principled" politics by centralizing the administrative process and blocking the access of interest groups to it is conducive to the spirit and habits of republican self-government. Near the end of *Democracy in America*, Tocqueville specifically considers the possibility of a form of government "which is unitary, protective, and all-powerful, but elected by the people," so that centralization is combined with popular sovereignty. Such a form satisfies the democratic demand that all people be treated equally, and all special privileges be abolished. But it ultimately destroys the conditions that make self-government possible. Far from accepting the view that freedom consists simply in the right to elect one's rulers, Tocqueville argues "that liberty is less necessary in great matters than in tiny ones." Those nations that attempt to reconcile popular sovereignty with hierarchical administration, he predicts, "will soon become incapable of using the one great privilege left to them." Once having abolished all limits to the scope of governmental regulation, and having accustomed themselves to meekly obeying in their private lives the dictates of a centralized state, they will lose the very capacity to exercise deliberative choice in "great" affairs.[55]

The American administrative state, as it has developed in the twentieth century, is not infrequently an awkward and clumsy affair. As Lowi argues, empowering statutes have sometimes been drawn in such loose terms as to deprive administrative agencies of meaningful mandates, while the systematic coherence of government policies is weakened by the conflict of diverse interest groups.[56] The role that interest groups play in the administrative process is ultimately, however, a reflection of the democratic pluralism that Madison cited as a salutary check on tyranny. The complexities of contemporary administrative policymaking are an inevitable result of grafting an expanded program of governmental activities onto a pluralistic society. As James Q. Wilson observes, "The larger the role of government, the more diverse the range of interests which it must reconcile and the greater the scope of administrative discretion—de facto if not de jure."[57] It is difficult to conceive how a truly representative regime whose policies affect so many interests as the American national government could avoid allowing the practice of informal representation to enter the administrative process. Tempting as "juridical democracy" may seem to reformers of the left or right, one may reasonably fear that the remedy is far worse than the disease it is designed to cure.

Postscript: On Pluralism

Much of the moral force of Lowi's argument for juridical democracy arises, as we have seen, from his critique of the deficiencies of pluralist political theory and its supposed influence on government. Lowi makes that critique more plausible, however, by focusing his analysis on the abstract version of pluralist doctrine advanced by such twentieth-century political scientists as David Truman, which he blames for the reign of "interest-group liberalism," rather than on what Lowi acknowledges as its more profound antecedent, the writings of Madison and Tocqueville.[58] Since neither of the earlier thinkers can justly be accused of subscribing to a simplistic "invisible hand" theory, which denies the need for statesmen to *regulate* and adjust the rivalry of conflicting interests on behalf of the public good, it is not evident that Lowi's argument refutes their position.

There is, however, a profound difference between Lowi's criterion of political legitimacy, or his conception of the proper scope of politics in a liberal polity, and the views of Madison and Tocqueville. Of critical importance here are Lowi's denial that there is any "natural distinction between the functions of government and the functions of nongovernmental institutions" and his claim that "power and control" are "ubiquitous" in modern society (33). Lowi, quite simply, rejects the American Founders' notion of limited government (one that is limited in principle by its ends, not merely by varying pragmatic considerations). And he evinces none of Tocqueville's concern with buttressing the social and political barriers that defend individual and local liberty against an otherwise omnipotent, centralized state.

I cannot undertake here to try to decide the controversy between Lowi and his liberal predecessors. Instead, I limit myself to posing some questions that bear on it. First, is it really plausible to equate as Lowi does the "power and control" exercised by nongovernmental

institutions with that exercised by government, in view of Lowi's own
acknowledgment that the latter is unique in its possession of the legitimate right to practice coercion? (In other words, is there not a
fundamental difference of kind between the "power" exercised, e.g.,
by a giant corporation—which leaves people legally free to work, or
buy products, elsewhere, or to establish competing businesses—and
the power exercised by government when it forbids people to do something, and backs up that prohibition with the threat of physical punishments or mandatory fines?)[59] Second, is there not an essential link
between the civil liberties which Lowi apparently prizes (293–94)
and the economic liberty that is threatened by the potentially all-
inclusive state that his argument seems to legitimize?[60]

Like other aspects of his position, Lowi's denunciation of interest-
group influence ultimately derives from Woodrow Wilson's understanding of American politics. Wilson's critique of governmental secrecy
and of the effects of "private" influence on government was aimed, as
Robert Eden has observed, at "alter[ing] the limits imposed on popular leadership by older liberal suspicions," as articulated in *The Federalist.*[61] In reducing the opportunities for "private" government, Wilson
sought at the same time to enhance the opportunity for independent
"opinion leaders" like himself to articulate and shape "public" opinion.[62] Does not this sort of effort to shape public opinion into ideological doctrines that elected governments are then compelled to execute
systematically amount to what Eden calls "a new kind of private
government by unelected representatives"—academics, media person-
alities, and self-styled "public interest" advocacy groups—whose heightened influence really makes government less truly republican?[63]

The principle of equality has a particular appeal to modern intellectuals, as Tocqueville recognized, because it harmonizes with their
ambition to regulate political affairs on the basis of "general ideas."
From a simply egalitarian perspective, all local or individual variations can be made to seem irrational and therefore unjustifiable.[64] Lowi's
own critique of interest-group liberalism derives its moral appeal from
the seeming unfairness that some individuals or groups have a greater
influence on governmental policies than others do. But since no system can insure an equal influence to all individuals (to reduce the
opportunities for "informal" private influence would, as Woodrow
Wilson anticipated, increase the influence of those who possess greater
rhetorical ability), perhaps this is not the decisive issue. Moreover,
the abstract demand for an equality of political influence neglects the
fact that the majority's *collective* power in a democracy may far ex-

ceed that of the most influential individuals.[65] As political philosophers from Aristotle on have recognized, the most important criterion
of a good government is not its achievement of some formal, mathematical distribution of wealth, influence, or other goods, but its overall conduciveness to the common good: that is, to a rough balance
among the interests of the various classes or social groups, such
that each group feels that the existing order is generally conducive
to its well-being.[66] As various aspects of the institutional system
created by the Founders have been further democratized, one
might plausibly argue that the sort of interest-group influence
decried by Lowi constitutes a needed counterweight to the egalitarian
bias of our present regime, helping to preserve its balance. (This is
not, of course, to say that such influence is benign in all instances—
but then, neither is the influence of government itself.) Pluralism alone,
as both Madison and Lowi recognize, can never supplant the need for
a practice of statesmanship that looks at the good of the whole. But
the mutually checking influence of interest groups may be the precon-
dition for providing members of the government with the freedom to
pursue a vision of that good, while ensuring that it remains accountable to its constituents.

Lowi's critique of pluralist theory thus reflects a deeper disagreement between him and Madison over the proper relation between the
public and private spheres. As followers of John Locke, Madison and
the other Founders believed a system of liberty to be most conducive
to the well-being of all individuals—both because of the intrinsic value
of freedom, and because of the contribution that economic liberty makes
to economic growth, and thus to raising everyone's standard of living. Hence they limited the goal of government to securing people's
equal rights (including the right to pursue happiness), rather than
empowering it to make them equal in wealth, influence, or other substantive goods. Without being simplistic proponents of laissez-faire,
they were unembarrassed to acknowledge that the security of liberty
depends on the capacity of government to defend the rights arising
from people's "different *and unequal* faculties of acquiring property."[67] Far from agreeing with this understanding, Lowi in *The End of
Liberalism* seems to regard inequalities in such goods as wealth, or
living in a desirable neighborhood, as if they were unearned "privileges" bestowed by government, and therefore subject (in principle)
to being redistributed in whatever fashion democratic leaders deem
appropriate. Such an erasure of the distinction between public and
private might truly constitute the end of liberalism.

Notes

1. David Stockman, *The Triumph of Politics: Why the Reagan Revolution Failed* (New York: Harper & Row, 1986), 32. A 1976–77 survey of members of the American Political Science Association listed Lowi as the political scientist who had made the most significant contribution to the discipline during the 1970s; of the several books Lowi had published by then, *The End of Liberalism* (the first edition of which had appeared in 1969) undoubtedly was the work most responsible for this estimation. See, on the indirect but substantial influence of *The End of Liberalism* on the development of federal regulatory policy during the 1970s, Alfred Marcus, "Environmental Protection Agency," in *The Politics of Regulation*, ed. James Q. Wilson (New York: Basic Books, 1980), 269–70; Donald R. Brand, *Corporatism and the Rule of Law: A Study of the National Recovery Administration* (Ithaca, N.Y.: Cornell University Press, 1988), 7–8, 317–18; and David Vogel, *Fluctuating Fortunes: The Political Power of Business in America* (New York: Basic Books, 1989), 106–7. Not acknowledging such influence, Lowi himself contended as of 1993 that the situation he decried in *The End of Liberalism* had only grown worse in subsequent decades: "Two Roads to Serfdom: Liberalism, and Administrative Power," in *A New Constitutionalism*, ed. Stephen Elkin and Karol Soltan (Chicago: University of Chicago Press, 1993), 149–73. On the continuing significance of Lowi's argument in the 1990s, see Brian Cook, *Bureaucracy and Self-Government* (Baltimore: Johns Hopkins University Press, 1996), 165–70.

2. All parenthetical citations in the text refer to Theodore J. Lowi, *The End of Liberalism: The Second Republic of the United States*, 2d ed. (New York: Norton, 1979).

3. Theodore J. Lowi, *The End of the Republican Era* (Norman: University of Oklahoma Press, 1995), 238, 249n, 251, 257.

4. See Friedrich Hayek, *The Road to Serfdom* (Chicago: University of Chicago Press, 1945), chap. 6; idem, *The Political Order of a Free People* (Chicago: University of Chicago Press, 1979), chap. 12.

5. In contrast, Hayek expressly distinguishes the issue of the limits of administrative discretion from the limitation of governmental authority by law, and even suggests that legislatures err by unnecessarily *constricting* the discretion of administrative agencies. In his view "The problem of discretionary powers as it directly affects the rule of law is not a problem of the limitation of the powers of particular agents of government but of the limitation of the powers of the government as a whole" (Hayek, *The Constitution of Liberty* [Chicago: University of Chicago Press, 1960], 212–13). Cf., on Lowi's selective use of Hayek's rule of law argument, Donald R. Brand, "Three Generations of Pluralism: Continuity and Change," *Political Science Reviewer* 15 (1985): 129n.

6. For findings challenging the "capture" theory, see Wilson, *The Politics of Regulation*, 149–51, 301–3, 391–92, et passim; Paul H. Weaver, "Reg-

ulation, Social Policy, and Class Conflict," *The Public Interest*, no. 50 (Winter, 1978): 45–63; Brand, *Corporatism*; Martha Derthick and Paul J. Quirk, *The Politics of Deregulation* (Washington, D.C.: Brookings Institution, 1985). Regarding the feasibility of Lowi's proposal, see Wilson, "Juridical Democracy versus American Democracy," *P.S.: Political Science and Politics*, 23 (1990): 570–72.

7. Theodore J. Lowi, *The Politics of Disorder* (New York: Basic Books, 1971), xviii.

8. My argument here is not intended, I emphasize, to deny the desirability of "downsizing" the federal government, devolving many of its activities to the state and local level and contracting the overall scope of governmental regulation, as many Republican leaders and some Democratic ones have recently urged. It simply seems unlikely, even after the fullest possible contraction of federal activities, that the size of the national government can be returned to anything like what it was in the pre-1933 era, given the extent of America's involvement in world affairs and the complexity of contemporary economic and social issues.

9. Lowi's interpretation of pluralism and capitalism here is curious for several reasons. First, he cites no thinker who maintained the supposed "capitalist notion that government is the only source of power and control"; is this notion any more than a straw man? Nor does Lowi attempt to show that his prototypical pluralists (Madison and Tocqueville) would have agreed with his anti-"capitalist" inference from their thought. Finally, Lowi himself emphasizes only a few pages later that the state *is* distinguished from other institutions by its *"legitimate use of coercion"* (*The End of Liberalism*, 37 [emphasis in original]). Such a distinction clearly differentiates political power from the forms of "power and control" exercised by nongovernmental institutions, and might well be thought to justify setting limits to the end and consequent scope of the former, as does John Locke, for instance, in his *Two Treatises of Government*. (I return to this point in the postscript.)

10. In *The End of the Republican Era* (e.g., 237), Lowi adopts a far more favorable view of pluralism, but only in regard to the religious and cultural sphere, which he wishes to defend against conservative moralism. He does not address the possible dependence of this sort of pluralism on that which is criticized in *The End of Liberalism*. (See *Federalist* 10 and 51, and the postscript to the present chapter.)

11. See, e.g., Grant McConnell, *Private Power and American Democracy* (New York: Knopf, 1966), 158–65 et passim, a work frequently cited by Lowi; C. Wright Mills, *The Power Elite* (New York: Oxford University Press, 1956), especially 125–26n and chap. 11; and William E. Connolly, ed., *The Bias of Pluralism* (New York: Atherton, 1971), which includes Lowi's original critique of interest-group liberalism.

12. Lowi, *The Politics of Disorder*, 185. For some apparent second thoughts regarding the effect of such "radicalism" on liberal governance, see *The End of the Republican Era*, 70–71, 77–78.

13. Cf. Brand, "Three Generations of Pluralism," 128; Harvey C. Mansfield Jr., "Disguised Liberalism," in *The Spirit of Liberalism* (Cambridge:
Harvard University Press, 1978), 31–32.

14. Nor is it clear that Hamilton "lost his war" even in the short run, by
Lowi's own account: in his notes accompanying a reprinting of relevant portions of the *Report*, Lowi remarks that Hamilton therein "identifies those
policies which were going to characterize American national government for
nearly a century after the Founding," and provides the rationale "for what
later became a national program of 'internal improvements'" (Lowi, ed., *Private
Life and Public Order: The Context of Modern Public Policy* [New York:
Norton, 1978], 111, 121). Consider further, in contrast to Lowi's claim regarding the disregard of the need for "administration" that supposedly characterized the original American government, Hamilton's forthright account
in *The Federalist* of "energy in the executive" as "a leading character in the
definition of good government (no. 70: 423, in Hamilton et al., *The Federalist*, ed. Clinton Rossiter [New York: New American Library, 1961]), his broad
definition of "administration" (no. 72: 435–36), his judgment "that the true
test of a good government is its aptitude and tendency to produce a good
administration" (no. 68: 414), and his initial warning "that the vigour of
government is essential to the security of liberty" (no. 1: 35). How can a
Constitution advertised as reflecting such principles possibly have been rat-
ified by a people whose ideology rejected "the idea of conscious and systematic application of legitimate controls on conduct" as Lowi claims (*The End
of Liberalism*, 21)?

In suggesting that the overall expansion of the federal government's economic activities has accorded with Hamilton's broad intentions, I do not mean
to assert that Hamilton would have approved of the specific forms those activities have taken; the issue here is simply the applicability of Hamilton's
constitutional understanding to the activities of twentieth-century government.

15. *The Federalist*, no. 47: 300–8; no. 48: 308–13; no. 51: 320–23. Cf.
the useful discussion of the Founders' "relaxed" interpretation of the separation of powers doctrine in John A. Rohr, *To Run a Constitution: The Legitimacy of the Administrative State* (Lawrence: University of Kansas Press,
1986), chap. 2; also James W. Ceaser, "Doctrines of Presidential-Congres-
sional Relations," in *Separation of Powers and Good Government*, Bradford
P. Wilson and Peter W. Schramm, eds. (Lanham, Md.: Rowman & Littlefield, 1994), 94–95.

16. *The Federalist*, no. 48: 309; no. 51: 322–25; cf. David Epstein, *The
Political Theory of "The Federalist"* (Chicago: University of Chicago Press,
1984), 142–43.

17. *The Federalist*, no. 71: 432; no. 63: 384.

18. Ibid., no. 78: 469.

19. In a later book, Lowi expressly aims to "build down" the presidency,
while attacking the remaining "nonmajoritarian" aspects of Congress (*The
Personal Presidency* [Ithaca, N.Y.: Cornell University Press, 1985], 205).

20. *The Federalist*, no. 78: 470.

21. Ibid., 467.

22. *The Federalist*, no. 10: 79–80; cf. Epstein, *The Political Theory of "The Federalist,"* 60, 90.

23. Cf. Lowi's attacks on "privilege" (107, 297), with Tocqueville's account of the sources and dangers of such attacks in modern democracy: *Democracy in America*, ed. J. P. Mayer, trans. George Lawrence (New York: Harper & Row, 1966), I.ii.2: 164; I.ii.5: 183; II.ii.1, 473–76. Lowi reassures his audience that "[j]uridical democracy is not popular totalitarianism in disguise," since it "does not dictate a particular definition of justice, of virtue, or of the good life" (311); but he holds at the same time that no particular policy "outcome" may be tolerated that "would threaten to violate democratic notions of citizenship and equal treatment" (299). Compare Lowi's criticism of interest-group liberalism for allowing "some [to] escape their fate better than others" (297), along with other references to "escape" cited in the text, with Nathan Glazer's observation of how the recurrent usage of the terms "escape" and "flee" in federal court opinions on busing reflects a transformation in the understanding of civil rights "from one in which the main note is the expansion of freedom, into one in which the main note is the imposition of restrictions" by judicial command (Glazer, "Is Busing Necessary?" *Commentary* 53.3 [March 1972]: 45).

24. *The Politics of Disorder,* xvii–xviii (emphasis added).

25. Ibid., 183–84.

26. *The Federalist*, no. 10: 81.

27. On this distinction, see Joseph M. Bessette, "Deliberative Democracy: The Majority Principle in Republican Government," in *How Democratic Is the Constitution?* ed. Robert A. Goldwin and William A. Schambra (Washington, D.C.: American Enterprise Institute, 1980), 102–16.

28. Significantly, Lowi criticizes interest-group liberalism in his concluding chapter for "weakening *democratic* forms," not the specific "forms" of American constitutionalism, (311 [emphasis added]). Contrast Harvey C. Mansfield Jr.'s discussion of the importance of the substantive "forms" contained in the Constitution for promoting genuine political deliberation or self-government, in *America's Constitutional Soul* (Baltimore: Johns Hopkins University Press, 1991), chaps. 1, 13–15. See also, on the significance of the "constitutional space" established for public officials by the Constitution (consistently with the right of *consent to* government specified in the Declaration of Independence), in contrast to the French Declaration of the Rights of Man and of the Citizen, Mansfield, "The Unfinished Revolution," in *Three Beginnings: Revolution, Rights, and the Liberal State*, ed. Stephen Englehart and John A. Moore Jr. (New York: Peter Lang, 1995), 23–24.

29. "Cabinet Government in the United States," in *The Papers of Woodrow Wilson*, 69 vols., ed. Arthur S. Link (Princeton: Princeton University Press, 1966–1994), I, 507. Even in his later writings such as *Constitutional Government in the United States*, after he abandoned his earlier ambition to have the Constitution amended, Wilson still endeavored, as Robert Eden has pointed out, to make the president more of a "Parliamentary" officer whose

power would derive chiefly from his personal capacity to shape public opinion and bring it to bear on congressional deliberations rather than from executive authority bestowed on him by the Constitution (Eden, "The Rhetorical Presidency and the Eclipse of Executive Power: Woodrow Wilson's *Constitutional Government in the United States*," *Polity* 28, no. 3 [Spring 1996]: 357–78; chapter 8 in this book).

Lowi himself has subsequently argued that "the presidency must be turned into a more parliamentary office" (*The Personal President*, 210).

30. "Cabinet Government in the United States," in Link, ed., *Papers*, I, 506.

31. Ibid., I, 510 (emphasis in original).

32. Link, ed., *Papers*, 18, 539.

33. Wilson, "The Study of Administration," *Political Science Quarterly*, 56 (December 1941; originally published 1887), 493, 504.

34. Ibid., 491, 497, 499. Note also Wilson's interpretation of democracy as entailing that "all structures of policy" be based "upon the major will," in contrast to the Founders' standard of securing the rights of all citizens or promoting the *common* good (ibid., 502).

35. For the most thorough analysis of Wilson's argument and its ambiguities, see Kent Aiken Kirwan, "The Crisis of Identity in the Study of Public Administration: Woodrow Wilson," *Polity*, 9.3 (Spring 1977), 321–43.

36. Storing, "Political Parties and the Bureaucracy," in *Political Parties, U.S.A.*, ed. Robert A. Goldwin (Chicago: Rand McNally, 1964), 143.

37. See, on the continuing influence of the politics–administration dichotomy and its departure from the political thought of the Founders, Jeremy Rabkin, "Bureaucratic Idealism and Executive Power: A Perspective on *The Federalist*'s View of Public Administration," in *Saving the Revolution,* ed. Charles R. Kesler (New York: Free Press, 1987), 185–202; chapter 6 in this book.

38. *Federalist,* no. 51: 324–25.

39. Lowi's recommendation that coercive desegregation policies be directed against the well-to-do, who are "most likely to respect the law" and to obey it (260), invites reflection on the causes, and the limits, of such respect: cf. Mansfield, "Disguised Liberalism," 50; Brand, "Three Generations of Pluralism," 137. Cf. also Lowi's acknowledgment in *The Politics of Disorder* (182) that "the politics of law" that juridical democracy would engender is "far more potentially conflictive" than alternative modes of governance, with note 53 infra.

40. Cf. Martin Diamond, *The Founding of the Democratic Republic* (Itasca, Ill.: Peacock, 1981), 70–78.

41. Storing, "The Problem of Big Government," in *A Nation of States,* 2d ed., ed. Robert A. Goldwin (Chicago: Rand McNally, 1974), 83–87 [citing *Federalist,* nos. 62–63]; cf. Storing, "Political Parties and the Bureaucracy," 147–56. Storing's suggestion is interestingly developed in Rohr, *To Run a Constitution*, chap. 3. Consider also Hugh Heclo's account of how such "bureaucratic dispositions" as "gradualism, indirection, [and] political caution" may promote the long-range effectiveness of government: *A Government of*

Strangers (Washington, D.C.: Brookings Institution, 1977), 142–48, 173–80. See further, on the potential capacity of the upper echelons of the civil service to foster a broadly based understanding of the public interest so as to compensate for the deficiencies of a merely "pluralistic," interest-based politics, Marc K. Landy, Marc J. Roberts, and Stephen R. Thomas, *The Environmental Protection Agency: Asking the Wrong Questions from Nixon to Clinton* (New York: Oxford University Press, 1994), 13 et passim; also Brand, *Corporatism*, 314–16.

For a thoughtful nineteenth-century account of the potential role of the civil service as a locus of statesmanship in modern democracy, see Sir Henry Taylor, *The Statesman*, ed. David Lewis Schaefer and Roberta Rubel Schaefer (Westport, Conn.: Praeger, 1992; originally published 1836 and 1878).

42. Cf. Brand, "Three Generations of Pluralism," 139; Antonin Scalia, "The Judicialization of Standardless Rulemaking: Two Wrongs Make a Right," *Regulation*, 1, no. 1 (July-August 1977), 38–41. By 1993 Lowi himself was decrying the surfeit of "proceduralism": "Two Roads to Serfdom," 158.

43. Rabkin, *Judicial Compulsions: How Public Law Distorts Public Policy* (New York: Basic Books, 1989); see also R. Shep Melnick, *Regulation and the Courts* (Washington, D.C.: Brookings Institution, 1977). Although Lowi attributes the courts' practice of "rewriting" many congressional statutes in the process of interpreting them to the vagueness with which they were written (300), Rabkin documents many instances in which judicial reinterpretation has been used to alter the intent of the statutes rather than merely to make them more precise.

44. This is not to deny the possible validity of another argument Lowi develops at greater length in *The End of the Republican Era* (50–51, 250–51) to the effect that in drafting legislation of extremely broad generality such as that which established the Environmental Protection Agency, Congress generated expectations that could not reasonably be satisfied, and hence set the stage for popular disenchantment with pragmatic liberalism. But his telling point here concerns presidential and congressional overreaching rather than the delegation of administrative discretion per se. In fact, the authors of an authoritative study of the Environmental Protection Agency find that while Congress has sometimes drafted environmental statutes that are "excessively vague," it has also erred in the opposite direction by introducing "too many cumbersome requirements"; the provision of the Clean Air Act that "forbids the EPA administrator from considering costs when setting ambient standards" is cited, for instance, as "a regrettable example of congressional micro-management" depriving the EPA of "the discretion it needs to think and act strategically" (Landy, Roberts, and Thomas, *The Environmental Protection Agency*, 332–33). See also Eugene Bardach and Robert A. Kagan, *Going by the Book: The Problem of Regulatory Unreasonableness* (Philadelphia: Temple University Press, 1982), chap. 4, "The Perverse Effects of Legalism"; and, for a popular treatment of the problem, Philip K. Howard, *The Death of Common Sense: How Law Is Suffocating America* (New York: Random House, 1994).

45. As evidence against the proposition that narrowing delegations of statutory authority will promote popular accountability, consider Michael Malbin's observation of how the vast increase in the size of congressional committee staffs has promoted the influence of "ideological" staff members, "experts without constituencies." The power of such "experts" enables them to advance "ideas and slogans whose main political support initially comes only from the fact that staff people and journalists are interested in listening to them" (Malbin, *Unelected Representatives: Congressional Staff and the Future of Representative Government* [New York: Basic Books, 1980], 249). Lowi's demand that legislation be drafted with greater specificity would probably require substantial further growth of committee staffs (cf. *The End of Liberalism*, 307). See also Brand, *Corporatism*, p. 317; Rabkin, *Judicial Compulsions*, 310n.8.

The duty of administrative officials themselves in governmental organizations like the EPA to engage in public education (as distinguished from politically self-serving oversimplification of policy issues) so as to strengthen the capacity of citizens to participate in self-government is usefully discussed in Landy, Roberts, and Thomas, *The Environmental Protection Agency*, 7–8, 310–13, et passim.

46. In *The End of the Republican Era*, however (65), Lowi acknowledges the tremendous growth in the number of administrative rules in recent years, as manifested by "the explosion of the number of pages in the *Federal Register* during the 1970s," but views this growth as symptomatic of the trends that engendered "the end of liberalism." From this perspective, it appears, the problem in Lowi's view is the delegation of excessive authority to administrative agencies, whether or not the agencies themselves then adopt rules to guide their operations.

47. Cf. Lowi's reference to the "almost total democratization of the Constitution" that had already occurred during the 1960s and 1970s, and its failure to reduce the public's "sense of distrust toward public objects" (50). The obstacle to legitimating the (further) expansion of governmental activity is not the lack of democratization, but the lack of formalism. Cf. also Lowi's objection to the system of delegated power for enabling "[e]veryone . . . to feel that he is part of one big policy-making family," and his wish to make "access to some areas of government a bit more difficult to acquire" (93, 311). The latter modification would help to overcome the resistance of "popular majorities" to "change" on issues like busing (267) or affirmative action, where government policy has been driven in recent decades by ideologically motivated elites in the courts, the academy, and particular public agencies.

For a different explanation of the legitimation "crisis" of our "democratized" national government that stresses the deficiency of contemporary views of democratic representation, see Ralph A. Rossum, "Representation and Republican Government: Contemporary Court Variations on the Founders' Theme," in *Taking the Constitution Seriously*, ed. Gary L. McDowell (Dubuque, Ia.: Kendall-Hunt, 1981), 417–34, especially 428–29.

48. In *The End of the Republican Era*, apparently chastened by the drift

of recent electoral politics, Lowi retreats from expressing hopes for such a transformation; but even while acknowledging that the "radicalization" of the Democratic party in the 1960s may have contributed to its subsequent electoral defeats, he still applauds the left for challenging such "morally reprehensible" aspects of American society as "the second-class status of women" and "the spread of poverty despite plenty" (77). At the same time he urges his readers, "for the sake of the republic," "to accept [a] liberal hegemony" that would overturn "morality laws" that criminalize abortion or other ostensibly "victimless" crimes (256–59). The critical aspect of continuity with *The End of Liberalism* in this regard is Lowi's wish to insulate government from popular objections to the agenda of "enlightened" liberal policymakers (258).

49. Stockman, *The Triumph of Politics*, 33; see also the quotations from the epilogue of that book in Lowi, *The End of the Republican Era*, 93. Cf., on the disposition of both liberals and conservatives, when in power, to lament the Constitutional separation of powers and the resultant difficulty of achieving rapid, radical change, James Q. Wilson, "Why Reagan Won and Stockman Lost," *Commentary*, 88.2 (August 1986), 17–21. And see also, on Stockman, Donald J. Maletz, "The Place of Constitutionalism in the Education of Public Administrators," chapter 11 in this book.

50. *Democracy in America,* I.ii.4: 161.

51. Ibid., 161–63.

52. In *The End of the Republican Era* (60), Lowi repeats his judgment that the Supreme Court in 1937 "conclusively settled . . . that in a democracy there can be no effective substantive limit to the scope of governmental power"; but he now argues that "an enlightened liberal republic" guided by the rule of law standard should constrain the scope of its undertakings by an awareness of "the limits of liberalism," generating a government that is "smaller" but more principled (251, 259). He insists, however, that liberal government be constrained only by the "formal" principle of rule of law, not by any "substantive moral content" (250). Subsequently, the Supreme Court, notably in its 1995 decision in *U.S. v. Lopez* striking down the "Gun-Free Schools Act" for lacking adequate grounding in Congress's constitutional authority to regulate interstate commerce, has indicated that it may endeavor to restore substantive limits to the national government's authority.

53. Compare Lowi's recommendation of heightened judicial advocacy on behalf of his conception of the rule of law in *The End of the Republican Era* (252). While acknowledging that this would encourage "frequent conflict at the level of constitutionality," he holds that such conflict "would make for superb civic education," without seeming to take account of its problematic political effects. Cf. the comments of Brand, "Three Generations of Pluralism," 136–37, regarding Lowi's curious faith "that the cultivation of disorder and conflict in civil society leads to order when mediated by the state," whereas (Brand observes) the rule of law seems in actuality to depend on "a spirit of moderation and compromise . . . among conflicting groups."

54. On the manner in which the American party system has promoted consensus while periodically articulating fundamental policy alternatives, see Harry

V. Jaffa, "The Nature and Origin of the American Party System," in *Political Parties U.S.A.*, ed. Goldwin, 59–83. Such an articulation of fundamental alternatives may be reoccurring in the 1990s, although not in a way to Lowi's liking, as he makes evident in *The End of the Republican Era*.

55. *Democracy in America*, II.iv.6: 668–69. Compare, in this regard, Lowi's ambition to achieve the "complete destruction of the fiction of local citizenship and the sanctity of local boundaries" with Tocqueville's stress on the value of local autonomy as a check on majority tyranny, and as a means of nourishing the spirit of liberty through active civic participation (ibid., I.i.8: 147–48; I.ii.8: 241–42). Consider also, with reference to Lowi's wish to limit administrative discretion, Tocqueville's remarks on the desirability of *buttressing* the independence of subordinate officials, as a means of protecting individual rights against the democratic bias in favor of centralization and uniformity (ibid., II.iv.7: 670–71).

Tocqueville's praise of administrative decentralization should not be confused with the principles underlying the program of client "participation" in the federal poverty program of the 1960s, some of the faults of which are aptly described by Lowi (*The End of Liberalism*, chap. 8). As Catherine Zuckert observes, in order for decentralization to have the desired effect in the administration of public spending programs, it is essential that "the connection between participation, benefits, and taxpaying" not be severed: "Reagan and that Unnamed Frenchman [De Tocqueville]: On the Rationale for the New [Old] Federalism," *Review of Politics*, 45.3 (July 1983): 421–42.

56. The latter effect is no less visible, however, in the legislative sphere— witness the difficulties encountered by recent presidents and Congresses in addressing the budget deficit—than in the administrative one. Consider also, on the good reasons that sometimes exist for statutory vagueness, Kenneth Culp Davis, *Discretionary Justice: A Preliminary Inquiry* (Urbana: University of Illinois Press, 1971 [originally published 1969]), 43; Louis Fisher, *The Constitution between Friends: Congress, the President, and the Law* (New York: St. Martin's Press, 1978), 27–28, 31–33.

57. Wilson, *The Politics of Regulation*, 392. Prior to his appointment to the Supreme Court, Antonin Scalia, who agreed with Lowi's criticism of vague congressional statutes, nonetheless defended administrative agencies' practice of consulting relevant interest groups as a second-best way of fleshing out their legislative mandates, since "the process of accommodating public desires, including the ardent support or vehement opposition of interest groups most proximately affected, is an essential part of the democratic process, however untidy and unanalytic it may be" ("The Judicialization of Standardless Rulemaking," 40).

In *The End of the Republican Era* (250–51), Lowi denies that the complexity of modern society excuses Congress's tendency to draft legislation in vague terms, since state legislatures in the early nineteenth century enacted statutes that had "much more legal integrity" even though the legislatures lacked significant staff or research assistance. He attributes Congress's disposition to delegate policy issues to the civil service to the difficulty it encounters in "work[ing] out compromises" among the demands of conflicting groups, but takes this fact to mean that Congress is ducking its job. Lowi's argument passes over the possibility that such delegations may improve the policymaking process by enabling administrative agencies to work out specific policies in the light of experience with their day-to-day operation: it is easier for agencies to alter rules they have established on the basis of such experience (subject, of course, to congressional oversight) than to rely on Congress to make such alterations each time they seem necessary. Hence the authors of the EPA study cited earlier recommend that "because Congress is good at investigation, it need not and ought not try to use legislation to accomplish oversight objectives" (Landy et al., *The Environmental Protection Agency*, 332).

Contrary to Lowi's assertion, it is by no means clear that "the analysis of Congress show[s] the shortcomings of efforts to gain administrative accountability through legislative oversight" (*The End of Liberalism*, 307). On the utility of a model of congressional deliberation that starts with analysis of "the specific impact" of an existing program to illuminate "what the general words of a statute or regulation mean in practice," rather than trying "to begin by thinking in terms of general principles," see Malbin, *Unelected Representatives*, 247, including the quotation from Richard Fenno therein.

58. For a critique of Lowi's position, that persuasively argues that pragmatism rather than pluralism is the real cause of the developments Lowi laments, see Brand, *Corporatism*, chap. 1 and conclusion. It is curious that Lowi, who does tellingly cite the scientific imprecision of twentieth-century pluralist theories that purport to explain *all* of political life by reference to the conflict of groups or "potential" groups (35–37), nonetheless softens his criticism of pluralist theory in the end by claiming "that modern pluralistic political science brought science to politics" (312). This attempt to balance his denunciation of the political evils supposedly wrought by pluralist theory with hyperbolic praise of its intellectual achievement perhaps indicates that Lowi's quarrel with theorists like Truman and Bentley (whose political opinions, after all, were not very different from Lowi's) is less serious than he makes it out to be.

For more systematic critiques of pluralist theory on theoretical rather than partisan grounds, see Leo Weinstein, "The Group Approach: Arthur F. Bentley," in *Essays on the Scientific Study of Politics*, ed. Herbert J. Storing (New York: Holt, Rinehart, and Winston, 1962), 151–224; Dennis F. Hale, "Arthur F. Bentley: Politics and the Mystery of Society," *Political Science Reviewer*, 13 (1983): 1–42 (see 23n, 27–35 for discussion of Bentley's Progressive politics).

59. Precedent for Lowi's attempted erasure of the distinction between public and private power may be found in Franklin Roosevelt's programmatic Commonwealth Club Address of 1932 (*The Public Papers and Addresses of Franklin D. Roosevelt*, ed. Samuel Rosenman [New York: Random House, 1938]: I, 742–56). On the rhetorical strategy of that address and its questionable

reinterpretation of American history, see Robert Eden, "On the Origins of
the Regime of Pragmatic Liberalism: John Dewey, Adolph A. Berle, and FDR's
Commonwealth Club Address of 1932," *Studies in American Political Development*, 7 (Spring 1993): 74–150.

60. Cf. Harvey Mansfield, "On the Political Character of Property in Locke,"
in *Powers, Possessions, and Freedom*, ed. Alkis Kontos (Toronto: University
of Toronto Press, 1979), 36–38; Clifford Orwin and Thomas L. Pangle, "Restoring the Human Rights Tradition," *This World*, 3 (Fall 1982): 23–25, 38–39.

Lowi stops short of advocating "true socialism," warning that the attempt
to establish such a system in the United States would require sacrificing our
civil liberties; but he is ambivalent as to whether this sacrifice is essential
to socialism or only an "interim" problem, and he counterbalances his warning by asserting that liberal capitalism is itself characterized by a "contradiction between civil liberties and economic privilege" (*The End of Liberalism*,
294).

61. Robert Eden, *Political Leadership and Nihilism: A Study of Weber
and Nietzsche* (Gainesville: University of Florida Presses, 1984), 6. Cf., on
the Founders' fears of popular political "leadership" as antithetical to liberty, James Ceaser, *Presidential Selection: Theory and Practice* (Princeton: Princeton University Press, 1979), 52–61. For Wilson's attack on secrecy, see,
e.g., "Cabinet Government in the United States," *Papers*, I, 494–96; also
"Committee or Cabinet Government?" (1884), ibid., II, 629–30.

62. Cf. Wilson's letters to Ellen Axson of 30 October 1883 and 24 February 1885 (*Papers*, II, 499–502 and IV, 287); his unpublished manuscript on
leadership (in *The Political Thought of Woodrow Wilson*, ed. E. David Cronon
[Indianapolis: Bobbs Merrill, 1965], 20–21); and his address "Ideals of Public Life" (*Papers*, 17, 498–500; also the published version reprinted in Cronon,
123–24). Compare Lowi's remark: "There is no necessary conflict of economic interest between the poor and the powerful. It depends on who the
powerful are" (*The End of Liberalism*, 234).

63. Eden, *Political Leadership*, 12, with references in note 44; cf. Brand,
Corporatism, 318. See, on the detrimental impact of the media's demand for
"open government" on formal, political representation and deliberation, Harvey C. Mansfield Jr., "The Media World and Constitutional Democracy," in
America's Constitutional Soul, 169–76. Mansfield makes a valuable distinction between the principles of the American Constitution and of the French
Declaration of the Rights of Man and of the Citizen in this regard: whereas
the French declaration was in principle more "opposed to private interests"
than the U.S. Constitution, in practice "it was more open to the influence of
private interests that can succeed in claiming to express the will of the nation than the American Constitution that was more tolerant of private interests but less likely to be seized by any particular interest" (Mansfield, "The
Unfinished Revolution," 24–25).

On Tocqueville's effort to buttress republican politics against the impact
of the ideological doctrines generated by intellectuals, see James Ceaser, *Po-

litical Science and Liberal Democracy (Baltimore: Johns Hopkins University Press, 1990), chap. 7.

64. *Democracy in America,* II.i.2–4:7; *The Old Regime and the French Revolution,* trans. Stuart Gilbert (Garden City, N.Y.: Doubleday, 1955), 147, 162; Ceaser, *Political Science,* 154–59. See also, with reference to Lowi's argument, John C. Koritansky, "Prudence and the Practice of Government," *Southern Review of Public Administration,* 6.1 (Spring 1982), 118–19.

The bias in favor of uniformity is reflected in Lowi's identification of the requisite of justice as the derivation of an action "from a preexisting general rule or moral principle" (296), an understanding that severely circumscribes the role of prudence. Contrast Aristotle, *Nicomachean Ethics,* 1134b18–1135a4, and the account of prerogative in Locke, *Two Treatises of Government,* II, xiv; also Taylor, *The Statesman,* chap. 16; and cf. Eugene F. Miller, "Prudence and the Rule of Law," *American Journal of Jurisprudence,* 24 (1979): 181–206. The Rousseauean-Kantian identification of justice with universal moral rules typifies the thought of revolutionary France rather than of the American Founders, as Terence Marshall points out: "Separation of Powers, Human Rights, and Constitutional Government: A Franco-American Dialogue at the Time of the Revolution," in *Separation of Powers and Good Government,* ed. Wilson and Schramm, 29–31.

65. Cf. Donald R. Brand, "Corporatism, the NRA, and the Oil Industry," *Political Science Quarterly,* 98 (Spring 1983), 99–118.

66. Aristotle, *Politics,* III.9–10, 13; IV.9, 12; VI.5; cf. Harry V. Jaffa, "Aristotle," in *History of Political Philosophy,* 2d ed., ed. Leo Strauss and Joseph Cropsey (Chicago: Rand McNally, 1972), 112–15; Delba Winthrop, "Aristotle and Theories of Justice," *American Political Science Review,* 72. 4 (December 1978): 1201–16. Compare Lowi's denunciation of the disposition to "[p]urchase support for the regime by reserving an official place for every major structure of power" (297), which seems to leave open the question of how such support *is* to be obtained; cf. note 39 supra.

67. *The Federalist,* no. 10: 78 (emphasis added). On the meaning of this passage see Epstein, *The Political Theory of "The Federalist,"* 74–75, 79–80. Not to be forgotten, of course, is Madison's assertion in the same essay that "the principal task of modern legislation" consists in "[t]he *regulation* of these various and interfering [economic] interests" (79 [emphasis added]). But see L. Peter Schultz, "Congress and the Separation of Powers Today," in *Separation of Powers and Good Government,* ed. Wilson and Schramm, 88–89, for a plausible challenge to Lowi's interpretation of this remark.

Part Two

Administration, Political Institutions, and the Constitution

Introduction

The problems and issues raised by the practice of public administration can rarely be resolved by abstract theory. Both the administrator's proper loyalty and his perception of the political dimension
of his work are best understood as constitutional. The chapters in
this section look to the Constitution's creation of political institutions for the formation of the distinctive character of administration
in America.

Jeremy Rabkin in chapter 6 shows that the authors of *The Federalist* had a more sophisticated understanding of human nature and its
relation to political life than later administrative theorists. The idealism of modern political theory from Immanuel Kant through Max Weber
aims to make bureaucratic activity mechanical on the basis of a peculiar, compulsive moralism. Facts and values, administration and politics, are to be rigorously separated in the name of an inhuman moral
purity. *The Federalist*, Rabkin argues, is more realistic in its acceptance of the inevitable mixture of politics and administration. It is
more accepting of the truth about the mixed character of human nature. Impersonal norms, in truth, cannot suffice as the basis of good
administration.

David Nichols examines in chapter 7 a number of key Supreme
Court decisions to determine the constitutional foundation of administrative responsibility. He argues that the modern administrative state
is not an aberration, but the logical outgrowth of the character of the
Constitution of 1787. The Constitution provides ample justification
for administrative discretion, as long as it is exercised with deference

149

to the administrator's constitutional superiors, the three branches of the national government.

In chapter 8, Robert Eden corrects the common interpretation of Woodrow Wilson's project for transforming the Constitution so as to enhance presidential power. That power was to come through opinion leadership, not executive action. Executive action was to be demoted to a subordinate status, to mere administration. For Wilson, one meaning of the separation of politics from administration was the freeing of the nation's moral leader from the drudgery of the details of implementation.

Donald Brand in chapter 9 elaborates the distinction between political devotion and cosmopolitan detachment as another way of looking at the distinction between politics and administration. He contrasts President Richard Nixon's political and moral understanding of the cold war with his key adviser Henry Kissinger's rather detached and amoral view of that conflict. Brand also considers Kissinger's academic distrust of President Ronald Reagan's moralism about the Soviet empire. Brand concludes that advisers from an academic or scientific background are and ought to be subordinated, under the Constitution, to the prudence of statesmen with a broadly political orientation.

Gary Bryner shows in chapter 10 how administrative discretion is properly shaped and limited by administrative law. He criticizes today's congressional Republicans for aiming only at a smaller government, not a more effective one. He criticizes the Democrats for neglecting both effectiveness and efficiency. Bryner recommends a loosening of the procedural requirements imposed on administrative agencies, as a means of facilitating a regulatory system that would be more comprehensive yet less cumbersome than the present one.

6

Bureaucratic Idealism and Executive Power: A Perspective on *The Federalist*'s View of Public Administration

Jeremy Rabkin

The term "bureaucracy" had not yet entered the English language when *The Federalist* set out to defend the new Constitution of the United States. Not only the term, but the notions now associated with it seem remote from the analyses offered in *The Federalist*. In nothing more than this, perhaps, does *The Federalist* seem so removed from the perspective of modern political science and the preoccupations of contemporary politics.

Today, commentators speak respectfully of "the bureaucracy" as "the fourth branch" of government.[1] *The Federalist*, like the Constitution it defends, seems to recognize only the legislative, executive, and judicial branches. Today, it is common to think of "bureaucracy" as the essential substratum in all modern governments, so that the development of any country's state bureaucracy can be regarded as the touchstone of its modernization.[2] From this perspective, the difference between parliamentary and presidential systems—even the difference between free countries and communist tyrannies—can seem altogether secondary.[3] *The Federalist* presents an improved "science of politics," which seems to regard the organization of "administration"—in the modern sense—as an altogether secondary matter. *The Federalist* is most anxious to show that the American executive is "republican," rather than modern. It is most concerned to show why the executive must be "energetic" rather than efficient, or expert, or impartial.

The seeming naïveté of *The Federalist* nonetheless has much to teach us. If *The Federalist* appears naïve in comparison to modern theorists of administration and bureaucracy, perhaps that is because

The Federalist possesses more sophistication about politics: Publius sees clearly many things that modern theorists have done their best to forget.

Bureaucracy by Any Other Name

If the term "bureaucracy" was unknown to *The Federalist,* the term "administration" appears often enough. The latter term had already acquired its predominant contemporary meaning of managing details in accord with the will or aim of another. Thus, on the eve of the American Revolution, William Blackstone's *Commentaries* relied on established usage in discussing the "administration" of estates or business concerns by court-appointed "administrators."[4] The "administrator" was charged with managing and maintaining property until bankruptcy claims could be satisfied or inheritances properly distributed. The "administrator" was not an owner and was certainly not free to dispose of property or business in his care as if he were the owner.

The Federalist plays on this usage but plainly conceives governmental administration in wider terms. Thus, in a famous dictum, Publius proclaims that "administration of government in its largest sense, comprehends all the operations of the body politic, whether legislative, executive or judicial," and only in "its most usual and perhaps most precise signification" is it "limited to executive details fall[ing] peculiarly within the province of the executive departments."[5] In itself, "administration" suggests implementation rather than intention, means rather than ends. *The Federalist*'s appeal to "administration in its largest sense" makes sense only on the understanding that "all the operations of the body politic" are a trust from the people, necessarily limited in their ends. In other words, all government can be conceived as "administration" only if government is first conceived as limited government. But within the bounds of limited government, *The Federalist* suggests that ends and means, policy and implementation, are not so readily separated.

The modern term "bureaucracy" has different roots and different implications, which make the concept—as much as the phenomenon—very hard to assimilate to limited government. The term combines the French word for desk or office with the Greek word for political rule. In its "most precise signification," then, "bureaucracy" is an alternative to democracy or aristocracy or autocracy.

The term was first employed in France in the last years of the *ancien régime* and was already well established in French when Publius offered his definition of "administration in its largest sense." Unlike Publius's use of "administration," the original French usage of *bureaucratie* was satirical. The more important difference was that the French term was not premised on liberal notions of limited government but was rather, from the outset, seen as implying a repudiation of limited government.

The original satirical connotations of "bureaucracy" are easy to appreciate. To a large extent they remain evident in contemporary American associations of the term "bureaucracy" with wheelspinning and red tape. The term had more of an edge in the eighteenth century, however, when educated people were more imbued with classical learning and more receptive to the Aristotelian teaching that every type of ruler—whether the common people (the *demos*) in a democracy or the few best (the *aristoi*) in an aristocracy—tries to shape the whole city in its own image and in accord with its own interests. When the notion of "ruling" was taken more seriously, there was something particularly comical and incongruous in the suggestion that a great nation might be ruled in accord with the outlook and interests of deskbound clerks.

It was the very scale of the French monarchy's governing ambitions that made this joke seem half plausible, however. During the course of the seventeenth and eighteenth centuries, French kings had greatly strengthened their control over the provinces through a network of purely administrative officials, men who owed their authority to direct royal appointment rather than inherited estates, purchased titles, or local status. But the range of local matters under the control (and the detailed control) of these officials made them difficult to direct from the center. The term *bureaucratie* thus seems to have been coined by a royal minister of commerce, evidently intending to express with this term his frustration in trying to get trade liberalization measures implemented by royal officials in the provinces.[6]

_ In the course of the nineteenth century, the term lost much of its satiric edge, just as the prestige of liberal or limited government began to decline in continental Europe. It was particularly among German writers, never renowned for their light wit and rarely satisfied with liberal principles, that *Bürokratie* came to be employed in a neutral, often indeed in a respectful sense. As the claims of government to order and direct on a large scale became more accepted, the institutional machinery for accomplishing these larger ends could no longer be regarded as a subject for ridicule. New conceptions of government—and a more radical "science of politics" than that espoused by Publius—made the notion of "bureaucracy" seem both plausible and necessary.

To place the thought of *The Federalist* in proper perspective, then, it is appropriate here to undertake a brief digression to trace the connection between German idealism and contemporary conceptions of "bureaucracy." For it was largely through the influence of German theorists that contemporary notions of bureaucracy entered American discourse in this century and helped obscure and corrupt the constitutional legacy of *The Federalist*.

The German Problem

The modern usage of "bureaucracy" as a neutral descriptive term of social analysis is usually credited—with much reason—to the work of Max Weber. Weber is often described as the founder of modern social science because of his insistence that "scientific" analyses of social phenomena must focus on observable effects, without obtruding the assessments or concerns of the "scientist." More generally, Weber insisted on the necessity of sharply distinguishing "facts" from "values" in social science inquiries[7] and his analysis of "bureaucracy" does indeed have a curiously abstract, disembodied character.

Weber presents the growth of bureaucracy in the modern world as one of the principal manifestations of the increasing "rationalization" of social institutions in modern life. He does not say that modern forms of social organization are more reasonable—that would be expressing a "value" judgment. He simply claims that bureaucratic organization is the most rational means of securing any given goal or standard—however arbitrary or unreasonable the standard may be. Weber himself draws a sharp distinction between "formal rationality"and "substantive rationality," parallelling his larger distinction between rational calculation about means, and judgments (or in his case, non-judgments) about the reasonableness of ends.[8] But his own account of bureaucracy tends to obscure this distinction by focusing all attention on the "rationality" and "efficiency" of bureaucracy in achieving its official goals.

Thus, Weber presents bureaucracy as the most developed form of authority grounded in "rational-legal norms." He contrasts this with "traditional" authority (where people accept a certain ordering of affairs because they have always been ordered that way) and with "charismatic" authority (where people uncritically accept the directives of a particular leader because of their mystical faith in his superhuman power and wisdom).[9] Distinctions between ends and means are readily lost in this peculiar framework, which inevitably suggests that bureaucracy bears the same relation to alternative governing forms as modern chemistry bears to medieval alchemy or modern medicine to ritual folk remedies. In fact, Weber explicitly compares bureaucracy with "precision machinery," which yields a "particularly high degree of calculability of results."[10] These characterizations derive from Weber's vision of bureaucracy as the systematic, hierarchical organization of specialists, each governed by rules and professional norms appropriate to his own delimited sphere of competence or authority.

Weber portrays the specialized expertise of officials as again a matter of pure technical capacity, with no necessary connection to particular ends or goals. The hierarchical organization of such specialists yields a bureaucratic machine that is highly resistant to "arbitrary" or irrational deflections from its given goals. Thus, even "the tendency of officials" to adopt "a utilitarian point of view in the interest of those under their authority" is tempered by the compulsion to proceed through "measures which themselves have a formal character and tend to be treated in a formalistic spirit. . . . Otherwise the door would be opened to arbitrariness."[11] For similar reasons, control of bureaucracy "is possible only in a very limited degree to persons who are not technical specialists. Generally speaking, the trained permanent official is more likely to get his way in the long run than his nominal superior, the cabinet minister who is not a specialist."[12] But this is hardly an objection, for "the purely bureaucratic type of administrative organization . . . is, from a purely technical point of view, capable of attaining the highest degree of efficiency and is in this sense formally the most rational known means of carrying out imperative control over human beings."[13]

Some critics have suggested that Weber's account of bureaucracy betrays an excessive credulity for the particular conceits of the Prussian state bureaucracy in the decades before the First World War, when Weber did most of his writing.[14] But Weber was not, in fact, an uncritical enthusiast of bureaucracy. He wrote eloquently of the spiritually deadening effects of expert administration and warned that the impersonal, legalistic ethos of bureaucracy would encourage a world of "specialists without vision and voluptuaries without heart."[15] It is scarcely an exaggeration to say that he viewed as somewhat regrettable his own finding that the "dominance of a spirit of formalistic impersonality . . . without hatred or passion and hence without affection or enthusiasm" is most conducive to administrative "efficiency."[16]

Regrettable or not, Weber's claims about the superior efficiency of bureaucracy are not actually very persuasive as factual descriptions. Armies do not win victories and business corporations do not win profits by following fixed rules in a "spirit of formalistic impersonality." Even governmental bureaucracies usually depend on much more flexibility and inspiration than Weber allows—as is suggested by the phenomenon of the "rule book slowdown," where public employees, rather than going out on strike, paralyze government operations by fastidiously observing every official rule to the letter. In Weber's account of bureaucracy, questions of motivation, morale, or initiative simply disappear. Managers face no awkward trade-offs between inspiration and control, between creativity and reliability, between flexibility and predictability. All their considerations seem to disappear because the actual goals to be served are always out of view. In Weber's account, the most orderly administrative scheme always seems to be the most efficient and the most rational.

Weber's claim to this effect surely did not derive from empirical observation, then, any more than from patriotic enthusiasm for the government of Wilhelmine Germany. He seems to have felt compelled to assert the superior rationality of bureaucratic organization, first, because of his peculiar—though by now rather prevalent—conception of "values." Insisting on the complete disjunction between "values" or goals, on the one hand, and "facts" or consequences on the other, Weber conceived of "values" as occupying a realm beyond reason or argument. This conception frees "rationality" to focus entirely on instrumental calculations, while disallowing a whole range of objections (regarding side effects or excessive social costs, for example) as mere "value" judgments.[17] Technical expertise is powerful for Weber precisely because it is so single-minded.

One might object that the citizenry, or the legislature, or the sovereign—the authority that provides ultimate goals for the state bureaucracy—is rarely so single-minded in its expectations. But Weber's account of bureaucracy does not simply depict impersonal devotion to rules and professional norms as a guarantee of superior effectiveness. It continually slides between this notion and the rather different notion that devotion to impersonal rules and norms is an essential attribute of legitimate authority in modern society.[18] But the latter claim, after all, is only another way of saying that bureaucracies must blind themselves to certain consequences of their decisions, just as courts must, to a large extent, blind themselves to the peculiarities of particular cases to lend an artificial clarity and an artificial air of absolute correctness to legal decisions. In Weber's idealized conception of "bureaucracy," as in ordinary law courts, prudence—the careful balancing of competing goals with an eye to particular circumstances—seems excluded almost entirely by the demand for fixed, impersonal formulas.

Weber's larger outlook has been described as "Kantian" for its insistence that "values" must be treated as ends to themselves, not susceptible to modification or adjustment in the light of instrumental calculations.[19] In truth, Weber's account of bureaucracy is marked throughout by the spirit of Immanuel Kant. Where Weber's sociology merges power and legality in the impersonal forms of bureaucracy, Kant's political philosophy merges freedom and legality in the impersonal norms of morality.

Kant's moral teaching revived the ancient notion that people are not truly free if they allow themselves to be compelled by physical appetite or blind passion. But in his determination to make freedom the absolute end of human conduct, Kant demanded a morality cleansed of any taint of personal feeling or calculation of advantage. He thought this could be achieved by defining morality as adherence to impersonal, universal rules, rules that can be followed in every case without exception. This uncompromising moralism is premised on the assertion that true morality must be indifferent to circumstances and consequences in particular cases, no matter how awkward or tragic.[20] Kant's moral teaching is, in other words, already an explicit celebration of the "spirit of formalistic impersonality." It seems to cast the conscientious bureaucrat as the archetype of human perfection. It was, in fact, well received in the higher reaches of the Prussian state bureaucracy in the late eighteenth century.[21]

Kant himself did not hesitate to apply his moral teachings to politics and to the proper conduct of public officials. Two examples from Kant's legal writings may be useful in illustrating their spirit. On the one hand, Kant's uncompromising moralism leads him to insist that the laws must always be fully enforced, punishment fully exacted, "and woe to him who rummages around in the winding paths of a theory of happiness looking for some advantage to be gained in releasing the criminal from punishment or in reducing the amount of it. . . . If legal justice perishes, it is no longer worthwhile for men to remain alive on this earth."[22] On the other hand, Kant's legalism leads him to assert that the state may not properly punish the murder of an illegitimate baby: "A child born into the world outside marriage is outside of the law (for this is [implied by the concept of] marriage) and consequently it is also outside the protection of the law. The child has crept surreptitiously into the commonwealth (much like prohibited wares) so that its existence as well as its destruction can be ignored (because by right it ought not to have come into existence this way)."[23]

Kant's obsession with adherence to impersonal norms suggests, on the plane of politics, that the laws and those charged with enforcing the laws must uphold obligations transcending the interest and opinions of the citizens—just as, on the plane of morality, moral laws must transcend the selfish interests and personal feelings of the individual who adheres to them. Kant indeed warns that "the well-being of the state must not be confused with the welfare or happiness of the citizens of the state."[24]

In the course of the nineteenth century, a succession of German theorists, beginning with Hegel, drew out the potential implications of this thought. If the state has a higher object than the welfare or happiness of the citizens, then the servants of the state—the professional administrators—must have higher, and more disinterested motives than do ordinary citizens.[25] Weber's account of bureaucracy retains strong elements of this mode of thought in its repeated suggestions that legality and impersonal formalism—rather than public approval—underlie the legitimacy of governmental bureaucracy. At the same time, Weber reverts to the comprehensive spirit of Kant's moralism by suggesting that the rationality or impersonality of government bureaucracy is simply the most prominent feature of a larger trend toward rationalization—and consequent bureaucratization—of all aspects of social life. But perhaps it was true by Weber's time that great masses of Germans had imbibed the notion that discipline and obedience to rules were somehow good in themselves.

It is always dangerous to judge thinkers by their followers, and thoughts—or rather the mental habits and slogans derived from serious thought—by its consequences. Still, it may not be altogether out of place to recall that Weber's conception of bureaucracy did, after all, find its most hideous fulfillment in Germany. Adolf Eichmann, who greatly disapproved of spontaneous or unauthorized violence against Jews, pursued his program of mass murder in a "spirit of formalistic impersonality . . . without hatred or passion. . . ." He claimed to have had no personal ill will toward Jews and invoked Kant's teachings by name in explaining why he felt a moral obligation to follow out his monstrous official orders in a conscientious and devoted manner.[26] However bizarre and demented it may seem, this plea is a chilling reminder that the mechanical spirit of bureaucracy has roots, after all, in a peculiar, compulsive moralism.

Politics and Human Nature

Impersonal norms do not loom so large in the world of classical liberalism. The American Founders felt no compulsion to invest law— at least human law—with a high moral dignity. Regarding government as properly founded in consent—the consent of actual human beings—they saw no need to elevate the dignity of "the state" above the private concerns of ordinary citizens. Law can be limited in its moral authority for the founders because government is limited in its moral ambitions. It is almost sufficient for the laws to protect private property and personal liberty.

In a curious way, the limitation of government proves a liberation for politics in the liberalism of the founders. Only the judiciary, the special guardian of private property and private rights under the law, must be above or outside of politics. Kant, while acknowledging in theory the classic threefold separation of powers, insists that executive officials must, like the judges, have life tenure in office and must follow the law unswervingly. The legislature is reduced to highly abstract generalities.[27] Weber's sociology, while purporting to describe rationalizing tendencies rather than pronounce moral imperatives, similarly depicts bureaucracy as resistant to control by political officials or parliamentary bodies—just as the logic of German idealism, more and more of government tends to be judicialized in spirit.[28]

By contrast, the American founders were more accepting of politics in government because they were more accepting of human nature. They did not think it possible or desirable to exclude all selfish passions from government, except in the very limited confines of judgment in individual lawsuits. They were, in consequence, less hostile to politics. This is perhaps only another way of saying that the American founders had limited expectations for law. "Parchment barriers" might be sufficient to shield individuals from particular intrusions, because judges might be detached and impartial in contemplating individual cases.[29] But "parchment barriers" could not be relied upon to stop political designs backed by the passion and interest of many.

By their own standard, looking to the natural rights of people, the founders were quite aware that justice could be threatened by every part of government. As *The Federalist* puts it: "what are many of the most important acts of legislation but so many judicial determinations, not indeed concerning the rights of single persons, but concerning the rights of large bodies of citizens? And what are the different classes of legislators but advocates and parties to the causes which they determine?"[30]

Still, it did not occur to the American Founders to try to solve the problem of factional self-dealing in government with an autonomous bureaucracy. In the same decade that Kant published his celebration of impartial legalism in Prussia, *The Federalist* dismissed the notion out of hand: "creating a will in the community independent of the majority—that is, of the society itself" would be "but a precarious security" for minority rights because "a power independent of the society may as well espouse the unjust views of the major as the rightful interests of the minor party and may possibly be turned against both."[31] Nor did it occur to the founders to claim that impersonal detachment— the protection for rights in lawsuits—could be a standard for good performance in government by itself. They assumed that a government dedicated to protecting rights would have to be responsive to the personal concerns—one might even say, selfish concerns—that rights in turn protect.

The Federalist thus praises the continental scale of the federal government for embracing such a variety of competing interests that no one faction will be able to impose its selfish designs. The multiplicity of interests does not make legislators indifferent to particular interests or particular constituencies, but it can provide a check on extreme partiality. Similarly, *The Federalist* praises the arrangement of powers in the federal Constitution precisely because it does not depend on "better motives" but rather summons personal "ambition" or "the interest of the man" to animate the duties of the official.

Locke on the Executive Power

The institutional implications of this perspective are already apparent in John Locke's *Second Treatise*, which deserves a brief glance here for the way it prefigures the argument of *The Federalist*. Locke stresses the importance of "settled, standing laws" so that individuals may be secured against arbitrary assaults on their persons or property.[32] The law must be general to ensure that it does not become an instrument of oppression. And the legislative power should be separated from the executive to ensure that those who make the laws cannot place themselves above the law.[33] But the enforcement or execution of laws is not simply governed by impersonal norms in Locke's account. It is not even governed by single-minded devotion to the particular standards proclaimed in the laws. Rather, inasmuch as laws are designed for the protection of personal rights, the executive has an independent claim to act for the same end.

In the state of nature, according to Locke, each person already has rights to protect his own life and property and the duty to respect the rights of others. Consequently, each person has a power to demand compensation for wrongs against him and also a distinct power to punish those who do wrong to others. In civil society, the laws must protect the right to seek personal redress by establishing impartial judges to hear such claims. But Locke never suggests that each person has an *obligation* to seek redress for wrongs against that person—as a German jurist argued, quite seriously, in the nineteenth century[34]—because, in Locke's scheme, rights serve the end of allowing each person to judge his own interest for himself. And it is not always in one's own interest to insist on full redress and bear the cost of obtaining it. In the same way, Locke argues that the civil magistrate, who inherits the original power of each person to inflict punishment for wrongs against others, need not insist on punishment in every case. Where Kant questions the propriety of any sort of pardon power, Locke takes it for granted that the executive must have the power to remit penalties where punishment is not necessary to deter future wrongdoing.[35]

More generally, it does not occur to Locke to demand, as Kant would later do, that officials must blind themselves to the tragic consequences of full adherence to the law in particular cases. Where the ultimate purpose of the law—"the preservation of [the life, liberty and property of] all as much as may be"[36]—is better served by leniency or by departing from the letter of the law, it is obvious, for Locke, that the executive must follow his own best judgment about "the publick good."

In practice, of course, it is rarely obvious *when* "the publick good" will be better served by departures from the law. Locke almost always refers to the executive in the singular, as if it were one person. Even in Locke's day, no king or minister could personally direct ev-

ery aspect of law enforcement. But Locke's personification of the
executive—whereas judges, by contrast, are often described in plural[37]—draws attention to the element of personal choice and personal
responsibility in executive actions. Locke is not interested in the logic of institutions. He is, on the other hand, quite voluble about the
necessity for the executive to exercise discretion—that is, to make
choices.

The chapter in the *Second Treatise* on executive "prerogative" is
indeed remarkable for the extent to which it collapses the distance
between ordinary and extraordinary occasions and obscures all the
distinctions a legalist might offer among routine discretion within the
law, acts technically unauthorized by law, and acts clearly contrary to
law. Everything seems to come under Locke's definition of prerogative as a "power to act according to discretion for the publick good,
without the prescription of law and sometimes even against it." And
Locke's enumeration of the justifications for such power has a comparable sweep:

> since in some governments the Lawmaking Power is not always in
> being and is usually too numerous and so too slow for the dispatch
> requisite to execution: and because also it is impossible to foresee
> and so by laws to provide for, all accidents and necessities that may
> concern the publick; or to make such laws as will do no harm if they
> are executed with an inflexible rigour on all occasions, on all per-
> sons that may come in their way, therefore, there is a latitude left to
> the Executive power, to do many things of choice, which the Laws
> do not prescribe.[38]

This generous view of executive authority might seem rather difficult to reconcile with Locke's claim, earlier in the *Second Treatise*,
that the executive has "no Will, no Power but that of law."[39] But Locke's
point in this claim is that the executive has "no right to obedience"—
no coercive authority over the liberty and property of private citizens—"otherwise than as the publick person vested with the Power
of the Law." It is only in this capacity that the executive has "no
Will, no Power but that of Law." Similarly, Locke warns that "Wher-
ever Law ends Tyranny begins," but immediately adds the qualification, "if the law be transgressed to another's harm"[40]—in a context
where "harm" refers to immediate threats to life and property.

While these qualifications take care of the problem of leniency or
executive actions not directly affecting private rights, they do not, of
course, fully solve the problem of reconciling forceful emergency actions

with "law." Nor can there be much reassurance from Locke's acknowledgment that the legislature may have open-ended prerogatives "defined by positive law":[41] these cannot be much constraint while there continues to be a residual prerogative to "act for the publick Good . . . even against . . . the prescription of law." Locke seems to place ultimate reliance, then, not on legal norms but on the authority of the legislature to replace the holder of executive power and "to punish for any mal-administration against the laws."[42] And beyond this, he points to the inherent right of individuals to revolt against tyrannical government—"this operates not, till the inconvenience is so great, that the majority feel it" and "this the Executive Power or wise princes never need come in danger of . . . [as] 'tis the thing of all others, they have most need to avoid. . . ."[43]

The ultimate check on the executive, then, is political rather than legal, and Locke seems equally comfortable with the resulting implication: the executive must act with discretion to retain political support—for himself and perhaps ultimately for the whole government. The occasions for emergency and action outside the law may be rare, but in pointing to them Locke reminds us why there must be executive discretion regarding smaller matters within the law: "the publick good"—and the rights of individuals standing behind it—cannot always be secured by fixed rules.

Good Administration and the Executive

The Federalist follows very much in the spirit of Locke. It does not begin with a philosophic discussion of the state of nature and the rights people may claim from nature. But five of the first ten papers of *The Federalist* (5, 6, 7, 8, and 9) dwell on the dangers of disunion and civil strife, among the states and even within them. And the moral is clear: government is artificial and governing is, therefore, always a challenge. People will never entirely agree on what it is right for government to do, for "as long as the reason of man continues fallible and he is at liberty to exercise it, different opinions will be formed. . . . The diversity in the faculties of men, from which the rights of property originate, is not less an insuperable obstacle to a uniformity of interests."[44] A government devoted to protecting liberty and property must therefore be strong enough to contend with faction and division—but also nimble enough to retain support.

The duties of the executive, as *The Federalist* presents them, thus

go beyond—and sometimes even beneath—the conscientious application of existing laws. The famous celebration of "energy in the executive" in *Federalist* 70 is strikingly reminiscent of Locke's account
of prerogative. Like Locke, *The Federalist* is eager to associate emergency interventions with routine discretion, dramatic political stands
with narrow administrative decisions:

> Energy in the executive is . . . essential to the protection of the
> community against foreign attacks; *it is not less essential to the steady
> administration of the laws;* to the protection of the community against
> those irregular combinations which sometimes interrupt the ordinary
> course of justice; to the security of liberty against the enterprise and
> assaults of ambition, of faction and of anarchy.[45] [emphasis added]

In the same spirit, *The Federalist* praises the Constitution's provision for unlimited presidential pardon power on the seemingly modest
ground that "without an easy access to exceptions in favor of unfortunate guilt, justice would wear a countenance too sanguinary and
cruel. . . ." But the same passage then moves quickly forward to the
more momentous consideration that "in seasons of insurrection or re-
bellion . . . a well-timed offer of pardon to the insurgents may restore
the tranquility of the commonwealth. . . ."[46]

The Federalist offers no systematic distinction between executive
power and administration. So, for example, a paper on the presidency
asserts that all executive officials "ought to be considered as the as-
sistants and deputies of the Chief Magistrate and on this account they
ought to be subject to his superintendence."[47] Like Locke, *The Federalist* generally refers to "the executive" as if it were one person
and is still more explicit about the basic rationale for unity in the
executive: there must be clear responsibility because executive operations demand continual choices.

But the responsibility of the president, as *The Federalist* presents
it, extends beyond executive details and this also turns out to be true
of "administration." In an early paper, Publius observes that "as a
general rule . . . confidence in and obedience to government will
commonly be proportioned to the goodness or badness of its administration."[48] The observation would be wildly implausible if "administration" referred only to the small details of executive implementation:
people do not, "as a general rule," develop feelings of confidence
and obligation toward governments that execute absurd or onerous
laws with meticulous care. And indeed *The Federalist* stipulates in a
subsequent paper that "administration of government in its largest sense,

comprehends all the operations of the body politic" and only "in its most usual and perhaps most precise signification" is it "limited to executive details. . . ."[49] The Constitution's chief executive, with his veto power assuring him an official role in legislative action, is plainly not "limited to executive details." The "administration" subject to the president's "superintendence" seems no more readily confined.

The linking of administration "in its most precise signification" with administration "in its largest sense" not only extends the reach of the former, however, but makes it, in some ways, hostage to the latter. Administration "in its largest sense" must be political because it rests, in the end, on consent. Thus, the president will be unlikely to exercise the veto power over legislation unless "stimulated . . . by the probability of the sanction of his constituents" or "encouraged by . . . a very respectable proportion of the legislative body whose influence would be united with his in supporting the propriety of his conduct in the public opinion."[50] And this is so, notwithstanding that "the mischiefs of . . . inconstancy and mutability in the laws . . . form the greatest blemish in the character and genius of our [republican] governments."[51] It seems equally clear that in "executive details," too, the "energy" of administration must be tempered by "great caution" for the sake of good administration "in its largest sense." In other words, the fact that confidence and obedience "will commonly be proportioned to the goodness or badness of administration" means that administration must sometimes be adjusted to maintain confidence and obedience.

The Federalist thus calls attention to the fact that even "steady administration" requires an "energetic executive": methodical administrators are not enough. But to sustain its energy the executive must also be cagey and politic. It must cajole and seduce, as well as threaten. And *The Federalist* is quite candid that the benefits of an enlarged federal administration in providing more resources will win support: "The more [federal administration] circulates through those channels and currents in which the passions of mankind naturally flow, the less will it require the aid of the violent and perilous expedients of compulsion."[52]

In sum, *The Federalist* suggests at least three reasons why impersonal norms cannot be the basis of "good administration." First, because government is established to secure definite ends—"private rights" and "the publick good"—the executive will be held responsible for results and not merely for selfless intentions. Second, given human nature and the natural diversity of interests in a free country, opinions about satisfactory results or attainable results are bound to differ. Third, in a free country what the executive can achieve is, in any case, much dependent on the cooperation of others, both within the government and outside: the executive cannot simply order and threaten to realize its objectives. All of these reasons reduce to this: "administration in its largest sense" cannot be fully separated from administration of "executive details" because politics cannot be separated from government. In accounts of bureaucracy inspired by German idealism, political strife and political calculation do indeed seem to disappear. But neither the subjects, nor the beneficiaries, nor the participants in administration are any longer recognizable as full human beings in their accounts.

Administration and the Party System

The large view of administration in *The Federalist* suggests a role for the executive as a kind of central balance wheel in American government. Alexander Hamilton, who wrote the largest share of essays in *The Federalist* (and all the papers specifically devoted to the presidency), did indeed try to implement this vision as President Washington's treasury secretary. It is necessary to recall, however, that Hamilton's conduct soon aroused much alarm and condemnation among leading figures of the founding era. And a prominent place in this opposition was occupied by James Madison, who had earlier collaborated extensively with Hamilton on the essays collected in *The Federalist*.[53]

Hamilton's opponents organized themselves as the "Republican" party—using the name to stress their opposition to the allegedly "monarchist" tendencies of Hamilton and his followers. The Republicans charged that Hamilton was systematically manipulating treasury policy—that is, "executive details"—to win the favor of commercial interests in the cities and mobilizing this political constituency in turn to shape a compliant "administration party" in Congress. While no clear-cut abuses were ever proved against Hamilton, the Republicans did arouse sufficient suspicion and concern to mobilize a powerful opposition party across the country—and in Congress—and their efforts finally drove Hamilton himself to resign from office.

In particular, the Republicans organized a system of congressional committees that kept a watchful eye on "executive details" and allowed Congress to make careful, independent assessments of the otherwise intimidatingly well-"digested" budgetary and legislative recommendations of the treasury secretary and other executive officials.

By 1800, the Republicans had gathered enough popular support to place their own candidate in the presidency, and a succession of Republican presidents thereafter helped to enshrine the Republican view of the Constitution: Congress is the ultimate guardian of the public good and the whole duty of executive officials is simply to enforce the will of Congress. Yet it did not occur to the Republicans to establish or encourage an autonomous professional bureaucracy. They did not seek to extend judicial controls over administrative activity or encourage a judicialized spirit in administrators. This could have run contrary to their own populist outlook, their demands for a government closely accountable to the people. On the contrary, therefore, the Republicans demanded that executive officials pay close heed to the promptings and preferences of congressional committees—committees that were anything but nonpartisan and professional. At the height of their power in 1820, the Republicans even passed a law imposing fixed limits on tenure in all administrative posts, ensuring a continual turnover of patronage and a check on the authority and ambition of experienced officials.[54]

In a number of ways, however, the Republican vision of administration—which has long outlasted the original Republicans—has proved curiously complementary to the Hamilton vision of *The Federalist*. In some ways, the Republican outlook has even helped to sustain the alternative Hamiltonian outlook through all the ups and downs of our constitutional history. For in practice, the Republicans, like *The Federalist*, could not be satisfied with administration carried on by impersonal norms in total isolation from larger political currents. Even in the nineteenth century, therefore, "energetic" presidents like Jackson and Lincoln built support for their larger policies in Congress by systematically catering to party factions in patronage and smaller administrative decisions. On the other hand, presidents could, even in the nineteenth century, enhance their authority by posing as the champions of administrative honesty and efficiency against the partisan or factional promptings of congressional committees.[55] Republican rhetoric about administrative fidelity to law, though usually trumpeted in the halls of Congress, could easily be turned against Congress—a fact the Founders certainly anticipated and one of the principal reasons they went to such lengths to devise a mode of selection for the president that would make him independent of Congress.[56]

The administrative system that has come down to us indeed still bears the impress of the Founders' handiwork and still in many ways follows the expectations of *The Federalist*. The movement for civil service reform in the decades after the Civil War did—as intended— eventually remove the mass of lower-level federal jobs from the patronage coffers of party politicians.[57] Compared to the leaders of almost any other Western democracy, however, a new American president appoints an enormous number of new administrative officials, implanting his personal or partisan followers rather deeply into the permanent departments and agencies.[58] Conversely, whereas parliamentary majorities must support "their" cabinets in Western Europe, the American Congress can scrutinize, criticize, prompt, and pressure executive agencies with abandon—and it usually does. The system may not often allow for the sort of masterful presidential coordination sometimes suggested in *The Federalist*'s papers on the executive. But it does display the logic that *The Federalist* itself has made famous—the logic of a system where power is widely distributed, where "ambition" is "made to check ambition" so there is less need to rely on "enlightened statesmen" and "higher motives."

Politics and Administration

There has plainly been a good deal of foreign influence on our thinking in this century that has also marked our current patterns of governmental administration. For several decades after the turn of the century, the new academic discipline of "public administration"—many of whose founding figures studied in German universities in their formative years—continually preached the need to separate "politics" from "administration."[59] The predictable and very much intended effect of this division was to narrow the range of political debate and limit the opportunities for political compromise, while elevating the authority of the ostensibly impartial, administrative expert.

This ideological program was most influential in municipal politics, where the abuses of low-level patronage politics were often quite flagrant in the early decades of this century.[60] But it has left some important legacies in federal administration, as well. Among the most notable are the independent regulatory commissions, most of which were established in the 1930s, amidst the great expansion of federal controls associated with the New Deal.

The commissions are "independent" in the sense that the president cannot remove commissioners at will, as he can with all policy-level officials in executive agencies and departments. When the Interstate Commerce Commission, the prototype of the other commissions, was established in the late nineteenth century to regulate interstate railroad rates, nothing was said about the president's power to remove the commissioners.[61] The "independence" of the commissions was not fully established, in fact, until the 1930s, when President Franklin D. Roosevelt tried to remove a Republican appointee to the Federal Trade Commission over disagreements on basic commission policy.

In an ensuing court challenge to this action by the deposed commissioner, the Supreme Court ruled against the president. The FTC commissioner, it held, was "an officer who exercises no part of the executive power vested by the Constitution in the president" because the commissioners were "charged with no policy except the policy of the law."[62] Since "the policy" of the Federal Trade Commission Act was little more than a vague prohibition on "unfair methods of competition," this ruling expressed remarkable confidence in the ability of commissioners to discern the true nature of unfairness and adhere to their own insights unswervingly. In the same year, in fact, the Supreme Court struck down a prominent New Deal statute authorizing the president to promulgate binding regulations defining standards of "fair competition" in large sectors of the economy. This, the Court held, was an unconstitutional delegation of legislative power to the executive, because the legal standard for executive action was so vague and open-ended.[63] Plainly the Court's willingness to accept an almost equally open-ended power in the Federal Trade Commission reflected its hope that the commission could be insulated from politically motivated "policy."

As a matter of fact, the commissions were no better insulated than most executive agencies from the pressures and promptings of congressional committees. If anything, they may have been (and continue to be) more exposed. Celebrations of administrative expertise, so prominent a theme in New Deal rhetoric,[64] did not greatly intimidate congressional committees intent on gaining accommodations for particular constituencies.[65] But they may have eased some misgivings about extended federal administrative controls into more and more new fields. By the 1960s, appeals to "expertise" did not even go far in soothing consciences. Educated people were more likely to smile with knowing condescension at the notion that officials could be trusted to determine sound policy by impersonal, expert norms. By the late 1960s, liberal opinion had embraced many of the charges popularized by anti–New Deal conservatives, who had characterized "bureaucracy" as sluggish, self-serving, and overly attentive to powerful "special interests."

Liberal opinion in the 1960s and 1970s was still entranced, however, with the notion that politics could be removed from government. Ralph Nader and other champions of the new "public interest" movement denounced the influence of "special interests" and appealed for aid to what they viewed as a more reliably impartial institution— the federal judiciary. Thus courts began, for the first time, to allow suits charging—on behalf of "the public"—that regulatory agencies had not enforced their mandates vigorously or comprehensively enough.[66] When Congress enacted sweeping new controls on air and water pollution in the early 1970s, it included remarkable provisions authorizing "any citizen" to sue administrative officials to compel full enforcement or proper implementation of these measures.[67] This legislative sanction naturally did nothing to deter the courts from allowing such suits against a wide variety of programs where they had not been explicitly authorized by statute.

It is notable, however, that suits demanding more vigorous enforcement of the criminal law have continued to be rejected by the courts without exception.[68] Perhaps old doctrines of executive discretion have been too firmly attached to this core executive function. But it may also be that criminal law enforcement is too vividly associated with force and coercion for contemporary Americans to think of it as a process that can be governed by entirely impersonal, expert norms. In many regulatory fields, like pollution control, enthusiasts can suppose that higher "values" are at stake, which should properly exempt administrative programs from pressures for political compromise, from recognition of awkward policy trade-offs in the real world. Thus, the purpose of judicial intervention in contemporary "public interest" cases, says a prominent professor of law, is "no longer primarily to protect private rights but instead to facilitate identification and implementation of the values at stake in regulation."[69]

The longing to separate politics from administration is, then, still very powerful. And the current appeal to "values" is not, after all, so removed in its theoretical roots from an earlier generation's appeal to "expertise." None of this is altogether surprising. As our expectations for federal administration have expanded, we find it hard to know how to judge its performance. We grasp for authoritative standards—though the expansion of federal administration in this century has plainly been driven forward by the denial that there are any authoritative limits on government.

Our contemporary confusions would probably not have surprised the authors of *The Federalist*. They understood that "the latent causes of faction are sown in the nature of man."[70] The most that could be done to remove division, without ending liberty, would be to remove the most dangerous sources of division—such as "a zeal for different opinions concerning religion"[71]—from the responsibility of government altogether. They might not have been surprised that, as we ask more of government than we used to, we have come to think that "politics" should concern itself with "values" or "ideals" that soar far beyond the details of administration. Still, they would probably have been astonished by the contemporary notion that the "goodness or badness" of our "administration" can be settled by impersonal, nonpolitical standards.

Notes

1. See, e.g., Peter Woll, *American Bureaucracy*, 2d ed. (New York: Norton, 1979).
2. See, e.g., Gabriel A. Almond and G. Bingham Powell Jr., *Comparative Politics: A Developmental Approach* (Boston: Little, Brown, 1966), 155 ("bureaucracy as the core of modern government") and 158 ("Other governmental structures, such as political executives, legislatures and courts, must be viewed in relation to the functioning of bureaucracy").
3. For a penetrating elaboration of this strangely myopic perspective, see Samuel H. Huntington, *Political Order in Changing Societies* (New Haven: Yale University Press, 1968).
4. William Blackstone, *Commentaries on the Laws of England*, vol. 2, facsimile of the first edition, 1765–1769 (Chicago: University of Chicago Press, 1979), 496.
5. Hamilton, Madison, and Jay. *The Federalist*, ed. Clinton Rossiter (New York: New American Library, 1961), 72: 435.
6. Fritz Morstein Marx, *The Administrative State: An Introduction to Bureaucracy* (Chicago: University of Chicago Press, 1957), 17.
7. Weber's fullest discussion of the need to separate "values" from social science analysis appears in a paper on scientific method, originally delivered in 1913, which can be found in translation as "Value-judgments in Social Science," in *Max Weber: Selections in Translation*, ed. W. G. Runciman (London: Cambridge University Press, 1978). The most celebrated critique of this position is in Leo Strauss, *Natural Right and History* (Chicago: University of

Chicago Press, 1953), 36–78, which, however, focuses on other examples in Weber's sociological work and does not pursue the consequences of this perspective for Weber's view of bureaucracy.

8. Talcott Parsons, ed. and trans., *The Theory of Social and Economic Organization* (New York: Oxford University Press, 1974), 339. The distinctions are not quite the same because Weber uses "formal rationality" to mean the achievement of given, subsidiary objectives or the satisfaction of given, subsidiary standards, as contrasted with the attainment of ultimate goals or standards (which he calls "substantive rationality"). But ultimate goals or "values" cannot, in Weber's view, be rational, and this is what makes them ultimate: they do not serve some further or higher objective.

9. Ibid., 328–29, 341–45, 358–63.

10. Ibid., 337, 339–40.

11. Ibid., 340.

12. Ibid., 338.

13. Ibid., 337.

14. See, e.g., Carl Friedrich, "Some Observations on Weber's Analysis of Bureaucracy," in Robert K. Merton, ed., *Reader in Bureaucracy* (New York: Free Press, 1952).

15. Weber's personal and political reservations about the spirit of bureaucracy in general—and the state bureaucracy in his own Wilhelmine Germany, in particular—are reviewed in J. G. Merquior, *Rousseau and Weber: Two Studies in the Theory of Legitimacy* (London: Routledge & Kegan Paul, 1980), 117–21.

16. Parsons, *The Theory of Social and Economic Organization,* 340.

17. By Weber's own terminology, objections regarding undesired side effects would not be "value" judgments unless they concerned ultimate goals. But once an ultimate goal or "value" is itself the goal, Weber's view implies that no objection can be admitted without compromising the ultimate status of "values." In other words, there is no rational basis in politics for preferring the statesman to the ideologue, the reasonable or prudent person to the fanatic. And Weber's entire discussion of bureaucratic "rationality" and "efficiency" abstracts from the question of what sort of people or what sort of government directs the bureaucracy at the top—as if this made no difference to the merits of bureaucratic organization.

18. Note that Weber's most extended discussion of bureaucracy, in *The Theory of Social and Political Organization,* occurs in the context of a larger exposition of "types of legitimate authority," where "bureaucracy" is presented as the characteristic manifestation of "rational-legal authority." Where unquestioned tradition or devotion to a mystically anointed leader are the only alternatives to the bureaucratic mode of authority, the claims of bureaucracy to "rationality" are bound to seem more than merely formal.

19. Strauss, *Natural Right and History,* 60, n. 22.

20. The most notorious illustration is Kant's claim that it is wrong to lie even when necessary to save another's life ("On a Supposed Right to Lie from a Benevolent Motive").

21. Hans Rosenberg, *Bureaucracy, Aristocracy and Autocracy: The Prussian Experience, 1660–1815* (Boston: Beacon Press, 1966), 189.
22. Kant, *The Metaphysical Elements of Justice,* trans. John Ladd (Indianapolis: Bobbs-Merrill, 1965), 100.
23. Ibid., 106.
24. Ibid., 83.
25. Hegel thus denounced the "vulgar presupposition" that representative assemblies were more to be trusted than the permanent civil service. This notion, "characteristic of the rabble," ignores the fact that representative assemblies "start from isolated individuals, from a private point of view, from particular interest," which they are inclined to pursue "at the expense of the general interests," while the civil servants "explicitly take up the standpoint of the state from the start and devote themselves to the general end" (*Philosophy of Right,* trans. T. M. Knox [Oxford: Clarendon Press, 1952], p. 196).
26. Hannah Arendt, *Eichmann in Jerusalem* (New York: Viking Press, 1965), 136–37.
27. See Kant, *The Metaphysical Elements of Justice,* 96.
28. Thus Hegel distinguishes "the monarchy" from "the executive" in order to separate the personal willfulness of the sovereign—as in exercising his power to pardon—from the duties of civil servants. He then does not hesitate to include the judiciary in the "the executive"—an "executive" now sufficiently purified of personal willfulness to be a fit home for judges. See *Philosophy of Right,* 188. On the importance of "public law" training and thinking for German notions of administration in the century after Hegel, see Kenneth Dyson, *The State Tradition in Western Europe* (New York: Oxford University Press, 1980).
29. The phrase "parchment barriers" has become famous. But it is often forgotten that it first appears (in *Federalist,* 48: 308) not in connection with guarantees of particular civil rights but in the context of a warning about the difficulty of separating the different powers of government from each other. Each power can only "be effactually restrained from passing the limits assigned to it [a]fter discriminating . . . in theory the several classes of power, as they may in their nature be legislative, executive or judiciary. . . ." The independence of the judiciary, therefore, can only be effactually defended against legislative encroachments when powers "in their nature" judicial have been distinguished in theory from the overall power of government. And there powers must be rather limited. Indeed, in No. 51, where this discussion of the need to maintain each power in its place reaches its immediate culmination, *The Federalist* still concedes that in "republican governments, the legislative authority necessarily predominates" (322). And the ultimate culmination of the argument, it might be said, comes in No. 84 where the omission of a bill of rights from the Constitution is defended on the grounds that the proper arrangement of powers within the Constitution is "in every rational sense and to every useful purpose a bill of rights" (515). Where efficacy or usefulness is the standard of "every rational sense," "parchment barriers" and judicial devotion to parchment provisions can have only a limited role to play.

30. *Federalist*, 10: 79.

31. *Federalist*, 51: 323–24.

32. John Locke, "An Essay Concerning the True Original Extent and End of Civil Government" (*Second Treatise*), in *Two Treatises of Government*, ed. Peter Laslett (New York: New American Library, 1965), ¶137: 405; ¶136: 404; ¶131: 398; ¶124: 396.

33. Ibid., ¶143: 410.

34. This position was urged by Rudolf von Ihering in *Der Kampf ums Recht* (trans. John J. Lalor, *The Struggle for Law* [Chicago: Callaghan, 1879]). Ihering was a proponent of "interest jurisprudence," often regarded as the forerunner of "sociological jurisprudence" in America in the early decades of this century. Ihering held to the seemingly hardheaded, "realist" view that law could be understood as a reflection of the power of dominant groups in society, that is, that the law's assignment of rights and duties should be seen as part of a larger scheme for ordering society from the top down. But then with characteristic German earnestness, he held that every citizen, in his capacity as a bearer of rights, had an obligation to enforce his own rights in every case to see that this scheme was upheld.

35. Locke, *Second Treatise*, ¶11: 314.

36. Ibid., ¶159: 421.

37. E.g., Ibid., ¶136: 404; ¶131: 399. The term "judge" is used in the singular in describing situations where there is no "common judge" or "no judge on earth"—where the singular reinforces the allusion to the One who renders ultimate judgment from above the earth; and the earthly counterpart here below does not seem to be the members of the judiciary but the legislative or supreme lawmaking power. See ¶89: 369; ¶181: 436; ¶240–41: 476.

38. Ibid., ¶160: 422.

39. Ibid., ¶156: 414.

40. Ibid., ¶202: 448.

41. Ibid., ¶163: 423.

42. Ibid., ¶153: 415.

43. Ibid., ¶168: 427.

44. *Federalist*, 10: 78.

45. *Federalist*, 70: 423.

46. *Federalist*, 74: 447, 449.

47. *Federalist*, 72: 436.

48. *Federalist*, 27: 174.

49. *Federalist*, 72: 435.

50. *Federalist*, 73: 445.

51. *Federalist*, 73: 444.

52. *Federalist*, 27: 176.

53. Two recent accounts, devoting close attention to party doctrine, are Richard Buel, *Securing the Revolution: Ideology in American Politics, 1789–1815* (Ithaca: Cornell University Press, 1972), and Lance Banning, *The Jeffersonian Persuasion* (Ithaca: Cornell University Press, 1978), but neither is entirely convincing in its explanation of Madison's apparent change of heart.

54. Leonard White, *The Jeffersonian: A Study in Administrative History, 1801–1829* (New York: Macmillan, 1956), 348–57, 387–90. White notes that while Jefferson and his immediate successors preferred to appoint "gentlemen"of good social standing, they were under tremendous pressure from congressmen and party leaders to extend the circle of appointees more broadly.

55. See Wilfred Binkley, *President and Congress,* 3d rev. ed. (New York: Vintage Books, 1962), 180–204, describing popular reaction against the Senate "oligarchy" in the Grant administration and the authority this gave to Presidents Hayes, Arthur, and Cleveland in resisting senatorial patronage and clientalist service demands.

56. The founders' concern for executive independence as a safeguard of administrative order and integrity is emphasized in Charles Thach, *The Creation of the Presidency, 1775–1789,* Johns Hopkins University Studies in Historical and Political Science, vol. 40 (Baltimore: Johns Hopkins University Press, 1922), esp. 554–79. Thach's book was reissued by Johns Hopkins in 1969.

57. The dominant concern of civil service reform advocates in the decades after the Civil War was not corruption but waste and expense in administration, as the patronage system provided continual incentives to expand the number of federal offices and fill them with untrained people. Even in later years, it was not so much the corruption of administration that troubled the reformers as the corruption of politics—as politicians, so it was charged, became preoccupied with thousands of low-level patronage appointments, nearly to the exclusion of basic policy concerns. See Leonard White, *The Republican Era: 1869–1901, A Study in Administrative History* (New York: Macmillan, 1958), pp. 295–301.

58. J. W. Macy, Bruce Adams, and J. Jackson Walters, eds., *America's Unelected Government* (Cambridge, Mass.: Bollinger, 1983) reports 4,000 direct presidential appointees in the federal administration, but this figure includes diplomatic and advisory posts. Hugh Heclo, *A Government of Strangers* (Washington, D.C.: Brookings Institution, 1977), 38, estimates 3,800 "political" appointees in the regular federal bureaucracy, though not all these appointments are made directly in the name of the president. For a suggestive survey of the differences in civil service career paths in the United States compared with Western Europe, see Edward C. Page, *Political Authority and Bureaucratic Power* (Knoxville: University of Tennessee Press, 1985), 15–30.

59. Frank Goodnow, for example, often credited as the "father of public administration" as an academic discipline in the United States, was one of the earliest exponents of the need for a strict separation between "politics" and "administration." Goodnow studied administrative law in Germany in his youth and his turn-of-the-century text on comparative administrative law is particularly striking for its strange pairing of administrative patterns in Imperial Germany and the United States, which it sets in contrast to "parliamentary" systems like Britain and France. On the general influence and appeal of German patterns in American thinking about administration before the First World War, see Barry Karl, "Executive Reorganization and Presidential Power," in *The Supreme Court*

Review: 1977, ed. Philip Kurland (Chicago: University of Chicago Press, 1978), 1–37.

60. For a dismayed account of municipal corruption by an otherwise rather admiring foreign observer of the period, see James Bryce, *The American Commonwealth*, vol. 2 (New York: Century, 1889), 111.

61. Robert Cushman, *The Independent Regulatory Commissions* (New York: Oxford University Press, 1941), 65.

62. *Humphrey's Executor v. U.S.*, 295 U.S. 602 (1935) at 628, 624.

63. *Schechter Poultry Corp. v. U.S.*, 295 U.S. 495 (1935).

64. See, e.g., James M. Landis, *The Administrative Process* (New Haven: Yale University Press, 1938), esp. 23–26.

65. Marver P. Bernstein, *Regulating Business by Independent Commission* (Princeton: Princeton University Press, 1955), chap. 3.

66. The most important early cases were *Office of Communication of United Church of Christ v. FCC*, 359F.2d 994 (1966) demanding that the Federal Communications Commission withdraw a TV broadcasting license from a station charged by the appellant with poor service to the public, and *Scenic Hudson Preservation Conference v. FPC*, 354F.2d 608 (1966), demanding that the Federal Power Commission deny a license for constructing a power plant that appellants charged would disrupt the scenic splendor of the surrounding area.

67. See, e.g., §304 of the 1970 Clean Air Act Amendments, now codified at 42 U.S.C. §7604.

68. See *U.S. v. Nixon,* 418 U.S. 683 (1974) at 693; *Linda R.S. v. Richard D.,* 410 U.S. 614 (1973) at 619; and most recently, *Nathan v. Smith,* 737F.2d 1069 (1984) at 1079.

69. Cass Sunstein, "Deregulation and Hard Look Doctrine," *Supreme Court Review* 177 (1983): 178.

70. *Federalist*, 10: 79.

71. Ibid.

7

Administrative Responsibility and the Separation of Powers

David K. Nichols

To whom are administrators responsible? There are three possible answers to this question: to the laws as passed by Congress and interpreted by the courts, to the chief executive who is their boss, or to themselves based upon their political independence or technical expertise. There is some truth to be found in each of these answers, but the relative merits of each of these claims must ultimately be judged in light of our constitutional system. The Constitution created and defined the powers of the national government, and it remains the best guide for understanding the operation of our political system.

The most important feature of our constitutional system is the separation of powers. Although it is the most important feature, it is not the best-understood feature. First, many people fail to appreciate the importance of the distinction between a separation of powers and a separation of power. Those who understand our system as a separation of power generally believe that power is one dimensional, and always dangerous. From this perspective, power is divided in order to decrease its potential danger. There is much support for this view in the writings of the Founders.[1] There is no mistaking their belief that the creation of different branches of government would create a safer and more restrained government.

But this understanding suffers from one serious drawback. It fails to take into account the fact that the Founders did not just divide power, they also took great pains to define different types of power. They created a separation of powers, not merely a separation of power. The different branches of government that reflect these different kinds of power would check and balance one another to ensure a due restraint on the part of those wielding power. But they would also serve another function; they would make the government more efficient and more effective. We too often forget that the Constitution was written in 1787, not 1776. It was written after years of experience with a weak central government, and it was written because of the growing recognition that a government that was too weak might be as dangerous to liberty as a government that was too powerful. Thus, the reason for the separation of powers was in part to encourage a government more capable of exercising power effectively in the name of liberty.

The Founders understood that the tasks of government were not simple and that no one organizational structure was well suited to performing all of these various tasks. Representation of diverse opinions and interests could best be handled by a multimember legislature elected for a relatively brief term. The execution of the laws would be more effective if it were under the direction of a single voice. The impartiality of the law could best be protected by a judicial branch that was insulated from immediate popular opinion. These were not the only considerations, but they are illustrative of the ways in which the definition of different powers, and their placement in different branches designed with their distinctive functions in mind, would help to overcome the problems that had led the delegates to Philadelphia in 1787.

How does the doctrine of the separation of powers help us to come to grips with the issues of administrative responsibility? Does it not instead show us the limitations of the separation of powers? Administration does not fit neatly under the umbrella of any of the three branches of government. It would appear to lie at the intersection of executive and legislative power. Administrators carry out the laws, and therefore serve Congress. However, the execution of general laws in specific circumstances usually leaves room for discretion. One reason for the creation of an independent executive branch was to provide a coherent direction for the exercise of that discretion. Without a unified executive branch, the execution of the laws would be ineffective and inefficient. Thus, both the legislative and executive branches have a claim to control administration.

We are frequently left at an impasse when these claims come into conflict. Imagine you are a career civil servant sitting in your office at the Department of Housing and Urban Development. You receive a call from the chair of the Senate committee in charge of your program telling you to do one thing. Then you receive a call from the

White House telling you to do the opposite. What do you do? This is not an abstract problem. It requires a clear and immediate answer. The senator contends that we have a government of laws, and that Congress must therefore have the final say. The president argues that the legislature is institutionally incapable of overseeing an effective execution of the laws. As an administrator you are asked to choose between two competing views of our constitutional system. You must choose either a system based on the rule of law (but that may be unable to respond to particular circumstances) or a system capable of exercising power effectively, but lacking the restraint and protection of law. You could say in theory that there is some truth to each position, but that does you no good in practice. You must know what to do.

One alternative is to ignore both claims and simply do what you think is best. You have a job virtually for life. You were hired because of your expertise in this area, and you have no particular political agenda. Would not the country be best served if you simply did the job the best way you know how, and ignore politics? Perhaps, but there is one problem with this approach. To whom are you responsible? "To thine own self be true" may be good advice to individuals, but is it the proper principle to guide a political system? What happens to democracy in such a system? Without some mechanism of political accountability, administrators would become a class of philosopher kings. This might be wonderful in theory, but few would want to accept it in practice.

So where should the administrator turn in practice? He should turn to the Constitution. It is in the Constitution that we can learn of the different types of power and of the ways in which those powers are to be held politically accountable. From the Constitution we learn that the question of administrative responsibility is complex, but that the institutional arrangements created by the Constitution provide mechanisms to ensure responsibility. They also embody principles that help us to evaluate the competing claims to control the discretion of administrators.

Of course, one of the most important institutional mechanisms is the independent judiciary, one of whose functions is to defend the Constitution against the short-term political interests of the political branches. The Court performs this function by serving as the voice and conscience of the Constitution, but the Court does not perform this function flawlessly. Judicial politics, as we will see, often gets in the way. Advocates of judicial restraint may be reluctant to deny to

the executive or the legislature the right to interpret their own powers. They may be tempted to leave disputes between the legislature
and executive to be settled in the political arena, labeling such disputes as political questions. Judicial activists may see the Court as
merely another political branch. According to this view, constitutional interpretation is merely a guise under which minority interests are
to be protected or "good" policy promoted, when the political branches
fail to do their job or act too slowly.

Nonetheless, I think that by examining a series of Supreme Court
decisions on the separation of powers, we can come to better understand the constitutional perspective on administrative responsibility.
In my opinion, the Court has erred in a number of these cases. But by
coming to grips with the Court's difficulty in recognizing its own
position in the separation of powers framework, we will shed important light on the question of the relationship between discretion and
law that lies at the core of the issue of administrative responsibility.

We will look first at the two crucial cases on the removal power,
Myers v. United States and *Humphrey's Executor v. United States*, to
find the Court's defense of an independent executive branch with
discretionary authority. Although the Court does establish the principle of executive independence in these cases, it leaves open some
important questions regarding political responsibility. We will turn
next to the majority opinions in the independent counsel and sentencing commission cases. In these cases, the Court fails to take seriously the significance of the separation of powers, and thus allows
the creation of institutions lacking accountability or responsibility.
We will then look at two dissenting opinions by Justice Scalia that
point us back to a constitutional understanding of the separation of
powers. We will also attempt to explain how partisan politics and
judicial politics have thwarted the attainment of such an understanding, and therefore undercut the principle of political accountability.

The Removal Power and the Principle
of Executive Independence

The power to remove subordinate officials is one of the most important in establishing responsibility. An employee has an obvious
interest in heeding instructions from the person who can fire him.
That is why the question of whether the president could remove executive branch officials without Senate approval led to some of the

most dramatic confrontations between the Congress and the president in the nineteenth century. Although James Madison successfully argued in the first Congress that the president possessed a unilateral removal power, there was no explicit mention of it in the Constitution.[2] Even such a renowned supporter of a strong executive as Alexander Hamilton contended in *The Federalist Papers* that the Senate would have to approve removals just as it approved appointments.[3] Andrew Jackson's removal of his secretary of the treasury, contrary to the wishes of the Senate, led to his censure, and Andrew Johnson's violation of the Tenure of Office Act, passed explicitly to establish the right of the Senate to veto removals, led to Johnson's impeachment. However, it was not until 1926 and the case of *Myers v. United States* that the Supreme Court rendered an opinion on this subject.

Myers had served as postmaster of Portland, Oregon, for several years, but in an effort to redistribute spoils, the Democratic Party under Woodrow Wilson ordered Myers's removal. Rather than go quietly, Myers protested, claiming that, by statute, the president could not remove a postmaster without the approval of the Senate. Chief Justice William Howard Taft, writing the majority opinion of the Court, accepted most of the arguments that had been made earlier by Madison and Jackson. He claimed that Senate participation in removal would be an unconstitutional infringement on the legitimate sphere of executive authority, because it would rob the president of the authority necessary to carry out his constitutional responsibilities as head of the executive branch. Taft was clear that the doctrine of legislative supremacy was inconsistent with the constitutional separation of powers.

Taft, however, recognized some limits on the president's removal powers. Congress could have legitimately restricted the removal power of the president over inferior officers, just as it had done in the creation of the Civil Service. There were limits on the president's removal power, but, according to Taft, they did not apply in this case. The reason they did not apply, Taft argued, was that first-class postmasters were appointed by the president with the advice and consent of the Senate:

> Congress deemed appointment by the President with the consent of the Senate essential to the public welfare, and, until it is willing to vest their appointment in the head of the Department, they will be subject to removal by the President alone, and any legislation to the contrary must fall as in conflict with the Constitution.[4]

According to Taft, the appointment and removal power are essentially executive and may be limited only under certain specific circumstances spelled out in the Constitution. Under the Constitution, the president is empowered to appoint the heads of departments and other important executive branch officials with the advice and consent of the Senate. The president's power is limited only in regard to inferior officers, who may be appointed by the president alone, the heads of departments, or the courts. Congress may place limits on presidential removal only when it has determined:

> first that the officer is inferior, and second that it is willing that the office shall be filled by appointment by some other authority than the President with the consent of the Senate.[5]

The *Myers* case clearly does not meet the second criterion. It is more analogous to the conditions described in *Shurtleff v. United States* (1903). There the Court concluded:

> Congress has regarded the office of sufficient importance to make it proper to fill it by appointment by the President and confirmed by the Senate. It has thereby classed it as appropriately coming under the direct supervision of the President.[6]

Taft's opinion, I believe, fails in only one particular. He is willing to concede that the postmaster of Portland is an inferior officer, but in so doing, Taft appears to create a third category of office—"important inferior offices." These important inferior offices are identified by the fact that they are to be appointed by the president with the advice and consent of the Senate. But this new category of offices is not found in the Constitution.

If these offices are of "sufficient importance" to warrant presidential appointment and senatorial consent, why should we not consider them to be principal offices? Would it not be more logical to conclude that the method of appointment was the clearest way to distinguish between principal and inferior offices under the Constitution? Offices appointed by the president with senatorial consent are principal offices, and those appointed by other means are inferior. Rather than create this strange hybrid of "important inferior offices," it is more logical to conclude that when Congress decides that an office is of sufficient importance to warrant presidential appointment and Senate consent, it has determined that such offices are principal offices. It might seem odd to speak of a Portland postmaster as a principal executive officer, and that fact might lead Congress to reconsider its decision to use presidential appointment and Senate consent in this instance. Nonetheless, the failure of Congress to use the appropriate method of appointment in this case in no way undermines the principle that the method of appointment is the best indicator of the importance of the office.

Although Taft did not suggest that the method of appointment be used as a dividing line between principal and inferior offices, he clearly accepted the rationale that the Constitution associated important executive offices with presidential appointment and senatorial consent. Moreover, he concluded that it was only within the sphere of inferior executive offices that limits on the president's removal power are found.

These possible qualifications on the removal power came to light more clearly in the 1935 case of *Humphrey's Executor v. United States.* William Humphrey was a member of the Federal Trade Commission during the New Deal. President Franklin Roosevelt, however, thought that Humphrey was thwarting New Deal policies and should be replaced. When Humphrey refused to offer his resignation, FDR removed him from office. Humphrey died shortly after his removal, but his wife brought suit claiming that FDR had no power to remove a member of an independent regulatory commission. Independence could be maintained only if the president were forbidden to remove commissioners for political reasons.

Many thought that the opinion in the *Myers* case provided support for FDR's action. If members of the executive branch were to be held politically responsible through the president's removal power, then that power must extend to all important members of the executive branch, including members of independent regulatory commissions (IRCs). After all, they were appointed by the president with the advice and consent of the Senate. But the Court decided that the IRCs were not simply part of the executive branch. They exercised "quasi-legislative and quasi-judicial functions." Moreover, the reason for their creation was to take certain areas of regulation out of the political arena. Political independence and in some cases technical expertise were to provide the grounds for decision. The threat of presidential removal, it was argued, would inevitably lead to repoliticization.

This decision does raise some troubling questions for maintenance of the separation of powers. The IRCs, by the Court's definition, do not fit neatly into the separation of powers framework. Because they do not, there is no clear means of establishing political responsibili-ty.[7] The IRCs are truly the most elitist institutions in our government.

Although the constitutional status of the IRCs is ambiguous, the Court was drawing, at least indirectly, on some constitutional quali-fications on the president's removal power. The IRCs do perform a quasi-judicial function, and the Constitution recognizes the need for judicial independence. Even though the president may appoint judg-es, he has no power of removal over them. The distinction between inferior and principal offices also comes into play. The reason the president is given less control over inferior offices is that such offic-es are largely involved in carrying out ministerial functions. It is only at the higher levels of administration that significant political discre-tion is exercised. Although in practice it is hard to argue that the IRCs do not exercise considerable political discretion, at least in theory one could claim that in some cases their decisions are based on technical expertise rather than political considerations. Tech-nical decisions may have far-reaching political consequences, but they are more ministerial than political in character. The technician tells us how a political goal can best be achieved but not what the political goal should be. In this sense, the member of the IRC might be seen as an inferior officer, a higher-level version of a civil ser-vant. He is a technical instrument for use by the political process. He can serve his function only if he maintains a certain degree of inde-pendence.[8]

The IRCs point to nonlegislative restraints on the exercise of ex-ecutive power and on the president's power to control appointees. The independent discretionary authority of members of an IRC stands outside the executive branch when it is used to perform a judicial function, but coexists within the executive branch when it is used to perform the technical tasks of an inferior officer. Such discretionary authority does restrict the president's authority. But what is even more interesting is the fact that these pools of discretion do not come un-der the direct power of the legislature, and may even aid the presi-dent in checking the legislature. This discretionary authority is another example of the limits of law. A government of laws cannot work without the existence of individuals wielding discretionary authority. Thus, executive branch discretion, even when beyond the immediate reach of the president, enhances executive power and restricts legislative power.

The judiciary and the IRCs only serve to amplify the point that we can never have simply a government of laws. The laws passed by the legislature provide a framework, a set of guidelines for the exercise of political authority, but both the Constitution and the laws give rise to the exercise of legitimate discretionary authority. While *Myers* established the principle that the administrators are to be held politically accountable to the president, *Humphrey's* leaves open the question of whether there is to be administrative discretion beyond the reach of political control. It is this possibility that ultimately lies behind the decisions in *Morrison v. Olson* and *Mistretta v. United States.*[9]

Morrison and *Mistretta:*
Undermining Responsibility

The independent regulatory commissions grew out of the Progressive belief that "politics" could be replaced by professionalism. According to the Progressives, "political" considerations were partisan and self-interested. They look to the good of special interests and not to the public good. To the extent that decisions could be taken out of the hands of politicians, the Progressives believed, the public good would be better served.

This idea has continued to be influential throughout this century. Whenever the political system is faced with a particularly difficult or divisive issue, there are inevitably calls to stop "playing politics" and act instead to serve the public good. We all understand the motivation for such sentiments. There is something inherently distasteful when politicians address issues only in terms of personal or partisan advantage, with no regard to the substantive policy question itself. The irony is that it is often these self-serving politicians who are first in line to remove a difficult problem from the political realm and place it in the hands of a bipartisan commission or independent agency. These politicians do not act out of some newfound respect for the public interest; they act instead to avoid responsibility. By removing the issue from the political arena, they neutralize the possibility that they will be held accountable for the decision. The issue is addressed by people with no political ax to grind, and the politicians support the solution because it insulates them from criticism.

The problem arises from the fact that it is very difficult to find people who have no political interests or beliefs that may color their decisions. It is difficult to find people who simply know the public interest and how to realize it. From the standpoint of democracy, what is most disturbing is that ultimately such apolitical mechanisms are not accountable to public opinion. That is ultimately what it means to take the politics out of government. It means that the mechanisms of democratic accountability are removed. The desire to stop "playing politics" leads us to deny the important role politics plays in a democracy, the role of ensuring accountability.

Unfortunately, the Court has not always appreciated this problem sufficiently. In the 1988 case of *Morrison v. Olson*, the Court concluded that political independence was the only way to deal with potential political corruption in the executive branch. The Court's majority did not appreciate the extent to which this decision might undermine the ability of the executive to carry out its legitimate constitutional functions or the extent to which it would undermine the principle of democratic accountability.

Theodore Olson was assistant attorney general for the Office of Legal Counsel. The chair of the House Judiciary Committee sent a report to the attorney general requesting the appointment of an independent counsel to investigate allegations that Olson had given false and misleading testimony to Congress. Under the Ethics in Government Act of 1978, the attorney general is required to appoint an independent counsel if there are "reasonable grounds" to believe that further investigation or prosecution is warranted. Attorney General Edwin Meese, assuming that it would be impossible to say there were no reasonable grounds for further investigation, given the Judiciary Committee's request, called for the appointment of a special prosecutor. As provided by the statute, a Special Court of Appeals appointed Alexia Morrison as independent counsel. When Morrison asked a grand jury to issue a subpoena to Olson, Olson moved to quash the subpoena, on the grounds that the independent counsel provisions of the act were unconstitutional. He argued that the existence of an independent counsel not under the control of the attorney general and the president was an unconstitutional violation of the separation of powers.

Writing for a seven-judge majority (Justice Anthony Kennedy recused himself), Chief Justice William Rehnquist defended the creation of the independent counsel. Rehnquist claimed that the constitutionality of the independent counsel should rest on the distinction in *Myers* between inferior and principal executive officers. Principal executive officers must be removable by the president because they exercise political discretion, but inferior officers, such as civil servants, may be insulated from immediate political control. According to Rehnquist, independent counsels fall clearly into the category of inferior officers.

Even though Morrison might not be simply subordinate to the attorney general insofar as she possessed independent discretion, Rehnquist first argued, her possible removal by the attorney general does indicate some degree of inferiority. Second, she was to perform only certain limited duties, such as the investigation and possible prosecution of certain federal crimes. Third, her jurisdiction is limited, because the act applies only to certain federal officials. Finally, although there is no precise time limit on the appointment, her tenure is limited to the time necessary to complete her specific task.

Rehnquist was aware of several objections that could be raised against his position. He noted that the decision to vest the appointment of the special prosecutor in the judiciary would violate the principles of the separation of powers if there were some "incongruity between the functions normally performed by the courts and the performance of their duty to appoint."[10] But given the fact that the act forbids judges of the Special Division to participate in any matters related to the special prosecutor they have appointed, Rehnquist concluded that there was no conflict. He also recognized that some might object to the fact that the restriction of the removal power to "good cause" would undermine the president's control of the executive branch. In the *Humphrey's* case, the quasi-legislative and quasi-judicial functions of the IRCs were said to justify limiting the removal power. But the independent counsel is exercising what is unambiguously an executive power. Nonetheless, Rehnquist claims that the "good cause" restriction on removal need not be limited to those performing extraexecutive functions. The real test is "whether the removal restrictions are of such a nature that they impede the president's ability to perform his constitutional duty. . . ."[11]

Similar arguments were made by Justice Harry Blackmun in *Mistretta v. United States* (1989). The Sentencing Act of 1984 created the U.S. Sentencing Commission within the judicial branch with seven voting members (three of them federal judges) appointed by the president. The purpose of the commission was to eliminate the wide disparity in sentences resulting from the broad sentencing discretion allowed to judges under existing federal laws. John Mistretta was sentenced for selling cocaine under guidelines established by the commission. Mistretta appealed to the Supreme Court, claiming that the sentencing commission was unconstitutional. He argued that Congress violated the nondelegation doctrine by granting excessive legislative discretion, and violated the separation of powers doctrine by placing the commission in the judiciary, including sitting federal judges on a commission that performed a rule-making function, and giving the president the power over appointment and removal.

Justice Blackmun, writing for an 8 to 1 majority, claimed that Congress was not delegating too much authority in establishing the commission, but merely seeking assistance from its coordinate branches. As for the violation of the separation of powers, Blackmun responds that the Framers rejected the idea that the three branches must be entirely separate and distinct. The judiciary is free to make administrative decisions within its own sphere and to establish rules of procedure for judicial proceedings. The sentencing commission is merely an extension of this principle. Blackmun also pointed out that while there is a constitutional provision prohibiting legislators from serving in the executive or the judiciary, there is no comparable provision directed toward members of the judiciary. Finally, the president has no power to coerce members of the commission, because his removal power is limited to removal for "good cause." They are insulated from political pressure just as members of IRCs are insulated from such pressure.

The problem with the majority opinions in *Mistretta* and *Morrison* is that they fail to provide any guidance as to how or when the principle of separation of powers would limit or direct the operation of government. Blackmun tells us that there is no excessive delegation in the *Mistretta* case, but he fails to establish a standard by which to make that determination. He concludes that while the separation of powers was important to the Founders, they did not require a strict separation. But where does one draw the line? To say that there is some flexibility implies that there are also limits to that flexibility. Blackmun fails to tell us at what point the separation of powers would be violated.

In *Morrison*, Rehnquist suggests that restrictions on the executive power are acceptable as long as they do not "impede the president's ability to perform his constitutional duty." While this may not be a bad place to begin, it is not clear how seriously even Rehnquist takes this standard. Without argument he concludes that the conduct of investigations and prosecutions against executive branch officials does not impede the exercise of the executive power. One is at a loss after such a conclusion to postulate what exactly would impede the President's execution of his office.

Perhaps the most troubling question to arise from these two cases is, what happens to the principle of responsibility? Do we want individuals to be prosecuted by an independent counsel, with virtually no political checks? Do we want the appropriate sentences for crimes to be determined by an independent commission rather than the legislature? Finally, do we want judges to use discretion in individual cases, or do we want that discretion controlled by an independent commission with no knowledge of the particular circumstances of the case?

A Dissenter's Defense of the Separation of Powers

The lone dissenter in both *Morrison* and *Mistretta* was Justice Antonin Scalia. Only Scalia was willing to take seriously the centrality of the separation of powers to the operation of constitutional government. He alone offers a theory that allows "delegation" and also offers standards for when delegation is unconstitutional. In *Mistretta* he explains:

> The whole theory of lawful "delegation" is not that the Congress is sometimes too busy or too divided and can therefore assign its responsibility of making law to someone else; but rather that a certain degree of discretion, and thus of law-making, *inheres* in most executive or judicial action, and it is up to Congress, by the relative specificity or generality of its statutory commands, to determine—up to a point—how small or large that degree shall be. . . .[12]

Congress can thus leave room for the exercise of discretionary authority by its coordinate branches. But Scalia concluded that "strictly speaking, there is *no* acceptable delegation of legislative power."[13] Congress may recognize the discretionary authority that inheres in executive and judicial power, and leave room for the exercise of such discretion, but it cannot abdicate its essential function, the function of lawmaking. According to Scalia, there is no mistaking the purely legislative character of the sentencing commission: "The lawmaking function of the Sentencing Commission is completely divorced from any responsibility for execution of the law or adjudication of private rights under the law." The commission is exercising neither executive nor judicial authority. It is neither executing the law nor dealing with the rights of particular individuals under the law. It is making law.

Scalia is ultimately concerned that the decision in *Mistretta* will make the delegation of lawmaking functions to "expert" bodies much more appealing in the future. It will allow Congress to escape difficult political issues by "delegat[ing] various portions of its law-making responsibility."[14] But in escaping such responsibility, Scalia believes that Congress will undermine the principle of democratic accountability. The Constitution created a government of the people, by the people, and for the people, not a government of the experts, by the experts, for the people.

Scalia, however, clearly believes that there is room for more than legislative authority under the Constitution. In *Morrison*, Scalia provides a defense of executive power. He complains that the majority opinion attacks the very heart of the principle of an independent executive. Scalia argues that the decision in *Morrison* should turn on two questions: (1) Is criminal investigation and prosecution a purely executive power? (2) Does the statute deprive the president of the United States of that power? What is most remarkable to Scalia about the majority opinion is that the majority appears to answer yes to both of these questions, but nonetheless upholds the constitutionality of the statute.

The majority argues that a "balancing test" must be applied. Executive power can be removed from the control of the president as long as it does not "impede the President's ability to perform his constitutional duty. . . ." But Scalia asks, "What are the standards to determine how the balance is to be struck, that is, how much removal of presidential power is too much?"[15]

The only answer offered by the majority is: the wisdom of the judges. For Scalia, however, the Court must ground its decision in some intelligible constitutional principle. It must ground its decision in a principled understanding of the separation of powers. According to such an understanding, the executive power is placed in the hands of the president with only such exceptions as are specifically laid out in the Constitution.

Judicial Politics and Partisan Politics

At least until the confirmation of Clarence Thomas, Scalia's influence among his brethren was very limited. Increasingly he was depicted merely as an "extreme" conservative. But it is not apparent that his view of the separation of powers is reducible to some version of conservative ideology. To the contrary, it would appear that Scalia's theory of the separation of powers is neutral in regard to the policies to be pursued. Those who see a defense of executive power as necessarily conservative have little historical sense or little appreciation of recent political changes.

Many conservatives were surprised by the 7 to 1 majority in *Morrison*. Why would so many conservative justices reject the position of the Reagan administration? Blackmun suggested that the administration position was so clearly in error that only the most ideological of the justices, Scalia, would dare to defend it.[16] But I think another explanation is more plausible. In rejecting the position of the Reagan administration, most of the conservatives on the Court were following the doctrine of judicial restraint in relation to Congress. The doctrine of judicial restraint had grown in strength on the conservative wing of the Court during the Reagan years. The restraintists believed that the Court should defer to the legislature, even if that meant going against a conservative president and defending a liberal legislature.

Conservatives saw an activist judiciary as one of the primary means of promoting liberal policies. As long as members of the Court thought their role was to make policy rather than apply specific constitutional restrictions in specific cases, the growth of liberal government would continue. Conservatives believed that they had a chance to win the ideological war on the battleground of public opinion, the ground on which the president and Congress operated. But unless they could restrict the activities of the Court, they would ultimately be doomed to failure. The best way to restrict judicial activism was to deny power to the Court and defer to the more political branches.

Because advocates of judicial restraint favor deference to legislative judgments, they tend to see government strictly in terms of laws. Discretion can be an engine for unchecked growth of government. Discretionary authority might support an activist conservative president but might also support an activist liberal Court. Thus, conservatives often reject discretionary authority, contending that the Constitution establishes a "government of laws." Even Scalia is influenced by this conception of government when he speaks of lawmaking authority that "inheres in most executive and judicial action." Here he speaks as though legitimate authoritative action is synonymous with lawmaking. But Scalia goes on to show us that there is more to government than lawmaking or legislation. There are distinctive types of authority exercised by the other branches of government. To deny that fact is to undermine the greatest source of restraint in the Constitution, the separation of powers.

The mistake of the conservatives can be explained in terms of their view of judicial restraint, but the liberal position is more difficult to explain. No doctrine of judicial restraint held the liberals back from overturning these laws. They are defenders of judicial discretion and

judicial activism. Why would they not also defend executive prerogatives? The most likely answer is political. Although liberals had
traditionally supported an activist government, including an activist
judiciary and an activist presidency, they did not see such activism as
an outgrowth of the constitutional separation of powers. To them the
constitutional separation of powers was an obstacle to activist government, an obstacle that could only be overcome by an appeal to
democratic values.

By the time of *Morrison,* the presidency was increasingly identified with the Republican Party. The Reagan presidency was the bastion of opposition to liberal activist government. Having no
constitutional standard for their defense of institutions, the liberal
justices now turned against the executive because Reagan was the
president, and the presidency had become anathema to the policy
position of the liberals.

What the liberals seem to have forgotten is that the kind of active
government they desire requires the exercise of discretionary authority. The public may not be as shortsighted as they think. If the liberals' attack on discretionary executive authority succeeds (as well as
their more recent attack on "conservative judicial activism"), they may
find themselves at a great disadvantage if they begin to win the presidency on a regular basis. Their own arguments and positions will
undermine their ability to govern effectively. The only restraint they
see for "conservative activism" of any kind is political. Their short-
sightedness is due to their failure to appreciate the power of the
Constitution in American politics. They believe that liberals created
a powerful presidency by means of popular leadership, completely
neglecting the constitutional supports for executive power that were
ultimately responsible for their success.

Conservatives, on the other hand, have failed to appreciate that
discretionary authority and limited government are not irreconcilable.[17]
To the contrary, the major support for limited government is the constitutional separation of powers. But that separation becomes meaningless if it is not the product of distinctive types of power. Without
such distinctions the branches will collapse into one another. Conservatives fail to recognize this because they tend to emphasize the limits of government. They want a limited government of laws, rather
than a government of people wielding discretionary authority. They
have become too enamored of the belief that laws serve to limit whereas
discretion serves to expand power. Conservatives need to learn that
laws are the ultimate means of extending power, and that discretion

in their implementation may serve to restrain the overreaching of the legislature.

The modern administrative state is not an aberration. It is a logical outgrowth of modern constitutional government. If we fail to understand this fact we will never be able to understand what limits can and should be placed on its growth and operation. The legislature can directly limit administrative discretion by passing specific legislation. More often, however, it will recognize the desirability of discretion. It will circumscribe the sphere of executive discretion, but it will not seek to eliminate it. The ultimate threat of a funding cutoff or more specific legislation serves as the legislature's most effective although more indirect means of control.

The administration has independent power, and to the extent that power is politically responsible it is subject to presidential control. It is possible that subordinate officers may have discretion based on their immediate experience or technical knowledge. The extent of political responsibility for this type of discretion is open to question, but its existence points to the need for some sphere of discretionary authority at the core of government, no matter how well circumscribed. This kind of authority is not a denial of the principles of liberalism, but is necessary in order to implement those principles.

When making a decision, administrators must look to their own knowledge and expertise, but they must also look to their political and constitutional superiors, the president, the Congress, and the courts. When these different considerations come into conflict, it will help if the administrator has an appreciation of the constitutional principle of the separation of powers. He will then be better able to appreciate to whom he owes allegiance in any given circumstance. If the law is clear, there is little room for argument. If there is discretion given in the execution of the law, then his allegiance must go to the head of the executive branch. But ultimately, his allegiance, like that of all government officials, including the members of the legislature, must be to the Constitution.

Notes

1. See particularly Madison's arguments in *Federalist* 47 and 51. Alexander Hamilton, James Madison, and John Jay, *The Federalist*, ed. Jacob E. Cooke (Cleveland: Meridian Books, 1961), 323–31, 347–53.

2. *Annals of Congress* 515–16, 519 (1789). See also "Letter to Edmund Pendleton," June 21, 1789, *The Papers of James Madison*, vol. 12, ed. by

Charles F. Hobson and Robert Rutland (Charlottesville: University of Virginia Press, 1979) 251–53.

3. In *Federalist* 77, Hamilton says explicitly, "The consent of [the Senate] would be necessary to displace as well as to appoint" (Alexander Hamilton et al., *The Federalist*, 515).

4. *Myers v. U.S.*, 272 U.S. 51 (1926).

5. Ibid.

6. *Shurtleff v. U.S.*, 189 U.S. 311, 315 (1903) as quoted in *Myers v. U.S.*, 163.

7. This was the argument made by the Brownlow Commission. See, the President's Committee on Administrative Management, *Administrative Management in the Government of the United States* (Washington, D.C.: Government Printing Office, 1937), 36.

8. This point is stressed by the Hoover Commission Report. Commission on the Organization of the Executive Branch of Government, *Task Force Report on Regulatory Commissions* (Washington, D.C.: Government Printing Office, 1949).

9. *Morrison v. Olson*, 487 U.S. 654 (1988) and *Mistretta v. U.S.*, 488 U.S. 109 (1989).

10. *Morrison v. Olson.*

11. Ibid.

12. *Mistretta v. U.S.*

13. Ibid.

14. Ibid.

15. *Morrison v. Olson.*

16. This comment was made to me by Justice Blackmun who, by chance, was my seat-mate on a flight between Washington and New York.

17. Terry Eastland makes a similar point regarding conservative ambivalence toward executive power. See Eastland, *Energy in the Executive: The Case for the Strong Presidency* (New York: Free Press, 1992), 2–3.

8

The Rhetorical Presidency and the Eclipse of Executive Power in Woodrow Wilson's *Constitutional Government in the United States*

Robert Eden

Many citizens still think of the American presidency as the place where "the buck stops"—Harry Truman's brisk image of executive responsibility. Yet, while "the executive office" remains at the apex of the federal government and retains the formal responsibilities assigned to it by the Framers, since Woodrow Wilson the presidency has been the focus of new expectations, not least those that our presidents (and presidential scholars) bring to the office. It is not clear where executive power fits in the novel expectations we have come to associate with "the rhetorical presidency."[1]

Most political scientists who have studied Wilson's writings have assumed that his exaltation of presidential political power must carry with it an affirmation of executive power. This essay questions that view. My account stresses Wilson's novel conception of opinion leadership. I shall focus on Wilson's writings, rather than on his tenure in office, because his political science seems to offer a more perspicuous account of his intentions in this matter.

To understand why Wilson fostered "the rhetorical presidency," it is necessary to consider his doubts about the presidency as an executive office and to examine his argument for thinking of the presidency as an office divorced from executive power. The opinion-forming responsibilities that Wilson assigned to the American president were not, as he saw them, mere additions or augments to executive power. Rather, Wilson sought to bring about a shift in the ranking of opinion leadership and executive power. If the highest office of constitutional governance could be reshaped into an office for opinion leadership, he thought the United States could be raised toward a higher, more advanced stage of representative government. In assuming that executive power gains strength in this new mode of governance, historians and political scientists have overlooked Wilson's attempt to demote executive action to a subordinate status. In doing so I believe we underestimate his originality, misunderstand the progress he envisioned, and narrow the scope of his reform project.

Wilson's Intentions

The best accounts of Wilson have striven to do justice to the impressive scope of his project. Thus, James W. Ceaser begins by observing:

> Wilson believed that nothing less than a complete transformation of the political system could save representative government in America. As a first step in this transformation, it was necessary to undermine the reverence Americans felt for the Constitution and the Founders. Wilson sought to expose the outmoded "Newtonian" theory of static checks that had informed the Founders' thought, contrasting it with the modern "Darwinian" theory that recognized the need for growth and change. . . . This was a prelude to his plan for a new institutional arrangement that would embody the proper understanding of representative government. Although Wilson changed his mind about which form of government was best, shifting from a proposal for cabinet government to a plan of presidential dominance, his basic objectives remained the same: to establish a greater capacity in the government for change through dynamic leadership and to make the relationship between the leader and public opinion the focal point of the new system.[2]

Yet even Ceaser's penetrating and lucid interpretation accepts the doctrine that Wilson's intention was to strengthen and enhance executive power:

> What Wilson called the "living constitution"—the actual regime as fixed not only by constitutional provisions, but by opinion and practice—would have to be changed by means of a basic transformation of the public's views under which the people would come to regard the executive as the most legitimate source of political authority.[3]

Ceaser speaks of "Wilson's plan to transform the Constitution by increasing the power of the executive"; he advocated a "change to a more powerful executive."[4] Ceaser implies that Wilson adopted Alexander Hamilton's argument for a strong executive office.

> Hamilton's two chief arguments for unity—the greater energy possessed when power is given to a single individual and the greater ease with which one person can be watched and held accountable— are both incorporated into Wilson's concept of leadership. But Wilson went much further than Hamilton, proposing in effect to do with political power in its entirety what Hamilton had sought for the executive power alone.[5]

Hence, Ceaser invites us to "wonder whether the executive is not too powerful" under Wilson's scheme.[6]

Many passages in Wilson's 1908 book *Constitutional Government in the United States* seem to confirm Ceaser's view that he intended to enhance the executive power of the president. These come to a kind of crescendo toward the end of the book:

> I have pointed out in previous lectures that opinion was the great, indeed the only, coordinating force in our system; that the only thing that gave the President an opportunity to make good his leadership of the party and of the nation as against the resistance or the indifference of the House or Senate was his close and especial relation to opinion the nation over, and that, without some such leadership as opinion might sustain the President in exercising within the just limits of the law, our system would be checked of all movement, deprived of all practical synthesis by its complicated system of checks and counterpoises.[7]

This has been taken as a statement about executive leadership, on the assumption that Wilsonian opinion leadership has all the "force" of presidential executive power. Yet when we reread the "previous lectures" to which Wilson refers us here, they assert Wilson's distinction between executive action and opinion leadership, and they envision the subordination of the president's executive functions:

> No one else represents the people as a whole, exercising a national choice; and inasmuch as his strictly executive duties are in fact subordinated, so far at any rate as all detail is concerned, the President represents not so much the party's governing efficiency as its controlling ideals and principles. He is not so much part of its organiza-

tion as its vital link of connection with the thinking nation. He can dominate his party by being spokesman for the real sentiment and purpose of the country, by giving direction to opinion, by giving the country at once the information and the statements of policy which will enable it to form its judgments alike of parties and of men.[8]

For Wilson, good government is constitutional government, but energy in the executive—qua executive—is by no means a leading feature in his definition of constitutional government.

The consent of the governed is no longer guessed at or risked upon some blind calculation. It is systematically ascertained. That is "constitutional government." When we speak of a constitutional government we mean a government so constituted that those who govern and those who are governed are brought by some systematic and efficient means into concord and counsel; and in which law, accordingly, is made and enforced in conformity with principle and by methods agreed upon between them.[9]

Wilson's problem in *Constitutional Government* is the Constitution and the kind of executive it establishes: a constitutional executive whose power and authority derive from a formal document. Wilson knows that the American president is not a party executive like the British prime minister, whose power is drawn from an informal source, a political party. As Ceaser implies, Wilson was as determined as ever to put American politics on the progressive track toward something equivalent to the British system as he understood it.[10] He was able to create a path toward such constitutional government in the United States in part because he was not committed to modern executive power on either the British or the American model; his preference for the British model did not rest on its claim to a superior executive.

Wilson's strategy in *Constitutional Government* is not to deny the existence of the formal constitutional presidency. Rather, he combines a selective account of the formal document with a presentation of the president as party leader so that the existing American executive office initially appears to the reader as the mixed product of two quite different conceptions. On the one hand, there is an original, static, and rigid Constitution, shaped by the Framers' mechanical, Newtonian theory. On the other, there is a subsequent historical development, shown especially in the growth of the American party system, which according to Wilson was driven by necessities the Framers did not anticipate.[11] The first conception is formal and doctrinaire; the second informal, empirical, and responsive to national needs. Because the conceptions are antithetical, their mixture in practice is unstable and generates momentum for change. It should be evident how Wilson intended to influence standards of public judgment regarding the office of the president: he encouraged readers to welcome the motion away from the formal constitutional executive toward a presidency of national opinion leaders.

Wilson presents himself in these lectures as an interpreter of constitutional government generally and only derivatively of constitutional government in the United States. He does not claim that the Framers of the American Constitution interpreted constitutional government as he will do, and like much of Progressive social science, his account is meant to supplant rather than supplement *The Federalist*. Wilson intended that his general understanding of constitutional government would supersede the Framers' understanding, and come to be regarded as authoritative in American public discourse.[12] If he is successful, his account will supplant competing theories. Accordingly, he makes no mention in *Constitutional Government* of John Locke.[13]

Evolutionary Political Science

As an apostle of evolutionary progress, Wilson made it a part of his mission to educate Americans in a historical understanding of their Constitution, interpreting the thought of the Framers from the perspective of a steadily evolving Anglo-Saxon tradition of constitutionalism. As Wilson presented it, American constitutional history was entirely a story of unforeseen or unintended consequences; he gave the Framers no credit for anticipating or providing for novel contingencies and emergencies. In particular he ignored the role executive power was to play in meeting such crises under their Constitution.[14] A grand optical illusion is conveyed: Wilson's reader is convinced that it is impossible to reconcile the Framers' Constitution with subsequent historical developments or the necessities that led to them.

Under the guidance of Wilson's political science, by contrast, it will be possible for the president to play a major role in lengthy reformations of the whole political order, in accordance with historical necessities. Wilson claims to be able to teach "the elements of practical politics."[15] His historical philosophy of politics trains leaders to seize the opportunity presented by circumstances, to understand the political need that they may serve, and to make use of them in sequence to carry out a long-term program.

> The object of constitutional government is to bring the active, planning will of each part of the government into accord with the prevailing thought and need, and thus make it an impartial instrument of symmetrical national development, and to give the operation of the government thus shaped under the influence of opinion and adjusted to the general interest both stability and incorruptible efficacy.[16]

Undermining respect for the Framers' political science was a crucial step in making such long-range guidance of American political development possible. Wilson thereby sought to precipitate a choice (or perhaps we should say a long sequence of choices) that would bring into being a very different kind of constitutional government. This is clear in his 1902 notes on leadership:

> Common elements: Ordinary ideas, extraordinary abilities (W. Bagehot). The habitual ideas of the governing group or class or of the existing task as performed in the past, and a power of effective presentation, progressive modification, a power to conceive and execute the next forward step and to organize the force of the State for the movement.[17]

As this note suggests, what is being "executed"—although Wilson does not often use that loaded term—is the transition to a new stage of constitutional government.

Wilson believed that transition could be helped along by his reshaping of the terms of political discourse. No one was more fascinated than Wilson by the power of names and their potential to engender new realities. Consider, for example, how he refined his terms regarding the executive office. In *Congressional Government*, the relevant section was entitled "The Executive."[18] Later he recognized this as an error or inconsistency. In *Constitutional Government*, the corresponding section is called "The President of the United States." Wilson had discovered in the interim that the president did not have to be "the executive." By being "The President," he could transcend the limits of the separation of powers and of his office. However, that did not enhance his executive power; instead, he was free to become something more—and other—than the executive.

This is evident in Wilson's conception of the "stages" of government. In *Constitutional Government*, Wilson identifies a primitive stage, in which executive power is identified with government in its entirety: "What used to be called the Government, we now speak of only as the 'Executive,' and regard as little more than an instrumentality for carrying into effect the laws which our representative assemblies originate."[19] He also recognized that in great crises constitutional government seems to revert to this primitive stage; thus he speaks of "the Civil War and Mr. Lincoln's unique task and achievement, when the executive seemed for a little while to become by sheer stress of circumstances the whole government."[20] He treats outbreaks of strong executive action, as under Andrew Jackson, as lapses into a more primitive and regrettable mood.[21] Evidently Wilson thought a mature constitutional government would never revert to this more primitive stage.[22]

Wilson seems to envision a gradual formalization of the informal standing of party government; this would result from an increasing reliance (by both party leaders and presidents) on the opinion-leading powers of the modern American president.[23] In due course, constitutional government in the United States will be converted into cabinet government on the British model; this will happen so reassuringly, conforming so closely to American customs and prejudices, that the transformation will hardly be noticed.[24] The result will seem so distinctively American that the armature of British arrangements will be entirely invisible. If this is so, Wilson must be seen not as changing his mind after *Congressional Government* about the basic direction of constitutional development, but rather as engaging in a subtle tactical adjustment.

Wilson believed that if this were done properly, the scale and scope of administrative activity would expand dramatically, so that in the aggregate result, much more would be accomplished through "executive action" at every level. Wilson regarded opinion leadership as a more comprehensive activity in part because it created the boundary conditions for effective execution. By consolidating the shared political understandings of a community, opinion leadership preserves the deference to governmental authority that executives (on his view) need in order to do their work smoothly and expeditiously. Thus, the subordination of executive governance does not by any means result in

less administration or less executive action. On the contrary, such
subordination makes it possible to expand the public sphere and to
establish administration as a wide field for able and ambitious professional civil servants.

But this interdependence does not work to strengthen the presidency as a locus of executive power. On the contrary, by making the
president responsible, in his capacity as a leader of national opinion,
for securing the support of majority opinion, Wilson may make it harder
for the president himself to engage in executive action. We shall return to this problem.

These observations on the structure of Wilson's argument indicate
the weight of his prefatory warning that *Constitutional Government*
was not an academic treatise but rather a tract for the times.[25] As
Wilson conceived them, his works were themselves instances of
leadership. He understood himself to be reshaping the elements of
practical politics as he oriented the reader toward them, reforming
institutions and practices by reshaping opinion about them. The transformative developmental picture he presents is an active element in
the political change he promotes. He is striving, in accordance with
his own understanding of the objective of constitutional government
and of the purposes of leadership, to lead the way toward the next
stage in the progress of democratic politics.

Wilson's rhetorical strategy, with regard to the presidency, in *Constitutional Government*, exhibits a twofold interpretive movement. He
simultaneously lowers the executive to the level of a mere instrument
of legislative will, and elevates the president beyond the status of an
executive, by interpreting his political powers as informal and strictly personal faculties for understanding popular thought or opinion and
for articulating it. The result is the presidency as an office for opinion leadership, almost divested of its original connection to the responsibilities of the Framers' constitutional office. Wilson's effort to
subordinate or exclude executive power is most evident in his accounts of two aspects of the Constitution: the provisions relating to
the president's cabinet and the constitutional oath of office.

The President's Cabinet:
Executive Power "In Commission"

One of the peculiarities of the account of the executive powers of
the president in *Constitutional Government* is the description of the

president as holding his executive powers as the chairman of a commission. Wilson began by identifiying the constitutional executive with the formal or "legal" aspect of the presidency. While Wilson says the Constitution "thinks" of "the President" as a singular officer, he denies that it is possible to think of him in this way:

> As legal executive, his constitutional aspect, the President cannot be thought of alone. He cannot execute laws. Their actual daily execution must be taken care of by the several executive departments and by the now innumerable body of federal officials throughout the country.[26]

What the Constitution formalized as a singular office, Wilson reinterprets as a delegation of executive power to subordinate officers. In practice, Wilson claims, this necessarily yields a plural executive headed by the president as chairman of a commission:

> In respect of the strictly executive duties of his office the President may be said to administer the presidency in conjunction with the members of his cabinet, like the chairman of a commission. He is even of necessity much less active in the actual carrying out of the law than are his colleagues and advisors.[27]

This is an observation about necessity. The widely accepted view of Wilson would lead us to expect necessity to work in the direction of strengthening the executive power at the apex of government. But instead, he says that it works in the opposite direction, of delegating executive power away from the president. And Wilson offers a general formula that suggests a quasi-legal formalization to firm up the new practical arrangement:

> It is therefore becoming more and more true, as the business of the government becomes more and more complex and extended, that the President is becoming more and more a political and less and less an executive officer. His executive powers are in commission, while his political powers more and more centre and accumulate upon him and are in their very nature personal and inalienable.[28]

What does it mean that the president's executive power is "in commission"? Wilson was fully aware that his description had no reference whatever to American public law. He was deliberately borrowing suggestive if rather esoteric language in order to displace American constitutional terms, and to insinuate a British understanding of the nature of the American executive. This becomes evident from *The State*:

> But in the reign of George I, the great office of Lord High Treasurer was, in English phrase, put permanently "into commission": its duties, that is, were intrusted to a board instead of to a single individual. This board was known as the "Lords Commissioners for executing the office of Lord High Treasurer," and consisted of a First Lord of the Treasury, the Chancellor of the Exchequer, and three others known as Junior Lords. Evolution speedily set in, as in other similar English boards. That is, the board ceased to act as a board. Its functions became concentrated in the hands of the Chancellor of the Exchequer; the First Lordship, occupied almost invariably since 1762 by the Prime Minister, gradually lost all connection, except that of honorary chairmanship, with the Treasury Commission, its occupant giving all his energies to his political functions.[29]

In the model case Wilson has in mind, putting an authority "into commission" was merely an interim measure prior to removing it from the (original) holder and thus freeing it from the shared understandings regarding sovereignty that informed the original commission or grant of power. It struck Wilson as singularly apt for his purpose, because what was taken from the individual officer under the British constitution was the responsibility for executing his office. That is what was put into the hands of a commission, acting in his stead. The lord high treasurer eventually lost all connection to Treasury duties, and was free to become prime minister, "giving all his energies to his political functions" as Wilson hopes the American president will do. The quasi-legal characterization opens to view a long perspective in which one sees the "elements of practical politics" as parts of a puzzle that the statesman is assembling: Wilson has in view a sequence of choices, a process of development, which would bring into being a very different kind of constitutional government in the United States.

In Wilson's hands, factual description is transformative: it displaces one theory and insinuates another. Here we see him taking something that he thinks has great powers of growth, removing it from its original British stem, and grafting it onto American stock. It is a high-minded Wilsonian graft, but graft nonetheless.

In practice, the rhetorical presidency is a progressive abandonment of executive power. As he becomes less and less an executive officer, Wilson's president will treat the presidency less and less as an executive office. Wilson's phrasing indicates that this will entail an exchange of one kind of power for another; the president no longer exercises executive powers, and executive power migrates away from the office of the president:

> the President is becoming more and more a political and less and less an executive officer. His executive powers are in commission, while his political powers more and more centre and accumulate upon him and are in their very nature personal and inalienable.[30]

It is not clear what Wilson means here by "political powers," but a few observations may be ventured. Surely he means to include the president's powers as a leader of public opinion. The president as executive does not, on Wilson's reading, have access to extraordinary powers that are not strictly executive in the instrumental sense. The political powers of the president as a leader of national thought or opinion are not, according to Wilson, extraordinary executive powers; they are powers of persuasion and of preeminence in counsel.

Although he intimates that one key to good constitutional government is the formation of an executive body within the government, Wilson is careful to describe the supreme tasks of governance without reference to execution or executive power.[31] They are tasks of opinion leadership, of persuasion in the context of political deliberations. Wilson's president seems to perform such tasks without having recourse to extraordinary powers, that is, executive powers not strictly executive in the instrumental sense. While the president's instrumental executive powers are delegated downward to subordinates, the remainder of the executive power vested in the president disappears from Wilson's account. Wilson is quite careful in his choice of formal terms; he preserves the title "The President," but disassociates it from executive power and finally drops the term "executive" entirely as an indicator of presidential powers and responsibilities.

Wilson offers us an explanation of the personal power that presidents acquire and exercise; he tells us that the president cannot merely "execute" in the sense of performing the formal duties assigned under Article II, Section 2 of the Constitution. There is a need for the "dominant individuality" of a strong president, Wilson explains, but it is the need for persuasive leadership, for the interpretation of the national thought.

When we survey all these contentions together, it is evident that Wilson has reduced the executive functions of the president or prime minister to a position so completely subordinate as to be practically invisible. And indeed, in some formulations, Wilson envisions the president or prime minister delegating "executive action" entirely to subordinates. Leadership of thought is meant to prevail through the dominant individuality of the leader, but in Wilson's understanding of the modern democratic state, the capacity for "executive action" need not be an element in this "dominant individuality." By freeing his president from executive duties, Wilson intends to free him for ampler responsibility: "The man who is full of persuasive counsel is kept for his native uses—for forming the thought of the nation."[32] As Wilson understands the modern tasks of governance, deliberation supersedes execution and keeps it subordinated. The executive functions of government, the tasks of execution, become the handmaiden of such opinion leadership and can therefore be delegated to energetic lackeys or messenger-boys.

Wilson's preference for the British practice of constitutional government rests primarily on his belief that it represented this advanced stage in assigning categorically different responsibilities to different human types. Although he was impressed by British prestige and success, Wilson did not arrive at his preference for their mode of government by admiring their efficiency in governance and then seeking its causes. He certainly read Walter Bagehot's book on the British constitution, but he differed with Bagehot on the crucial issue. Bagehot did not attempt to integrate opinion leadership into the British constitution as Wilson did. Bagehot did not, like Wilson, distinguish categorically between individuals preeminent in counsel and those with executive capacity. Instead, he argued that men like Richard Cobden— Wilson's model of the gifted opinion leader—should be required to develop administrative skills.[33] In contrast to Bagehot, Wilson thought the British system produced success because it elevated deliberative opinion-leading individuals like William Gladstone to the prime ministership. He presumed that adopting a similar arrangement in the United States would increase efficiency and expand executive capacity, not because the executive power would be strengthened, but because stronger opinion leadership at the apex of government would create greater scope for administration.

Reinterpreting the constitutional provisions on the cabinet is thus a Wilsonian reform initiative. Following in Wilson's footsteps, a school arose in American political science favoring cabinet government and seeking to transform the American executive accordingly. But since Wilson's disciples have not always appreciated his originality, let us pause to underscore it. Good grounds could be supplied for Wilson's judgment identifying executive power with the primacy of decision (and the subordination of deliberation).[34] Wilson was correct in thinking that to elevate deliberative politics to the apex of constitutional government, it would be necessary to subordinate executive power.[35] To do so consistently would require surgery on the executive. This reordering might take a different form in Britain because the British understood the separation of powers somewhat differently, but the principle would require a far-reaching reinterpretation of the British constitution no less than the American. Once the primacy of deliberation is accepted, Wilson may confidently proceed to reinterpret the tasks of the American president and denigrate executive activity. That ranking would require a parallel understanding of the British prime minister. The exercise of his veto, his powers of dissolving parliament and calling for elections, his prerogatives in initiating legislation and managing its passage—all these aspects of the executive power (some of which have counterparts in the American Constitution) would have to be reinterpreted as prerogatives or tasks of persuasive leadership in the context of a sovereign deliberative body. Among other things, that meant executive prerogative could have none of the dimensions it had in John Locke's interpretation of the British constitution; prerogative ceases to be an aspect of executive power and becomes "political."

The account of the executive office that Hamilton developed in *The Federalist* drew on a long tradition of modern political science. That tradition began with Machiavelli, as Harvey C. Mansfield Jr. has shown; later liberals like Locke and Montesquieu modified the ferocity of the Machiavellian executive while accepting the primacy of decision over deliberation in constitutional government.[36] Wilson breaks with this tradition on the crucial question of the ranking of deliberation. It is therefore not strange that the modern argument for the unification of executive power in a single individual is abandoned by Wilson. When he speaks of the more efficient executive, as he occasionally does, Wilson has in mind a plural executive body, such as a cabinet. The unifying qualities he seeks do not require that one individual embody executive power; it is quite sufficient, indeed preferable from Wilson's standpoint, that executive power be shared. Nothing that Wilson wrote on this topic requires that the executive body be "one body" in the strong sense of "some one."[37] While it happens that one person is elected president and that the executive in the American Constitution is united in a single human body, Wilson's argument strongly suggests that there is no inherent reason that it should continue to be so. Although Wilson speaks of the executive body of government as an essential unifying faculty, and he insists upon the presidency as a focus of national opinion, Wilson does not equate the president with the executive body. Only the president, Wilson insists, is the focus of national opinion; he alone is elected by the nation as a whole. But on Wilson's developmental understanding of constitutional government, that arrangement is surely subject to revision. In principle, nothing prevents the executive body as a whole from becoming subject to national elections, as it was in Britain; and insofar as Wilson's reasoning turns on the dependence of the American parties on the president as party leader, here too the singularity of the president is coincidental; Wilson argues that the entire form of American parties is likely to change dramatically.[38]

Thus, Wilson's account of the cabinet in *Constitutional Government* is perhaps best understood as a comprehensive effort to shift the locus of executive power away from the constitutional office of the president. Wilson reshapes the office through reinterpretion to create "the rhetorical presidency," a new kind of office invested with novel expectations. Conversely, the old expectations, focused on the president's singular responsibility as the bearer of the executive power, are interpreted away. The tract gives a fair indication of how Wilson envisioned the possibility of transforming the office. There are duties assigned to the president by the Constitution that Wilson did not intend that presidents should consider to be duties, and that he effectively excused them from performing.

> It is through no fault or neglect of his that the duties apparently assigned to him by the Constitution have come to be his less conspicuous, less important duties, and that duties apparently not assigned to him at all chiefly occupy his time and energy. The one set of duties it has proved practically impossible for him to perform; the other it has proved impossible for him to escape.[39]

The Constitutional Oath of Office

Had he intended to strengthen the executive power, Wilson could easily have said that the president "embodied" the executive power. Wilson would surely have used such vigorous and graphic language if he agreed with its point. I suggest that he chose quite consciously to avoid such phrasing. His reasons for avoiding it may become clearer as we consider his treatment of the oath of office.

How does Wilson read the Constitution as it bears upon the powers and duties of the President? The clearest text answering this question is from *The State*.[40] In a section titled "Duties and Powers of the President," Wilson repeats most of Article II, Section 2.[41] But he leaves the matter there. This exclusion indicates that according to Wilson's interpretation, the only duties and responsibilities that the president has under the Constitution, or in commission from it, are those spelled out in Section 2.

The first thing one should reflect upon, then, is Wilson's omission of the first section of Article II. That section begins by ordaining that the entire executive power shall be vested in a president (a feature that Wilson thought had been superseded, as we have seen). Section 1 ends by stipulating an oath of office that every president must swear or affirm. The terms of the clause are noteworthy for their emphasis on execution:

> Before he enter on the execution of his office, he shall take the following oath or affirmation: I do solemnly swear (or affirm) that I will faithfully execute the office of President of the United States, and will to the best of my Ability, preserve, protect, and defend the Constitution of the United States.[42]

This is a commission. The presidency is an office, an office bearing the executive power. Contrary to Wilson's argument from informal "realities," and notwithstanding the necessity to delegate tasks to his subordinates, the president is invested with the totality of executive power. Wilson's guiding notion is that all the duties enumerated in Section 2 of Article II can be delegated because they require executive capacity, but not the skills in government by debate and deliberation that Wilson thinks those who occupy the highest offices of a constitutional government should possess. He thought it irrational to frame a constitutional order upon the conjunction of both executive and political ability in a single individual. All the executive duties that the Constitution assigns to the president are, in Wilson's view, merely administrative duties that ought to be fully subordinated to "political" leadership. He then treats the duties and powers of the president that are not "merely" executive (or do not carry out someone else's orders) as though they were not executive in any sense and were no part of "the executive power" vested in the president. They vanish from his account, to be reinterpreted and gathered up into the political responsibilities of the president. On Wilson's understanding, those responsibilities were not envisioned by the Framers of the Constitution but come to light through subsequent events.

The beauty of this rhetorical solution to the problem of executive power lies in the presumption it insinuates. The presumption is that any authority that a Wilsonian president exercises must come "directly" from the nation, that is, not from the Constitution but rather from the authority by which the Constitution was originally authorized. Among other things, this means that presidential authority is not divided by functions; it is neither executive, nor judicial, nor legislative (if these could be distinguished); instead it is "political."[43] Conversely, however, the authority that the American president could invoke by claiming the whole executive power is diminished.

Scholarly interpreters have been duly impressed with Wilson's discovery of powers that the executive was not granted or expected to exercise under the U.S. Constitution. But they have overlooked a corresponding diminution, which follows from Wilson's suspicion of that Constitution; they have hardly noticed that Wilson virtually encouraged the American president not to claim the powers that were formally his. The most dramatic example of this erosion of presidential claims to authority and executive power is Wilson's silence on the president's constitutional oath.

If Wilson's project had been less comprehensive, he might have argued that his preferred tasks of persuasive leadership were commissioned by the Constitution when it required the president to affirm that he would execute the office and defend the Constitution. Wilson was aware of Abraham Lincoln's exemplary use of the president's duty in this regard; he could have invoked the oath as a grand "commission" from the Constitution that would cover most of the political arts of persuasion a president might employ. Since he was keen to demonstrate that the restraints on those arts that had grown up around the American presidency were merely customary and without constitutional authority—he was eager to restore George Washington's practice of addressing Congress—it is striking that Wilson did not invoke the sanction of the president's constitutional oath. Instead, he deliberately tried to persuade presidents to find a new purpose in the office and to disregard its executive character:

But we can safely predict that as the multitude of the President's duties increases, as it must with the growth and widening activities of the nation itself, the incumbents of the great office will more and more come to feel that they are administering it in its truest purpose and with greatest effect by regarding themselves as less and less executive officers and more and more directors of affairs and leaders of the nation,—men of counsel and of the sort of action that makes for enlightenment.[44]

In thus revising the president's oath, Wilson envisions the presidency as invested with certain broad duties "for action of the sort that makes for enlightenment." The striking feature of Wilson's exposition is that he does not find any basis for the comprehensive responsibilities of his president in the Constitution. To the contrary, according to Wilson, the Constitution denies the president such responsibilities: "It may with a great deal of plausibility be argued that the constitution looks upon the President himself in the same way. It does not seem to make him a prime minister or the leader of the nation's counsels."[45]

Wilson's exclusion of the constitutional oath of office is one of his least subtle omissions; it is evidently meant to be noticed. It is consistent with Wilson's account of the whole subject. If scholars have noticed such omissions, they have assumed they were intended to strengthen the executive power of the president. That the effect may in certain cases have been to enlarge the scope and reach of the presidency may be granted, however, without prejudice to our inquiry. Wilson's abandonment of the executive office may free presidents from the confines of the American constitutional tradition, and loosen the hold of many customary constraints that had deterred earlier presidents from "claiming the silences of the Constitution." But Wilson accomplishes this primarily by dissolving the fixed points of reference, such as the president's oath, which defined the constitutional space occupied by the president.

The result is by no means simply to expand the boundaries of the office; it may equally result in contracting those boundaries or collapsing them entirely. Wilson makes the space available to the president depend almost entirely on his peculiarities or "individuality"—"his political powers more and more centre and accumulate upon him and are in their very nature personal and inalienable." The result is, as Wilson claims, that the office can be as large as the man who occupies it:

We can never hide our President again as a mere domestic officer.
We can never again see him as the mere executive he was in the
[eighteen] thirties and forties. He must always stand at the front of
our affairs, and the office will be as big and as influential as the
man who occupies it.[46]

But it can also be as small, and that might be very small indeed. If
the constitutional space occupied by presidents is not independent of
the occupant to a considerable degree, it is difficult to imagine how
any citizen other than the president could act to protect the office.
Wilson rules out one method: he ignores impeachment because the
power was seldom used in the United States and had passed out of
usage in Britain. He discounts the commission to impeach a president who does not fulfill the duties of the office, which other officers
receive from the Constitution. If one regards the oath as a serious
commission and a solemn undertaking, Wilson's silence is striking,
particularly in an author known for moral high-mindedness. No president who took his bearings by Wilson's *Constitutional Government*
or *The State* would consider the constitutional oath a guide to presidential duties and responsibilities.

Instead of providing the basis for the concentration of executive
power in the presidency, Wilson's mode of argument provides on the
contrary for the circumvention of the president by Congress, and for
the supervision of the cabinet officers and all subordinate administrators by Congress. If all the "merely executive" duties of the president may be turned over to subordinates, does it not follow that the
legislative branch (whose laws or commands are to be executed) will
hold these subordinates to be executing the will of the legislature?
The massive involvement of Congress in the details of administration
that developed after 1960 is thus consistent in spirit with Wilson's
reshaping of constitutional government, and particularly with his se-
questration or sublimation of executive power. The danger that the
president may thereby lose control over all administration does not
perturb Wilson, I suspect, because it merely brings home to the president that he must dominate the course of legislation and make himself the master of the legislature through his leadership of public
opinion.[47] Wilson strips the president of his constitutional office in
order to endow him with new resources. Wilson seeks to enlarge the
informal powers and authority of the president, but he is convinced
that he can do so only by overriding or canceling the formal duties of

the constitutional office. As a political scientist, Wilson does not know how the executive could draw strength from the formalities of his constitutional office.

Conclusion

These, then, are Wilson's leading opinions about the presidential office and executive power. Had he been a proponent of executive power, as most interpreters assume, it is safe to say he would have done his best to promote the kind of public opinion that presidents need so long as they must work within the separated and counter-poised powers of the American Constitution. They need "the help of some general understanding favoring strong executive power to resist legislative usurpation and its partner, overbearing bureaucracy."[48] Although Wilson stressed the importance of "shared understandings" for the functioning of constitutional government, he did not devote his powers of persuasion and public instruction to the task of consolidating such an understanding of executive power. Surprisingly, in *Constitutional Government* he did just the opposite, strengthening the dictionary definition of the executive—as an agent who carries someone else's resolutions into effect—that would reduce the executive to an instrument of the legislature. Wilson's revaluation of the potential of the presidential office is not a defense or assertion of the executive power and does not advance a shared understanding favoring strong executive power. All his faculties of persuasion were directed toward creating a public climate favorable to strong opinion leadership, along the lines we have considered. On Wilson's understanding, the president gains political power by transcending, mastering, or abandoning executive power.

We may summarize by saying that in *Constitutional Government*, Wilson transferred political responsibility to opinion-leading politicians by minimizing or dismantling their political responsibility as executive officers. The political dimension of executive governance, which had been foremost in the political science of executive power from its invention by Machiavelli through its sublimation into Hamiltonian "administration" in *The Federalist*, is left darkling by Wilson's interpretation. In the writings here examined, execution is either demeaned by eliminating its political dimension and reducing it to what Wilson calls the "merely executive" function, or else it is absorbed into and utterly eclipsed by the "political," opinion-leading tasks of Wilson's prime ministers and presidents. In either case, the executive power is beyond the horizon of political science—out of sight because it is out of mind.

Few students of the history of American political science dispute that Woodrow Wilson's impact upon presidential studies in the United States has been deep and lasting. Yet even the most careful students of his influence, who have articulated Wilson's teaching on "the rhetorical presidency," have underestimated his originality; they have agreed with Wilson's proponents in representing his doctrine as a way of strengthening executive power.[49] Wilson's purpose, as we have demonstrated, was to subordinate executive power and transfer it away from the office of the president. Students of the presidency may choose to accept responsibility for this purpose, or place their thought on different foundations.

Notes

1. For an introduction to the term and to the school of presidential studies that stresses Wilson's effort to reshape the presidential office, see Jeffrey K. Tulis, *The Rhetorical Presidency* (Princeton: Princeton University Press, 1987), 117–44.

2. James W. Ceaser, *Presidential Selection: Theory and Development* (Princeton: Princeton University Press, 1979), 171.

3. Ibid., 172 (my emphasis).

4. Ibid., 173.

5. Ibid., 179.

6. Ibid., 182.

7. Woodrow Wilson, *Constitutional Government* (hereafter cited as CG) in *The Papers of Woodrow Wilson*, vol. 18, ed. Arthur S. Link (Princeton: Princeton University Press, 1972), 181 (all emphasis added). The *Papers* will be cited by volume and page as follows: PWW 18:181.

8. CG, PWW 18:114 (all emphasis added).

9. Woodrow Wilson, 31 August 1901, "The Real Idea of Democracy," PWW 12:175–79.

10. Ceaser, *Presidential Selection*, 171.

11. CG, PWW 18:105–7, 109, 112, 114–15, 117, 200–202, 204–5, 207–9, 213–15.

12. Compare the lecture on "Democracy" (1891), PWW 7:367.

13. The omission of Locke from *Constitutional Government* represents a rhetorical advance: in his earlier accounts, Wilson had been particularly attentive to Locke's treatment of executive prerogative. See PWW 7:132 on prerog-

ative power in his lectures on Locke, and compare Wilson's treatment of the prerogatives of the British executive body in "Four General Chapters from *The State*," 3 June 1889, PWW 8:259–61. The early volumes of Wilson's papers are punctuated with criticism of Locke's theory of contract, which he associates with Rousseau. See for example, letter to Horace Elisha Scudder, 10 July 1886, PWW 5:303–4, 384.

14. See "Nature of Democracy in the United States," PWW 6:232; "Democracy," PWW 7:350–54, *Constitutional Government*, PWW 18:78, 96–97, 99–100, 106–7, 109, 115, 123, 204–5, 207–9, 215.

15. The subtitle of Wilson's work on comparative government, *The State*, was "Elements of Historical and Practical Politics." See Woodrow Wilson, *The State: Elements of Historical and Practical Politics*, rev. ed. (Boston: Heath, 1906).

16. CG, PWW 18:78 (emphasis added).

17. Woodrow Wilson, "A Memorandum on Leadership" 5 May 1902, PWW 12:365 (emphasis added). For a fuller account of the themes of this memo, see Robert Eden, "Opinion Leadership and The Problem of Executive Power: Woodrow Wilson's Original Position" *The Review of Politics* 57, no. 3 (Summer 1995): 483–503.

18. PWW 2:134–60.

19. CG, PWW 18:78.

20. CG, PWW 18:107.

21. CG, PWW 18:107; "Marginal Notes," 29 December 1889, PWW 6:34.

22. This may raise the question of whether by Wilson's interpretation, "the [entire] executive power" would be "vested" in a president, as it had been under the Framers' Constitution.

23. CG, PWW 18:214–15.

24. CG, PWW 18:213–16; consider the effect of Wilson's introduction to *Constitutional Government*, in which British development since Magna Carta becomes the broad framework for understanding American constitutional development, PWW 18:69–85.

25. "My object in the following lectures is to examine the government of the United States . . . with an eye to practice, not to theory" CG, PWW 18:69.

26. CG PWW 18:113.

27. CG PWW 18:113.

28. CG PWW 18:113 (emphasis added).

29. Wilson, *The State: Elements of Historical and Practical Politics*, Section 870, p. 385 (emphasis added).

30. CG PWW 18:113 (emphasis added). Wilson's repeated efforts to reinterpret the Declaration of Independence, lead me to think that he chose his wording—from the most familiar phrases of the Declaration—quite carefully here. The things that are in their very nature personal and inalienable are not the things in which men are equal but rather those distinctive features of a dominant individuality that enable him uniquely to rule and persuade other men. See "Spurious versus Real Patriotism in Education" (1899): "What is

equality? We no longer entertain the opinions that we used to entertain about the Declaration of Independence literally; but we don't, we take it now in a Pickwickian sense" (PWW, 11:259). Further, "The authors and signers of the Declaration of Independence," 4 July 1907 (PWW, 17:248–59), and "A Fourth of July Address," Independence Hall, Philadelphia, July 4, 1914 (PWW, 30:248–55).

31. Compare CG PWW 18:97 where Wilson speaks of the British cabinet as "the working executive of the country" with the strong uses of executive in "Government Under the Constitution" (1893), PWW 8:259–61. Wilson's deliberate use of "leadership" to replace the exercise of executive power is highlighted by his account at the beginning of *Constitutional Government* of Frederick the Great and Queen Elizabeth as leaders rather than as princes or monarchs, PWW 18:91. Similarly the terms to describe the task of American presidents will be not execution but "leadership and control" (18:105), and "synthesis of parts" (PWW 18:108), contrasted with "legal executive" (PWW 18:105). Compare *Congressional Government*, where Wilson quotes Roger Sherman in the Constitutional Convention of 1787: "he considered the executive magistracy as nothing more than an institution for carrying the will of the legislature into effect" (PWW 4:147).

32. "The Modern Democratic State" (1885), PWW 5:89; "The Eclipse of Individuality" (1887), (PWW 5:483).

33. Wilson of course accepted Bagehot's point about practical experience: "Of the Study of Politics" (1886), PWW 5:399. See further his criticism of Bagehot's inability to accept popular government, "Lecture on Walter Bagehot" (1889), PWW 6:353.

34. See Harvey C. Mansfield Jr., *Taming the Prince: The Ambivalence of Modern Executive Power* (New York: Free Press, 1989): 51–53, 55–56, 63, 68–71, 153, 184–85.

35. Mansfield, ibid., 251–52, 261, 268–70, 273–74.

36. Mansfield, op. cit.

37. Compare Mansfield, ibid., 127, 133–34, 140, 142, 238. These observations require us to qualify Ceaser's judgment likening Wilson to Hamilton, especially regarding unity in the executive. See note 6 above.

38. CG PWW 18:214–15.

39. CG PWW 18:114.

40. The same answer is suggested in *Constitutional Government* at PWW 18: 113–14, but I believe Wilson intended this to be read in conjunction with the corresponding passages in *The State*.

41. Woodrow Wilson, *The State: Elements of Historical and Practical Politics*, Sec. 1329:543. In the 1918 edition, this is on 375.

42. Article I, Section 1 (my emphasis).

43. Mansfield, op. cit., 262.

44. CG PWW 18:123 (emphasis added).

45. CG PWW 18:120.

46. CG PWW 18:121.

47. That this is the thrust of Wilson's understanding of sovereignty, which would effectively make Congress the sovereign, is clear from Wilson's 1891 lecture, "Political Sovereignty"—"On the whole, however, it is safe to ascribe sovereignty to the highest originative or law-making body of the State—the body by whose determinations both the tasks to be carried out by the Administration and the rules to be applied by the courts are fixed and warranted. . . . As for the Executive, it is the agent, not the organ, of Sovereignty." PWW 7:341.

48. Mansfield, op. cit., 16.

49. See the remarks on Ceaser and Tulis above.

9

Presidents and Their Cosmopolitan Advisers: The Nixon-Kissinger Dialogue

Donald R. Brand

Ever since Franklin Roosevelt tapped a number of academicians to serve as his informal "brain trust" in crafting the New Deal, presidents have returned to this well in selecting prominent administrative advisers and aides. However familiar it may now seem, this pattern is somewhat peculiar, for the university and the political arena differ fundamentally, and intellectuals and politicians would therefore appear to have little in common. Intellectuals tend to pride themselves on their skepticism regarding parochial traditions, pointing in particular to the detachment they have achieved from the time and place in which they were raised. Politicians tend to remain more firmly wedded to the principles and traditions of their country and their era. This attachment is a source of their electoral strength and of their capacity to move nations.

The attempt to achieve a universalistic perspective is intrinsic to the philosophic enterprise and dates back to the ancient Greeks. It was not until the Enlightenment, however, that the cosmopolitanism of philosophy was directly coupled to political aspirations. Intellectuals, hoping to reform political practice, either sought political power themselves or encouraged politicians to adopt their virtues by becoming more cosmopolitan. The distinction between the realms of theory and practice began to blur. By the twentieth century, this cosmopolitan project, in significantly modified forms, had revolutionized world history.

The Enlightenment sought a fundamental transformation in the character of political regimes. A regime grounded in reason must detach

219

itself from alternative grounds such as tradition or religion. This "transvaluation of values" alters the ends pursued by political actors. When this revolutionary undertaking is pursued immoderately, it cannot hope to be popular. It becomes fundamentally a war against recalcitrant popular ignorance and prejudice and degenerates into tyranny. The Soviet Union under communism is a chilling example of where this project can take us.

Some countries have been more successful than others in taming the Enlightenment impulse to create a wholly cosmopolitan society. The American Framers recognized the importance of factors specific to the United States in shaping our political culture. Hence they fashioned a republican government tailored to the republican mores of its citizens. In deference to the parochial loyalties of the former colonists, they also carved out a place for states in the new, enlarged *federal* republic. The regime they founded was a mixture of cosmopolitanism and localism. Abstract theory attenuated but did not eradicate particular attachments.

Any and all concessions to parochialism weaken the influence of intellectuals as a class. In the American mixed regime, the political role of intellectuals depends on their willingness to moderate their cosmopolitan political aspirations by distinguishing between theoretical and practical wisdom. With this distinction they might come to appreciate the reasonableness of their fellow citizens' devotion to religion and tradition as indispensable antidotes to tyranny.

I will use the distinction between cosmopolitan intellectuals and parochial citizens to analyze Henry Kissinger's relationship with Richard Nixon. While Kissinger and Nixon agreed on the general direction of American foreign policy during the Nixon presidency, differences that subsequently emerged as each played the role of elder statesman suggest that their earlier policy agreement was not derived from shared worldviews. Kissinger was a liberal realist, ultimately a disciple of Thomas Hobbes. Kissinger's conception of relations among states in the international arena resembles Hobbes's description of relations among individuals (as well as states) in the state of nature, and like Hobbes, he tended to view all politics as a struggle for power. Hobbes's teaching is cosmopolitan in its denial of the relevance of moral, religious, partisan, or other qualitative human distinctions to the construction of a rational state. In contrast, Richard Nixon remained a citizen whose political horizon was defined by the American regime.

Liberal Realism in Political Science

The philosophical orientation of Kissinger's political science is evident in his preference for cosmopolitan statesmen. In his first book, *A World Restored*, he praises Prince Metternich as the finest statesman of his day. By Kissinger's account, the peace settlement that Metternich fashioned at the end of the Napoleonic Wars made him in effect the prime minister of Europe, the highest practical approximation to cosmopolitan rule possible in that day: "Metternich with his cosmopolitan education and rationalist philosophy, Austrian only by the accident of feudal relationships, could be imagined equally easily as the minister of any other state."[1] In Kissinger's view, statesmen can function most effectively in an arena where nations define their self-interest narrowly and concretely. But the achievement by such nations of a stable balance of power requires cosmopolitan diplomatic virtuosity.

According to Kissinger, a sound statesman's judgment requires overcoming the love of one's own nation that blinds individuals and peoples to the fundamental similarities among nations. Americans typically are less cosmopolitan than Europeans because they are committed to a belief in American exceptionalism. The tendency for American foreign policy to vacillate between an unrealistic isolationism and a misguided messianic interventionism can be traced to the belief "that the United States possessed the world's best system of government."[2] Kissinger finds a similar parochial pride responsible for Russian and Soviet expansionism, noting that "like Americans, Russians thought of their society as exceptional" (142).

Kissinger's preference for cosmopolitan statesmanship is Hobbesian. Hobbes dismisses the guidance of parochial traditions and turns instead to unassisted and universal human reason. According to Hobbes, effective theorists must become skeptical of the moral judgments of their fellow citizens, and he formulated a systematic methodology for achieving the required detachment. He begins by relativizing our understanding of good and evil. According to Hobbes

> whatsoever is the object of any man's appetite or desire, that is it which he for his part calleth *good*: and the object of his hate and aversion, *evil*; and of his contempt, *vile* and *inconsiderable*. For these words of good, evil, and contemptible, are ever used with relation to the person that useth them: there being nothing simply and absolutely so. . . .[3]

For Hobbes the acceptance of this moral relativism is only a prelude to the construction of a new conventional moral horizon. For many of those who have followed in his footsteps, however, Hobbes's critique of traditional morality has taken on a life of its own. Utilitarian students of Hobbes, like Hans Morgenthau, the author of *Politics Among Nations*, a widely read textbook on international relations that has gone through seven editions since first being published in 1948, have claimed that political life would be healthier if we would eschew the distinction between good and evil and make the distinction between the advantageous and the disadvantageous the touchstone for political analysis.[4] Judgments of virtue and vice should be replaced by judgments of interest because a politics based on the good and its corollary, the virtues, will lead to interminable conflict that will be harmful to all. In developing this line of thought, Morgenthau and other "liberal realists" had in mind the destructive religious wars that had engulfed Europe after the Protestant Reformation.

Liberal realists often conceal rhetorically how radical their project really is. Under the guise of traditional language, they sought to abolish the moral horizon. While they appeared to be pouring new wine into old skins, they were moral prohibitionists who encouraged people to abstain from moral reasoning altogether. Calculations based on concrete interests were to replace abstract moral speculations, which were too prone to sophistic manipulation or casuistry.

Morgenthau was the founder of the liberal realist school in America, but Kissinger is the most prominent contemporary spokesman of liberal realism and its most illustrious practitioner. Contrasting the European and American diplomatic traditions, Kissinger argues that the former has been dominated by a sensible realpolitik approach, which eschews moral judgments and replaces them with calculations of power based on national interest. Such calculations maximize the possibility of establishing stable balances of power and achieving relative peace. In contrast, Kissinger argues, the American tradition has allowed moralism to distort and mask a clear perception of interests.

For Kissinger, the fundamental mistake Americans make is to apply the same ethical norms that they apply to individual behavior to the behavior of states. The result of this mistaken procedure is that America has "tormented itself over the gap between its moral values, which are by definition absolute, and the imperfection inherent in the concrete situation to which they apply" (22–23). Kissinger's assertion that moral values are absolute entails the conclusion that they are unsuited for providing guidance in the imperfect world of international relations.

On the surface, Kissinger is not calling for an amoral power politics. He contrasts Otto von Bismarck's late-nineteenth-century attempt to establish a balance of power based exclusively on amoral calculations of power unfavorably with Metternich's attempt to fashion a balance based simultaneously on an equilibrium of power and a shared sense of legitimacy. Bismarck's attempt foundered because calculations of power are inherently imprecise. Hence, the balance of power he constructed was too fragile and too dependent on his own statesmanship to survive. But Metternich succeeded because the 1815 Congress of Vienna achieved a congruence of "power and justice" and thereby established a consensual framework within which a stable equilibrium of power was possible.

In fact, however, Kissinger is not nearly so critical of Bismarck as he first appears to be. Bismarck is portrayed as a rational statesman in an irrational world. He is faulted not for pursuing power in the international arena, nor for ignoring justice in his pursuit of German interests, but for failing to institutionalize his system of power politics. Bismarck needed to secure the legitimacy of his accomplishments, to make them rest more on consent and less on force, by justifying them in terms of consensually shared "values." But since some consensually shared values would not have sanctioned Bismarck's achievements, Kissinger implicitly denigrates those values. Kissinger would praise as "enlightened" only those consensually shared values that accommodate the rational calculations of international power politics.

The highest task of statesmanship, Kissinger holds, is to promote enlightened values. Bismarck failed because of this limitation of his statesmanship. The publication of *Diplomacy* was Kissinger's attempt to rectify the same shortcoming in his own career by disabusing Americans of the idealist illusions that prevented them from appreciating his accomplishments and building upon them.

Religion, according to Kissinger, is one of the most prolific sources of values that subvert rational power calculations. In his history of diplomacy, the age of diplomacy and the attendant practice of realpolitik follow the age of religion. The European balance of power system arose from the ruins of the seventeenth-century wars of religion and the final collapse of the "medieval aspirations to universality" derivative from the universality of the Catholic church. Rational politics became possible only when religion was demoted to the private sphere of individual conscience and the public sphere became emphatically secular.

When religion does intrude into the public sphere in the modern world, Kissinger invariably portrays it as an eruption of the irrational. Thus, Russian expansionism is traced to the influence of the Russian Orthodox Church:

> Nationalist Russian and Pan-Slavic writers and intellectuals ascribed the alleged altruism of the Russian nation to its Orthodox faith. . . . Unlike the states of Western Europe, which Russia simultaneously admired, despised, and envied, Russia perceived itself not as a nation but as a cause, beyond geopolitics, *impelled by faith*, and held together by arms. (143; emphasis mine)

Kissinger goes on to describe communism as a form of secular religion and to suggest that after the 1917 revolution, "the passionate sense of mission" associated with Russian orthodoxy under the czars "was transferred to the Communist International" (143). In the American context religion is similarly disruptive. Kissinger describes Woodrow Wilson as a "prophet-priest" and characterizes his World War I intervention as a "global crusade," which allowed Wilson to "proselytize for a new and better approach to international affairs." Wilson inappropriately tried to make "altruism," a value closely associated with religion, the animating spirit of American foreign policy because "the altruistic nature of American society was proof of divine favor" (45–47). Wilson's religiosity is the source of his diplomatic failings, which Kissinger would describe as a lamentable messianic internationalism and a naive faith in international law and collective security.

For liberal realists, moralism can manifest itself not only in naive idealism but also in a truculent response to a foe perceived as evil. Thus, Kissinger has criticized not only idealists like Woodrow Wilson and Jimmy Carter, but tough-minded anticommunists like Harry Truman and Ronald Reagan as well. Kissinger describes Truman as a president who "rejected balance of power, disdained justifying American actions in terms of security, and sought whenever possible to attach them to general principles applicable to all mankind and in keeping with the new United Nations charter. Truman perceived the emerging struggle between the United States and the Soviet Union as a contest between good and evil, not as having to do with spheres of political influence" (446–47).

Kissinger cites Truman's inaugural address of 20 January 1949, and its subsequent elaboration in the policy of containment, as typical examples of an open-ended American commitment to the moral principle of national self-determination, without regard for the limits of American resources or its specific national interests (662). Truman gave America the impossible and debilitating task of world policeman.

Kissinger's analysis of Reagan's foreign policy focuses on similar themes. Reagan described the Soviet Union as an "evil empire" that had to be resisted. To refuse to shoulder the burdens of national defense was to "remove yourself from the struggle between right and wrong and good and evil."[5] Noting this dimension of Reagan's approach to the Soviet Union, Kissinger compares Reagan, with his "insistently confrontational style," to Wilson. Moralists like Reagan and Wilson fail to understand politics in terms of realistic geopolitical analysis, and their inflammatory rhetoric subverts diplomacy. Reagan brought détente to an end during his first term in office by issuing "a direct moral challenge from which all of his predecessors would have recoiled" (767).

Kissinger's suggestion that Reagan's approach to the cold war differed from that of his predecessors must be properly understood. Kissinger does not mean that whereas Reagan was a moralist, most of his predecessors had been realists. In fact, only Theodore Roosevelt and Nixon among twentieth-century presidents qualify as realists in Kissinger's typology. Hence, Reagan "was closer to classical patterns of American thinking than Nixon had been." Reagan differed quantitatively from most of his predecessors in the stridency of his rhetoric, but it was Nixon who differed qualitatively from his predecessors and successors in the realism of his worldview. According to Kissinger, "Nixon would not have used the phrase 'evil empire' to describe the Soviet Union. . . ." (785).

Kissinger's critique of Reagan's foreign policy is actually a thumbnail sketch of his critique of American foreign policy throughout the cold war:

Reagan overrode conventional diplomatic wisdom, and he oversimplified America's virtues in pursuit of a self-appointed mission to convince the American people that the East-West ideological conflict mattered and that some international struggles are about winners and losers, not about staying power or diplomacy. (813)

Preserving a balance of power, not victory over competitors, is the goal of a rational foreign policy.

Kissinger's realpolitik approach is also evident in his recommendations for a foreign policy in a postcommunist world. Kissinger's focus on geopolitical realities leads him to downplay the significance of the kind of political regime that succeeds communism. Kissinger notes with concern that

> American policy has been based on the premise that peace can be ensured by a Russia tempered by democracy and concentrating its energies on developing a market economy. In this light, America's principal task is conceived to be to strengthen Russian reform, with measures drawn from the experience of the Marshall Plan rather than from the traditional patterns of foreign policy. (814)

According to Kissinger, "students of geopolitics and history are uneasy" with a foreign policy that is primarily directed at securing the success of Russian domestic reforms. Communism had only exacerbated the problem of Russian imperialism, a problem rooted in Russian geography and history. With the fall of communism there are grounds for optimism that the Russian Federation can be integrated into a stable balance-of-power arrangement, but greater realism concerning the nature of this nation is needed if we are to achieve this outcome. The Russian Federation is still "the heir to one of the most potent imperial traditions" (815).

Kissinger stresses that Russia will not be America's friend just because we provide aid to it during a difficult time of transition. The rational calculation of self-interest, not feelings of friendship or enmity, is the proper foundation for conducting foreign policy. We should expect the Russians to proceed on this basis, and we should do the same. The Russians, following the self-interested dictates of human nature to maximize power, have already exploited the weakness of the new nations that have spun off from the former Soviet Union. But the United States, whose national interest dictates keeping Russia weaker and shoring up the independence of the former Soviet colonies, has not been responding to this threat to our interest in a rational manner (815).

Kissinger attributes the failure of American foreign policy to properly respond to the post–cold war world to our characteristic idealistic moralism. It leads us to evaluate other nations in terms of our conjectures about their intentions [a category of moral analysis] rather than an analysis of the likely consequences of their actions:

With respect to no other country [than Russia] has American policy been geared as consistently to an assessment of its intentions rather than to its potential or even its policies. Franklin Roosevelt had staked his hopes for a peaceful postwar world to a considerable degree on Stalin's moderation. . . . Even Reagan placed great stock in what amounted to the conversion of Soviet leaders. Not surprisingly, in the aftermath of the communist collapse, it has been assumed that hostile intentions have disappeared, and, since the Wilsonian tradition rejects conflicting interests, American post–Cold War policy has been conducted as if traditional foreign policy considerations no longer apply. (813)

To reinforce his claim that "Wilsonian concepts like 'enlarging democracy' [cannot] serve as the principal guides to American foreign policy," Kissinger argues that the attempt to foster democracy in the Russian Federation is problematic. Western-style democracies flourish in countries that have strong, relatively homogeneous societies with a fundamental consensus of values. Such countries can restrict the role of the state, decentralize power, and safely permit political parties to contest elections. In other parts of the world with different historical backgrounds, a strongly centralized authoritarian state may be the only alternative to anarchy. For Kissinger, the fundamental question is how a regime conducts itself in the international arena, and he denies that democracies are the only regimes that act moderately and prudently. Kissinger recommends that we "bolster the obstacles to Russian expansion" and "not place all the chips on domestic reform" (817).

Consistent with these principles, Kissinger portrays the former Soviet leader Mikhail Gorbachev in a more favorable light than Boris Yeltsin. While acknowledging that Gorbachev was a communist who sought to reform communism rather than subvert it, Kissinger stresses that there was a fundamental change in the behavior of the Soviet Union under Gorbachev. "Gorbachev was the first Soviet leader . . . to proclaim coexistence as an end in itself" (789). Under Gorbachev, the Soviet Union had transformed itself from a revolutionary state seeking to subvert the international order into a status quo power that sought peace so it could turn its energies inward. Whereas Gorbachev accepted the dissolution of the Soviet empire in Eastern Europe, "the reformist Russian government of Boris Yeltsin has maintained Russian armies on the territory of most of the former Soviet republics . . . often against the express wish of the host government" (815).

The detachment from questions of regime that Kissinger displays in his approach to the Soviet Union under Gorbachev and the Russian Federation under Yeltsin is linked to the detachment from moral valuations that we have identified as a premise of liberal realism. Regimes are constituted by shared conceptions of the good. If judgments of good and evil are to be avoided for the sake of rational policy, then we must develop a mode of political analysis that abstracts from regime questions in examining political conflict. But only a cosmopolitan scientist can approach the world in this way. Citizens are too wedded to conventional notions of good and evil and too inclined to identify with regimes that share their conception of the good, or hostile to regimes that differ from their own. Citizens approach international relations from the vantage point of friends and enemies.

Richard Nixon: Citizen

Just as Kissinger's cosmopolitan commitments are visible in his choice of Metternich as a statesman to honor and emulate, Nixon's more parochial commitments are visible in his choice of statesmen to honor in his book *Leaders*. If there is one quality shared by all the men whom Nixon chooses for his list of twentieth-century statesmen, it is that they embody the spirit and character of their nation, and they identify their interests with the interests of the nation. Typical is his assessment of Charles de Gaulle:

> Just as the ancient Chinese viewed China as the "Middle Kingdom"—the center of the world, beyond which all was merely peripheral—so de Gaulle saw France as a sort of middle kingdom. The rest of the world had meaning only as it affected France. He could be cold-eyed and farsighted in analyzing the affairs of the world but his policies were solely those designed to advance or protect the interests of France.[6]

Wedded to the American regime as he was, Nixon could appreciate other statesmen who were wedded to their regimes in turn. To Nixon a cosmopolitan statesman was an oxymoron.

For Nixon, the political horizon was defined by American national interests broadly understood. Nixon believed that the Soviet Union represented the most fundamental threat to those interests, and the ultimate goal of his foreign policy was to contain the Soviet threat. Nixon's overtures to China can be understood in this way. Nixon contrasted China and Russia, arguing that China unlike Russia had not historically been an imperialistic or expansionist nation. Believing that these historical traditions would color the character of communism in each nation, Nixon concluded that China was less of a threat in the long run and that it shared an interest with the United States in containing the Soviet Union.[7] The effect of the establishment of American relations with China was a more stable international system, but Nixon's primary intention was a system serving American national interests.

Kissinger, on the other hand, saw the creation of a stable international system as a valuable end in itself. His biographer, Walter Issacson, accurately captured this cosmopolitan dimension of Kissinger's statesmanship when he described Kissinger's goal in the opening to China as an attempt "to create a triangular diplomacy rather than simply to enlist a new ally in the old bipolar game."[8] Kissinger believed that bipolar systems were less stable than multipolar systems, a cosmopolitan concern that Nixon did not share.

The differences between Kissinger and Nixon are particularly visible when we recall Kissinger's criticisms of Reagan for believing that "some international struggles are about winners and losers, not about staying power or diplomacy," and Kissinger's suggestion that Nixon would never have used the term "evil empire" to describe the Soviet Union. But Nixon did describe the conflict between the Soviet Union and the United States as a real conflict in which the United States should seek *victory*, albeit primarily by nonmilitary means:

> And it [victory] does require a firm unflagging faith, as Lincoln would put it, that we are on God's side, that our cause is right, that we act for all mankind.
>
> It may seem melodramatic to treat the twin poles of human experience represented by the United States and the Soviet Union as the equivalent of Good and Evil, Light and Darkness, God and the Devil; yet if we allow ourselves to think of them that way, even hypothetically, it can help clarify our perspective on the world struggle. As the British writer Malcolm Muggeridge has pointed out, "Good and evil . . . provide the theme of the drama of our moral existence. In this sense, they may be compared with the positive and negative points which generate an electric current; transpose the points and the current fails, the lights go out, darkness falls and all is confusion."[9]

Judging from this postpresidential statement, Nixon was much closer to Reagan than Kissinger had believed.

The differences between Nixon and Kissinger are also visible in
their respective attitudes toward the religious foundations of political
life. As we have observed, Kissinger is a typical child of the Enlightenment, arguing that religion exacerbates political conflict and that a
secular, philosophically grounded approach to political life is a pre-
condition for respectable political practice. In contrast, Nixon retro-
spectively presents the struggle between the United States and the
Soviet Union in a religious framework:

> The Soviet Union began by banishing God. The United States began
> as a community of people who wanted to worship God as they chose.
> Many factors contributed to the outcome of the Cold War. One cru-
> cial but underrated factor was that a system that attempted to blunt,
> deny, and even punish the spiritual aspirations of its people could
> not survive because it was fundamentally at odds with human na-
> ture. Man does not live by bread alone. Those in the United States
> whose desire to create a strictly secular society is as strong as Len-
> in's was should study this Cold War lesson closely. Communism was
> defeated by an alliance spearheaded by "one nation under God."[10]

The struggle between democracy and tyranny or between communism
and capitalism was more fundamentally a struggle between Christian
civilization and atheism. "Democracy and capitalism are just techniques unless they are employed by those who seek a higher purpose
for themselves and their society,"[11] and Americans have traditionally
understood democracy and capitalism as means for securing the freedom to worship.

The differences between Nixon and Kissinger not only shaped their
approaches to the cold war; they also carried over into their perspectives on the post–cold war world. In contrast to Kissinger's sympa-
thetic portrayal of Gorbachev, Nixon stresses that Gorbachev was a
committed Marxist who sought to reform communism rather than
overthrow it. Nixon concedes that Gorbachev's reforms paved the way
for the collapse of communism, but he emphasizes that this was an
unintended consequence of reforms that unleashed forces Gorbachev
could not control. As of 1992, Nixon focused "on what [had] not
changed" in the Soviet Union under Gorbachev, and emphasized that
the Soviet Union still posed a serious threat to America, potentially
a more serious one than it had under more cautious leadership. Under
Gorbachev, the Soviet military had modernized and the Soviet Union
continued to spend 20 percent of its GNP on the military in contrast
to the 6 percent spent by the United States. Under Gorbachev, Mos-

cow continued to provide aid to communist regimes in Cuba, Afghanistan, Vietnam, and Nicaragua, and it sold arms to regimes that exported international terrorism.[12]

Nixon maintained that even Gorbachev's most conciliatory gestures were strategic moves calculated to advance Soviet interests and weaken the collective resolve of the West to stem the tide of communism. By making the Soviet Union appear less threatening, Gorbachev could weaken "the glue that holds the anti-Soviet alliance together." By accepting the collapse of the Soviet empire in Eastern Europe, Gorbachev could "make a play for a far more important target—the psychological disarmament of Western Europe." A seemingly more peaceful Soviet Union could gain access to Western technology and financial assistance to further its domestic reforms. But, Nixon argued, a successfully reformed Soviet Union might simply be a more dangerous adversary since "the hallmark of his [Gorbachev's] 'new thinking' in foreign policy has been shrewder tactics, not kinder *intentions*" (emphasis mine).[13]

As we have noted, to a practitioner of realpolitik like Kissinger, Nixon's focus on the intentions of the leaders of the Soviet Union is misguided. A geopolitical approach, Kissinger argues, resists the tendency to personalize foreign policy because "foreign policy builds on quicksand when it disregards actual power relationships and relies on prophesies of another's intentions" (301). Kissinger had faulted Woodrow Wilson for understanding German behavior in the World War I through the lens of the Kaiser and his intentions, a lens that caused him to respond moralistically (49, 245). A similar judgment applied to the interwar period:

> The West's obsession with Hitler's motives was, of course, misguided in the first place. . . . *Realpolitik* teaches that, regardless of Hitler's motives, Germany's relations with its neighbors would be determined by their relative power. The West should have spent less time assessing Hitler's motives and more time counterbalancing Germany's growing strength. (294)

Nixon's evaluation of the Russian Federation under Yeltsin also diverged from liberal realist principles. Insisting that American national interests, broadly construed, include an interest in the fate of reforms in the Russian Federation, Nixon concludes that the failure of reforms would "have a profoundly negative impact." If Russia slips back into autocracy, this would "give inspiration to every dictator and

would-be dictator in the world." Nixon asserts that the linkage between domestic regime and foreign policy is closer than Kis-singer
concedes: "Since an authoritarian Russia would be far more likely to
adopt an aggressive foreign policy than a democratic Russia, freedom's failure would threaten peace and stability in Europe and around
the world."[14]

Nixon acknowledges that it will take time for the Russians to successfully institutionalize democracy, and in the interim tough measures may be needed to preserve order. If the United States is to play
a constructive role in encouraging democracy in Russia, it must develop discriminating judgment so as to distinguish between the harsh
means that may be necessary to secure democracy and the arbitrary
repression of authoritarianism. Attempting to use such judgment, Nixon
praises Yeltsin's generally positive role in fostering democracy and
capitalism. While cautioning against identifying America's interests
with Yeltsin's in ways that could harm us when Yeltsin is replaced,
Nixon nevertheless sympathetically contrasts Yeltsin's achievements
with those of his predecessor, Gorbachev. Kissinger's insistence that
we regard Russia as a potential foe, even if democratization succeeds,
stands in contrast to Nixon's hopes:

> basing our policy on such a contingency would require an element
> of cynicism that would violate American foreign policy traditions.
> We did not act this way toward Germany and Japan after World War
> II, and we should not act this way toward Russia after the Cold War.
> . . . It would be the height of hypocrisy for any Western statesman
> who spoke movingly of the plight of the Soviet people living under
> the communist yoke to withhold the hand of friendship from the Russian
> people now that communism has been defeated. (56)

Nixon thus divides the world into friends and enemies. Under communism the Soviet Union had been our enemy. As an emerging democracy, the Russian Federation was our friend. Liberal realists like
Kissinger insist that atheoretical categories like friend and enemy do
not apply to international relations because nations act out of
self-interest, not out of friendship or enmity. Thus, according to Kissinger, when Franklin Roosevelt tried to befriend Joseph Stalin and
establish a new world order at the end of World War II, Roosevelt
was misguided not because Stalin was a poor choice of friends but
because nations cannot be friends. Befriending Winston Churchill was
just as misguided.[15]

Conclusion

Given the significant differences in the worldviews of Nixon and Kissinger as elder statesmen, what is striking is their agreement on the proximate objectives of foreign policy during the Nixon presidency and their ability to work together to achieve shared goals. Liberal realists should weigh the significance of this. In the seventeenth century when the foundations for the liberal realist school of thought were being developed, philosophers like Hobbes were convinced that nothing less than the displacement of religious moralism by Hobbesian political science would suffice to fortify the influence of reason in the world. This conclusion became an article of faith for liberal realists, who have asserted ever since that an analysis of international relations grounded in concepts of good and evil, a bipolarity inherent in all forms of religious moralism, is inherently simplistic.

Yet why should an analysis framed in terms of the distinction between good and evil be *inherently* more simplistic than an analysis framed in terms of the distinction between the advantageous and the disadvantageous (an analysis framed in terms of interest)? Each distinction *can* be applied in an oversimplified manner if the analysis is crude. If statesmen are appealing to a public, they must simplify *any* form of subtle analysis to get their point across and arouse an appropriate response. But neither of these points undercuts the possibility of a subtle analysis of international relations framed in terms of good and evil. Medieval political thought from Augustine to Aquinas was dominated by the contrast between good and evil, yet it was anything but simplistic.

Liberal realists have assumed that a moral conception of international relations will be lacking in prudence. The natural tendency of moralism, it is asserted, is simplistic universalism. If democracy is valued as a moral goal, then a moralistic foreign policy will imprudently seek to establish democratic regimes even where the prerequisites for stable democratic government are lacking. Liberal realists point to Wilson's foreign policy as confirmation of this alleged propensity. Certainly, liberal realists are on solid ground in warning of the dangers of moralism. But as the preceding analysis of Nixon makes clear, liberal realists have underestimated the possibilities of avoiding moralism within a moral framework. Because Kissinger and other liberal realists have not faced up to this possibility, they have mistakenly categorized Nixon in the camp of the realists.

Kissinger might have had a better understanding of Nixon if he had thought through the implications of Nixon's decision to hang Wilson's portrait prominently in the Oval Office (54). Instead Kissinger dismissed this as a puzzling anomaly. Kissinger assumed that since Nixon's foreign policy did not manifest the characteristic vices of Wilsonian moralism, Nixon's conception of politics must have been amoral. Since Nixon argued that "making the world safe for liberty . . . does not mean establishing democracy everywhere on earth," and since he did not want the United States to become the world's "policeman,"[16] his analysis of foreign policy must, in Kissinger's view, have been grounded simply in the concepts of power and national interest. This conclusion would be sound only if prudence and morality are antithetical, and this is not the case.

If presidents who have a moral worldview can nevertheless be prudent and accept advice from liberal realists who eschew moral conceptions, then liberal realists may have to reconsider their strategies for achieving political influence. Throughout his magnum opus *Diplomacy*, Kissinger expresses the hope that Americans will come to understand the virtues of realpolitik and contain their propensities for moralism. Kissinger longs for the day when realpolitik will become an acknowledged public philosophy, and liberal realists will rule. He insists that Americans give up their prideful claim of American exceptionalism and become cosmopolitans. But there are weighty reasons for believing that liberal realism cannot rule in a democracy, because its cosmopolitan detachment and amoral calculations of power offend widely held beliefs.

Once we recognize the utopian character of the demand that the citizenry at large embrace a realpolitik perspective, we can begin to investigate alternative ways of incorporating some of the important insights of the liberal realists into American political discourse without presupposing a revolutionary transformation of perspective. The strength of realism has always been its capacity to rein in our hopes by forcing us to examine the limited resources at our disposal for realizing those hopes. Realism encourages moderation.

Liberal realism may be most effective playing a supporting role, tempering the propensities to moralism that reside in any moral worldview without seeking to displace good and evil as an orienting framework. Kissinger's own career demonstrates that liberal realists can achieve influence without realpolitik becoming a public philosophy. Although Kissinger is optimistic that America "can still accomplish more than any other society if it can only learn its limits," he never demonstrates that the adoption of realpolitik is the only or even the most certain path to a recognition of limits (834). Unless such a demonstration can be produced, we should conclude that although liberal realists can make good national security advisers and good secretaries of state, they would make poor presidents.

Notes

I wish to thank Tom Baldino, Ashim Basu, Peter Lawler, Dan Mahoney, and David Schaefer for their help in developing this paper.

1. Henry Kissinger, *A World Restored* (Boston: Houghton Mifflin, 1964), 321.
2. Henry Kissinger, *Diplomacy* (New York: Simon and Schuster, 1994), 18. Parenthetical citations in the text refer to this book.
3. Thomas Hobbes, *Leviathan* (New York: Macmillan, 1962), chap. 6, 48–49.
4. In *Politics Among Nations,* Morgenthau does not distinguish the use of good and evil as concepts of judgment from the claim to have absolute knowledge of good and evil. Morgenthau rhetorically labels the latter claim blasphemous and dismisses it as epistemologically untenable, "morally indefensible," and "politically pernicious." Morgenthau then goes on to argue that "the concept of interest defined in terms of power . . . saves us from both that moral excess and that political folly." See Hans Morgenthau and Kenneth W. Thompson, *Politics Among Nations,* 6th ed. (New York: Knopf, 1985), 13.
5. Cited in Lou Cannon, *President Reagan: The Role of a Lifetime* (New York: Simon and Schuster, 1991), 317.
6. Richard Nixon, *Leaders* (New York: Warner Books, 1982), p. 83.
7. Richard Nixon, *In the Arena* (New York: Simon and Schuster, 1992), 329; also, *The Real War* (New York: Simon and Schuster, 1980), 128–29, 132, 136, 146–47.
8. Walter Issacson, *Kissinger* (New York: Simon and Schuster, 1992), 403.
9. Nixon, *The Real War,* 313–14.
10. Richard Nixon, *Beyond Peace* (New York: Random House, 1994), 20–21.
11. Ibid., 21.
12. Nixon, *In the Arena,* 316–17.
13. Ibid., 318–20.
14. Nixon, *Beyond Peace,* 40.
15. Kissinger, *Diplomacy,* 412, 417–18.
16. Nixon, *The Real War,* 312–13.

10

Limiting Bureaucratic Discretion: Competing Theories of Administrative Law

Gary C. Bryner

Dissatisfaction with government bureaucracy has been a staple of American political life, but criticisms reached a new level by the mid-1990s. Federal bureaucrats were blamed for a host of governmental failures and social ills. Candidates built political careers by bashing bureaucrats; collecting bureaucratic horror stories became a high priority for members of Congress and the media. Some criticism culminated in acts of violence aimed at federal agencies and officials. Bureaucracy is regularly scolded as being out of touch with the needs of states and communities, mired in red tape, and ensnared in old ways of thinking. Academics, analysts, and policy advocates leveled their aim at agencies, administrative procedures, agency rulemaking, litigation, and a host of other shortcomings in the process of formulating and implementing public policies.[1] The new Republican leadership of Congress, elected in 1994, provided a focal point for dissatisfaction with government and led a frontal assault on government, from environmental regulation to welfare, in bills that were passed as part of the House Republicans' Contract with America and the Senate's agenda.

Regulatory agencies and bureaucrats, not surprisingly, often bear the brunt of attacks against government. Bureaucrats and agencies are caught in the middle of the ideological and policy debate over the size and role of government, and what specific actions governments should or should not take. They also occupy a tenuous position in the American constitutional system, as they exercise important policy-making powers without enjoying the legitimacy that comes from express constitutional creation.

237

Some criticism of bureaucracy is rooted in the separation of powers and institutional conflict inherent in the structure of government.
Administrative decisions and actions are expected to conform to notions of the rule of law and consistency with relevant statutes, to be
responsive to direction given by Congress and by the president, to
accommodate judicial norms and standards of due process, and to
efficiently and effectively reduce environmental risks. Agencies are
also expected to accommodate demands for access to agency officials and to the decision-making process for a variety of interests as
well as to be guided by expertise and professional norms and values
and by objective policy analysis. Much of the dissatisfaction with
government agencies is a result of their inability to satisfy inconsistent and, to some extent, mutually exclusive expectations.[2]

This chapter explores the role of administrative law in bridging
the gap between constitutional expectations and the practical imperatives of governing. It examines the origins of administrative law and
its evolution in response to criticisms and changes in the size and
scope of the federal government, and then reviews the current debate
over whether and how administrative law ought to be "reformed."

The Rise and Evolution of Administrative Law

Until the 1930s, the era of the Great Depression and the New Deal,
most of the governing that took place in the United States occurred at
the state and local levels. The federal government, apart from its responsibility for foreign affairs, was primarily interested in promoting
commerce, agriculture, and industry; primary responsibility rested with
the states for the regulation of social and economic life—public health,
criminal laws, banking and credit regulation, property laws, regulation of water and other natural resources, licensing of professions,
creation and regulation of schools, and electoral laws.[3]

The decentralized nature of this governmental activity permitted
much of the policy-making power to be exercised directly by elected
officials and citizen groups rather than administrative bodies. That
began to change after the Civil War, however, as state governments
began creating regulatory bodies in response to perceived failures or
limitations of market exchanges. Demand for state regulation of public health, pollution, and other byproducts of industrialization and ur-
banization was stimulated during the last part of the nineteenth century,
as individual communities could no longer control their own quality

of life. State government bureaucracies, staffed by economists and other professionals, became increasingly important during this time, as these problems were no longer seen as amenable to resolution by direct political processes. Great confidence was placed in the ability of experts and professionals to manage and direct economic and social behavior. Some of these regulatory tasks eventually came to be viewed as outside the scope even of effective state action, and attention was directed toward the federal government. The first major federal regulatory agency, the Interstate Commerce Commission, was created in 1887. Subsequent agencies such as the forerunner of the Food and Drug Administration, formed in 1907, and the Federal Trade Commission, organized in 1914, were also given regulatory responsibilities. All of this represented a significant growth in government, and especially administrative government, at all levels.[4]

The federal government was itself transformed in the 1930s, as it assumed new functions, in ways that have had profound consequences for public administration. First, the federal government became the center of regulatory and redistributive power, accompanied by the conflict and political controversy that inevitably surround the exercise of those powers. Fundamental choices concerning economic activity and the regulation of community health and safety were increasingly viewed as federal rather than state responsibilities. Second, Congress increasingly began delegating broad policy-making powers to the executive branch and particularly to administrative agencies.[5]

Many political leaders in the early nineteenth century emphasized accountability as the primary criterion for good government. The Jacksonian theory was that government is and ought to be simple enough to be run by the ordinary citizen. The persons selected by the victorious political party would conduct the affairs of state at an acceptable level of efficiency and effectiveness, while remaining fully accountable to the electorate. Civil service laws from 1883 until the 1960s shifted the focus toward efficiency by removing political parties from the recruitment process, while at the same time developing norms of professional public service through job classification and examination.The goal of accountability, while never absent, was subordinated to efficiency and was made to appear consonant with efficiency through the theory of the "neutral civil servant," which held that professionally competent and dedicated civil servants will accept and zealously implement the policies and goals to which the victorious party is committed. The expansion of the federal govern-

ment in the 1930s firmly embraced the ideal of expertise and efficiency, but as the size of bureaucratic government expanded, concern
over accountability also grew.[6]

Administrative law has been shaped and formed by legal doctrines
developed by the courts and by legal scholars as well as by broader
ideas of political theory.[7] Progressivism, with its faith in expertise
and in the concentration of governmental powers, contributed to the
development of an administrative law that largely deferred to administrative expertise. Judicial review was limited by the presumption that
agency decision making was due great deference and that there was
little for judges to do in monitoring the administrative process. By
1900, administrative law was typically viewed as being comprised of
two elements: (1) public law, focusing on the organization, jurisdiction and powers of agencies, and (2) private law, providing remedies
for violations of individual rights by governmental officials.[8]

Early in the twentieth century, the Supreme Court, in two important cases, provided the first of a number of constitutional principles
that have helped to shape administrative procedures. In the first case,
Londoner v. Denver (1905), the Court found that a local government's
tax board decision had unconstitutionally deprived individuals of their
property because the decision had "exceptionally affected . . . a relatively small number of persons" without providing the due process
protection of a hearing before the board.[9] Seven years later, in *Bi-
Metallic Investment Co. v. Colorado*, the Court ruled that an administrative rulemaking proceeding, which "applies to more than a few
people" and "where it is impracticable that everyone should have a
direct voice in its adoption," need not provide a hearing for those
affected by the administrative action; rights are not to be protected
through hearings, Justice Oliver Wendell Holmes argued, but through
the electoral process.[10]

The administrative process could be viewed as either judicial or
legislative in nature, each with different constitutionally based procedural requirements. An administrative hearing, much like a court
suit brought against individuals by the government, was required when
governmental action was directed at individuals. When the administrative process assumed the characteristics of a legislative process,
no hearing was required, and affected parties were expected to appeal
to political oversight for redress of their grievances.

The second principle developed by the Court was the broad definition given to administrative law and its interaction of administrative and judicial proceedings. Felix Frankfurter, in one of the earliest

administrative law casebooks, had emphasized the differences between adjudication and administration, and called for the development of legal principles to guide the administrative process that rested upon a "highly professionalized civil service . . . easy access to public scrutiny, and a constant play of criticism by an informed and spirited bar."[11]

The third principle offered by the Court is that standards of due process for administrative decisions were to be set by the legislature, as long as they were consistent with constitutional standards. In *North American Cold Storage v. Chicago*, a 1908 case involving the destruction by a city public health agency of unwholesome food, the producer of the food claimed that the law under which the agency acted violated the requirement of due process. The Court rejected his claim, finding that it was "within the legislative discretion as to whether any hearing need be given before the destruction of unwholesome food."[12] The acceptance by the Court of the role of the legislature in defining procedural rights was an essential part of its acquiescence to broad delegations of power to administrative agencies.[13]

The legal profession, however, through the organized bar, responded to the growth of administrative agencies by calling for the development of a system of administrative law, and charged the American Bar Association with the responsibility to lead the way. Elihu Root wrote:

> If we are to continue a government of limited powers these agencies of regulation must themselves be regulated. The limits of their powers over citizens must be fixed and determined. The rights of the citizen against them must be made plain.[14]

Nonetheless, little attention was given to the call to create a system of administrative law until the 1930s and the onset of the New Deal. Spurred by the promises and actions of Franklin Roosevelt during his first hundred days in office, the American Bar Association in 1933 created the Special Committee on Administrative Law. The committee argued that the judicial branch of government was being undermined by the creation of administrative agencies that tended to

- decide issues without a hearing
- make decisions on the basis of opinions and prejudices
- disregard jurisdictional limits
- yield to political pressure at the expense of the law

- take action arbitrarily for administrative convenience at the expense of important interests
- fall into perfunctory routine
- take other actions inconsistent with the committee's idea of law.[15]

In 1941, the definition of administrative law was narrowed significantly by the Attorney General's Committee on Administrative Procedure (established in response to the creation of the New Deal agencies), which characterized administrative law as the "power to determine, either by rule or by decision, private rights and obligations."[16] This shift in orientation from administrative law as a system of public powers to one of private rights has had major consequences for the development of the administrative process, as it focused on the right of private parties to sue agencies rather than taking a broader view of the administrative process. The organized bar was opposed to many of the substantive goals of the New Deal and was joined by business groups and conservatives who saw in legal restraints and procedures a way to weaken and delay agency actions. It argued that administrative proceedings ought to be structured by legal experts and be based on the adversary process as the most appropriate means for assuring fairness and the most effective mechanism for discovering the truth.[17]

The reports of the ABA's Committee on Administrative Law and of the attorney general's committee provided the basis for a number of bills introduced in Congress, and they eventually led to passage of the Administrative Procedure Act (APA) in 1946. The APA rests on four important values sought by its sponsors.

First, Congress explicitly endorsed the idea of independent regulatory commissions that enjoyed some autonomy within the executive branch. They were to be supervised primarily by the federal courts as well as through congressional oversight. Second, the right to seek judicial review was extended to "any person suffering legal wrong because of agency action, or adversely affected or aggrieved by agency action within the meaning of the relevant statute."[18] Third, different standards of review were provided for different types of administrative actions. Informal proceedings could be set aside by reviewing courts if they were found to be "arbitrary, capricious, an abuse of discretion, or otherwise not in accordance with the law . . . [or] in excess of statutory authority." Courts were to give greater deference to decisions made in formal hearings, where more procedural protections were provided affected parties, and to reject only actions that were "unsupported by substantial evidence" in the record compiled by the agency.[19] Fourth, administrative proceedings were divided into rule-making and adjudication: an informal process of formulating rules (agency actions having "general or particular applicability and future effect designed to implement, interpret, or prescribe law or policy") required only that the agency provide notice of its intention to issue a rule and provide an opportunity for interested persons to submit comments. If the substantive statute demanded formal rule-making, or rule-making on the record, hearings and other procedures were required. Formal adjudicative proceedings (defined as "a final disposition . . . other than rule making") also required the procedures for formal rule making, but no procedures were mandated for informal adjudication.[20]

Administrative law, as reflected in the APA, treated bureaucratic discretion largely as a legal problem that could be solved through traditional procedural devices and judicial supervision. Little attention was directed toward how legal restrictions on administrative power might constrain efforts by Congress and presidents to influence agency officials. Legal requirements conflict with inherent bureaucratic concerns of efficiency and hierarchical control, and resources used in adversarial proceedings are not available for other agency efforts. Despite its shortcomings, and criticisms aimed at its provisions,[21] the APA provided the essential framework for the federal administrative process until the late 1960s.

In the mid-1960s, as new laws were enacted that significantly increased the power of the federal government, Congress also began to write procedural requirements for agency actions that went beyond the APA. As the rule-making powers of agencies were expanded, part of the compromise included more procedural protections, such as hearings, for potentially affected parties. Decisions by federal courts played an even greater role in expanding procedural provisions: requiring more hearings and cross-examination of agency officials, relaxed standing rules so that parties unhappy with agency decisions could more easily challenge them in federal courts, and a heightened level of review by the courts, giving agency decisions a "hard look" to ensure that agencies have "genuinely engaged in reasoned decision making."[22] By 1978, however, the Supreme Court tried to rein in the activist review of lower courts as it argued that

absent constitutional constraints or extremely compelling circumstances
the administrative agencies should be free to fashion their own rules
of procedure and to pursue methods of inquiry capable of permitting
them to discharge their multitudinous duties.[23]

In 1984, it ruled that where statutes are ambiguous, reviewing courts
must defer to any reasonable interpretation offered by the implementing
agency.[24]

One observer described the shift in judicial review of administrative agencies as a transformation of administrative law into a "surro-
gate political process" that widened the scope of participation in agency
decision making and sought to ensure "fair representation for all affected interests in the exercise of the legislative power delegated to
agencies."[25] Some agencies even created public participation programs
that reimbursed nonbusiness groups for the costs of participating in
agency hearings. Critics, however, found that this form of judicial
activism pressured agencies to make decisions that were inconsistent
with their underlying statutory authority.[26]

Criticisms of rule-making procedures became intertwined with
broader appraisals of federal regulatory policy that arose during the
1980s. Regulatory decision making, particularly the issuance of rules
and technical guidance documents for state agencies and regulated
industries, was for some too slow and cumbersome. Agencies were
often not given adequate resources to accomplish their assigned tasks;
while new programs were regularly delegated to them, funding did
not keep pace.[27] Other problems centered on the means employed to
achieve policy goals and the inefficiency of the nationwide rules and
standards that failed to account for regional differences or create
incentives for preventing problems or developing new, more efficient
technologies. Agency officials were excoriated for failing to ensure
that the rules they issued generated benefits that exceeded their costs.[28]

The process of issuing regulations has become cumbersome and
slow.[29] Because of procedural requirements and administrative shortcomings, some risks remain unaddressed.[30] Adversarial legal proceedings
require such a high burden of proof on agencies that the number of
risks they can address is very limited.[31] Agencies are blamed for failing to engage in careful, systematic review of scientific evidence, relying
instead on political judgments.[32] The administrative process has also
been disparaged as too adversarial and contentious. Regulatory agencies in the United States operate in a much more litigious context
than their counterparts in Canada, Japan, and Western Europe.[33]

Congressional and White House oversight adds greatly to the procedural requirements agencies must follow. Officials from large agencies are subject to oversight inquiries and hearings from House and Senate appropriations committees, numerous and overlapping authorization and government operations committees, and the General Accounting Office, the Congressional Budget Office, and other congressional support agencies. Bill Clinton, in one of his first official acts as president, abolished the vice president's regulatory review apparatus that had played a major role in the Reagan and Bush administrations' efforts to control the rule-making process, but created another regulatory review scheme. Under Executive Order 12866 (1993), each regulatory agency is required to submit to OMB's Office of Information and Regulatory Affairs a regulatory plan outlining the most important regulatory actions it intends to take during the coming year. If elements of the plan are found by OMB officials to be inconsistent with the president's twelve principles of regulation, negotiations are triggered until the problems are resolved. When specific regulations having a major impact (an economic effect of $100 million or more, or other major economic repercussions) are proposed, they must be screened by OMB desk officers to ensure that agencies rely on the "best reasonably obtainable scientific, technical, economic, and other information concerning the need for, and consequences of, the intended regulation"; design regulations that are the most cost-effective means of achieving the regulatory objective; and provide a "reasoned determination that the benefits of the intended regulation justify its costs."

The history of bureaucracy in America is largely one of efforts to find a way to achieve both efficiency and accountability in administration. Increasing the representativeness of the civil service, enhancing efficiency and accountability through organizational or structural reform, developing executive branch management and budget techniques, overseeing of agencies by Congress, and supervising the administrative process through judicial review have all been central to the quest for efficiency and accountability. Are we any closer today to striking a satisfactory balance between the discretion necessary for efficient and effective government, and the oversight necessary to ensure democratic accountability?

The Contemporary Debate over
Administrative Discretion

The frustration and dissatisfaction that have characterized the modern administrative state perhaps reached a new high in 1994 with the election of the first Republican-controlled Congress in over forty years. The response of the newly empowered Republicans was to try to reduce the size and authority of administrative agencies. The backlash against bureaucracy was part of the movement toward smaller government, more reliance on markets, and fewer restraints on individuals and business. It was rooted in the Reagan-era efforts to reduce the size of the federal government, but unlike those efforts that were limited to administrative and managerial changes, the new Congress sought legislative changes.

The 1994 House Republican Contract with America promised to "roll back government regulations and create jobs."[34] The Job Creation and Wage Enhancement Act, introduced at the beginning of the 104th Congress, included provisions aimed at changing administrative law and the rule-making process for major rules to ensure that more scientific and economic analyses are performed; to increase opportunities for regulated industries to help shape the provisions; to ensure that only relatively serious risks are regulated; and to require a demonstration that the benefits resulting from these regulations exceed the cost of compliance with them and that the regulation proposed is the most cost-effective option.

Other changes included:

- A regulatory moratorium on the issuance of new regulations until the regulatory reform agenda is enacted

- A regulatory "budget" that places a cap on compliance costs to be posed on industry; changing the way federal programs are funded, so that unfunded federal mandates require additional votes by Congress

- Requiring federal agencies to compensate property owners for losses in property values resulting from environmental regulation

- Increasing procedural protections for those subject to regulatory inspections and enforcement, such as a right to have counsel present during inspections and legal actions that can be taken against regulatory officials.

Additional reforms that were proposed as part of Congress's regulatory agenda include (1) delegating more autonomy and responsibility to states to formulate and implement policies; (2) giving Congress the power to review and overturn proposed regulations by enacting a joint resolution of disapproval that would be subject to presidential veto; (3) holding "correction days" to take up proposals for legislation to eliminate existing federal rules that are considered "obnoxious or burdensome to state or local governments," to be proposed by a congressional task force that would identify possible regulations, confer with the relevant committees, and (if there were broad support) bring them to the House floor for an up-or-down two-thirds majority vote; and (4) creating a "regulatory burden commission" to propose legislation on an industry-by-industry basis.

The Clinton administration sought to counter the Republican initiatives with several changes in regulatory policy in early 1995. It ordered federal agencies to review their regulations and identify those that are "obsolete or overly burdensome," negotiate with regulated businesses and local governments rather than dictate to them, and not evaluate inspectors by how many citations they write. In March, the administration offered a new round of initiatives in response to the House bills that would give small businesses 180 days to correct violations before being fined, waive punitive fines if the businesses agreed to use the money to correct the violation, and institute new record-keeping and reporting requirements for businesses and local governments.[35]

The Republican proposal that may have the greatest impact on administrative procedures is one requiring agencies to conduct cost-benefit and risk analyses before issuing regulations. In March 1995, the House passed H.R. 9, which would require the EPA and eleven other agencies, when proposing regulations with an expected cost of $25 million or more, to (1) assess the nature of the risk being regulated, including the range of risk; (2) compare the risk at issue with similar risks, including everyday risks such as auto accidents; (3) assess how effectively the rules would reduce risks to the public, based on detailed scientific analysis; (4) assess risks that might occur if alternatives are substituted for the substance or practice to be regulated; and (5) demonstrate that the costs of compliance are justified by the expected benefits and that the proposal is the most cost-effective option.

Judicial review of agency actions would be expanded under H.R. 9 so that any party could sue the agency for failing to follow any of the risk or cost-benefit assessments. The cost-benefit requirement would override any existing statutory provision: if a less costly alternative than the proposed rule were identified, it would have to be substituted by the agency. The agencies would be required to convene external committees, including representatives of regulated industries, to review the risk and cost assessments accompanying regulations with an impact of $100 million or more. Agencies would be required to perform a series of analyses for any proposed rule with an expected impact of $50 million or more to demonstrate that the projected benefits outweigh the costs. Emergency situations, military readiness-related activities, and federal approval of state programs and plans would be exempt from these requirements.

In contrast, the Senate proceeded more slowly on risk and cost-benefit legislation. After several days of debate and three votes to cut off further consideration of the bill, the leaders withdrew the bill. The House regulatory reform bill was subsequently attached to a debt limit extension bill passed by Congress but vetoed by Clinton in November 1995. The Clinton administration and environmental groups were quite successful in labeling this and other Republican initiatives as antienvironmental, and Congress took no further action in that session.

Republicans tried again in the 105th Congress to change the regulatory process, moving much more slowly and cautiously. The Senate took the lead in 1997 with a bipartisan regulatory reform bill sponsored by Senators Fred Thompson (R-Tenn.) and Carl Levin (D-Minn.) that, as with earlier proposals, would require agencies to perform new cost-benefit and other regulatory analyses and permit regulated industries to challenge those analyses in federal court. The Clinton administration and environmental groups continued to attack the proposal as a weakening of regulatory protection, but by March 1998, the Senate Commerce committee appeared ready to push the bill forward.[36] The other bill aimed at changing the regulatory process was a property rights bill that passed the House in October 1997 and the Senate Judiciary Committee in February 1998. That bill would increase significantly opportunities for developers and landowners to sue federal agencies for compensation if regulations placed limits on their use of their land.[37]

The contentiousness of these issues has demonstrated that there is a yawning gap between most Republicans and most Democrats on how the administrative/regulatory process ought to be "reformed." Democrats argued that the Republican bills were "the all-time case of throwing the baby out with the bath water. . . . [The risk assessment proposal] makes no distinction between the rules we need and the rules we don't." Republicans proclaimed that "if we have some gridlock on the regulatory agencies . . . the American people will stand up and say, 'Yeah! Hallelujah!'"[38] Speaker Newt Gingrich, in a 1995 speech, claimed that "we've spent far more money than we've gotten results; we've caused far more economic dislocation [from environmental regulation] than we've gotten results." The United States, he contended, had created a "Soviet-style bureaucracy," and the EPA was the "biggest job-killing agency in inner-city America."[39] Former Democratic Senator Edmund Muskie retorted that "this bill is not reform, it is repeal. [It] would turn the clock back to the days when the special interests made the rules and the people absorbed the risk."[40]

While it is uncertain whether any such reforms in administrative procedures will eventually be enacted by Congress, they reflect widespread criticism of and unhappiness with the federal government and, in particular, with federal agencies. Unfortunately, however, such reforms are not likely to balance effectively the competing concerns of accountability and efficiency. One of the primary objectives of House proponents of the new procedural requirements was simply to slow down the process of issuing new regulations. Much of the motivation was hostility to regulation and the federal bureaucracy. Representative Gerald Solomon (R-N.Y.), for example, seemed to have "getting even" with bureaucrats in mind:

> The Republican Congress is about to turn the tables on the regulators in Washington. . . . For years, business and industry have been forced to jump through hoops to satisfy regulators in the bureaucracy. Well, if this legislation becomes law, we are going to turn that around.[41]

The primary purpose of the regulatory reform proposals was unambiguous: House Republicans were convinced there are too many regulations. Or, as a *Wall Street Journal* reporter put it, "That Americans swim in a regulatory ocean is undeniable. . . . Under the cost-benefit bill, for good or ill, that ocean would become a puddle—and possibly a desert."[42]

From industry's perspective, increased procedural requirements and judicial review of agency actions may be counterproductive. A recurring complaint of regulated industries is the inflexibility of rules and the adversarial, litigious, snail-like pace of the regulatory process. Industry officials who want more flexibility in regulation, more use of market-based regulatory instruments, more predictable and consistent regulations, and more cooperation between government and industry are not likely to find those things in the risk and cost-benefit analysis bills Congress has debated during the past few years. "This legislation sets up a system where everybody can say no and virtually nobody can say yes," a former industry trade association official observed. "Because it creates so many opportunities for gridlock and stonewalling, it's going to be very difficult for industry or environmentalists or the government to get a yes answer." Which means that the country won't get a yes answer.[43] Additional procedures will also likely create an opportunity for businesses to use petitions and judicial review to get advance information about new products and processes that are being developed by their competitors.

Requiring risk assessment and cost-benefit analysis, despite the hope of sponsors for regulations to be grounded, "objective" science underlying regulation is no panacea. There is usually little agreement about what costs and benefits to include in the calculations. Should the costs of environmental regulations, for instance, be limited to the cost of new pollution control equipment, for example, or should they include the impact on individuals who lose their jobs when industries cannot afford to meet regulatory requirements? The benefits in terms of lives saved or illnesses prevented are similarly difficult to measure. Disagreements also focus on how to assess the distribution of costs and benefits across generations, and whether the current monetary value of costs and benefits should be discounted in comparing their long-term value. Cost-benefit analysis also provides little help in determining the advantages and disadvantages for different industries subject to regulation. While virtually everyone involved in the regulatory reform debate calls for improved analysis, simply adding an exhaustive set of requirements and then subjecting each of them to judicial review is not likely to achieve that goal. The contributions cost-benefit analysis can make as a way to frame issues and aggregate relevant information are considerable; it is not a replacement for political judgments.[44] Demands for new procedures, analyses, and increased judicial review of agency decisions fail to recognize that agency decision making, particularly risk assessment and cost-benefit analysis, requires political judgments that are not simply objective, neutral, technical calculations. Regulatory policymaking is a struggle of ideas over how to define and distribute risks, costs, and benefits. Behind every policy proposal is a set of choices that reflect differing interpretations and values.[45]

Scholars have demonstrated that risk assessment is a political process. Sheila Jasanoff concluded in her study of the interaction of scientific committees and regulatory agencies that such committees cannot supply an unambiguous "scientific" basis for policy, and that the "scientific component of decision making" cannot be "separated from the political and entrusted to independent experts."[46] Mark Rushefsky's study of cancer policy also found that risk assessment efforts were heavily influenced by the policy agendas of those involved, and that scientific and political judgments could not be easily separated.[47] The courts are not well suited to make the kinds of political judgments that are involved in risk assessment. Fundamental value choices are inescapable, even when unambiguous, quantitative risk data are available. For example, are health risks posed to the aged more or less serious than health risks posed to infants? Are risks of cancer to be treated as more or less serious than threats to reproductive processes?

Howard Latin has argued that the implementation of regulatory laws "has seldom conformed to legislative expectations and rarely if ever achieved the desired degree of protection."[48] The difficulty of the issues involved, the complexity and scientific uncertainty, the diversity of interests, and the conflict in values all combine to place limits on the ability of Congress to compel regulatory agencies and regulated industries to conform to its detailed statutory mandates. Latin attributes the failure to achieve policy goals to the inability to offer an affirmative response to any of the following questions: Can Congress expect regulatory agencies to make politically controversial choices if the legislature itself will not provide clear direction? Can Congress insist that administrators develop a comprehensive, consistent, proactive approach to all regulatory issues? Can Congress ask agencies to resolve disputed scientific issues despite the absence of a reasonable scientific consensus? Can Congress effectively instruct regulators to achieve the best possible results under severe resource constraints, or will agencies tend to allocate budgets and attention in whichever ways are likely to create the appearance of bureaucratic competence? Can Congress reasonably demand that agency officials ignore constant criticism and other forms of negative feedback from regulated parties? Can Congress compel regulators to act expeditiously when they must consider all facets of remarkably complicated problems and when any major decision may be challenged in appellate proceedings?[49]

Rather than making laws more procedure-bound, or more explicit and detailed, a more promising change may lie in giving agencies more discretion, loosening the procedural bands that have been placed on them. Administrative law, despite its history of "reform," has ultimately failed to produce either efficient or accountable government. Greater administrative discretion may be necessary in order to strike a more effective balance between these two expectations.

The more complex the world, Richard Epstein argues, the less likely lawmakers and rule writers will know how things interact and will be able to anticipate possible developments. The more complex law becomes, the less efficient and effective it is. Part of the inefficiency lies in the endless litigation spawned by the regulatory state.[50] While Epstein calls for the use of a legal framework based on principles of the common law rather than for heightened administrative discretion, his criticism of the shortcomings of the current system is compelling.

Philip K. Howard argues that law in general has become too prescriptive, and too detailed, and has collapsed under its own weight as it tries to anticipate every problem and prevent all harms, instead producing delay, increased costs, rigidity, paralysis, and frustration with government. The root problem for Howard is the fear of administrative discretion, the excessive fear of waste and abuse, and the belief that detailed rules will prevent them. Americans typically believe that accountability comes through detailed mandates, that paperwork will prevent corruption. We have great faith in regular procedures and try to limit administrative discretion at almost all cost. As a result, "We seem to have achieved the worst of both worlds: a system of regulation that goes too far while it also does too little."[51] Although the goal of lawmakers to provide specific legal standards to check governmental power and provide clear guidelines for citizens was reasonable, Howard contends that approach has failed: "Human activity can't be regulated without judgment by humans."[52] Excessive reliance on procedures is a result of the naive belief that "one correct or best answer will emerge if the process is extensive enough."[53] But the adversary system is not designed to get at the truth, but to advance the interest of one's client. Causing delay, confusion, and doubt are part of the effort. A strict reliance on process has no natural closure and is too open-ended to permit effective government.

Discretion is required for efficient and effective policies and also (as Woodrow Wilson argued more than a century ago) for responsibility. Wilson's complaint about the separation of powers was that it was inconsistent with the idea of democratic accountability. For Wilson, there was no contradiction between administrative efficiency and political accountability: "Large power and unhampered discretion seem to me the indispensable conditions of responsibility." If power is divided, it is likely to become obscured: "if it is obscured, it is made irresponsible. . . . There is no danger in power, if only it be not irresponsible."[54]

The responsible use of government power is an important expectation in our political system, and due process is only one of many tools to achieve it. Sound governance cannot come from a primary reliance on procedural requirements.[55] Administrative agencies need to negotiate, compromise, and find flexible solutions that achieve goals in the most efficient ways possible. Fair procedures are important, but they cannot substitute for clear goals, the power to achieve them, and oversight aimed at ensuring accountability to those goals. Accountability comes when goals are clearly expressed and accountability to achievement of those goals is aggressively ensured. Just as regulators need to provide clear goals and flexible means to regulated industries to ensure efficient, effective compliance efforts, the regulators themselves need some deregulating in order to achieve the goals given them.

A major theme in the literature on regulation has been the need to set priorities, both to ensure that the most serious problems are met and to ensure that scarce resources are used more effectively so that other resources are available for other policy concerns. A related theme is that regulation should achieve necessary goals at the lowest cost, to minimize the burden on economic activity. Perhaps the most frequently voiced criticism of regulatory policy is that the goals established by Congress and the way they are implemented by federal agencies fail to address the most serious problems.[56]

One option is for the executive branch to develop a broad, comprehensive, and less stringent regulatory strategy than the current approach. Agency efforts and resources could be redistributed and regulatory decision making greatly streamlined so that more hazards can be addressed, but at less stringent levels of regulation. Agency resources would be spread more broadly in investigating more potential hazards instead of concentrated in developing data for a few stringent standards that will have to be defended in court. An administrative body could take responsibility for developing a coherent system for regulating risks that could be used by all agencies, helping to make recommendations for setting priorities among agency programs, and making shifts in resources across agencies in order to ensure that regulatory efforts reach the most serious risks.[57] Congress will likely resist permitting agency officials to set their own regulatory agendas. It could, however, require the EPA to prepare a long-term regulatory agenda that would outline the results of its analysis of comparative risks and propose what direction the agency should take. Since agency priorities based on such analysis reflect basic choices about how to compare and rank risks, Congress must be involved. Since this approach might conflict with current statutory requirements, Congress may need to engage in some reconciliation of statutes with the agreed-upon regulatory agenda, much as occurs in the budget process. The framework for such an exercise in interbranch priority setting is already in place under the executive orders discussed above. Congress would work with agency officials in negotiating a program that responded to the conclusions from comparative risk assessments. Congress would also have to increase funding for the agencies' research resources so that their capacity for such assessments is enhanced.

Proponents of less government and opponents of specific policies have been happy to use procedural provisions to weaken agencies and reduce their impact on regulated interests. The Republican Congress has aimed its reform efforts at producing a smaller state, but not a more effective one. Democrats have largely failed to engage in the difficult debate of how to make regulatory and other programs more efficient and effective. One of the most serious threats we face is that another round of regulatory relief efforts, dressed up as regulatory reform, will make it more difficult to devise ways of making regulation more effective and efficient and increasing government's capacity to accomplish important public purposes.

Notes

1. These criticisms are summarized and assessed in Charles T. Goodsell, *The Case for Bureaucracy: A Public Administration Polemic*, 3d ed. (Chatham, N.J.: Chatham House, 1994).

2. See Gary L. Wamsley et al., "A Legitimate Role for Bureaucracy in Democratic Governance," in *The State of Public Bureaucracy*, ed. Larry B. Hill, (Armonk, N.Y.: M. E. Sharp, 1992), 59–86; and John A. Rohr, *To Run a Constitution: The Legitimacy of the Administrative State* (Lawrence: University Press of Kansas, 1986).

3. See Theodore Lowi, *The End of Liberalism,* 2nd ed. (New York: Norton, 1979), chap. 3; Lowi, *The End of the Republican Era* (Norman: University of Oklahoma Press, 1995), chap. 1.

4. James Q. Wilson, ed., *The Politics of Regulation* (New York: Basic Books, 1980); Francis Rourke, *Bureaucracy, Politics, and Public Policy* (Boston: Little, Brown, 1984).

5. Lowi, *End of Liberalism*, chap. 5.

6. Emmett Redford, *Democracy in the Administrative State* (New York: Oxford University Press, 1969).

7. Martin Shapiro, *Who Guards the Guardians? Judicial Control of Ad-*

ministration (Athens: University of Georgia Press, 1988).

8. Oskar Kranes, *The World and Ideas of Ernst Freund: The Search for General Principles of Legislation and Administration* (University: University of Alabama Press, 1974).

9. 210 U.S. 373 (1905).

10. 239 U.S. 441 (1915).

11. Felix Frankfurter and J. Forrester Davidson, *Cases and Other Materials in Administrative Law* (New York: Commerce Clearing House, 1931), 266.

12. 221 U.S. 306 (1908).

13. For a critical assessment of this practice, see David Schoenbrod, *Power Without Responsibility: How Congress Abuses the People Through Delegation* (New Haven: Yale University Press, 1993).

14. Elihu Root, *Public Service and the Bar*, reprinted in Frankfurter and Davidson, *Cases and Materials in Administrative Law*, 266.

15. American Bar Association, *American Bar Association Report* (Littleton, Conn.: 1938), 540.

16. Attorney General's Committee on Administrative Procedures, *Final Report* (Washington, D.C.: U.S. Government Printing Office, 1941), 7.

17. Morton Horowitz, *The Transformation of American Law* (Cambridge: Harvard University Press, 1978), 253.

18. 5 U.S.C. 702.

19. 5 U.S.C. 706.

20. 5 U.S.C. 706.

21. See K. C. Davis, *Discretionary Justice* (Baton Rouge: Louisiana University Press, 1969), and James O. Freedman, *Crisis and Legitimacy: The Administrative Process and American Government* (Cambridge: Cambridge University Press, 1978).

22. *Greater Boston Television Corp. v. FCC*, 444 F.2d 841 (1970); cert. denied 403 U.S. 923 (1971).

23. *Vermont Yankee Nuclear Power Corp. v. Natural Resources Defense Council*, 435 U.S. 519 (1978).

24. *Chevron U.S.A., Inc. v. Natural Resources Defense Council*, 467 U.S. 837 (1984).

25. Richard Stewart, "The Reformation of American Administrative Law," *Harvard Law Review* 88 (1975): 1712.

26. See, for example, R. Shep Melnick, *Regulation and the Courts: The Case of the Clean Air Act* (Washington, D.C.: Brookings Institution, 1983); and Jeremy Rabkin, *Judicial Compulsions* (New York: Basic Books, 1989).

27. Walter A. Rosenbaum, *Environmental Politics and Policy* (Washington, D.C.: Congressional Quarterly Press, 1995); and Marc K. Landy, Marc J. Roberts, and Stephen R. Thomas, *The Environmental Protection Agency: Asking the Wrong Questions from Nixon to Clinton* (New York: Oxford University Press, 1994).

28. Stephen Breyer, *Regulation and Its Reform* (Cambridge: Harvard University Press, 1982); and Robert E. Litan and William D. Nordhaus, *Reforming Federal Regulation* (New Haven: Yale University Press, 1983).

29. Cornelius M. Kerwin, *Rulemaking: How Government Agencies Write Law and Make Policy* (Washington, D.C.: Congressional Quarterly Press, 1994).

30. Stephen Breyer, *Breaking the Vicious Circle: Toward Effective Risk Regulation* (Cambridge: Harvard University Press, 1993).

31. John M. Mendenhoff, *The Dilemma of Toxic Substance Regulation: How Overregulation Causes Underregulation* (Cambridge: MIT Press, 1988).

32. Lester B. Lave, ed., *Quantitative Risk Assessment in Regulation* (Washington, D.C.: Brookings Institution, 1982).

33. Alan Peacock, *The Regulation Game* (London: Basil Blackwell, 1984); and David Vogel, *National Styles of Regulation* (Ithaca: Cornell University Press, 1986).

34. See Ed Gillespie and Rob Schellhas, eds., *Contract with America* (New York: Times Books, 1994), 125–41.

35. "Regulation: Clinton, Browner Would Back Moderate Reform," *Greenwire*, 9 March 1995.

36. 105th Congress, S. 981 (1997).

37. 105th Congress, H.R. 1534, S. 1204 (1997).

38. "Regulation: House Expected to OK Moratorium Today," *Greenwire*, 24 February 1995.

39. "Policy: Gingrich Talks Env't; Browner, Chafee Answer," *Greenwire*, 17 February 1995.

40. Natural Resources Defense Council, press release, 1 March 1995.

41. Bob Benenson, "House Easily Passes Bills to Limit Regulations," *Congressional Quarterly Weekly Report*, 4 March 1995, 682.

42. Timothy Noah, quoted in "Regulation: House Approves Risk, Cost-Benefit Mandates," *Greenwire*, 1 March 1995.

43. Terry Yosie, former director of EPA's Science Advisory Board, former vice president of American Petroleum Institute, interview in *Greenwire*, 22 February 1995.

44. Edward M. Gramlich, *A Guide to Benefit-Cost Analysis*, 2d edition, (Prospect Heights, Ill.: Waveland Press, 1990), 2–6

45. Deborah Stone, *Policy Paradox* (New York: Norton, 1997), 8–12.

46. Sheila Jasanoff, *The Fifth Branch: Science Advisers as Policymakers* (Cambridge: Harvard University Press, 1990), 16–17.

47. Mark E. Rushefsky, *Making Cancer Policy* (Albany, N.Y.: SUNY Press, 1986).

48. Howard Latin, "Regulatory Failure, Administrative Incentives, and the New Clean Air Act," *Environmental Law* 21 (1991): 1647.

49. Ibid., 1650.

50. Richard Epstein, *Simple Rules for a Complex World* (Cambridge: Harvard University Press, 1995).

51. Philip K. Howard, *The Death of Common Sense* (New York: Random House, 1995), 10.

52. Ibid., 11.

53. Ibid., 88.

54. Woodrow Wilson, *Congressional Government* (1885), reprinted in Christopher H. Pyle and Richard M. Pious, *The President, the Congress, and the Constitution* (New York: Free Press, 1984), 56.

55. See John J. DiIulio Jr., *Deregulating the Public Service: Can Government Be Improved?* (Washington, D.C.: Brookings Institution, 1994), and Christopher F. Edley Jr., *Administrative Law: Rethinking Judicial Control of Bureaucracy* (New Haven: Yale University Press, 1990).

56. These and other criticisms are summarized in National Academy of Public Administration, *Setting Priorities, Getting Results: A New Direction for EPA* (Washington, D.C.: NAPA, 1995).

57. Breyer, *Breaking the Vicious Circle*, 59–61.

Part Three

Rebuilding Public Administration

Introduction

The contributors to this section consider the place of personal responsibility or morality in the activity of the American public administrator. They ask what constitutes just and legitimate political action for administrators, and what sort of moral and political education prepares administrators best for the responsible exercise of political discretion.

In chapter 11, Donald Maletz argues that contemporary public administrators are not adequately educated in constitutionalism. The Constitution, as a result, tends to disappear in the ideologically driven debates among public officials. Maletz maintains that ethical responsibility for a public administrator entails an attitude of political moderation that depends on an understanding and appreciation of constitutional liberty.

William Richardson and Lloyd Nigro in chapter 12 return to the political thought of the Founders and Woodrow Wilson so as to consider their concerns about ethical behavior by public officials. Administrators must be led to reconcile their own interests with the common good. Indispensable to their doing so is recognition of the fact that they are properly animated by honor.

John Rohr considers in chapter 13 the problem of administrative discretion arising from the civil servant's authority to fulfill sometimes nebulous mandates. Bureaucrats must understand the functioning of the separation of powers under the Constitution. Although they need to work effectively with all three branches of government, they often are compelled by the nature of their office to make ethical decisions in light of their own understanding of the Constitution.

Mark Blitz expands the horizon covered by the idea of responsibility in chapter 14. Responsibility means understanding one's duty in a comprehensive way, not merely following rules. Responsibility is not merely accountability but effective action in light of the American republic's overall, liberal purposes.

11

The Place of Constitutionalism in the Education of Public Administrators

Donald J. Maletz

There is an unduly neglected element in the education we offer to prepare men and women for public service in the United States. This element is an understanding of constitutionalism, considered to include principles defining standards, ends to be pursued, and authoritative practices established over time. Inattention to constitutionalism is not complete. The American Society for Public Administration's 1984 Code of Ethics, to its credit, concludes by stating the need for professional administrators to "respect, support, study, and when necessary, work to improve federal and state constitutions, and other laws which define the relationships among public agencies, employees, clients and all citizens."[1] This provision of the code is the only one that refers to a distinct writing or text as an authority to respect and to study, if the administrator wants some guidance in matters of ethics. Another impetus to connect public administration and constitutionalism is provided in the work of John Rohr, whose writings have done much to restore constitutional themes to view as a crucial element in the field of public administration.[2] These developments nevertheless struggle against a long-established tendency to gloss over constitutionalism, a tendency that has important theoretical roots and that has helped to shape an approach to administrative education that gives the study of constitutional practice a marginal role.

It is not my purpose here to develop an account of the content of constitutionalism, except in a very general way, but rather to reflect on the ideas that led to a certain lack of interest in the issue within public administration and that still today affect the way we view the task of educating administrators in principles by which to guide their work. I contend that a turning away from constitutionalism is not accidental, as I will show by examining Woodrow Wilson's classic essay, "The Study of Administration." And I contend that more recent discussion of ethics in government often lacks a distinct connection to constitutional principles; Dennis Thompson's "The Possibility of Administrative Ethics" will help to illustrate this point.[3] In the movement from Wilson's 1887 study to Thompson's 1985 call for a new emphasis on ethics in administration, we can see both the arguments for marginalizing constitutionalism and why an otherwise persuasive plea for the "possibility" of administrative ethics remains potentially quite formless when not linked with constitutional principles and practices. Finally, I turn to a distinctly less theoretical work, the memoir by David Stockman (President Ronald Reagan's first budget director), which was revealingly entitled *The Triumph of Politics*. Stockman's career exemplified the path of a certain type of mind (an increasingly common type of mind) in public service and still today illustrates why that type of mind could profit from a deeper education in constitutionalism. Constitutionalism, properly understood, contributes at least a partial antidote to the tendency toward "ideology" that Stockman and others harbor and whose consequences he tried to explain.[4]

Wilson's "Study of Administration" makes the case for professionalized administrative study. The attractiveness of this notable essay still lies in Wilson's attempt to consider the largest issues of principle that must be faced in trying to combine American constitutional government with the need of a new era for more competent and expansive administration. His argument centers on the need for a distinction between "politics" and "administration," designed to allow administration its own distinctive sphere within which it can profit from the cultivation of, literally, businesslike methods. Wilson's argument tries to *create* this distinction within an American governmental outlook that he takes to be too comprehensively democratic or populist in tone. He boldly pronounces what verges on a critique of democracy in America, arguing that popular controls are too intrusive and that the public is too distrustful of expertise and such intrusions in the daily issues of government.[5] Wilson's critique has, for my present purpose, two features worth noting. First, he argues that fundamental questions of authority and sovereignty are the truly central questions of politics and precede administrative problems in importance. But these questions, he insists, can eventually be settled in a relatively final way for all practical purposes. Once a people settles the issue of who should rule, then proper attention may be paid to administrative problems and their more competent resolution.[6] Sometimes, however, this closure is difficult to reach. "Once a nation has embarked on the business of manufacturing constitutions, it finds it exceedingly difficult to close out that business and open for the public a bureau of skilled, economical administration."[7] The obsession with popular control through legislative oversight plus freedom for political criticism of officials can combine to become obstructive, once that moment is reached when administrative development should become a focus of attention. Anticipating the end-of-ideology thesis (and utterly failing to anticipate the emerging challenges to constitutional democracy from the left and the right in the twentieth century), Wilson suggests that fundamental authority issues can be decisively resolved in relatively final ways. Such a moment has arrived in America, he maintains, alluding to the Civil War and its aftermath. Hence, we can now allow ourselves some criticism of populism and of the "fullness" with which we have "realized popular rule."[8] Because constitutional problems are more or less settled, a window of opportunity opens for American constitutional democracy to turn its mind to administrative competence, to problems which require the "methods of the counting house."

Yet the insufficiency of this thesis emerges in several distinct ways in Wilson's argument, which brings me to my second point concerning his criticism of nineteenth-century American democracy. Wilson finds himself obliged to admit, first of all, that administrative issues affect constitutional authority and, second, that even thoroughly skilled and effective administrators ultimately need some focus beyond their managerial craft. Those who understand administration, he argues, will reflect about the proper distribution of authority needed to do their jobs and will present claims for the discretionary authority that ought to be vested in the professional administration.[9] This cautiously worded admission might suggest certain dangers to an ordinary American populist, especially to those who notice Wilson's explicit readiness to adopt European, even Prussian, models. Anticipating this objection, Wilson asks what will prevent an "illiberal officialism," an "offensive official class," a "distinct, semi-corporate body with sympathies divorced from those of a progressive, free-spirited people, and with hearts narrowed to the meanness of a bigoted officialism"? "A great many very thoughtful persons" may choose to raise this issue.[10]

This altogether reasonable question is not, be it noted, a question about effective external controls over administrators. It is rather a question about the hearts of these administrators, about the spirit that will animate them and their work, and it implies a question about the ultimate ends that they serve. Will that spirit be "illiberal" or undemocratic? Wilson's answer to the question is that "administration in the United States [unlike in Prussia] must be at all points sensitive to public opinion," and administrators must have "steady, hearty allegiance to the policy of the government they serve."[11] He suggests the need to teach administrators a loyalty to something beyond professional managerial norms, so that their administrative competence coupled with significant discretionary authority can be felt by them and others to be in the service of something beyond their own professional interests. But the defect in Wilson's position should be clear. He relies on the amorphous concept of public opinion, which he has described in this very essay as too fluid, populist, and contemptuous of executive expertise (at least in the Anglo-American experience). He also fails to draw a distinction between what "public opinion" has firmly, coherently, and consistently authorized (for example, constitutional forms and procedures), and the more fluctuating opinions and passions by which it responds to current events.

A simple maxim of loyalty to public opinion cannot fully serve the purpose Wilson intends. He wants public administrators to have a distinct critical distance from intrusive populism and at the same time a visible loyalty to something higher than their own professional expertise. Wilson's wording unwittingly sacrifices the first aspect and carelessly endorses the overly democratic tendency he has earlier criticized. But his recognition of the need for some set of administrative loyalties outside those of the professional corps indicates a genuine need. That need can be addressed if we turn to the Constitution and constitutionalism less as a source of negative restrictions on government and more as an act, even perhaps an ongoing series of acts, by which the public authoritatively establishes norms, practices, and principles for their government.

If Wilson implicitly concedes the need for something beyond professional administrative norms, this is for him rather like an afterthought. What remains as his legacy is the vision of administration detached from "politics," enabled thereby to pursue the managerial skills that will permit more effective performance in public service. The influence of that model has been enormous, no doubt because it appeals to certain wider tendencies in the American approach to organizations and certainly also to some serious and legitimate needs. Some interesting consequences of this model, however, appear in the more recent attempt by Dennis Thompson to establish the "possibility" of administrative ethics.[12] Thompson's argument for the role of ethics in public administration begins with recognition that a case for administrative ethics must overcome a principled resistance to the idea that ethics is relevant. The objection does not come from Machiavellians who contest any useful connection between ethics and government altogether. Rather, Thompson addresses those who admit the possibility of an ethics relevant to government but deny it a place specifically in administration. They incline to think that administration in the proper sense "precludes the exercise of moral judgment," and they tend to hold this view for one of two reasons. Either they believe that administrative duties require a sort of neutrality, in the sense that the administrator should suppress personal moral conviction in order to follow organization aims, or they believe that moral responsibility belongs to the organization, not to the individual administrator, and that the individual administrator may not rightly be held morally accountable.[13] These positions are expressed in a manner more sophisticated than Wilson's, but they reflect the consequence of what he means by an administrative outlook proceeding with the mentality of business and without a vital connection to "politics."

Thompson skillfully outlines the weaknesses of these relatively common views. I will not here discuss his critical arguments against these views but want rather to consider the result emerging from them. Thompson would suggest that independent moral judgment cannot reasonably be eliminated from administration. His concluding word is that

> We are forced to accept neither an ethic of neutrality that would suppress independent moral judgment, nor an ethic of structure that would ignore individual moral agency in organizations. To show that administrative ethics is possible is not of course to show how to make it actual. But understanding why administrative ethics is possible is a necessary step not only toward putting it into practice but also toward giving it meaningful content in practice.[14]

It is correct that the problem of content is crucial. Once the arguments for avoiding moral responsibility are overcome, then the next issue must be: how are we to understand the content of moral responsibility? We should not uncritically assume that more awareness of moral responsibility is necessarily a good thing, in any and every situation, without regard to the content of the moral sense. It *may* be a good thing, but mention of the unattractive disposition called "moralism" serves to remind us of the possibility of excess, disproportion, and fanaticism in these matters.[15] Thompson's own examples of the moral conscience at work include situations that could have serious and harmful effects on organizations. Some draw on genuinely extreme instances where an administrator might feel justified in remaining in his job (rather than resigning) while being so opposed to an organization's policy that he would believe it right to pursue "covert obstruction."[16] Thompson mentions as well the ultimate in extreme methods, giving "secrets to enemy agents," an act which would "count as treason."[17] We can imagine conditions justifying such actions, but we can also imagine cases where a sense of entitlement to such steps is misused for misguided, more selfish, or more partisan purposes. Furthermore, to heighten the sense of moral responsibility, Thompson argues that administrators should be held accountable not only for what they do but sometimes for what they fail to do, that they are responsible for the outcome of policies and not just for their own personal intentions, and that they should be held to a "higher standard than that to which we hold ordinary citizens."[18] Thompson thus argues that administrative ethics is possible, but he also suggests that ethics could lead to extreme actions and that it places a heavy burden of responsibility. He is right to call attention to severe situations and unusual responsibilities, for ethics can lead in such directions. But this fact makes it plain that we need to learn not only the possibility of ethics but also how to educate the ethical sense. For not every extreme action accompanied by an appeal to "conscience" is really justifiable, nor is every imputation of responsibility defensible.

Thompson gives us an opening toward administrative ethics but little guidance on how to guide and shape what follows. The emptiness of the newly awakened administrative conscience he depicts is striking. It discovers the inadequacy of the antiethics based on administrative structure and neutrality and thereby acquires a receptivity to new issues, new problems, and surely, new levels of controversy. But once the administrator has recognized the right and the duty to make moral judgments, where then does he look for guidance in the proper formation of these judgments? It is insufficient to say: look into one's conscience. It should be obvious that many dangers lurk in the purely private conscience, which can be too easily confused with personal inclination. A doctrine of moral judgment and responsibility that relies purely on the sense of private conscience risks indulging those who confuse the intensity of their personal convictions with the defensibility of those convictions, as Thompson perhaps admits, though with insufficient emphasis.[19] Administrative ethics is possible, we must concede, but so is moral fanaticism. The point suggests not that ethics is unwise but that the ethical or moral sense requires a guide, requires instruction in the possibilities and limits of conscience, and requires an understanding that moral sincerity is not sufficient in and of itself. Ethics is an area that is necessary and yet also inherently controversial and even, in its way, obscure. It is an area where one can do worse than keep in mind the reasons once offered by James Madison for moderation in matters regarding our opinions: reason and passions have a "reciprocal" influence on each other, and the "institutions of man" are so imperfectly delineated that it is extraordinarily difficult to deal with them in terms that are precise and unequivocal.[20] When we learn the unavoidability of personal judgment, even within the context of large, well-structured organizations, we need next to ask: how does the sense of moral autonomy acquire a disciplined understanding of social, political, and historical context, so that it does not remain empty, merely formal, and possibly dangerously subjective? If we recognize the possibility of ethics, do we then proceed as if there are no standards beyond our private judgments? Or are there in fact authoritative, *public* principles to which the conscientious administrator owes some considered deference?

It is striking that both Wilson and Thompson (unlike the ASPA Code of Ethics) leave us with no clear sense of distinct and useful *public* standards in these matters. In Wilson's case, the reasoning seems to be that public standards are too blindly democratic to be of much use, but he himself concedes somewhat halfheartedly that a loyalty to public opinion may be necessary. However, he does not seem to make this element of loyalty to "public opinion" part of the real *study* of administration. As one example of the underlying difficulty, Wilson's own argument contains a critique of public opinion and its tendency toward inappropriate interference with certain operations of government. This factor alone illustrates that an official needs a refined sense of what public opinion is.[21] One element of education for public administration should be an investigation of what American constitutional democracy is and how one best practices a serious loyalty to the norms and goals that flow from its more considered opinions.

Thompson's argument shows the inadequacy of relying on a position of neutrality or of abandonment of responsibility to the organization. But this awakened conscientiousness is given no sense of authoritative guidance in matters of ethics. The resulting moral space can be filled, to be sure, by any number of competing doctrines available today, but then we are faced with the question of whether it is plausible to be uncritically open to all such doctrines, or whether we require a standard to apply in evaluating them and their suitability for public life and public business. If Wilson's argument culminates in a somewhat blind grasping for "public opinion" as touchstone, Thompson's arrives at a sense of openness to something beyond the organization while allowing us to believe that choice at this level is primarily personal and yet morally weighty. Neither of these arguments so much as hints at the thesis stated in the ASPA Code of Ethics, in the form of a professional obligation toward constitutionalism. Neither would appear to accept that public life is guided, in its actual operations, by principles that one could consider ethically authoritative.

In order to suggest more clearly why a new sense of constitutionalism as principle and end might be valuable, I want to consider the case conveniently presented by David Stockman's reflections on his experiences in a high administrative post. Stockman's example is quite instructive about certain common difficulties in ethics. His career illustrated well the mentality of a certain kind of talented, vigorous, and more or less well-educated young man (educated in the famous 1960s) who approached government with what could be described as an intensely active conscience. And yet he claimed to learn that his approach was somehow unsuited to constitutional government.

Stockman's story is that of a man of principle given the position from which he could pursue the implementation of his principles. He came into the Office of Management and Budget believing that he should pursue the program of supply-side economics. With great enthusiasm and enviable energy, Stockman struggled to achieve his cause, only to meet what he thought was a severe defeat. *The Triumph of Politics* is chiefly concerned with a rather detailed account of the machinations within the Reagan administration, and between the administration and Congress, as plans for the 1981 tax cut and then Federal budget reductions were formulated, presented to Congress, and fought through to victory or defeat or, in many cases, some sort of compromise. I do not intend to concentrate on this part of the tale here, but rather to consider the larger framework that Stockman gave to his experiences, for his book offers an overall interpretation— actually, two different interpretations—of what is going on in American government and of the likely fate that Stockman thinks will befall those who enter government with a strong commitment to principles. The first interpretation is suggested by the title. Stockman's title meant that "politics" will defeat—reason, sound economic planning, financial prudence, economic doctrine (such as the program of supply-side theory), and finally, most important of all, principle itself. "Politics" means the mentality of institutions like Congress, presented here as entirely the captive of powerful but hidden interest groups who cannot restrain themselves when given the opportunity to acquire benefits from the federal government. This hoary theme—"the special interests" and their malignant power—is given a treatment worthy of the welfare state by the fact that Stockman views social programs as just another part of the famous government pork barrel.[22] Stockman thinks that the special interests are, in the long run, certain to dominate institutions like the Congress and thus to permeate the very heart of government, with the result that those dedicated to principle will fail to achieve their programs.

Now, if this lesson is correctly derived from his experience, Stockman's message to those concerned with ethics might be of two possible kinds. One consequence could be the view that politics is so thoroughly controlled by self-regarding interests that it is utterly useless to care about principle. On this conclusion, perhaps the reasonable outcome would be a posture of cynicism: unable to defeat the interests, one might as well join them and play their game better than they do. Another possible result, however, might be to conclude that principle is so inefficacious in politics that one must adopt extreme methods, be they the methods of the covert obstructor or those of aggressive confrontation of the "system," attacking from the outside and with other means than debate and elections. On this conclusion, the adherent of principle would best become a protestor against the "system" itself. The Stockman story might be read to lead in either direction. But the story as first presented could hardly lead to the "conservative realism" that Stockman thought that he had learned from Reinhold Niebuhr and Walter Lippmann, and that served at one time as his reason for returning from the world of feverish student protest against the government to a quest for influence and competence within the government.[23]

We need to ask whether Stockman's experiences actually lead to these results or whether the lesson would be different if he had interpreted his situation more carefully. It is striking that at the end of the book, he reports that he is deeply troubled by the financial prospects of the United States, yet he does not seem to be either a cynic or an extremist. He may, perhaps, fail to see clearly where his own experiences lead. However that might be, to see why neither cynicism nor extremism is the proper conclusion to be drawn from this tale, let me draw attention to another aspect of Stockman's story, which allows us to correct the lesson he drew from these events. I suggest that the better conclusion to draw is not the victory of sordid "politics" over principle but a more interesting victory of "politics" in a different sense over "ideology" or, to put it in finer terms, of consent over doctrine. Indeed, in suggesting this point, I follow certain elements of the Stockman story that he himself proposed but did not reflect on sufficiently; they suggest the need for his second, rather underdeveloped interpretation of government.

Stockman's deeper difficulties derived not from the problems he had with Congress or with other members of the Reagan administration but from a certain way of thinking about American government and about the role of ideas like supply-side economics within it. The difficulty can be seen if we consider Stockman's reflections on "ideology," for an important element of his story could in fact be described as "the defeat of an ideologue." In *this* story lies an illustration of the difficulties faced by those who adhere enthusiastically to principle while derogating the established forms of constitutional democracy. These forms, the constitutional forms, erect significant barriers in front of the schemes of principled people, in a way that is itself based on a certain principle about how government must work in our circumstances.

Stockman begins his book with an important description of his education in politics and government. Disarmingly frank, he entitles this chapter "The Odyssey of an Ideologue." The word "ideologue" seems quite apt. Speaking of the celebrated *Atlantic Monthly* article about him by William Greider, he says that Greider rightly portrayed a "radical ideologue" who had "burst upon the scene of national governance" and whose approach was "principled," a case of "idealism" at work. The Stockman program "started out as an idea-based Reagan Revolution," or so he thought, but it ended with Stockman recognizing that the program belonged to himself and a "small cadre of supply-side intellectuals" and was "not Ronald Reagan's real agenda in the first place." Here are all the key words of the Stockman political universe: ideology, revolution, and intellectuals, set off against one of many politicians who give a verbal allegiance to the program but who are in the end more pragmatic, devious, or complex.[24] Stockman held a view requiring "relentless" battle in the name of principle against interests, embracing the value of the "creative destruction" that the market requires, preferring "theory" to "history," calling for "perpetual revolution."[25] This aggressive outlook, with its penchant for theories and abstractions, characterizes Stockman's entire political education. He moved from one "ideology" to another: fundamentalism, the soft-core Marxism of the student left, conservative realism, free-market economics, Lowi-ite opposition to "interest-group" liberalism (to which we shall return below), and finally supply-side economics. To be sure, an important part of Stockman's early development had to do with the rejection of a certain kind of "ideology." He abandoned the left, he says, because it contained too many who "wanted to bring about change with the barrel of a gun"; in the context, he recognized in himself a preference for "democracy" and its methods.[26] Nevertheless, like many who emerged from the charged climate of the sixties, he returned to the mainstream of American public life while retaining a taste for a politics dominated by "ideology," although it was now the economic theories of the right that moved him.

When Stockman talks about "ideology," he means a set of beliefs that are bookish and theoretical in origin, that provide a comprehensive "grand doctrine,"[27] that entail a set of policies and actions that need to be undertaken together (piecemeal approaches undermine the effectiveness of the ideology), that justify a decisive break with existing patterns of action and thought, and that should be subjected to as little compromise as possible. The authority of an ideology derives not from its degree of public support, the deliberate, free "consent" of those who may be governed by it, but from its intellectual plausibility. Ideologies can be anywhere on the political spectrum, right or left. In a number of amusing asides, Stockman draws examples and similes from *the* example of ideological politics in this century, the Soviet communist regime. Thus, he likens a gathering of senior House Democrats to a "Politburo of the Welfare State"; he refers to his own reluctance to compromise at one point in these terms, only half jokingly—"revolutionaries don't cut deals, they cut heads"; when he begins to have some doubts about supply-side orthodoxy, he calls himself the Trotsky of the movement.[28]

Stockman approached his tasks with a firm principle in mind, and he thought that principle—he would use the term "ideology"—required a determined, perhaps ruthless confrontation of existing programs, policies and institutions. Can we then say that Stockman illustrates "ethics" at work? He seemed "committed" to a principle, he rejected expediency, he sought higher ground than ordinary political dealmaking, he did not wish simply to conform but to shape policy in accordance with his views. He is of the right, not the left, but this makes little difference. The ideology to which he is committed is stated in terms of the general good, for he claims it sought the liberation of productive work, a method for rejecting "weak claims, not weak clients," and new brakes on the pursuit of special interests. Yet it seems inappropriate to call Stockman's case an illustration of ethics at work, precisely because his position is admittedly one driven by ideology, and it seems imperative to distinguish ideology from ethics.

There are a number of important reasons for making that distinction, but one of them is suggested, again, by Stockman himself. At certain points in his book, he hints at, but fails to develop, another account of what he encountered than the simple one of principle ["ideology"] confronting naked self-interest. For example, he eventually found himself forced to admit that his economic program was not merely a matter of financial planning but was at its base "a political revolution," which one would presume to mean, in Stockman's terms, not just an issue of principle versus interests but of one set of interests versus another set of interests.[29] This insight, if explored and deepened, might suggest the need to recognize that more is involved in the conflict than abstract truth in one set of hands and greed in the other. It might suggest that the problems of economic growth and balanced budgets involve issues not only of financial loss and gain but of political influence, goals, and power—on both sides—and that it is unwise to be dogmatic about the superior intellectual rigor of one's own views in such situations. More significantly, Stockman at the very end seems to grasp dimly the specific implications of this more political understanding of his failures. He sees that "the politics of American democracy made a shambles of my anti-welfare state theory," because that theory "rested on the illusion that the will of the people was at drastic variance with the actions of the politicians." Stockman means that his ideology led him to a profound misunderstanding of the popular will. He had thought that there were only narrow interests who pursued the welfare state, and that their errand-boys in the legislatures, once confronted and exposed, would lose influence to spokesmen for reduced government activities. But this was a mistake, he finally came to see. Those

who suggest the existence of an anti-statist electorate are in fact demanding that national policy be harnessed to their own particular doctrine of the public good. The actual electorate, however, is not interested in this doctrine . . . the spending politics of Washington do reflect the heterogeneous and parochial demands that arise from the diverse, activated fragments of the electorate scattered across the land. What you see done in the halls of the politicians may not be wise, but it is the only real and viable definition of what the electorate wants.[30]

These crucial admissions suggest one of the most important difficulties in the ideological posture that Stockman assumed. His doctrines made him blind to political reality. The welfare state was not an accidental creation of conniving politicians and obscure interests. It represented what the public has deliberately chosen; the people are "interested in getting help from the government to compensate for a perceived disadvantage."[31] If this is the case, then it follows that the supporters of the various government programs comprising the welfare state cannot be stigmatized merely as special interests. Stockman finally concedes that

> the triumphant welfare state principle means that economic governance must consist of a fundamental trade-off between capitalist prosperity and social security. As a nation we have chosen to have less of the former in order to have more of the latter. . . . Social democracy . . . encourages the electorate to fragment into narrow interest groups designed to thwart and override market outcomes. That these pressure groups prevail most of the time should not be surprising. The essential welfare state principle of modern American governance sanctions both their role and their claims.
>
> Viewed in this light, our political system performs its intended function fairly well. Its search to balance and calibrate the requisites of capitalism with social democracy's quest for stability and security has produced a surprising result. By any comparative standard, American politicians have created a more favorable balance between the two than in any other advanced industrial democracy.[32]

It should be obvious that this account constitutes an implicit repudiation of the ideology versus interests framework dominating the earlier parts of Stockman's book. It shows that the categories of the ideologue were highly deceptive about the character of democratic policies and political institutions. Stockman, it turns out, was hardly a conservative at all. The Congress acted conservatively in preserving the basics of the welfare state, in accordance with a certain firm if rough consent on the part of the public, while the Stockman program, as he often admits, was revolutionary in its attempt to overturn that existing consensus. This late turnabout in Stockman's understanding illustrates an important effect of constitutional forms—they make rapid and revolutionary change driven by ideological fashion quite difficult, and they force us to see that an established and settled policy is likely to be such because it more or less reflects the public mind. Or so it is wise to assume, until a convincing case is made to the contrary. "Ideology" blinds us to a certain deference that ought to be given in a constitutional democracy to both the processes of government designed to elicit deliberate consent and to the policies that come to be firmly established through deliberate consent. It cannot be that a proper code of "ethics" could require of us either self-deception about the actual state of affairs or indifference to the consent of the public. I would suggest that a critique of ideology or of the ideologue must be considered not only useful but in a certain sense a moral imperative following as a direct consequence from the democratic preference for government by deliberate consent. It is the reluctance of the ideologue to perceive that which is established by consent, the ideologue's inclination toward coercion and intolerance, that renders his orientation in public business so dubious; the same qualities lead to the excessive denigration of governing institutions such as repeatedly recurs in Stockman's account. It is self-evident that "ethics" involves the critique of narrow self-interest and therefore of processes of government dominated by self-interest. However, this point is insufficient for delimiting what ethics requires. By itself the criticism of selfish interests fails to draw the necessary distinction between criticism based on a potentially intolerant and coercive ideology (often concealing hidden, unreflective interests, while presenting itself as idealism) and criticism based on the deliberate sense of the community and its permanent and aggregate interests.

The position I have begun to sketch here suggests the need for a critique of the ideologue and of ideology for two different kinds of reasons. The first concerns the ineffectiveness in our context of the ideologue's approach. The abstract, inappropriately theoretical character of ideology distorts perceptions and hinders the prudence that enables one to judge accurately the difference between what is achievable and what is only to be wished for. The second is moral or ethical; it is based on the fact that we have freely established certain ways of governing that dispose us toward such methods as persuasion, the free solicitation and free giving of consent, and a process of negotiation and compromise in many (not all) situations. These same methods dispose us against the self-righteous coerciveness and dogmatism of the ideologue. They are methods based upon a "morality of consent," whose grounds go deep into the tradition of liberal theory and governmental practice.[33] They are methods the need for which is suggested by a late realization of Stockman's that, in the struggle for influence over policy, "raw hunger for power was as important a part of the equation as pure ideas."[34]

The view I have stated is susceptible to the objection that ideology is unavoidable, which can be extended into the proposition that even the methods of nonideological democratic politics contain a hidden ideology of sorts. This view is indeed the one advocated by Theodore Lowi in his very influential *The End of Liberalism*, a book that provides the framework to which Stockman turns when he seeks to put his experiences into perspective.[35] I shall conclude with a comment on this important book, because the ideas advanced in it make the case for my "critique of ideology" more difficult.

Stockman's progress was from the new left toward the right, but the road went through *The End of Liberalism*. To the extent that Stockman has an understanding of how American government works, apart from the notions afforded by supply-side economics, his ideas seem to be guided by Lowi's important thesis about the dominance of "interest-group liberalism" in the contemporary welfare state. Lowi calls into question the common view that American government fosters a politics discouraging ideology and favoring those who pursue their "interests" while knowing how to negotiate with others in order to give and get specific benefits. Lowi thinks the seeming pragmatism of American government masks deeper processes in which public philosophies form, shape perceptions, and finally control the general orientation of policies. He supports this thesis with ingenious and quite illuminating analyses of various policy areas, attempting to show the presence not so much of prudence, improvisation, or reasonable deliberation but rather an all-encompassing ideology called "interest-group liberalism."[36]

Lowi contends, and in this point lies the real passion of his book, that the result of "interest group liberalism" is an absence of "morality" in government and especially in administration.[37] The New Deal intellectuals, he suggests, wanted more government programs, more "administration," but were hesitant to allow the state to be too coercive. They preferred government and administration through negotiation or bargaining; in Lowi's account, they adopted a doctrinaire preference for bargaining processes, wanting formal legislation to set only the vaguest of standards while administrators work out through negotiation and compromise the vital specifics of programs.[38] The mentality behind this preference is what he calls "interest-group lib-eralism." It is condemned by Lowi for its fear of law, principle, and morality—that is, clear, distinct stands taken by lawmakers subject to democratic election. He sees at hand a new impoverishment of dem-ocratic politics, since delegating authority to faceless bureaucrats and permitting them to negotiate with the affected interests allows insuf-ficient opportunity for public control. The administrative process comes to substitute for "law," the authoritative stand taken by government in explicit formal rules.

It is not my purpose here to evaluate this thesis but rather to com-ment on Stockman's response to it. If Lowi is correct about a domi-nant public philosophy in the welfare state, or about what seems close to an ideology,[39] then it may be the case that the public world is permeated by ideology more deeply than old-fashioned pluralists have believed. And in that case, it may be that Stockman is on the right path in assuming that the way to fight an ideology is with a new set of ideas. This seems to be the world of Stockman and of those who inspire him, and it is perhaps Lowi's world as well. The approach has the merit of taking ideas seriously, and taking ideology seriously. My caveat is only this: those whose politics are energized by ideas need to include among them the idea of constitutional democracy.

Stockman came late to the realization that the structures of consti-tutional government, despite their untidiness, have produced a set of policies that in fact capture a tolerable balance between conflicting interests in a free economy and a welfare state. As such, these struc-tures have forced, at least on these issues, a certain practical level of agreement and policy effectiveness even when the principles applied are somewhat contradictory or conflicting. The structures create in-stitutional practices that elicit and establish consent and shape the sort of leadership capable of maintaining practical agreement. One might call this the ethic of constitutional government. It is an ethic that is operative, not a wished-for utopia, and one might suggest that an education in this ethic, toward which even Stockman seems final-ly to move, is precisely the step needed to inform the administrator whose conscience has been awakened. A politics centered on ideas, public philosophies, or ideologies will likely be a polarizing and confrontational politics. It need not be too much so, however, if a part of those ideas is the ethic of constitutional democracy, which requires attention to the building of a sustainable public disposition expressed in deliberate consent.

When persons in government become aware of the "possibility" of ethical responsibility and accountability, a vast domain opens. The domain can be filled by moral principles shallow or deep, ignorant or informed, idiosyncratic or tutored by public as well as private experience. As we can learn from the Stockman case, the "odyssey" of ideologues, of whom we have too many, is likely to be frustrated and ineffective while constitutional structures are in place. Those structures are designed to produce a certain degree of agreement and stable consent, often through methods of election and government, giving a surface appearance that is not very inspiring. Nevertheless, the achievement may be more successful government than any fashionable ideology, of the right or the left, can produce. On these grounds, we are entitled to suppose that constitutional structures possess a certain degree of authority precisely for those wanting to know what it is "right" to do. They serve to discipline ethical or moral idealism.

Now, I do not think this view is the last word; I would not argue that the norms of constitutional government are sufficient to define a completely satisfactory ethics. I would only suggest that they should be the starting point for those concerned not just to assert moral principles but to discern what principles have already been established, and to see that they are not weakened by attempts at a perfection that is, in practice, unavailable to us. A case like Stockman's is no accident. Managerial and technical norms replaced constitutional principle as the core of administrative education, following the injunction of Wilson and others. It was inevitable that later generations would see the inadequacy of these norms, but the critics of our time, like Thompson, point out their limitations while opening up only an undefined "possibility" of a more satisfactory ethics. In a situation of this kind, it is small wonder that people in public life, like Stockman, turn to one of the many available quasi-theoretical "ideologies" available. But American constitutional government is known for its capacity to make influence available primarily to those who move to the center and to refuse such influence to those who decline to move. It has, so far, tended to frustrate ideologues. If we search for some guidelines in public ethics, perhaps we need to concentrate on just this aspect of the constitutional system, and make it a deliberate object of explanation, cultivation, study, and defense. This aspect of constitutionalism is in essence an unwritten rule of democratic moderation, and it is even more the core of constitutional government than the changing doctrines of judicially expounded law.[40] It is, furthermore, still a real and established process, not merely an ideal. The American Society for Public Administration was wise to conclude its code of ethics with an exhortation to "respect" as well as "study" our constitutions, but what we need next is a vigorous, historically rich program to educate public administrators in what constitutionalism means.

Notes

1. American Society for Public Administration, Code of Ethics (Washington, D.C.: American Society for Public Administration, 1984), number 12. On the ASPA Code of Ethics, see Darrell L. Pugh, "The Origins of Ethical Frameworks in Public Administration," 9–33, in *Ethical Frontiers in Public Management*, ed. James S. Bowman, (San Francisco: Jossey-Bass, 1991).

2. John Rohr, *Ethics for Bureaucrats: An Essay on Law and Values*, 2d ed. (New York: Dekker, 1989); *To Run a Constitution: The Legitimacy of the Administrative State* (Lawrence: University Press of Kansas, 1986). Rohr acknowledges a debt to Herbert J. Storing, *What the Anti-Federalists Were For* (Chicago: University of Chicago Press, 1981), and "The 'Other' Federalist Papers: A Preliminary Sketch," *The Political Science Reviewer* 6 (1976), 215–47, as well as to Gordon S. Wood, *The Creation of the American Republic* (Chapel Hill: The University of North Carolina Press, 1969). See also Herbert Storing's "American Statesmanship: Old and New," in Robert A. Goldwin, ed., *Bureaucrats, Policy Analysts, Statesmen: Who Leads* (Washington, DC: American Enterprise Institute, 1981), pp. 88–113 [chap. 1 of this volume]; and "Slavery and the Moral Foundations of the Constitution," in *The Moral Foundations of the American Republic*, ed. Robert H. Horwitz (Charlottesville: University Press of Virginia, 1977), 214–33. And see Michael W. Spicer, *The Founders, the Constitution, and Public Administration: A Conflict in World Views* (Washington, D.C.: Georgetown University Press, 1995). An earlier version of Spicer's argument provided the occasion for a debate on constitutional issues. See Michael W. Spicer and Larry D. Terry, "Legitimacy, History, and Logic: Public Administration and the Constitution," with responses by John A. Rohr, Kenneth F. Warren, Camilla Stivers, Charles R. Wise, and Theodore J. Lowi, and a reply by Spicer and Terry, in *Public Administration Review* 53, 3 (May/June 1993): 237–67.

3. Woodrow Wilson, "The Study of Administration," *Political Science Quarterly* 56 (December 1941): 481–506 [reprint of the original article of 1887]. Dennis Thompson, "The Possibility of Administrative Ethics," *Public Administration Review* 45 (September/October, 1985): 555–61.

4. David Stockman, *The Triumph of Politics* (New York: Harper and Row, 1986).

5. Wilson, "The Study of Administration," 491–93.

6. Ibid., 482–85.

7. Ibid., 489.

8. Ibid., 491.

9. Ibid., 497.

10. Ibid., 500. Cf. the treatment of the "reform debate" in Rohr, *Ethics for Bureaucrats*, 24–29.

11. Wilson, "The Study of Administration," 500. Cf. Kent Kirwan's comments on the implicit political component in Wilson's understanding of administration, "The Crisis of Identity in the Study of Public Administration: Woodrow Wilson" *Polity*, 9, no. 3 (Spring 1997), 321–43 at 331–32.

12. See Dennis Thompson, "The Possibility of Administrative Ethics," and, more recently, *Political Ethics and Public Office* (Cambridge: Harvard University Press, 1987).

13. Thompson, "The Possibility of Administrative Ethics," 555.

14. Ibid., 560.

15. No discussion of ethics should overlook the important study by Suzanne Garment of excess in matters of ethics, *Scandal: The Culture of Mistrust in American Politics* (New York: Random House, 1991).

16. Thompson, 557–58.

17. Ibid., 558. One quite common method of covert obstruction is unauthorized disclosure of government documents, which Thompson suggests to be justifiable in some situations. An interesting case where most would agree that such a method of covert obstruction through leaks was highly disreputable is discussed by Fred I. Greenstein, *The Hidden-Hand Presidency* (New York: Basic Books, 1982). Recounting the attempts of President Eisenhower to deal with Senator Joseph McCarthy, Greenstein notes that at one point McCarthy openly urged the several million government employees to feel at liberty to reveal confidential materials to him (209–210). Context is essential, as Thompson notes in saying that certain methods by which officials express dissent "may be morally wrong except under extreme circumstances" (557).

18. Ibid., 560.

19. Ibid., 557.

20. See *The Federalist* 10 and 37. Cf. David Epstein, *The Political Theory of "The Federalist"* (Chicago: University of Chicago Press, 1984), chap. 4.

21. For a contrast to Wilson's views, see the comments on "democratic self-control" in Joseph Schumpeter, *Capitalism, Socialism, and Democracy* (New York: Harper and Row, 1975), 294–95.

22. Cf. Stockman, "The Social Pork Barrel," *The Public Interest*, no. 39 (Spring 1975): 3–30.

23. Stockman, *Triumph of Politics*, 24–26.

24. Cf. Stockman, *Triumph of Politics*, 11, contrasting his own preference for "exacting, abstract principles" with the politician's subordination of "ideology" to "the plight of real people." The same distinction is illustrated in a different way in Stockman's passion for economic theory and hostility to the "so-called social issues" (49). (Compare, on the relation between statesmen and intellectuals, Donald Brand's essay in this volume.)

25. Ibid., 11, 156–57 (citing Joseph Schumpeter), 136, 312.

26. Ibid., 23.

27. Ibid., 43.

28. Ibid., 121, 171, 302.

29. Ibid., 303–4.

30. Ibid., 376, 377.

31. Ibid., 377.

32. Ibid., 391–92.

33. See Alexander Bickel, *The Morality of Consent* (New Haven: Yale University Press, 1975), 17–20, 22–25, 100–111, 139–42; Robert K. Faulkner, "Bickel's Constitution: The Problem of Moderate Liberalism," *American Political Science Review* 72 (September 1978): 925–40; John Fischer, "The Unwritten Rules of American Politics," *Harper's Magazine*, 197 (November 1948): 27–36; and James Q. Wilson, "American Politics, Then and Now," *Commentary*, February 1979, 39–46, which drew my attention to Fischer's excellent article.

34. Stockman, *The Triumph of Politics*, 243.

35. Ibid., 32–33.

36. Theodore J. Lowi, *The End of Liberalism*, 2nd ed. (New York: Norton, 1979) chap. 3.

37. Ibid., 43, 93, 124–26, 291. Cf. his response to Spicer and Terry in the *PAR* forum cited in note 2 above, at pp. 261–64.

38. Cf. the views on bargaining in Lowi's chapters 3 and 5 with the more balanced account in James O. Freedman, *Crisis and Legitimacy* (Cambridge: Cambridge University Press, 1978), pp. 22–30, 32–35.

39. Wilson, "American Politics, Then and Now," stresses a prevalence of ideology in recent public life that may have permanently transformed the American scene (44–45). His recent article on Stockman, however, suggests the importance of "equity" as a concern possibly more powerful than ideology; see also his "Why Reagan Won and Stockman Lost," *Commentary*, August 1986, 17–21, at 21.

40. What I mean by democratic moderation is not totally unlike the "conservative realism" Stockman claimed to have learned from Niebuhr and Lippman (*Triumph of Politics*, 24–26), but it is not based on doctrines of original sin, and it is meant to reflect the "idealism," so to speak, which allowed the founders to believe that popular government and republican liberty could be made to work successfully. There is no reason why what is here intended could not be equally well described as "liberal realism."

12

The Limits of Ethics: Revisiting the Origins of the American Regime

William D. Richardson
and Lloyd G. Nigro

[The American regime] has its foundations in the willing use of human passions and interests, but it has also certain enduring excellences necessary to its fulfillment. Preserving that foundation and, at the same time, nurturing the appropriate excellences is the task of enlightened American citizenship and statesmanship. It is easy to fail; easy to indulge a preference for liberty that exults only in the free play of the passions and interests and easy to make utopian demands for universal excellences which ignore the limiting requisites of the American political system.[1]

American public administrators play a major role in the governance of the regime because they routinely exercise broad discretionary powers. Toward the end of his essay on the study of administration, Woodrow Wilson asked a question concerning the character of the American public administrator that is as salient today as it was in 1887:

The question for us is, how shall our series of governments within governments be so administered that it shall always be to the interest of the public officer to serve, not his superior alone but the community also, with the best efforts of his talents and the soberest service of his conscience? How shall such service be made to his commonest interest by contributing abundantly to his sustenance, to his dearest interest by furthering his ambition, and to his highest interests by advancing his honor and establishing his character?[2]

In the more than a century that has passed since Wilson posed this question, students of American public administration have worked to

283

provide answers. Government and civil service reform, professionalism, codes of ethics, legislative oversight, judicial review, and citizen participation have been put forward as ways to improve the chances
that public administrators will consistently serve the public interest.[3]
However, the explicit attention to the character of the public administrator for which Wilson has called received far less attention than
his desire for a "science" of administration.[4] At least in regard to the
ethical content of public administration, Wilson framed the issue in
a manner that placed it squarely in the founding tradition. The very
language used reveals an attempt to link 1787 and 1887 and, in so
doing, to clearly connect the science of administration with the ideas
that form the foundations of the American regime.

Recognizing and encouraging the development of those virtues or
excellences needed to sustain the American regime was of concern to
those who established the United States. A close look at the thoughts
of some participants in the founding, therefore, offers a partial answer to the question asked by Wilson in the essay that is generally
considered to have launched public administration as a self-conscious
field of study.[5] Accordingly, the focus here is on the potential contributions of founding thought to current efforts to define and establish
a public administration that is ethically excellent.

Citizen Character and Founding Thought

The "black letter text" of the Constitution of the United States offers
little if any explicit assistance to those seeking to understand the role
of citizen character in the thinking of the Founders. Since Article II
and related parts of the document do not go beyond general references to the powers, duties, and requirements of the executive branch, it
is not surprising that there is equal vagueness regarding the character
required of those who would administer the affairs of the new national government.[6] The Constitution's silence on these matters, of course,
is deceptive. The historical record, including the written works of those
who were delegates to the Constitutional Convention, reveals that their
expectations, fears, and aspirations concerning citizen character were
central to their deliberations over the powers and form of the new
government.[7] While interpretations differ, students of American political thought agree that the Constitution establishes a form of
government designed to rest on what the Founders understood to be
the bedrock realities of human nature. To sustain the new republic,

they also sought to encourage the development of certain "appropriate excellences" or virtues. Clearly related, but less closely examined, are the implications of founding thought on these matters for public administrators.[8] *The Federalist Papers* provides perhaps the clearest evidence that public administration was of great concern to several of the Founders, most notably James Madison and Alexander Hamilton. Publius argued that the federal executive should be energetic and competent, and govern in the public interest, and these attributes require that public administrators have certain appropriate character traits.[9] Public administration also had an important role to play in cultivating citizen character. Rejecting the Anti-Federalists' argument for small and administratively weak governments, Hamilton in particular asserted that a strong and competent public administration would command public support and "promote private and public morality by providing [the people] with effective protection."[10]

Public Virtue and the American Regime

There is, in short, ample reason to conclude that many of the most influential delegates to the Constitutional Convention believed that the character of public administrators was an important part of the foundation upon which the American regime would rest. A common theme that cuts across the well-documented disagreements among these delegates is their conviction that the survival of the new regime would depend heavily on the public virtue of those who governed and on the extent to which those governors could reliably be expected to serve the public interest. Often their debates revolved around the questions of what constituted public virtue and of how best to achieve it. Some contemplated a regime designed to produce an elevated form of public virtue involving "firmness, courage, endurance, industry, frugal living, strength, and above all, unremitting devotion to the weal of the public's corporate self, the community of virtuous men. . . . [E]very man gave himself totally to the good of the public as a whole."[11] Others urged constitutional arrangements predicated on the assumption that public virtue of this kind would be a rare commodity. Since a democratic republic of some kind was contemplated, there was also disagreement over the extent to which its citizens would be able to select virtuous governors. If ambitious, self-interested governors were to be the norm, what was necessary to assure that the consequences would not be fatal to the regime?

In finally choosing the constitutional arrangement to be proposed for ratification by the states, the Federalists' position set forth by Publius in *The Federalist Papers* prevailed. The constitutional framework advocated by Publius accepted the premise that the American character would be self-interested to the point that private interests would normally be more important than the general welfare in influencing people's behavior. In Publius's eyes, people were in the main ambitious and self-interested, and they should be expected to make the improvement of their own conditions the basis for political choices. Those who *govern* a free people, therefore, must seek to use and channel the motive of self-interest.[12] Hamilton bluntly made this point in the following terms:

> Take mankind as they are, and what are they governed by? Their passions. There may be in every government a few choice spirits, who may act from more worthy motives. . . . Our prevailing passions are ambition and interest; and it will ever be the duty of a wise government to avail itself of these passions, in order to make them subservient to the public good.[13]

Led by Madison and Hamilton, the Federalists sought to establish a regime in which "choice spirits" need not be the norm. They were emphatically unwilling to write a constitution based on the assumption that virtuous governors would always be available and in office. Since these governors were to be drawn from the ranks of the governed, Publius argued that they could be expected to resemble their fellow citizens in generally being self-interested. Thus, according to Martin Diamond, the Federalists' objective was "a durable regime whose perpetuation require[d] nothing like the wisdom and virtue necessary for its creation."[14] Robert Horwitz uses even stronger language: "Pushing questions of virtue aside, they sought to develop political arrangements and institutions that would insure 'the existence and security of the government, *even in the absence of political virtue.*'. . . . The guiding and energizing principle of the community would be the vigorous pursuit of individual self-interest."[15] Diamond, however, goes on to ask: "But does not the intensity and kind of our modern problems seem to require of us a greater degree of reflection and public-spiritedness than the Founders thought sufficient for the men who came after them?"[16]

This is the issue that Woodrow Wilson recognized and that other students of American public administration have raised more recently in a variety of contexts.[17] Does founding thought offer any guidance to those seeking ways in which the public-spiritedness or civic virtue of public administrators might be enhanced? We will argue here that it does have a great deal to offer, because the Founders did not simply jettison the idea of public virtue. They gave the term a distinctly modern definition, one stressing the compatibility of self-interest, moderation, and service to the community.[18] Working from this perspective, the Founders reasoned that the American regime would be capable of producing a steady stream of people dedicated to public service.[19] Thus, Publius wrote in *Federalist* 57:

> The aim of every political constitution is, or ought to be, first to obtain for rulers men who possess most wisdom to discern, and most virtue to pursue, the common good of the society; and, in the next place, to take the most effectual precautions for keeping them virtuous whilst they continue to hold their public trust.[20]

The writings of several delegates to the Constitutional Convention indicate that they shared the belief that the excellences of character needed to sustain the American regime originate in one or more of three mutually reinforcing sources: constitutional correctives, a concern for reputation or honor, and education. These writings increase our understanding of how the Founders proposed to enhance the probability that Americans would be served by *publicly virtuous governors* (a term that would include Wilson's public administrators).

Public Virtue and Constitutional Correctives in Founding Thought

As a group, the Founders were painfully aware of the administrative failings of the confederation, but they were divided over a series of questions relating to the jurisdiction and powers of its contemplated successor. All concerned recognized, at least in general terms, that these questions had serious administrative implications, since the new government—whatever form it took—would have to be capable of fulfilling its domestic as well as its international responsibilities. Citizen character was a centerpiece of the debate, in part because of disagreement between the advocates of institutional arrangements that depended on high levels of public virtue in the citizenry and those who believed, in John Adams's words, "that all projects of government, founded in the supposition or expectation of extraordinary degrees of virtue, are evidently chimerical."[21] There was, however, general agreement that constitutional arrangements should reflect certain assumptions about citizen character.

The Anti-Federalists argued that relatively small, homogeneous, and highly democratic states offered the best opportunity to *form* citizen character around public virtues that would nurture and protect republican government.[22] In their view, the long-term survival of the new republic would depend on citizens' adherence to community as opposed to individual interests. They believed that a primary function of government should be the cultivation of public or civic virtue, because "Republican government depends on civic virtue, on a devotion to fellow citizens and to country so deeply instilled as to be almost as automatic and powerful as the natural devotion to self-interest."[23] Here the Anti-Federalists tended to mirror the classical conception of the regime as a comprehensive system for the formation of character, in which the governors are to be judged by their commitment to the ethical purposes of the regime and their capacity to instill (and enforce) public virtues in the citizenry.[24]

Leaning heavily on the classical tradition, the Anti-Federalists opposed the extended commercial republic contemplated by the Federalists in part because they saw it as a threat to public virtue, and therefore, to a truly republican form of government.[25] They saw the small, homogeneous republic as a school of citizenship, a school that could not survive in the large, heterogeneous, and factionalized republic advocated by the Federalists.[26] If citizenship declined, they feared that popular control would be replaced by aristocratic rule. Accordingly, their arguments in opposition to ratification of the Constitution typically expressed sentiments like the following:

A republican, or free government can only exist where the body of the people are virtuous, and where property is pretty equally divided. In such a government the people are the sovereign and their sense or opinion is the criterion of every public measure; for when this ceases to be the case, the nature of the government is changed, and an aristocracy, monarchy or despotism will rise on its ruin.[27]

As expressed by Publius, the Federalist point of view maintained that a constitution applying a "composition" of federal and national principles to an extended republic was necessary because people were not "angels" and, left to their own devices, could not reliably be expected to select virtuous leaders. Publius's forceful criticism of classical republican approaches to public virtue—particularly their inability to homogenize the opinions, passions, and interests of a naturally diverse citizenry without destroying liberty—is well known. Publius's treatment of the causes of factional politics and the corrective functions of an extended commercial republic still stands as the clearest, most powerful statement of this perspective on the connections between citizen character and the American regime.[28] In this view, the belief that democratic citizens and governors would possess superior virtues simply could not be relied upon as the foundation of the regime. Accordingly, the alternative was to accept as the "bedrock" of the regime that character trait most commonly in evidence, self-interest.

In *Federalist* 51, Publius applied this point of view to the "interior structure of the government" to show how, under the Constitution, ambition counteracted ambition and the "interest of the man [was] connected to the constitutional rights of the place."[29] Robert Goldwin observes that ambition and self-interest are so fundamental to Publius's design that

> if officials in one part of the government should be insufficiently moved by ambition and self-interest, a necessary balancing restraint would be lacking. . . . As fundamental as separation of powers is as a principle in the Constitution, that office holders must be ambitious and self-interested is even more fundamental.[30]

As we have noted, the argument between the Federalists and Anti-Federalists over the proper constitutional approach to citizen character was resolved largely in favor of the Federalists' position. For those such as Madison and Hamilton, to channel human passions and interests effectively was the most important goal:

> because character formation was no longer the direct end of politics, the new science of politics could dispense with those laws [by means of which the ancient philosophers had sought to "high tone" human character] and, for the achievement of its lowered ends, could rely largely instead upon shrewd institutional arrangements of the powerful human passions and interests. Not to instruct and to transcend these passions and interests, but rather to channel them became the hallmark of modern politics.[31]

The Federalists recognized that self-interest was, by itself, an inadequate foundation for the regime they contemplated. Restraints were needed. They did not, however, choose to rely on an aristocracy of virtuous governors to achieve that restraint. Rather, citizens, elected governors, and administrators were to be restrained by constitutional correctives. In this regard, Herbert J. Storing has properly emphasized the need for citizens both to understand and to support these constitutional devices. His words suggest that public administrators have "special" responsibilities:

> This government is popular but not simply popular. It does not, however, rely on mystery or myth to check the fundamental popular impulse. "Nondemocratic" "elements" are at work . . . but they are out in the open. This government is like a glass-enclosed clock. Its "works" are visible to all and must be understood and accepted by all in order to function properly. . . . [T]he government . . . [the Framers] constructed was nevertheless understood by them all to be unusual in the relatively small demands it placed on a political aristocracy and in the relatively great demands it placed on the people.[32]

The Founders' system of constitutional correctives requires public administrators who both appreciate and actively support it. John Rohr, for example, argues that ethical standards derived from regime values should apply to bureaucrats because they are sworn to defend the regime. In this context, he cites the character-forming role of the Supreme Court. He points out that Supreme Court procedures and opinions often "teach" enduring principles, offer insightful interpretations of American values, have direct applicability to administrative actions, and raise questions "that are useful for reflection on fundamental values."[33]

Another constitutional corrective, the extended commercial republic with its multiplicity of interests (which Publius called "a republican remedy for the diseases most incident to republican government"), is seen by Stephen Bailey as a source of administrative obligation:

> A large part of the art of public service is in the capacity to harness private and personal interests to public interest causes. Those who will not traffic in personal and private interests (if such interests are themselves within the law) to the point of engaging their support on behalf of causes in which both public and private interests are served, are, in terms of moral temperament, unfit for public responsibility.[34]

The diffusion of powers among the branches of government established by the Constitution also guides the public administrator. Rohr concludes that upholding the Constitution "means that public administrators should use their discretionary power in order to maintain the constitutional balance of powers in support of individual liberty."[35] Since public administration applies the three powers of government, it has been placed in the position of being able to influence events by favoring one branch or another. As Rohr observes, this imposes a formidable responsibility: public administrators, as constitutional trustees, "must learn to think like judges, as well as like legislators and executives, because they are all three of these. In a regime of separation of powers, administrators must do the work of statesmen."[36]

The Constitution makes a "politics-administration dichotomy" a literal impossibility. The Weberian bureaucrat who, unlike the politician, finds honor only in the energetic and competent execution of a superior's orders (whether or not he agrees with them) does not fit comfortably into the founding scheme.[37] While Publius emphasized the need for ability as well as virtue on the federal level, he saw it as a means to a political end: building popular support for a new national government that, in certain important respects, would be in perpetual competition with the several states for the loyalties of the people. For Publius, the conduct of a national public administration deserving of public confidence was an enterprise essential to the vitality of the regime.[38] This line of reasoning helps us understand why American public administrators must be more than Weberian bureaucrats. They are constitutional representatives who should find honor through service to the regime and the values it represents. This is far more than "neutral" competence; it is a profoundly political role demanding a *"devotion* to public duty and an *understanding* of the principles of governmental structure and operation of the broadest and deepest kind."[39]

Public Virtue and Honor in Founding Thought

The Founders sought ways in which the passions of those who govern might be so channeled as to result in publicly virtuous behavior. Federalists such as Madison and Hamilton thought it only prudent to assume that the most reliable of passions would be self-interest and ambition. However, in Forrest McDonald's words, they also

> expected something better, for men are driven by a variety of passions, and many of these—love of fame, of glory, of country, for

example, are noble. When any such passion becomes a man's ruling passion, he must necessarily live his life in virtuous service to the public; and it was such men whom the nationalists counted on to govern others through their baser passions.[40]

For the statesmanlike governor, self-interest requires public virtue.[41]

McDonald, citing George Washington's example, suggests that the Federalists believed that "public persons are and should be governed mainly 'by the law of *honour* or *outward esteem.*'"[42] A desire for the esteem of those of high reputation should be the guiding standard of individuals in public life: "To others be true, seek the esteem of the wise and the virtuous, and it follows that thou cannot then be false to thyself—or to the republic."[43]

John Locke, who was widely read in the American colonies, also emphasized the individual's concern with reputation and its social uses. He argued that the "law of public opinion" was a powerful (indeed socially necessary) element in controlling behavior. He reasoned that the law of public opinion is so effective because people have a strong need to be held in high esteem and greatly fear public shame or disgrace.[44]

This sentiment was subsequently reflected in the influential works of Adam Smith, who assigned priority to the love of "praise-worthiness." His interpretation of the relationship between self-approbation and the approbation of others seems particularly relevant to the situation of the contemporary American public administrator:

> The love and admiration which we naturally conceive for those whose character and conduct we approve of, necessarily dispose us to desire to become ourselves the objects of the like agreeable sentiments. . . . Neither can we be satisfied with being merely admired for what other people are admired. We must at least believe ourselves to be admirable for what they are admirable. . . . Their approbation necessarily confirms our own sense of our own praise-worthiness.[45]

The significance of Woodrow Wilson's previously mentioned reference to the connection between advancing the honor of public servants and their service to the community can be understood in the context of the Founders' effort to use what they saw to be a basic human concern for reputation and praiseworthiness. Their constitutional design is one intended to channel the private passions into those public excellences appropriate to (and needed by) the American regime. However, if this channeling is fundamental to the regime's capacity to produce publicly virtuous or excellent public administrators, how can it be achieved in a regime that is now considerably more democratic than that contemplated by most of the Founders?

With regard to reputation, it has been a long time since civil servants have been held in high esteem by the general citizenry. Recently, public scorn, often fueled by the words and actions of elected officials, has reached the point where some in the community of public administrators have seen the need to publish "polemical" defenses of bureaucracy.[46] Efforts also have been made to provide (or at least to revive) constitutionally grounded justifications of the "administrative state."[47] Others have warned of an erosion of morale and of competence as government loses (as well as fails to attract) qualified personnel.[48] However, none of this is unique to the present time. Complaints about tyrannical, incompetent, and self-interested officials date from the colonial period, and the constitutional framework provides no explicit legitimation of bureaucratic power, however real that power may be. In the United States, civil service has never been an easy road to honor and high levels of public approbation.

To whom do contemporary public administrators look for approbation and, hence, whom do they seek to emulate? Clearly, the Founders intended that, within limits, "public opinion" be heard and heeded in a democratic republic. As Storing points out, they saw no need for an administrative aristocracy operating according to its own idea of the public interest and independent of the formative influence of majority public opinion. If they were correct in believing that public virtue is closely connected to reputation and approbation, must it necessarily suffer when those who want to be praised and to see themselves as praiseworthy are not reinforced by public approval?

In "The Study of Administration," Wilson recognized this issue. In the course of his argument for a highly professionalized corps of civil servants having extensive discretion, he asked:

> To whom is official trustworthiness to be disclosed, and by whom is it to be rewarded? Is the official to look to the public for his need of praise and his push of promotion, or only to his superior in office? . . . These questions evidently find their root in what is undoubtedly the fundamental problem of this whole study. That problem is: What part shall public opinion take in the conduct of administration?[49]

Wilson's answer placed the public in the role of "superintending" the legislative and executive policy-making processes while leaving the day-to-day public administration in the hands of specially schooled and efficiently organized civil servants. To those who might complain that he was advocating the creation of an "offensive official class," Wilson responded that "administration in the United States must be at all points sensitive to public opinion" and earn its praise through "hearty allegiance to the policy of the government."[50] Since the American regime rests solidly on the principle of majority rule, Wilson understood that any fundamental solution to the "problem" of public approbation would have to be grounded in that majority's opinion. His solution included a call for civil service reform and professionalism: "If we are to improve public opinion, which is the motive power of government, we must prepare better officials as the *apparatus* of government."[51]

Between 1887 and the present, Wilson's call for merit systems and a technically trained civil service has been in large measure answered affirmatively. However, the anticipated improvement in public opinion regarding the civil service itself has apparently not materialized. Charles Goodsell has colorfully described the current climate in the following terms.

> Bureaucracy . . . is despised and disparaged. It is attacked in the press, popular magazines, and best sellers. . . . It is assaulted by molders of culture and professors of academia. . . . It is charged with a wide array of crimes . . . failure to perform; abuse of political power; and repression of employees, clients, and people in general. In short, bureaucracy stands as a splendid hate object.[52]

Under these conditions, the founding strategy would appear to stand a better chance of success if the range of those to whom public administrators look for approval were narrowed. Along these lines, a favored approach in the United States has been to attempt to build a foundation for public virtue through professionalization and codes of ethics for public administrators. While the public service is now highly professionalized in the sense that it is staffed by a wide variety of experts, most students of the field believe that public administration itself still has not achieved the status of a recognized profession. The desirability of such a profession, of course, has been the subject of lively debate since Wilson's essay.[53] Despite this controversy, many academics and practitioners have urged that "professional" standards be adopted and applied uniformly for all administrators.[54] In part, the aim is to provide a reference group of professional peers to guide and evaluate behavior. What remains unresolved is the possibility that substantial differences between public opinion and professional norms could arise—even to the point that what Wilson called "an offensive administrative class" could emerge.

Stephen Bailey and Frederick Mosher are perhaps the best-known commentators on the tensions between professional standards and democratic norms.[55] Both accept the inevitability of a government dominated by professionals who exert significant influence on public policies. A problem may arise if these same individuals see little or no honor in serving democratic norms or constitutional principles. If professional peers are be the primary points of reference for public administrators, education may be the most effective way of orienting them to these standards:

> For better or worse—or better *and* worse—much of our government is now in the hands of professionals (including scientists). The choice of these professionals, the determination of their skills, and the content of their work are now principally determined, not by general governmental agencies, but by their own professional elites, professional organizations, and the institutions and faculties of higher education. . . . The need for broadening, for humanizing, and in some fields, for lengthening professional education programs may in the long run prove more crucial to governmental response to societal problems than any amount of civil service reform.[56]

Public Virtue and Education in Founding Thought

The importance of a "proper" education for those who would govern in the American regime was a central concern of the Founders. In addition to expressing their belief that the small republic was itself a school of citizenship, a number of the Anti-Federalists proposed the establishment of schools or seminaries where youth could be educated in the habits of public virtue. Citizens, they argued, should be broadly educated in morality and the useful arts and sciences. Such education would form virtuous citizens who, "instead of abusing [their liberty], would wade up to their knees in blood, to defend their governments."[57]

The Federalists were no less interested in the education of the regime's future leaders. Several among them, including Madison and Washington, proposed the establishment of a national university for this purpose. They hoped to foster the habits of public virtue through a combination of public and private sources of education. At least indirectly, certain aspects of Locke's commentaries on education are reflected in the Federalists' thinking. Locke, who wrote extensively on the subject of education, stressed the character-forming functions of the family and recommended methods by which gentlemen could instill public virtues in their children during their upbringing.

While civil law and religion have roles to play in morality, Locke thought that the socially derived standards of public opinion more powerfully affected individual conduct, including one's choice of occupation. Therefore, he stressed the need to educate children in the standards or opinions of the community. This early socialization teaches not only standards but also the idea of rewards or penalties associated with actions that uphold or violate them. In Locke's scheme, a successful education of this sort would control those who might otherwise casually break religious and civil law in the pursuit of self-interest:[58]

> it follows that governments, even though they are legitimately constituted by Lockian standards, will be ineffective unless they rest on a foundation of sound opinion. That in turn can be accomplished only if the content of public opinion is established through the proper education of those citizens on whom the proper functioning of the commonwealth depends.[59]

Locke's argument relies on the assumption that people are by nature acquisitive, ambitious, and self-interested. The task of a proper education, therefore, is not to change human nature, but to help channel it in socially beneficial directions.[60] Accordingly, education should be a process devoted to demonstrating the connections between public virtues and personal rewards. The pursuit of self-interest properly understood is a hallmark of Locke's well-educated gentleman.[61] Not surprisingly, the Federalists shared Locke's goals for the education of the citizenry:

> The major thrust of their activities would be toward the acquisition of property, whether through the careful management of land or through trade, commerce, or such professions as law, medicine, or the like. . . . They would be "men of business," in the broad seventeenth-century meaning of that term.[62]

Thomas Jefferson's influence on public administration thought has also received considerable attention, particularly in the "new public administration" literature.[63] His ideas regarding education are particularly significant in part because they are based on a treatment of self-interest that is arguably somewhat at odds with that of Locke and the Federalists. In his *Notes on the State of Virginia,* Jefferson considers his law establishing an educational system in the state to be one of his most important contributions because of the need for a public education that would prepare the people to defend their liberty against those who would seek to establish a new form of monarchy.[64] As a defense against ambitious despots, the government should provide for the basic education of the whole people.[65]

Contending that "people will be happiest whose laws are best, and are best administered, and that laws will be wisely formed, and honestly administered, in proportion as those who form and administer them are wise and honest," Jefferson set forth a plan to discover those "fitly formed" children "whom nature had endowed with genius and virtue."[66] After a selection process that grew progressively more rigorous as the students advanced in their studies, those students possessing the most superior "parts and disposition" were to be sent on for three years of advanced study at William and Mary College. It was this natural aristocracy that was to become public servants.[67]

Thus, along with constitutional correctives and honor, education was an important part of the Founders' thinking with regard to the goal of assuring that the American regime would be served by publicly virtuous governors. One hundred years later, Wilson made the connection between education and virtue in public administration a key element of his essay. Of course, he did not believe that "universal political education" would itself suffice to create competent public administrators. In 1887, conducting government required technical training as well: "It will be necessary to organize democracy by sending up to the competitive examinations for the civil service men definitely prepared for standing liberal tests as to technical knowledge. A technically schooled civil service will presently become indispensable."[68] But Dwight Waldo observes that "Wilson saw everything through a political lens . . . and was highly motivated to make the republican-democratic [experiment] succeed."[69] Wilson's lecture notes reveal that he had no intention of restricting public administration education to purely instrumental or technical matters. Constitutional principles, history, comparative government, practical politics, public law, as well as management were essential to a proper curriculum.[70] It is against this background that Wilson made the following statement:

The ideal for us is a civil service cultured and self-sufficient enough
to act with sense and vigor, and yet so intimately connected with the
popular thought, by means of elections and constant public counsel,
as to find arbitrariness or class spirit quite out of the question.[71]

Conclusion

We suspect that the Founders would not have disapproved of the
post-Wilsonian preoccupation with public administration as an instrumental field. But they likely would have considered it to be incomplete because it neglected the development of desirable public virtues.
The contemporary interest in ethics for public administrators is consistent with the Founders' concern that, left to itself, the citizenry
(including public administrators) would act in a narrowly self-interested manner. As we have noted, the regime requires public administrators who can be reliably expected to act on the public's behalf.

The Founders understood that the new nation required "certain
enduring excellences." While there is no reason to believe that the
Founders anticipated the size, scope, and complexity of today's administrative state, they did anticipate that the quality of public
administration under the Constitution would play a major role in determining the success of their experiment in republican-democratic
government. "Nurturing the appropriate excellences," therefore, is a
challenge of particular importance to American public administration.

Our reading of the Founders' intentions reveals a heavy reliance
on the interaction of constitutional correctives, honor, and education
to produce virtuous public officials who would serve the regime "with
the best efforts of [their] talents and the soberest service of [their]
conscience." Seen in this light, Woodrow Wilson's oft-quoted assertion that "It is getting harder to *run* a constitution than to frame one"
becomes far more than a call for rational organization and efficiency—it is also a reaffirmation of the Founders' belief that the promise
of the American regime could be fulfilled only if those who govern
are committed to preserving and strengthening the foundations upon
which it rests.

Public administrators should understand the importance and function of the constitutional correctives we have discussed. As Wilson
understood, this means that their education must encompass far more
than a simple description of the Constitution. The public administrator is well served by a thorough grounding in American political thought

and constitutional history and law.[72] Although public administration is an imprecisely defined field, open to many prescriptions regarding the preparation of its practitioners, in the American setting, no definition could sensibly exclude these topics and an examination of their applications to the administrative enterprise.

The study of the Constitution and the ideas that underpin it should provide a major element of public administrators' understanding of the duties and obligations that flow from a commitment to the regime. However, as Wilson said, particular attention must be paid to the problem of how best to integrate the self-interest of the public administrator with service to the community or public interest. (With the possible exception of Jefferson, the Founders had little confidence in noblesse oblige as the moral foundation of the Republic.)

As we have pointed out, concern for reputation—the desire for approbation or honor—is fundamental to the Founders' design. For those who govern, to be well educated meant a proper orientation to the "law of public opinion" or to the standards and judgments of those we are taught to admire. In contemporary terminology, public virtue is the result of orienting oneself to a reference group that values service to the regime, community, and others. On the one hand, it is to this group that the individual looks for guidance and approbation. On the other, it is their disapproval that is most feared and, therefore, to be avoided:

> Is it then unethical somehow to want to be honored by the public, to seek the esteem of one's peers? Clearly not. But . . . the relevant distinction is between doing right, helping people who need help, preserving democratic government, achieving some measure of excellence, on the one hand, and being honored for its own sake, on the other. In the end, then, the desire for honor, which is inherently selfish, can be redeemed only by seeking to satisfy it through service to others.[73]

The greatest irony of public administration since Wilson's essay may lie in the success of policies and practices designed to avoid the creation of anything resembling an American "administrative class." In combination with the emphasis on technical expertise or public management, the lack of any identifiable community of public administrators may have eroded the foundations upon which the Founders relied to assure that the regime would be served by publicly virtuous administrators capable of being effectively superintended by public opinion. At the very least, this is a matter that should be of concern to those who concern themselves with the proper governance of the American regime.

Notes

1. Martin Diamond, "The American Idea of Man: The View from the Founding," in *The Americans 1976, Critical Choices for Americans*, vol. 2, ed. Irving Kristol and Paul Weaver (Lexington, Mass.: Lexington Books; Washington, D.C.: Heath, 1976), 21–22.

2. Woodrow Wilson, "The Study of Administration," *Public Administration: Politics and the People,* ed. D. Yarwood (White Plains, N.Y.: Longman, 1987), 29.

3. The literature on these and related topics is extensive. For example, see Martin J. Schiesl, *The Politics of Efficiency: Municipal Administration and Reform in America* (Berkeley: University of California Press, 1977); Dwight Waldo, *The Administrative State* (New York: Ronald Press, 1948); Emmette S. Redford, *Democracy in the Administrative State* (New York: Oxford University Press, 1969); Barry Karl, *Executive Reorganization and Reform in the New Deal* (Cambridge: Harvard University Press, 1963); Paul H. Appleby, *Big Democracy* (New York: Knopf, 1949); Vincent Ostrom, *The Intellectual Crisis in American Public Administration* (University: University of Alabama Press, 1974); Paul Van Riper, *History of the United States Civil Service* (Chicago: Row, Peterson, 1958); Theodore Lowi, *The End of Liberalism*, 2d ed. (New York: Norton, 1979); and Laurence J. O'Toole Jr., "American Public Administration and the Idea of Reform," *Administration and Society* 16 (August 1984): 141–66.

4. Dwight Waldo, "The Perdurability of the Politics-Administration Dichotomy: Woodrow Wilson and the Identity Crisis in Public Administration," *Politics and Administration: Woodrow Wilson and American Public Administration,* ed. Jack S. Rabin and James S. Bowman (New York: Dekker, 1984), 231; and Gerald E. Caiden, "In Search of an Apolitical Science of American Public Administration," in *Politics and Administration,* 51–76.

5. Dwight Waldo, *The Enterprise of Public Administration* (Novato, Calif.: Chandler and Sharp, 1980), 10–12, 67–69.

6. Ibid., 66–67.

7. See *The American Founding: Politics, Statesmanship, and the Constitution*, ed. Ralph A. Rossum and Gary L. McDowell (Port Washington, N.Y.: Kennikat Press, 1981).

8. See, however, Robert A. Goldwin, ed., *Bureaucrats, Policy Analysts, Statesmen: Who Leads?* (Washington, D.C.: American Enterprise Institute, 1981).

9. Alexander Hamilton, James Madison, and John Jay, *The Federalist Papers* (New York: New American Library, 1961), nos. 1–4.

10. Herbert J. Storing, *What the Anti-Federalists Were For: The Political*

Thought of the Opponents of the Constitution (Chicago: University of Chicago Press, 1981), 42–43.

11. Forrest McDonald, *Novus Ordo Seclorum: The Intellectual Origins of the Constitution* (Lawrence: University Press of Kansas, 1985), 70–71.

12. Martin Diamond, "Ethics and Politics: The American Way," in *The Moral Foundations of the American Republic*, 2d ed., ed. Robert Horwitz (Charlottesville: University of Virginia Press, 1979), 47.

13. *The Records of the Federal Convention of 1787*, ed. Max Farrand (New Haven: Yale University Press, 1937), I: 82; see, also, McDonald, *Novus Ordo Seclorum*, 188–89.

14. Martin Diamond, "The Federalist," in *American Political Thought: The Philosophic Dimension of American Statesmanship*, 2d ed., ed. Morton J. Frisch and Richard G. Stevens (Itasca, Ill.: Peacock, 1983), 87.

15. Robert H. Horwitz, "John Locke and the Preservation of Liberty: A Perennial Problem of Civic Education," in his *The Moral Foundations of the American Republic*, 132–33 (emphasis added).

16. Diamond, "The Federalist," 88.

17. For example, see Brian J. Cook, "The Representative Function of Bureaucracy: Public Administration in Constitutive Perspective," *Administration and Society* (February 1992): 403–29; J. Patrick Dobel, "Integrity in the Public Service," *Public Administration Review* (May/June 1990): 354–66; H. George Frederickson, "Toward a Theory of the Public for Public Administration," *Administration and Society* (February 1991): 395–417; H. G. Frederickson and David K. Hart, "The Public Service and the Patriotism of Benevolence," *Public Administration Review*, 45 (September/October 1985): 547–53; Louis C. Gawthrop, "Civas, Civitas, and Civilitas: A New Focus for the Year 2000," *Public Administration Review*, 44 (March 1984): 101–7; David K. Hart, "A Partnership in Virtue among All Citizens: The Public Service and Civic Humanism," *Public Administration Review* (March/April 1989): 101–5; Hart, "The Virtuous Citizen, the Honorable Bureaucrat, and 'Public' Administration," *Public Administration Review*, 44 (March 1984): 111–20; Hart, "The Honorable Bureaucrat Among the Philistines," *Administration and Society*, 15 (May 1983): 43–48; Larry M. Lane, "Individualism, Civic Virtue, and Public Administration," *Administration and Society*, May 1988, 30–45; John A. Rohr, "Ethical Issues in French Public Administration: A Comparative Study," *Public Administration Review* July/August 1991: 283–97, and his *Ethics for Bureaucrats: An Essay on Law and Values* (New York: Dekker, 1978); and Camilla Stivers, "The Public Agency as Polis: Active Citizenship in the Administrative State," *Administration and Society*, May 1990, 86–105.

18. Diamond, "Ethics and Politics: The American Way," 56ff.

19. McDonald, *Novus Ordo Seclorum*, 188–91.

20. *The Federalist* 57: 350.

21. John Adams to Samuel Adams (1790), in *Political Thought in America: An Anthology*, ed. Michael B. Levy (Homewood, Ill.: Dorsey Press, 1982), 73.

22. Storing, *What the Anti-Federalists Were For*, 8.

23. Ibid., 15–23.

24. Ibid., 21.

25. Ibid. To understand the arguments over "virtue" in the new regime, it helps to clarify the distinction between "virtue" and "public" (or "political") virtue. The former is understood to mean the actual possession of a particular laudable attribute such as moderation. The crucial aspect of such a possession is that one acts moderately *because* one values moderation for itself. "Public virtue" is different in that while one may act moderately, one does so primarily because of the public honor or reputation attached to such a display.

26. Storing, *What the Anti-Federalists Were For*, 20.

27. Samuel Bryan, "Letter of Centinel, No. 1" (1787), in *Political Thought in America*, 115.

28. *The Federalist* 10, esp. 78–79. See also Diamond, "Ethics and Politics: The American Way," 39–72.

29. *The Federalist Papers*, 51: 322.

30. Robert A. Goldwin, "Of Men and Angels: A Search for Morality in the Constitution," in *The Moral Foundations of the American Republic*, 10.

31. Diamond, "Ethics and Politics: The American Way," 47.

32. Herbert J. Storing, "American Statesmanship: Old and New," in *Bureaucrats, Policy Analysts, Statesmen: Who Leads?* 92–93 (repr. in present volume, ch. 1, 5–32).

33. Rohr, *Ethics for Bureaucrats*, esp. 59 and 64–74.

34. Stephen K. Bailey, "Ethics and the Public Service," in *Public Administration and Democracy*, ed. Roscoe C. Martin (Syracuse: Syracuse University Press, 1965), 283–98.

35. John A. Rohr, *To Run a Constitution: The Legitimacy of the Administrative State* (Lawrence: University Press of Kansas, 1986), 181.

36. Ibid, 185. See also Dwight Waldo, *The Administrative State*, 2d ed. (New York: Holmes and Meier, 1984), 104–27.

37. See Max Weber, *Economy and Society*, ed. G. Roth and C. Wittich, (Berkeley: University of California Press, 1978), 1404.

38. Rohr, *To Run a Constitution*, 1–11; *The Federalist Papers*, 3, 17, 27, 46, 68; and Laurence J. O'Toole Jr., "Doctrines and Developments: Separation of Powers, the Politics-Administration Dichotomy, and the Rise of the Administrative State," *Public Administration Review* 47 (January/February 1987): 17–25.

39. Storing, "American Statesmanship: Old and New," 98 (emphasis added).

40. McDonald, *Novus Ordo Seclorum*, 189.

41. Ibid., 223.

42. Ibid., 198.

43. Ibid., 198–99.

44. Robert H. Horwitz, "John Locke and the Preservation of Liberty: A Perennial Problem of Civic Education," 139ff.

45. Adam Smith, *The Theory of Moral Sentiments* (Indianapolis: Liberty

Classics, 1976), 208–9. A related discussion of this issue is found in David K. Hart and P. Artell Smith, "Fame, Fame-Worthiness, and the Public Service," *Administration and Society* (August 1988): 131–51.

46. See, for example, Charles T. Goodsell, *The Case for Bureaucracy: A Public Administration Polemic* (Chatham, N.J.: Chatham House Publishers, 1983).

47. See Rohr, *To Run a Constitution.*

48. Bruce Adams, "The Frustrations of Government Service," *Public Administration Review* 44 (January/February 1984): 5.

49. Woodrow Wilson, "The Study of Administration," 26.

50. Ibid., 27.

51. Ibid. (emphasis added).

52. Goodsell, *The Case for Bureaucracy*, 11.

53. Waldo, *The Enterprise of Public Administration*, 61–62, 77–78.

54. *American Society for Public Administration Code of Ethics and Implementation Guidelines*, Supplement to *P.A. Times* (1 May 1985); John A. Rohr, "The Study of Ethics in the P.A. Curriculum," *Public Administration Review*, 36 (July/August 1976): 398–406; *Public Duties: The Moral Obligations of Government Officials*, Joel L. Fleishman, Lance Liebman, and Mark H. Moore, eds. (Cambridge: Harvard University Press, 1981); Rohr, *Ethics for Bureaucrats*, 50–51; and Ralph Clark Chandler, "The Problem of Moral Reasoning in American Public Administration: The Case for a Code of Ethics," *Public Administration Review* 43 (January/February 1983): 32–39.

55. Stephen K. Bailey, "Ethics and the Public Service," and Frederick C. Mosher, "The Professional State," in *Public Administration: Politics and the People*.

56. Mosher, "The Professional State," 198.

57. Storing, quoting Maryland Farmer VI, 5.1.82, in *What the Anti-Federalists Were For*, 21.

58. Robert H. Horwitz, "John Locke and the Preservation of Liberty," 139–41. See *The Educational Writings of John Locke*, ed. James L. Axtell (Cambridge: Cambridge University Press, 1968); and Nathon Tarcov, *Locke's Education for Liberty* (Chicago: University of Chicago Press, 1987).

59. Horwitz, "John Locke and the Preservation of Liberty," 141.

60. Ibid.

61. Locke's approach to the connections between self-interest and public virtue also found expression in Alexis de Tocqueville's concept of self-interest properly understood: "that by serving his fellows man serves himself in that doing good is to his private advantage. . . . [I]f it does not lead the will directly to virtue, it establishes habits which unconsciously turn it that way." (*Democracy in America*, J. P. Mayer, ed. [Garden City, N.Y.: Anchor Books, 1969], 525, 527.)

62. Horwitz, "John Locke and the Preservation of Liberty," 154–55.

63. H. George Frederickson and David K. Hart, "The Public Service and the Patriotism of Benevolence," *Public Administration Review* (September/October 1985); H. George Frederickson, *New Public Administration* (University: University of Alabama Press, 1980); and Richard J. Stillman II, "The Changing

Patterns of Public Administration Theory in America," in *Public Administration: Concepts and Cases*, 3d ed., ed. Richard J. Stillman (Boston, Mass.: Houghton Mifflin, 1984), 5–24.

64. David Tucker, "The Political Thought of Thomas Jefferson's *Notes on the State of Virginia*," in *The American Founding,* ed. Rossum and McDowell, 116.

65. Lynton Keith Caldwell, *The Administrative Theories of Hamilton and Jefferson: Their Contribution to Thought on Public Administration* (Chicago: University of Chicago Press, 1944), 110.

66. "Bill 79 of 1779 for the 'More General Diffusion of Knowledge,'" in *Thomas Jefferson and the Development of American Public Education*, ed. James B. Conant (Berkeley: University of California Press, 1962), 88–93.

Some contemporary commentators have also discussed the role of public administration in terms reminiscent of Jefferson. For example, H. George Frederickson and David K. Hart set forth a distinctly Jeffersonian point of view in their discussion of the moral obligations of American public administrators: They "define the primary moral obligation of the public service in this nation as the patriotism of benevolence. . . . [T]he primary duty of public servants is to be the *guardians* and *guarantors* of the regime values for the American public." ("The Public Service and the Patriotism of Benevolence," *Public Administration Review*, 45 [September/October 1985]: 549, 551 [emphasis added].) A related discussion of the role of public administration is found in Charles J. Fox and Clarke E. Cochran, "Discretion Advocacy in Public Administration: Toward a Platonic Guarding Class?" *Administration and Society* (August 1990), 249–71.

67. Thomas Jefferson, *Notes on the State of Virginia*, ed. William Peden (New York: Norton, 1972), 146–49.

For an argument that the *Notes* represent an Aristotelian detailing of the proper requisites for the new regime, see William D. Richardson, "Thomas Jefferson and Race: The Declaration and *Notes on the State of Virginia*," *Polity* 16 (Spring 1984): 447–66.

68. Wilson, "The Study of Administration," in Yarwood, 27.

69. Waldo, "The Perdurability of the Politics-Administration Dichotomy: Woodrow Wilson and the Identity Crisis in Public Administration," 225.

70. Ibid., 230–31.

71. Woodrow Wilson, in Yarwood, 27.

72. On these and related topics, see Waldo, *The Administrative State*, ix–lxiv; Waldo, *The Enterprise of Public Administration*, 49–64; H. George Frederickson, *New Public Administration*, 93–111; and Cooper, "The Wilsonian Dichotomy in Administrative Law," in *Politics and Administration: Woodrow Wilson and American Public Administration*, 79–94.

73. Fleishman, "Self-Interest and Political Integrity," 70–71.

13

Bureaucratic Morality in the United States

John A. Rohr

This chapter presents a brief overview of the problem of "bureaucratic morality" in the United States. The two words in quotation marks need some explanation. By "bureaucrat" I mean a public official who is hired, retained, promoted, and retired (or fired) through a merit system. I distinguish bureaucrats from officials who have been either elected or politically appointed. "Morality" is a broader term than "ethics." It captures nicely questions of character as well as the narrower concerns usually associated with ethics.

The chapter has two major sections. The first attempts to state the American version of the problem of bureaucratic morality. The second shows how certain peculiarities of American government affect the American problem of bureaucratic morality. The argument proceeds from the widely held opinion that administration is best understood as a function of regime and not as a universal science.

I

If one takes one's cues from American newspapers, one is tempted to conclude that questions of conflict of interest are at the heart of the American problem of bureaucratic morality. The case of President Reagan's close aide and confidant, Michael Deaver, is only one in a long string of spectacular stories of high-ranking public officials who are alleged to have violated statutory prohibitions governing their financial affairs during or after their terms of government service.

Important as questions of conflict of interest are, they have little to do with bureaucratic morality. For the most part, questions of this nature concern political appointees rather than career civil servants. One reason for this is that the high-ranking political appointees tend to hold their positions for only a short time—about two years on the average. Consequently, these officers maintain much closer relationships with the private sector than is the case with career civil servants. Political appointees, especially in Republican administrations, are quite likely to have just left lucrative positions in commerce or in industry and are likely to return to similar positions. Such men and women are likely candidates for conflict-of-interest troubles, far more so than are career civil servants with long-term governmental commitments and relatively modest and simple financial affairs.

The academic literature in the field of public administration virtually ignores the problem of conflict of interest and its companion issue, public financial disclosure that is intended to "detect and deter" conflicts of interest.[1] This is a remarkable phenomenon. The fact that these issues pertain more to political appointees than to career civil servants does not explain the lack of interest on the part of public administration journals. These journals regularly feature articles on political appointees who are not "bureaucrats" as I have defined the term above.

One reason for this neglect is the long-standing antipathy to the study of public law among American political scientists specializing in public administration.[2] Conflict of interest is a highly technical subject. Few practical problems are solved by invoking the "Caesar's wife" principle or the broad moral prohibition against using one's public office for private gain. These grand principles are soon forgotten when a decision must be made on whether a particular government official has actually violated a specific statute or an administrative regulation governing conflict of interest.

For example, an important point in the case of Michael Deaver is whether some of the persons with whom he communicated after leaving government service were members of the same "agency" as that in which Deaver had served. That question, in turn, requires a careful examination of how the Office of Government Ethics has defined the word "agency." These matters are important because the Ethics in Government Act of 1978 differentiates between a former employee's communications with members of his or her former agency and communications with other government officials.

These technical matters are not confined to highly visible figures like Deaver. Let us suppose, for example, that Smith and Jones are partners in a legal firm. Smith takes a position with the Bureau of Traffic of the Interstate Commerce Commission (ICC). Jones is approached by a client whose company is being investigated by that bureau. Can Jones take the case? Suppose Smith works for a different bureau in ICC, for example, the Bureau of Accounts. Does this change make a difference? Suppose the client were being investigated by an entirely different agency, such as the Antitrust Division of the Department of Justice. Could Jones then take the case? If Jones were permitted to take the case in any of these instances, could Smith share in the fees the partnership derives from Jones's efforts?[3]

When one descends to particulars of this sort, the possibility of generating significant moral reflection is considerably reduced. One is dealing with a question of purely positive law that has been purged of the most interesting questions of morality in public administration. Most of the scholars writing in public administration journals are themselves teachers who want to offer helpful guidance to their students. They find little hope of reaching questions amenable to serious moral analysis in the areas of conflict of interest and financial disclosure, since questions coming from these areas collapse all too quickly into shallow legalism. This is why the academic literature on ethics and morality in public administration tends to eschew conflict-of-interest issues.

This tendency is nonetheless somewhat surprising in view of the remarkably broad range of topics covered in this literature, for example, administrative responsibility;[4] corruption;[5] whistle-blowing;[6] education for the public service;[7] the use of language in moral argument;[8] the question of "waste, fraud and abuse";[9] ethics as related to management;[10] the specific moral problems for policy analysts;[11] fixing personal responsibility for an organizational decision;[12] the problem of "following orders";[13] the relevance of John Rawls's *A Theory of Justice* for public administration;[14] specific problems raised by the creation of the Senior Executive Service;[15] highly focused studies such as "An Ethical Framework for Human Resources Decision Making";[16] and the "Statement of Principles" of the American Society for Public Administration (ASPA) and the "Ethics Workbook" of the same organization.[17]

Despite this breadth of interest, there is one theme that dominates the literature, and that is the problem of administrative discretion. From the early days of the civil service reform movement at the end of the nineteenth century, Americans had been taught to draw a sharp distinction or even a dichotomy between policy and administration.

Elected officials made policy, and administrators carried it out. This distinction was crucial for legitimating the role of a career civil service in a democratic regime. Career civil servants are, of course, by definition, exempt from the discipline of the ballot box. The simplest way to justify this exemption in terms of democratic principles is to maintain that career civil servants do not govern but merely carry out the will of those who do. The real governing is done by elected officials. Public administration is purely instrumental. It is, in Woodrow Wilson's words, "the systematic execution of public law," and public law is made by elected officials. Policy is made by law; administration is a politically neutral technique grounded in scientific principles.[18]

This model of public administration was a matter of high doctrine in civil service circles for decades. With the dramatic growth of administrative agencies in the 1930s, however, the model came under attack. Political scientists began to point out that the laws that were being executed by administrators were not *commands* to perform specific acts but *empowerments* to govern significant areas of American life. Administrative agencies were assigned such nebulous mandates as "preventing unfair competition," "maintaining a fair and orderly market," or granting radio (and later television) licenses as "the public interest, convenience, or necessity" would indicate. Loosely drawn statutes of this sort conferred enormous discretion on administrators and weakened considerably the force of the dichotomy between politics and administration.

As it became increasingly clear that administrative behavior was characterized more by discretionary judgment than by slavish adherence to legislative prescription, thoughtful commentators began to worry about being governed by a bureaucracy that was not accountable to the electorate. At the same time it was recognized that the exigencies of a modern industrial state often precluded tightly drawn statutes that rigidly govern administrative behavior. Administration had to be flexible so as to meet rapidly changing circumstances without having to go back to Congress for new legislation. This, of course, is another way of saying there is a need for considerable administrative discretion. The moral problem for the bureaucrat is how to exercise his discretionary powers in a responsible manner even though he is not formally accountable to the electorate.

Variations on this theme of defining the moral problem for bureaucrats in terms of the responsible use of administrative discretion abound in the public administration literature. A consensus has emerged making this problem *the* central moral concern of this literature.[19] It is a moral problem because bureaucrats must play an active role in those institutional processes that authoritatively allocate values in American society. To put the same point in more traditional language, bureaucrats are called upon to promote the common good. This requires a certain capacity for sound political judgment, which is one important way of practicing the moral virtue of prudence.

II

At the same time that political scientists were discovering the discretionary character of public administration, they were also abandoning earlier beliefs in a "science" of administration. It was becoming increasingly clear that administration was a function of regime. Different political cultures had different administrative systems. What was appropriate administrative behavior in one part of the world might be quite dangerous in another part. All this is quite obvious today, but it was not always so.

The awareness of administration as a function of regime had a profound effect on how American scholars of public administration began to think about questions of morality in the profession of government. Instead of looking for universal principles of justice, the literature emphasized the norms and values peculiar to a liberal democracy. The New Public Administration movement and the social equity literature[20] of the late 1960s and early 1970s were cases in point. This literature gave little attention to arguments in support of liberal democracy. Liberal democracy was simply a given. The problem was how to move administrative practice in a direction that would make it more supportive of liberal democratic values.

In *Ethics for Bureaucrats*,[21] I distanced myself somewhat from the New PA/social equity literature because I thought it was insufficiently grounded in the American constitutional tradition. I thought (and still do think) that this literature did not go far enough in developing the logic of the insight that administration is a function of regime, and I suggested that we look to certain "regime values" embedded in the American constitutional tradition as the basis for normative reflection on appropriate attitudes and behavior for American administrators.

This approach presupposes a distinction between administrative ethics and political philosophy. Administrative ethics is supportive of the regime.[22] (By "regime" I do not mean the administration of a particular president but the fundamental American political order that came into being in 1789.) If administrative ethics and political philosophy are confused, one weakens the basis for a fundamental criticism of the regime. *Fundamental* criticism of regimes is the task of the political philosopher, as Aristotle has taught us. Administrative ethics is much less ambitious. Its focus is on improving in practice a regime that the administrator believes is fundamentally just. For the administrator who does not believe that his regime is fundamentally just, there can be no *administrative* ethics. The honorable course for such a person would be either to become a subversive or a revolutionary, or simply to drop out of public life. This involves, of course, questions of high politics that go far beyond the modest scope of administrative ethics. Genteel reform is in this instance an untenable middle ground. A regime that can be reformed is not *fundamentally* unjust. Questions of fundamental justice are questions of political philosophy. Questions of administrative ethics are second-level questions that arise only after one is satisfied that a particular regime is fundamentally just.[23]

The moral implication of the use of administrative discretion is not a problem peculiar to American administrators but, because of certain peculiarities of the American Constitution, the problem assumes some distinctively American characteristics. For example, American administrators carry out their responsibilities under a formal structure of separation of powers. This means they are quite properly accountable to two and sometimes even to three constitutional masters. This bifurcated responsibility raises some interesting ethical questions. These questions became salient during the Reagan administration because Ronald Reagan won his office through a 1980 campaign that was sharply critical of certain federal programs that continued to be administered after he had become president. Let us look at this issue concretely.

The Environmental Protection Agency (EPA) was a favorite target of Reagan's campaign rhetoric. The president's well-known opposition to environmental regulations put career civil servants at EPA in an uncomfortable position. On the one hand, they were members of the executive branch of government whose chief officer was President Reagan. In a certain sense, they and their agency worked for President Reagan, whom the American people approved in a resounding victory after a campaign in which environmental issues figured prominently. On the other hand, they were responsible for carrying out the environmental laws that had been enacted by Congress over the previous decade. Quite correctly, they sensed an atmosphere created by Reagan appointees at the head of the organization that discouraged serious enforcement of some environmental laws. No one would tell them to break any laws, but a tone was set that encouraged bureaucrats to use whatever discretion they had to reduce the scope of effective enforcement.

Eventually, high-ranking officials from the EPA's political leadership became so flagrant in disregarding their agency's mission to clean up toxic waste sites that career officials were able to "blow the whistle" to key congressional committees that undertook investigations that led to the resignation of four officials and a criminal conviction for a fifth.

The outrageous behavior at EPA was exceptional. Far more common and more effective were the subtle efforts by Reagan appointees to redirect agency policy through incremental changes in implementation. The Office of Surface Mining (OSM) in the Department of the Interior presents an illuminating example of subtle redirection of policy without any statutory changes.

OSM was created by the Federal Surface Mining Control and Reclamation Act that was passed during the first year of President Jimmy Carter's administration. One of the major purposes of the act was to restore lands that coal companies had ravaged by decades of strip mining. OSM was given generous inspection and regulating powers to achieve this goal. During the Carter administration, there was vigorous enforcement of regulatory policy that led to charges of excessive zealotry on the part of the OSM personnel. After President Reagan's election, his interior secretary, James Watt, announced that there would be a "new OSM" that would emphasize cooperation and persuasion rather than confrontation and coercion. Administrative regulations based on the statute were rewritten to reflect the more relaxed regulatory environment, and the number of inspectors was dramatically reduced. The upshot, not surprisingly, was a sharp reduction in the number of violations detected in the early years of the Reagan administration when compared with the Carter years. Although there had been no change in the statute that created OSM, its performance record changed markedly. This change escaped the attention of neither the Congress nor the environmentalists. OSM, which had been criticized for its zealotry under Carter, was now attacked for its laxity under Reagan. Secretary Watt and the cadre of political appointees surrounding him had successfully changed the administrative behavior of OSM personnel without any change in the law. It is quite clear that bureaucrats used their discretionary authority in a different way because of a new political environment.[24]

The National Highway Traffic Safety Administration (NHTSA) provides another example of administrators changing their discretionary judgments to accommodate the preferences of a new administration. Pursuant to the National Traffic and Motor Vehicle Safety Act, NHTSA promulgated a safety standard in 1977 that would have required all motor vehicles produced after 1982 to be equipped with passive restraints (automatic seat belts, air bags). In 1981, the first year of the Reagan administration, this standard was rescinded. The agency's action was challenged in court by insurance companies and consumer groups that were displeased with a change in policy that was unsupported by any statutory change (*Motor Vehicle Manufacturers Association v. State Farm Mutual*).

The agency defended its rescission on the basis of new "findings" that were made in 1981. In 1977, it had been assumed that automobile manufacturers would install air bags in 60 percent of the new cars made after 1982 and automatic seat belts in the remaining 40 percent. By 1981, the agency maintained, it had become clear that 99 percent of new cars would have automatic seat belts. However, these seat belts could be detached by the owners, and there was good reason to think a very high percentage of owners would actually do this. As a result, the new requirements would not achieve the life-saving potential that the agency had thought they would achieve in 1977. In effect, the passive restraints would not be mandatory at all. Passengers would still "buckle up" only if they so desired. Consequently, the new requirements would add a needless cost to producing automobiles, a cost that would eventually be passed on to the consumer. Therefore, the 1977 safety standard was abandoned.

The Supreme Court rejected the agency's line of reasoning. Although the obvious political basis of the agency's decision was not ignored by the justices, judicial propriety required them to take seriously the agency's account of its own decision-making rationale. The Court remanded the case to NHTSA and ordered the agency to show why it had rejected certain obvious alternatives to merely rescinding the standard. Why, for instance, did NHTSA not require air bags in all new cars? Or why not require manufacturers to make automatic seat belts that could not be detached? The Court was careful not to substitute its own judgment for that of the agency, but it insisted upon a "reasoned analysis" for the agency's action. This left the agency ample opportunity to justify its original decision, but it would have to make a better argument to do so.

These examples from EPA, OSM, and NHTSA portray a peculiarly American version of the universal problem of administrative discretion. American administrators must serve two and sometimes three constitutional masters because of the principle of separation of powers in the American Constitution. In all three cases an administrative agency changed its policies in response to a change in the presidency. There was no change in the statutes they administered. As members of the executive branch they are accountable to the president, but as the Supreme Court noted 160 years ago, administrative officers are also responsible to the statutes passed by Congress. It is a well-established principle of American constitutional law that Congress can (and very often does) impose legal responsibilities upon officers subordinate to the president. "In such cases," the Court held in 1838, "the duty and responsibility [of the officer] grow out of and are subject to the control of the law, and not to the direction of the President" (*Kendall v. Stokes*).

When the courts intervene, the administrator has a third master he must serve. In such cases, the administrator's discretion is focused on deciding which of three competing masters he will obey. Thus, separation of powers gives a peculiar American twist to the moral dimension of administrative discretion. This discretion involves deciding not only what one thinks is right, but which constitutional master to serve as well.

To date there has been very little research on how mid-level and high-ranking bureaucrats see the moral dimensions of their complex role under a government of separated powers. Court cases and congressional hearings do not examine these matters. One can hope that this issue will rise to the top of the ethics scholars' research agenda. It is an important issue and one that would link ethics research with broader ideas in political science, such as the idea that administration is a function of regime.

The constitutional doctrine of separation of powers has had an important effect on the "official" ethics sponsored by the Office of Government Ethics (OGE). To examine this matter, it is necessary to review the background of the establishment of the OGE.

Two of the most important issues in President Carter's 1976 presidential campaign were the need for civil service reform and the need for a new federal ethics act. Congress passed both pieces of legislation in 1978; there was an interesting connection between the two statutes.

The Civil Service Reform Act of 1978 abolished the Civil Service Commission that had been established in 1883. The problem with the commission was that it had been burdened with conflicting duties. On the one hand, it was supposed to serve as the personnel management office of the executive branch of government. On the other hand, it was expected to police the merit system against patronage raids by the president and his political appointees. Thus, the same organization was required to serve simultaneously as a managerial instrument of the president and as a check on his power—or as both lapdog and watchdog, to use more graphic language. The 1978 legislation created two new agencies. The first was called the Merit Systems Protection Board. It is an "independent" agency sheltered from presidential influence. Its task, as its title indicates, is to protect the integrity of the merit system. The second agency is the Office of Personnel Management. It is housed in the Executive Office of the President and again, as its title indicates, its task is to manage the personnel affairs of the executive branch.

The Ethics in Government Act dealt primarily with financial disclosure by high-ranking officials and secondarily with certain employment restrictions imposed on such officials after they leave government service. The act created the Office of Government Ethics to administer the ethics program developed in the statute. Quite significantly, the OGE was housed in the Office of Personnel Management. Thus, Congress looked upon ethics—at least the ethical issues involved in financial disclosure—as a function of management.

The shortcomings of this point of view became quite clear when the OGE began to go about its statutory obligation of deciding whether a new presidential appointee had to take some action concerning financial holdings that appeared in his or her disclosure statement. For example, if the president wanted to appoint a stockholder in Exxon to a responsible position in the Energy Department, OGE would require the appointee either to divest himself of the stock or to agree to recuse himself from matters affecting Exxon or to take some other action that would remove the obvious conflict of interest. That is, it was the responsibility of OGE to impose demands upon a presidential appointee that might not be particularly welcome to either the appointee or to the president.[25]

This issue became acute when President Reagan took office in January

1981. With the change in administration there came an enormous number of new high-ranking appointees in a relatively short time. To his credit, President Reagan kept in office the man President Carter had appointed as director of OGE, J. Jackson Walter. By letting a Democrat, Walter, evaluate the financial disclosures of incoming Republicans, President Reagan avoided any appearance of partisan collusion in allowing people with questionable financial interests to hold high offices in the executive branch.

Under federal law, many government agencies must be reviewed periodically by Congress to see if their function is still necessary and, if so, whether any legislative changes should be enacted to enable them better to fulfill it. OGE underwent such a review in 1983. By that time Walter had resigned, and President Reagan had appointed his own director of OGE, David Martin. One of the questions that arose during the congressional hearings centered on the independence of the director of the Office of Government Ethics. The Senate version of the bill renewing OGE added a significant change. The director would enjoy a five-year term of office during which time he could be removed by the president only "for cause." This provision was intended, of course, to give the director more independence from the president than he would have enjoyed had he continued to serve simply at the pleasure of the president.

The Justice Department opposed this provision vigorously. It argued that the provision was an unconstitutional infringement by Congress of the president's authority to remove "purely executive" officers. Almost fifty years earlier, the Supreme Court had held that Congress could put limitations on the president's removal power over officers whose functions were "quasi-legislative" or "quasi-judicial," but that the president had unfettered discretion to remove those officers whose functions were "purely executive" (*Humphrey's Executor v. the United States*, 1935). Thus, the argument centered on the nature of the responsibilities of the director of the Office of Government Ethics. The fact that this office is part of the Office of Personnel Management would seem to suggest that he is indeed a purely executive officer. The precise purpose, after all, for establishing the Office of Personnel Management was to put personnel matters squarely under the president's authority without any interference from independent agencies like the old Civil Service Commission or the newly established watchdog agency, the Merit Systems Protection Board, which was quite clearly beyond presidential control. Independence from the president was thought to be desirable when it comes to protecting the integrity of the merit system, but not when it comes to the management of personnel matters.

On the other hand, it is quite clear that the director of OGE had a serious statutory obligation to tell the president what no president wants to hear—that a person he has selected for high office cannot serve unless he is willing to make some serious changes in his financial holdings. To discharge such a task responsibly, it would seem that the director of OGE should have considerable independence from the president.

The final resolution of the issue came in a compromise in which the director was given by law a five-year term, which he fills at the pleasure of the president.[26] This means he serves for five years unless the president wants to get rid of him sooner! The five-year provision is not entirely meaningless, however. It signals the intent of Congress to confer some independence on the director of OGE. If a president were to remove a director who had served well, there would surely be a strong protest from Congress and the media. Eventually, the president would prevail, but he would have to pay a price.

Thus, the short history of OGE finds that office, like so many others, caught up in the byzantine intricacies of that overarching principle of American politics, the separation of powers.

The responsible exercise of administrative discretion within a government that espouses the principle of separation of powers creates an important and interesting set of ethical problems for high-ranking bureaucrats. We have it on good authority that "no man can serve two masters," and yet this is precisely what the administrator must do. At times he must even serve three, and all this while trying to exercise his discretionary authority in a manner that he thinks will promote the public interest. In the contemporary administrative state, American politics may well be best understood by taking as the central theme the struggle among president, Congress, and the courts to control the government bureaucracy. The administrators themselves are not merely feckless pawns in this struggle. They take sides and at times move their agencies now toward one constitutional master and now toward another. This helps to preserve the stability and reduce the chaos of a government built around the principle of separation of powers. To do this, of course, is to engage in politics, and to engage in politics is to promote (or retard) the common good. This is morally significant activity; indeed, it goes to the heart of the issue of bureaucratic morality in the United States.[27]

Notes

1. There are some exceptions; see J. J. Walter, "The Ethics in Government Action, Conflict of Interest Laws, and Presidential Recruiting," *Public Administration Review* 14 (1981): 659–65.

2. This tendency can be traced back to the first public administration textbook, Leonard D. White's (1926) *Introduction to the Study of Public Administration.*

3. J. A. Rohr, *Ethics for Bureaucrats: An Essay on Law and Values* (New York: Dekker, 1978), 6.

4. H. J. Spiro, *Responsibility in Government: Theory and Practice* (New York: Van Nostrand, 1967); T. L. Cooper, *The Responsible Administrator: An Approach to Ethics for the Administrative Role* (Port Washington, N.Y.: Kennikat Press, 1982).

5. M. Johnson, *Political Corruption and Public Policy in America* (Monterey, Calif.: Brooks Cole, 1982).

6. C. Peters and T. Branch, eds., *Blowing the Whistle: Dissent in Public Interest* (New York: Praeger, 1972); and E. Weisband and T. M. Frank, *Resignation in Protest* (New York: Grossman, 1975).

7. J. A. Rohr, "The Study of Ethics in Public Administration Curriculum," *Public Administration Review* 36 (1976): 398–406; M. T. Lilla, "Ethos, 'Ethics,' and Public Service," *Public Interest* 63 (1981): 3–17; J. T. Edwards, J. Nalbandian, and K. R. Wedel, "Individual Values and Professional Education," *Administration and Society* 13 (1981): 123–44; J. C. Koritansky, "Prudence and the Practice of Government," *Southern Review of Public Administration* 6 (1982): 111–22; N. F. Brady "Feeling and Understanding: A Moral Psychology for Public Servants," *Public Administration Quarterly* 7 (1983): 220–40; J. Worthy and B. Grumet, "Ethics and Public Administration: Teaching What Can't Be Taught," *American Review of Public Administration* 17 (1983): 54–86.

8. R. C. Chandler, "The Problem of Moral Reasoning in American Public Administration: The Case for a Code of Ethics," *Public Administration Review* 43 (1983): 32–39; F. Fisher, "Ethical Discourses in Public Administration," *Administration and Society* 15 (1983): 5–42; J. R. Killingsworth, "Idle Talk and Modern Administration," *Administration and Society* 16 (1984): 346–83; W. G. Scott, "Organization Revolution: An End to Managerial Orthodoxy," *Administration and Society* 17 (1985): 149–70.

9. R. P. Kusserow, "Righting Fraud, Waste, and Abuse," *The Bureaucrat* 12 (1983): 19–23; J. Gardiner and T. Lyrnan, *The Fraud Control Game: State Responses to Fraud and Abuse in AFDC and Medical Programs* (Bloomington: Indiana University Press, 1984); C. L. Dempsey, "Managerial Accountability and Responsibility," *The Bureaucrat* 12 (1984): 17–23.

10. L. C. Gawthrop, *Public Sector Management, Systems, and Ethics* (Bloomington: Indiana University Press, 1984).

11. D. F. Davis and E. B. Portis, "A Categorical Imperative for Social Scientific Policy Evaluation," *Administration and Society* 14 (1982): 175–93;

J. L. Foster, "Reflections on the Categorical Imperative," *Administration and Society* 14 (1982): 195–99; J. A. Rohr, "Applying the Categorical Imperative to Policy Evaluation," *Administration and Society* 12 (1982): 201–5; D. J. Amy, "Why Policy Analysis and Ethics Are Incompatible," *Journal of Policy Analysis and Management* 3 (1984): 523–61; G. Beneveniste, "On a Code of Ethics for Policy Experts," *Journal of Policy Analysis and Management* 3 (1984): 561–72.

12. D. F. Thompson, "Moral Responsibility of Public Officials: The Problem of Many Hands," *American Political Science Review* 74 (1980): 905–16.

13. M. S. Jackson, "Eichmann, Bureaucracy, and Ethics," *Australian Journal of Public Administration* 43 (1984): 301–7.

14. M. M. Harmon, "Social Equality and Organizational Man: Motivation and Organizational Democracy," *Public Administration Review* 36 (1976): 11–18; D. K. Hart, "Social Equity, Justice, and the Equitable Administrator," *Public Administration Review* 34 (1974): 3–11.

15. J. A. Rohr, "Ethics for the Senior Executive Service: Suggestions for Management Training," *Administration and Society* 12 (1980): 203–16; N. E. Long, "The S.E.S. and the Public Interest," *Public Administration Review* 41 (1981): 305–12; B. Rosen, "Uncertainty in the Senior Executive Service," *Public Administration Review* 14 (1981): 203–7.

16. D. W. Stewart, "Managing Competing Claims: An Ethical Framework for Human Resources Decision Making," *Public Administration Review* 44 (1984): 14–22.

17. H. Mertins and P. J. Henningan, eds., *Applying Professional Standards and Ethics in the Eighties: A Workbook and Study Guide for Public Administrators,* 2d ed. (Washington, D.C.: American Society for Public Administration, 1982).

18. W. Wilson, "The Study of Administration," *Political Science Quarterly* 2 (1887): 197–22.

19. W. A. R. Leys, "Ethics and Administrative Discretion," *Public Administration Review* 3 (1943): 10–23; J. A. Rohr, *Ethics for Bureaucrats: An Essay on Law and Values* (New York: Dekker, 1978); G. D. Foster, "Law, Morality and the Public Servant," *Public Administration Review* 41 (1981): 29–34; M. T. Lilla, "Ethos, 'Ethics,' and Public Service," *Public Interest* 63 (1981): 3–17; D. P. Warwick, "The Ethics of Administrative Discretion," in *Public Duties: The Moral Obligation of Government Officials,* ed. J. Fleishman et al. (Cambridge: Harvard University Press, 1981); J. C. Koritansky, "Prudence and the Practice of Government," *Public Administration Quarterly* 6 (1982): 111–22; N. F. Brady, "Feeling and Understanding: A Moral Psychology for Public Servants," *Public Administration Quarterly* 7 (1983): 220–40; R. C. Chandler, "The Problem of Moral Reasoning in American Public Administration: The Case for a Code of Ethics," *Public Administration Review* 43 (1983): 32–39.

20. F. Marini, ed. *Toward a New Public Administration* (Scranton, Pa.: Chandler, 1971); H. G. Frederickson, ed. "Symposium on Social Equity and Public Administration," *Public Administration Review* 34 (1974): 1–42.

21. J. A. Rohr, *Ethics for Bureaucrats: An Essay on Law and Values* (New York: Dekker, 1987).

22. I use "regime" as the best English equivalent of Aristotle's *politeia*. In that way I can avoid the difficult question of the distinction between state and society without necessarily denying the validity of the distinction.

23. This point might be clarified by considering questions of professional ethics in other fields. Physicians, for example, worry about the meaning and extent of the "informed consent" they should elicit from their patients. Conscientious lawyers agonize over the moral limits on advocacy. For instance, provided one did not suborn perjured testimony, might not a clever lawyer deliberately mislead a judge or jury with specious arguments leading to the acquittal of his client, whom he knows to be guilty? Indeed, would it be ethical for such a lawyer not to make such an argument? The clergyman properly worries about balancing the need for ritual integrity against the evangelical demand for charity toward one's neighbor. Should he, for example, permit a member of another Christian denomination to receive communion in the clergyman's own parish?

These are important ethical questions, but they are second-level questions. A more serious question for the thoughtful clergyman is whether there is indeed a personal God and, if so, whether He has made his definitive revelation in the person Jesus. Thoughtful lawyers will surely be troubled at some point in their careers about the principle of advocacy as the best means to achieve justice. Thoughtful physicians may well ponder the meaning of their experience, which teaches them that pain and illness often reveal a person's true nobility of character. Such matters are far more important than questions of professional ethics in law, medicine, and religion. Important as they are, however, they are also quite different from questions developing a field of professional ethics. If any progress is to be made in developing a field of professional ethics, the practitioner must learn to set aside temporarily these more profound questions. As patients, we do not want our physicians engrossed in contemplating how our illness might ennoble our souls. Most of us would prefer to have him heal our bodies and to save his philosophical reflections for another day, or at least another patient (Rohr, 1982).

24. D. C. Menzel, "Redirecting the Implementation of a Law: The Reagan Administration and Coal Surface Mining Regulation," *Public Administration Review* 43: 411–21.

25. J. J. Walter, "The Ethics in Government Act, Conflict of Interest Laws, and Presidential Recruiting," *Public Administration Review* 14 (1981): 659–65.

26. A separate budget line was created for OGE within the Office of Personnel Management. This gives OGE some independence from the leadership of OPM.

27. I have developed this point more fully in *To Run a Constitution: The Legitimacy of the Administrative State* (Lawrence: University Press of Kansas, 1986).

14

Responsibility and Public Service

Mark Blitz

The purpose of American government is to secure individual rights, equally. This effort liberates and depends upon an energetic spirit of acquisition, and upon citizens who defend self-government that is also limited government. We may combine these traits of private and public spirit and say that the purpose of our politics is to foster the education and actions of responsible individuals.

The human characteristics that any government strives to produce and establish are visible in those who govern and in the way that they govern. Because responsible individuals often flourish more impressively outside our day-to-day government than within it, however, and because a responsible individual is less defined by a specific field of action than is, say, a person devoted to virtue or faith, the link between who governs (and how) and that for which they govern is more obscure in liberal democracies than in other regimes. Nonetheless, the link still exists, and I will assert in this chapter that good government in America—government that serves worthwhile purposes in a worthwhile way—is essentially identical to responsible government (and, more narrowly, to bureaucratic responsibility) once we properly understand what this means. Responsible public servants help to achieve the purpose of the American regime and, at the same time, exemplify the actions and the limits of responsible individualism.[1]

Unattractive Responsibility

Whatever good things we might say about responsibility, there is also something dull and ponderous about it. Who wants to spend the

weekend with someone famous for his responsibility? "Be responsible" means "stop having fun." "Act responsibly" means "do not do as
you would like." Responsibility is a sober characteristic that we may
all grudgingly respect, but it is something only a teenager's father
could love. Concern with it is chief among the traits that make fathers seem heavy-handed, old-fashioned, humorless, and overbearing
in the few moments when they do not seem bumbling, woebegone,
hapless, and out of touch.

To add to the unattractiveness, the search for the responsible
figure is often the search for someone to blame. "Who is responsible" means "whom can I punish?" Not a day goes by in which congressmen are not planning or holding hearings to fix responsibility,
so that they may destroy careers and reputations, or at least make
someone suffer. After all, if they cannot find someone else accountable for Waco, Whitewater, or Ruby Ridge, then perhaps it will be
said that they themselves are accountable; at the least, they might
seem irresponsible if they did not live up to their "oversight" responsibility.[2]

Being responsible seems boring, and assigning accountability
looks mean-spirited. We rarely think that it is vicious or bad, of course,
but displaying and demanding it is often uninspiring, sometimes
narrow-minded, and occasionally hypocritical. Yet, unattractive as
responsibility may appear, consider what we think of bureaucracy.
"Bureaucrat" is a word to which "petty" attaches itself as surely as
rubber is glued to stamp. Government officials, some of us so often
believe, are narrow-minded, small-souled, officious, inflexible, rule-
mongering, paper-chasing weasels. Coupling responsibility with
bureaucracy may mean that the weasel no longer fecklessly whistles
while he works, or that he blames himself for losing your license application rather than scolding you for asking about it, but the coupling of bureaucracy and responsibility is hardly the exciting marriage
of the century.

Responsible Government as
Accountable Government

It might therefore come as a surprise that properly defining and
institutionalizing bureaucratic responsibility was for many years among
political scientists almost synonymous with providing good govern-

ment.[3]   Academics thought that bureaucracy was indispensable for modern life, but ordinary citizens thought that it was often undemocratic. Political scientists therefore needed to show how it could be democratic after all. "Not only must we reject the idea that democracy is opposed to bureaucracy," wrote a young political scientist who was later to become a dean of his profession,

> but we must recognize that the future of democracy depends upon its ability to maintain a fully organized bureaucracy. For the industrial system which demands it is with us for better or worse since the life of millions of human beings depends upon it. If a popular government is incapable of maintaining a bureaucratic hierarchy, it is bound to give way to a form of government which will accomplish that, whether it be the dictatorship of an individual or of a small group in the name of the nation, the people, or the proletariat.[4]

In order to show how bureaucracy could be democratic, political scientists considered how it might be made responsible. By democracy they largely meant representative democracy, by representation they largely meant responding to popular interests, and by responsibility they almost exclusively meant accountability. If the people and their representatives could hold bureaucrats to account for serving their interests, then bureaucracy and democracy could be reconciled.

This was and is a difficult task, for several reasons. Bureaucrats might have professional or scientific skills that make them hard to control and understand: indeed, it is often because of their expertise that we think they are useful in the first place. They might have a tendency to follow procedures with such scrupulous (or unthinkingly lazy) precision that they are beyond the reach of valid individual adjustments and exceptions: indeed, we believe that it is only by following careful rules that they can deal with great complexity and large numbers quickly and fairly. They might have selfish interests that would be easy to mask in a civil service system with weak internal controls, little professional esprit de corps, and hiring and firing dominated by individual politicians. And they might be practicing in an administration with such unclear direction that there is little to which they could be held to account: indeed, they might be practicing in a constitutional regime such as ours that appears designed always to check and frustrate clear direction.

The result of these possibilities is that bureaucrats seem to have more free rein—to be used lazily, automatically, venally, or in pursuit of their own sense of what is best—than is democratically healthy.

Scholars invented remedies for these ills. They asked civil servants to be accountable to professional norms, to take a sophisticated view of their jobs, and to involve local groups of interested citizens in their work. They argued for the importance of budget and personnel staffs that would speak to each other across the government, and allow mature coordination and control. Above all, they sought ways to turn elections into obvious referenda on policies and programs, so that the president and Congress would be more accountable to the people, less at odds with each other, and better able to control administrators. The high point of this effort was an explosion of support for doctrines of responsible party government, which in different degrees tried to assimilate America's Constitution to Britain's practices by subordinating to political parties with precisely defined programs both the separation of powers and the individual accountability of representatives to their constituents. "Party government would establish popular control over government by making the group of rulers in power collectively responsible to the people."[5]

Not all scholars and journalists made these arguments, of course, and several wrote against them. But the thrust was that modern life needs bureaucracy and that bureaucrats need to be responsible. These arguments and concerns remain relevant. We still worry that bureaucracies are heavy-handed and unresponsive, although we also are troubled when they unfairly deviate from standard procedures and give some people special privileges. And, although the courts and technology rather than bureaucracy as such are the focus of today's greatest concerns about irresponsible expertise, the conflicts between expertise and accountability remain vivid. The classic problem of the tension between the (possible and sought after) wisdom of the governors and the (necessary) consent of the governed cannot help but appear in every regime.

That said, today's immediate debate about bureaucracy has more to do with whether bureaucrats should do things at all than with how they can do them more responsibly, and today's discussion of responsibility has more to do with unwed mothers and absent fathers than with the accountability of political institutions. The crux of contemporary debate more visibly concerns what government must do for people and what they must do for themselves than it does how government can do what it does more responsively. If we are to discuss the issue of bureaucratic responsibility with greater acuity, therefore, we need an analysis of responsibility that allows us to relate the problem of accountability to the questions of the purpose, connection to character, and scope of democratic government.

Responsibility and Effectiveness

What is responsibility? Let us begin by distinguishing various meanings. First, as we have said, when we say that someone is responsible, we mean that he can be held to account. "Who is responsible for spilling this milk?" That is, whose fault is it, who can be blamed? It is in this sense that to feel responsibility means to feel "guilt," to feel worthy of blame and punishment. But why are we deservedly accountable? Because we are the cause. The second meaning of being responsible is to be the cause of something, the reason it happened.[6]

Accountability and guilt may make us think of sin and intention, vices of the heart and head. Responsibility's third main meaning, however, points in a different direction, for when we call a person responsible we mean that he is concerned with results, and takes care that the results are correct. A responsible physician or auto repairman sees his work through to its completion, and sees that it is done well. He is dependable and reliable: good intentions are not enough, and bad motives do not matter much if the job is always done right. While being responsible in the sense of being accountable often has a negative ring—Congress looks for the "responsible" official when it has a complaint, as we have said, and we hold people to account when they have made a mistake—when we call someone responsible in the sense of dependably and reliably completing tasks and carrying them through, we mean to praise him.

So, to be responsible is to be accountable for results, for outcomes. Accountable to whom, and for what? Primarily, when we think of responsible people as the ones who get results, we think of them as doing their jobs, and, more, as doing their jobs well by bringing about, by causing, the results we expect, when and where we expect them. They are accountable to themselves for doing their jobs, or, more obviously, they are accountable to the ones for whom they are doing them.[7]

The characteristics that enable such responsibility to occur, and that largely define it are (in addition to having a skill) those that allow one to do one's job effectively: the reliability, dependability, and steadiness that enable one to give oneself and others their due. Such responsibility often involves attention to the future, to what is necessary to permit oneself or one's enterprise to pursue its interests successfully over the long term. Indeed, when we call someone irresponsible we mean not just that he fails to do what is necessary to complete an immediate job, but, often, that he pays little attention to the consequences of his actions for his own or his business's overall success. Dropping out of school early, or yielding to the boss's immediate whim and firing an able but unpopular subordinate are, for this reason, "irresponsible."[8]

Responsibility, however, goes beyond simply doing one's own job, because we think of responsible people as the ones who take charge in situations in which it is unclear whose job it is, situations in which no one is accountable. Responsible people are the ones to whom everyone turns to get out of a tight spot, to take charge when one of the neighbors' children is hurt and no one knows what to do, to clean up debris after a storm when everyone else passes it by, to figure out how to frame a request to local government for street lights and see that they are installed, to organize the local PTA so that instruction in the neighborhood school is improved. Responsible people are the ones who attempt to bring results that are good for many, for others as well as for themselves, when it is no one's job in particular to do this. (When we call people who are responsible in this way to ask for a favor, we actually expect them to try to deliver.) Responsible men and women are precisely the ones often urged by their friends to enter politics.

Such responsibility is the most interesting kind because it goes beyond questions of accountability and obligation in any simple meaning. The responsible person in this sense takes on common tasks, or tasks that provide a common as well as an individual benefit. The responsible person takes on common tasks, takes charge of them, and sees them through. His actions go beyond doing his job, because he makes things his job. The characteristics that define such responsibility obviously include those that allow one to work effectively, but they go beyond these because the responsible person in the fuller sense is connected to the common good more visibly. The responsible person of this sort holds himself accountable (to himself and to others) when he need not, although in time everyone begins to expect him to act responsibly. He therefore needs more than the steadiness and reliability of someone who gives others their due, and needs something of the pride and nobility with which we are familiar, primarily from ancient writings, though as Winston Churchill's example shows, not exclusively from them.[9]

Responsibility and the Constitution

More than accountability, then, the heart of responsibility is to do one's own job effectively and to take charge of common tasks that belong to no one in particular. Now, in the United States responsible individualism and bureaucratic responsibility are promoted by a government that is formed by a Constitution. This observation is trivial, but if we reflect on it we will be able to understand bureaucracy and bureaucratic responsibility better by putting them in a broader frame.

The Constitution seeks to secure and advance equal liberty by assuring as best it can that those who govern consider and deliberate on a wide range of measures, but for limited purposes. To do this it must be a structure that looks to popular interests while controlling the possibility of majority tyranny, and that uses individual judgment and energy while controlling overweening individuals or dominant minority factions. It must divide and domesticate, but not eliminate, the proud and the able and disperse and redirect, but not eradicate, the self-interested and the cunning.

For our purposes, we can best see how the American Founders effected their intention by considering the separation of powers. Separation of powers means that government power is dispersed among offices. The people rule, but indirectly through representatives, and the representatives work through various offices that are filled by citizens in different ways at different times. Functions are not simply split among offices so that, for example, one and only one set of officials deals with financial or foreign affairs. Rather, no office has total control of any issue, several offices have some effect on many issues, and a few offices have some effect on all issues. But, for each office, the range, quality, and immediacy of its impact on issues vary, and they vary in ways that are connected to the Constitution's statement of the size, length of term, and powers of the offices, and, therefore, of the powers of those who hold them. The complexity and interplay among these offices make it difficult indeed for anyone, including a majority of the people, to have their way immediately, directly, and completely.

The apparently mechanical structures of the separation of powers come to life in two ways. One is through respect or even reverence for the Constitution itself, for the form that has been engendered by the understanding and intentions of the Founders.[10] This respect is not merely ceremonial. On the contrary, it is embodied in our practice as ordinary citizens, namely, the unusual degree to which we respect and obey the results of duly constituted forms for choice—elections, juries, presidential directives, congressional deliberations and votes— even when our immediate interests and desires have been thwarted. This devotion is much more remarkable than we usually believe.

Respect for constitutional results obviously does not determine the full substance of those results, although it surely limits the ordinary range of possibilities. Rather, the impetus comes from the variety of interests, opinions, and passions that government represents, and that the separation of powers structures with subtlety and complexity. Here, structure comes to life through the deliberation and persuasion that occur because our representatives, separated into their official responsibilities, take their jobs seriously, and because we expect them to. Attachment to their offices and attention to the range, powers, and purposes of these offices enable and force representatives to bring to bear a variety of immediate and extended considerations. When separation of powers works best, legislative compromise occurs in which representatives discover commonly acceptable solutions to generally perceived problems, and executive enterprise occurs in which representatives deal with wars or other direct threats to our settled rights; with circumstances that require congealed interests to be relaxed and overcome (as one might say that Franklin Roosevelt or Ronald Reagan acted to rescue or resuscitate economic enterprise); or with situations (such as the one Abraham Lincoln faced) that demand education, risk, and invention to protect or restore rights.

When representatives attach their protection of the people's liberties and interests to their offices, they are carrying out their constitutional responsibilities, and when citizens attach their interests and rights to their vote and to respect for constitutional forms, they are carrying out theirs. Doing one's job responsibly is not equivalent to the immediate accountability or responsiveness of representatives to citizens (or of a citizen to his own most immediate desires), because what our interests and liberties require is not always clear to us. Moreover, accountability, even to the extent that one can reasonably demand it, cannot be identical for all representatives, because the people judge them through varied elections at varied times. Representatives are held to account for different interests, or, at least, for measures that secure these interests over the long term. Senators, for example, as James

Madison argues in *Federalist* 63, deal with objectives that depend "on a succession of well-chosen and well-connected measures, which have a gradual and perhaps unobserved operation." It is in carrying out such objectives that they act responsibly, and it is for this that the people should hold them to account. By implication, responsible senators do this long-term job even if the people tend to judge them on more immediate grounds.

The matter is still more complicated. For if the result of any government vote or action taken as a whole reflects the clash of interests and objectives both long term and short, it might always look as if no representative has done just what the people might want.[11] By doing his job responsibly each representative may look as if he has failed, still another reason why his assumption of responsibility must go beyond his fear of accountability, and why the electorate must learn to respect thoughtful representatives, and not just those who appear to bring home the bacon.

This difficulty is a bridge to the sense in which not just accountability but even responsibility, as doing one's job, falls short. Why exactly should any citizen pay attention to the common interest, or stand for election, if immediate self-interest does not require it? Why, having decided to stand for election, should he risk the immediate wrath of his constituents by "failing" them in order to choose what is responsible over the long term? Whatever other motives may exist, responsibly assuming the tasks that are no one's and everyone's, and attending to the Constitution and its purposes as a whole within which one's particular responsibilities lie, are necessary to serve common interests well. Respect or responsibility for the whole is at some point indispensable.

But from where might responsibility emerge? Fortunately, our Constitution itself helps form the characteristics it needs. Our way of life encourages and directs a person's natural political ambition to satisfy itself through partial responsibilities that find their place in a deliberative whole, and it encourages and directs selfish interests that discover they must be satisfied in common to respect and attend to complex governmental responsibilities and their results. In this way, our constitutional form helps to produce the responsible characters it needs to be effective, even beyond what is promoted through laws and private education. When, for example, my desire to protect my property cannot be well satisfied without the public protection of laws and police, and when the interest I share with others to establish effective police power bears fruit only after extensive deliberation and discussion, the habit of respecting and attending to others' interests and of delaying or forgoing my own immediate satisfaction (through, say, crime) increases and grows. This respect for others and for what is common, moreover, is not just the result of persuasion, but is built upon the solid foundation of individual rights and interests. Similarly, when my desire to acquire and enjoy goods is deflected away from crime and easy satisfaction toward the regulated competition of markets, the spirit of acquisition begins to be expanded and enhanced at the very moment it is frustrated, and the overall wealth that it creates is increased. In the same way, by giving natural political ambition so many opportunities for private enterprises and public office, the Constitution at once calls it forth and limits it, frustrating (through competition) the tendency of any spirit to dominate, yet at the same time allowing and encouraging it to be more responsible, subtle, and complex, and expanding self-government generally.[12] The Constitution at once requires, stimulates, and limits (but in its liberation of economic self-interest also risks stunting) the assumption by at least some citizens both of clearly visible and, ultimately, of more remote, public responsibilities that belong to no one in particular.

We may sum up these reflections as follows. The accountability of elected officials to the people derives from the respect citizens and their representatives have for elections, offices, and other constitutional forms. These forms and this respect are allied to the goal of securing individual rights, and to liberating a widespread spirit of economic acquisition and self-rule. The laws and other measures that are most likely to secure rights and enhance public and private spirit are discovered through legislative and executive deliberation, compromise, and enterprise as these qualities are dispersed and called forth in a variety of positions. The clash among representatives who are accountable to voters at different places and times and who have different and sometimes only loosely defined ranges of political control brings about results that generally serve these purposes. Actually accomplishing one's job, loosely defined as this job sometimes is (rather than merely accepting blame for failure), being accountable by respecting the electoral limits and source of one's office (rather than by instantly bowing to constituents' immediate interests), and, as much as is possible, attending to remote and long-term considerations are what constitute the true responsibility of representatives, and their genuine responsiveness. By taking on public tasks that no more belong to them than to any other citizen, moreover, and by working in terms of (rather than outside of) a constitutional separation of powers that both frustrates and energizes them, representatives display and develop some of the controlled spirit (i.e., some of the character) whose liberation and enhancement is a goal of the measures that they enact.

Bureaucratic Responsibility

These accounts of responsibility and its constitutional framework will help us see more subtly than in our first discussion the link between responsibility and public service. My point will be that bureaucratic responsibility is not immediate accountability to the whims of superiors or the electorate. Nor is it bowing down to or recklessly implementing some abstract moral or professional standard. Nor, moreover, is it doing one's job with no attention to the actual results, or to whether these results in fact serve citizens' purposes and interests. Rather, bureaucratic responsibility is an attenuated version of the more subtle and complex responsibility of representatives that I have just discussed. It is attenuated because for most bureaucrats the job to be done and the guidance from superiors is more narrow and direct than it is for most representatives. The problem of bureaucratic responsibility is therefore not as important as the general question of the responsibility of representatives, but it is not different from it in kind.[13]

We will begin our present consideration of bureaucratic responsibility by noting and modifying the usual view of bureaucracy, turn next to a discussion of the limits of bureaucratic accountability and the use of responsibility in controlling bureaucratic failings, and conclude with a summary statement.

The textbook portrayal of "bureaucracy" depicts an organization that does its job by following public rules that are designed to treat each case identically, employing for this purpose large numbers of officials each of whom performs a precise task within a precise hierarchical structure. The virtue of such organizations is that they can do a large amount of business in a generally fair and reasonable way, and can make use of the division of labor and specialization of training that allow much of what is discovered technologically to become economically and militarily useful.[14]

The government agencies that we see around us, however, vary from this picture in many ways. A good public school, for example, treats everyone equally, but only up to the point where differences in talent demand differences in approach; pays as much attention to what works in educating students here and now as it does to pedagogical "rules";

uses employees (teachers) who perform countless tasks directed to whole children, not narrow tasks directed to discrete operations; and is not especially hierarchical. Most actual public schools are at least as close (and most likely closer) to this picture as to the standard bureaucratic one.[15] For bureaucracies such as schools, the tasks and the methods are not uniform and discrete but variegated and complex. Responsibility is surely something that we require, but blame is hard to mete out. We wish to have teachers who pay actual attention to their students' success—because of skill, competition, self-reliance, dependability, "pride," and respect, that is, because of elements of responsibility—rather than the kind of "democratic" accountability in which everyone looks over everyone else's shoulder.

The Limits of Bureaucratic Accountability

Another reason why the standpoint of effectiveness rather than of accountability is necessary for democratic public servants is that so much of what they do is hidden from public view, so much is hidden from timely judgment, and so much is hidden from any effective judgment at all. Who, for example, can measure the exact contribution of State Department diplomacy toward defeating Soviet communism? Perhaps the discipline and foresight of the Defense Department was decisive? Perhaps the sheer volume and tenacity of the military buildup of the Reagan years was central, largely independent of how well or poorly the Pentagon handled it? That is, perhaps President Reagan, or Defense Secretary Caspar Weinberger, or the senators they convinced, or the American people who elected them were more significant than any bureaucrat in any department? Yet, perhaps technology was more decisive than any contribution of management or politics, or the power of liberty and of those who died or even argued for it more significant still? Or perhaps Soviet leaders simply lost their will?

If we narrow the example to more concrete policies, it is easier to assign responsibility. It was these particular diplomats (and not others) who, for example, met with colleagues in Italy in 1983 to persuade them to stand firm on NATO's wish to locate intermediate-range missiles there, and these colonels and generals, not others, who grasped the capabilities of such missiles and planned to produce and buy them. But many other people in the State Department, Pentagon, and congressional staffs contributed to this success—or argued against the policy. How many of them were properly recognized or reprimanded? More, how could one tell how much this single policy truly affected matters, when compared to everything that happened before or after? Whether or not people are doing their job, how much this job contributes to the result, how much the result contributes to the larger aim, and how sensible the aim is in the first place—all this is often obscure.[16]

In addition to hiddenness or obscurity, and to the prevalence of bureaucracies that deal more with individual cases than with rules, a third limit to democratic accountability is the openness of bureaucratic tasks that stems from the breadth and imprecision of bureaucratic goals. Many bureaucracies have at least some elements of what we have described in schools. Usually, the lower down one goes in most organizations, the narrower and more defined the job. A clerk in the Justice Department performs more circumscribed tasks than the attorney general. Sometimes, however, even those far enough down in the hierarchy to be directly in the line of fire—a policeman walking the beat, or as we have said, a teacher in a public school—have jobs that are not very well defined.[17]

One's initial reaction to this problem might be to define the job better by writing an exhaustive job description and a set of rules to cover every possible engagement. But ill-defined jobs (and precisely the examples we are using) sometimes have large aims—preventing crime, keeping immediate peace, and promoting national security—that are not well met by defining the job precisely, narrowly, and restrictively, that is, "bureaucratically." Sometimes, too much depends on variable connections between nebulous outcomes and complex circumstances—what counts as peace or calm, for example; for how long must this calm be kept, who is causing the danger, what are one's immediate resources?—for restrictive definitions to allow the job to be done effectively. Other times—in genuine education, again—liberty of action is inherent in reaching the goal and in the very definition of it. Not everything can be reduced to precise rules to control precise activities that are precise means to precise ends.

How does responsibility help to relieve these difficulties? The hiddenness of much of what bureaucrats do, and the contingency and openness of many of their tasks, means that we cannot assure through close observation and control that everyone will do his or her job well. Even when bureaucrats' jobs are visible and strictly bounded, we still want them to act responsibly, that is, in a way that takes special circumstances into account, and therefore requires some freedom from following precise rules. Moreover, fear of punishment (assuming that we could observe better and that we wish to control more rigidly) will not produce sufficient energy and innovation among public servants, useful as it might be for limiting corruption.

Rather than fear and control, it appears that what is necessary for good public service is doing one's duty, performing one's obligations, acting on the basis of decent habits, friendship, or loyalty. Friendship and loyalty are insufficient, however, because so many organizations have such changeable membership. Bureaucracies usually are composed of people who are there voluntarily, with entrance and exit governed by contract, ambition, and economic opportunity more than by tradition, service, and attachment to land and family. And, although performing properly because of duty and obligation surely is desirable, "duty," strictly speaking, points to subservience to an occupation, profession, or religious or moral code that is either narrower or broader than service in the public interest in liberal democracies.

In contrast, responsibility is a phenomenon that speaks to the necessity of duty and loyalty in a way that captures the peculiar quality of modern bureaucracy and the modern purposes that it serves, in which obligations, friendships, and professions are all in the last analysis chosen voluntarily, and are in the service of energetic, acquisitive individualism. To be responsible is to do one's job well, not because of inherited attachments, but within a structure of rights, and of common tasks and interests that have been selected, not given. It is to do one's job well when one's job could be anyone else's, or, at least, when one did not have to choose it for oneself. It is this form of responsibility, more than mechanisms that might improve immediate accountability to the people and their representatives, that is crucial to meet bureaucracies' weaknesses and to help insure that bureaucrats do their jobs effectively.

Conclusion

We may sum up our reflections on bureaucracy and responsibility as follows. Public servants should be responsible, but this must and should mean more than being transparently or immediately accountable to the people and their representatives, and it rarely means being directly accountable to an extraconstitutional order, or to a professional code of practices and principles.[18] Rather, it involves the understanding of responsibility that we have been discussing, a sense that defines the responsibility of citizens and political representatives as well as of bureaucrats, a sense that is specified by characteristics that are at once means and ends of our regime. The responsibility that one needs from the public servant is that he actually does his own job as effectively as he can. Sometimes this will mean that he will exercise a freedom that seems too unregulated, or even seek to expand his responsibilities beyond what his job appears to require. The teacher who attends to each student differentially might be too harsh with some and too easy with others. The State Department official who is negotiating one element of a treaty may sometimes see and seize the opportunity to redirect arms control policy more generally than his brief stipulates. The government attorney who is writing an equal opportunity regulation may have in mind a result that will affect agencies other than his own. The check on such liberty must be others exercising their own liberty, citizens at the polls or in the courts, fellow bureaucrats, and above all, political executives. The spirit of responsibility cannot be limited mechanically to mere dependability any more than it can be captured through narrow accountability, for it often seeks new areas over which to take charge. Indeed, this connection of responsibility to effectiveness more than to accountability means that it is difficult to specify precisely or universally what all responsibility requires. The variety of tasks, abilities, and lengths and breadths of view means that we cannot ask every public servant, or everyone simply, to be equally responsible. To do so might limit what is best in responsibility.

Because so many bureaucracies live or attempt to live by the identical application of rules, they are too often places dominated by an ethic of narrow accountability rather than of effective responsibility. This problem is somewhat offset by the difficulties in assigning accountability, and by the competition among public servants who deal with similar issues, a competition that brings out, or even requires, responsibility in the more effective sense. Nonetheless, however truly responsible bureaucrats are, all bureaucrats save those at the very top are constrained by the actions and responsibilities of political executives and, in the end, depend for their own responsibility on the effectiveness of the discharge of responsibilities by these representatives, and by the people. However much government's laws and measures may, in turn, affect these, respect for the Constitution itself, and for the scope of private liberty, affect them still more.

Notes

1. I will use "bureaucrats" and "public servants" interchangeably.

2. These three cases—the degree of responsibility of the Departments of the Treasury and Justice and their relevant bureaus for the killing of well over a hundred Branch Davidians in Waco, Texas, in 1993, the level of accountability of the FBI for the killing of the wife of a "white separatist" in Ruby Ridge, Idaho, in 1993, and the responsibility of President Clinton (or, ostensibly, that of various banking agencies and bureaus) for possible special treatment given an Arkansas Savings and Loan—were current during the period when this essay was drafted.

3. This view is a significant part of the political science literature from at least the 1930s to the 1960s; the problem is evident as well in the work of Woodrow Wilson and in activity from the New Deal through the Eisenhower administration that sought to establish and defend a professional civil service and the kind of administrative staffs for presidents and cabinet officers that (until very recently) we have come to take for granted. Because bureaucracy (and administrative staff) was considered necessary for modern government, it had to be perfected or even established at the same time one tried to show that it could be responsible. For various discussions of these issues, see, among others Woodrow Wilson "The Study of Administration," *Political Science Quarterly* 2 (June 1887): 197–222; Arthur A. Maass and Laurence I. Radway, "Gauging Administrative Responsibility," *Public Administration Review* 9 (Summer 1949) 182–92; and J. Roland Pennock, "Responsiveness, Responsibility and Majority Rule," *American Political Science Review* 46 (September 1952): 790–807.

4. Carl Joachim Friedrich and Taylor Cole, *Responsible Bureaucracy* (Cambridge: Harvard University Press, 1932; reprinted by Russell and Russell, 1967), 28. Friedrich, later to become president of the American Political Science Association, is, according to the book's preface, the primary author of the chapter from which this passage comes.

5. Austin Ranney, *The Doctrine of Responsible Party Government* (Urbana: University of Illinois Press, 1962), 14. (The book was originally published in 1954, and the dissertation from which it was adapted was completed in 1948.) For additional elements of these arguments, see many of the readings collected in Dwight Waldo, *Ideas and Issues in Public Administration* (New York: McGraw-Hill, 1953). For the basic argument about political parties see, in addition to Ranney, the Committee on Political Parties of the American Political Science Association's report "Toward a More Responsible Two-Party System," *Supplement to the American Political Science Review* 44 (September 1950).

6. It is causation with a view, often, toward holding to account, but responsibility as accountability and responsibility as causation are not identical, because some causes are responsible without being accountable. The broken hose is "responsible" for the car's stalling: it is accountable only by extension.

7. It is in this sense that those who are responsible are often asked to be

responsive, that is, asked to pay more attention to the ones for whom they are working. It is also in this sense that we speak of our responsibilities as our "obligations," especially when we think of obligations simply as what we owe others, and do not have a fancy theory of obligation.

8. As the president of the San Francisco 49ers said, "We feel that it was not only inappropriate and irresponsible to match" the Dallas Cowboys' $30 million offer to cornerback Deion Sanders; "we feel that had we done so, it would have had a very destructive effect on the 49er team chemistry and the financial structure and sanity of this organization for years to come" (*New York Times*, 10 September 1995, section 5: 7). Good material alone is, of course, insufficient to guarantee responsibility, and institutions can themselves help to encourage it. This is a theme of my discussion, though I am not considering here the connection of specific policies to the development of character. (It should also go without saying that foresight in one instance demonstrates neither responsible character nor foresight generally.)

9. Although responsibility is in this way a term that points out a natural virtue in new language, more fundamentally it points up the transformation of ancient virtue in the modern world, just as my "interest" is similar to my "good," but is not identical with it because it belongs to a different way of seeking, finding, and holding. Our responsible people operate within a smaller field than do people of great pride, do what they do less because they are attracted to beauty and honor and more because they concentrate on being themselves, have less connection to the possibility of playful brilliance, and characteristically act in situations where the common benefit is also a more or less identical benefit to them, rather than acting because ruling a common enterprise is their own characteristic, natural field. In a very general way that is not linked specifically to politics, for the responsible person in the full modern sense, can implies ought.

10. Consider here *Federalist* 49.

11. And, of course, it is also usually difficult to separate one representative's contribution from others'.

12. In addition to *The Federalist Papers*, one should, for further consideration of these issues, examine John Locke, *The Second Treatise of Government*. I have discussed these questions further in an unpublished paper, "Self-interest and Responsibility."

13. The view that bureaucratic and political responsibility are different in kind would follow from the strict separation of politics and administration, a division that strikes many people as plausible at first glance. This separation is often associated with the work of Frank Goodnow. See Frank J. Goodnow, *Politics and Administration* (New York: Macmillan, 1900).

14. The classic discussion of bureaucracy occurs in the writings of Max Weber. A useful selection of Weber's writings has been translated by H. H. Gerth and C. Wright Mills, in *From Max Weber* (Oxford: Oxford University Press, 1958). The material on bureaucracy can be found on 196–244, with Weber's view of the characteristics of bureaucracy (roughly, what I am calling here the picture-book portrayal) to be found on 196–98.

15. A fine discussion of contemporary American bureaucracies can be found in James Q. Wilson, *Bureaucracy* (New York: Basic Books, 1989). For schools, consider, among others, Chester E. Finn Jr., *We Must Take Charge* (New York: Free Press, 1991); J. S. Coleman, T. Hoffer and S. Kilgore, *High School Achievement* (New York: Basic Books, 1982); Peter W. Cookson Jr., *School Choice* (New Haven: Yale University Press, 1994); and S. C. Purkey and M. S. Smith, "Effective Schools: A Review," *Elementary School Journal* 83 (1983): 427–52.

16. Consider here the categories of bureaucratic types that Wilson provides on 158–71 of *Bureaucracy*.

17. Consider Wilson, passim., as well as James Q. Wilson, *Varieties of Police Behavior* (Cambridge: Harvard University Press, 1983).

18. What such a code might properly require—that a government scientist not distort his results because a superior asks him to, for example—is not different from what effective service in a regime of varied offices and powers requires. If it is different, by what argument could one show it to be just that the professional should prevail over the political? Neither immediate accountability nor extra-political professional accountability, but, rather, political responsibility, should be the guide. To the degree that discussions of bureaucratic responsibility—such as the famous debate over half a century ago between Herman Finer and Carl Friedrich—are seen primarily as debates between unmediated accountability to popular interests and accountability to professional norms, the issue is miscast. See Carl J. Friedrich, "Responsibility and Policy Formation," in *Public Policy: 1940*, ed. Carl J. Friedrich and Edward S. Mason (Harvard University Press, 1940); and Herman Finer, "Administrative Responsibility in Democratic Government," in *Public Administration Review* 1 (1941).

Index

About the Contributors

Mark Blitz is Fletcher Jones professor of political philosophy at Claremont-McKenna College.

Donald R. Brand is associate professor of political science at the College of the Holy Cross.

Gary C. Bryner is professor of political science at Brigham Young University.

Robert Eden is professor of political science at Hillsdale College.

Richard T. Green is associate professor of political science and public administration at the University of Wyoming.

Marc K. Landy is professor of political science at Boston College.

Peter Augustine Lawler is professor of political science at Berry College.

Donald J. Maletz is associate professor of political science at the University of Oklahoma.

David K. Nichols is associate professor of political science at Montclair State University.

Lloyd G. Nigro is professor of public administration at Georgia State University.

Jeremy Rabkin is associate professor of government at Cornell University.

William D. Richardson is associate professor of political science and public administration at Georgia State University.

John A. Rohr is professor of public administration at Virginia Polytechnic Institute.

Charles T. Rubin is associate professor of political science at Duquesne University.

David Lewis Schaefer is professor of political science at the College of the Holy Cross.

Robert Martin Schaefer is associate professor of political science at the University of Mobile.

Herbert J. Storing (1929–1977) was Robert Kent Gooch professor of government at the University of Virginia.